SON AND LOVER

The Young D. H. Lawrence

SON AND LOVER

The Young D. H. Lawrence

PHILIP CALLOW

And departure is the opposite equivalent
of coming together; decay, corruption,
destruction, breaking down is the
opposite equivalent of creation.

D. H. Lawrence, 'The Crown'

STEIN AND DAY / *Publishers* / New York

First published in the United States of America, 1975
Copyright © 1975 by Philip Callow
All rights reserved
Printed in the United States of America
Stein and Day/*Publishers*/Scarborough House,
Briarcliff Manor, N.Y. 10510

Library of Congress Cataloging in Publication Data

Callow, Philip.
  Son and lover, the young D. H. Lawrence.

  1. Lawrence, David Herbert, 1885-1930—Biography.
I. Title.
PR6023.A93Z59   823'.9'12 [B]   75-9615
ISBN 0-8128-1819-9

To Michael Henshaw
book lover
remembering his kindness
and generosity

ACKNOWLEDGMENTS

The author gratefully acknowledges permission to quote extracts from the correspondence of D. H. Lawrence, from *Sons and Lovers* and *The White Peacock*, by courtesy of the Estate of the late Mrs Frieda Lawrence and Messrs Laurence Pollinger; and extracts from Jessie Chambers' *D. H. Lawrence: A Personal Record*, by courtesy of Mrs V. Wood and Messrs Jonathan Cape.

CONTENTS

LIST OF PLATES

Grateful acknowledgement is made to the following copyright owners for permission to reproduce illustrations:

Professor Harry Moore for Plate 1; James Bridgen for Plates 2, 3, 4, 5, 6, 11, 17, 18, 23 and 24; the Local Studies Library, Nottinghamshire County Library for Plates 7, 9, 10, 21 and 22; Professor J. T. Boulton for Plate 8; Messrs Jonathan Cape for Plate 12; the Radio Times Hulton Picture Library for Plate 13; Mrs Barbara Weekley Barr for Plates 14 and 15; Mrs J. Middleton Murry and the Society of Authors for Plate 16; and the English Theatre Guild Ltd. for Plate 20.

PREFACE

David Herbert Lawrence was twenty-eight when he was writing *The Rainbow*, and by the age of thirty-one had almost completed *Women in Love*. The rapid maturing of his gifts and the short span of his life, his extraordinary buoyancy of spirit and his sick body – these are factors we can study fruitfully but in the end only marvel at. He was a meteor, and the phenomenon was too much: the speed of his trajectory and his fiery brilliance blinded and confused his contemporaries, most of whom didn't perceive his uniqueness until he was dead.

Living as he did with the knowledge of his body's precariousness, he developed a craving for spring; both his own and the world's. Towards the end he hung, like a phoenix, in the midst of flames. Yet there was no pathos in him. Skin and bone, seething with death, he appeared virulently, brilliantly alive. This was an affront, and no one appreciated the malice of it more than Lawrence himself. The most astonishing thing of all was that this was happening in England, albeit an England of his own creation, which he carried around everywhere within himself, and that it had originated in the very middle, the mild Midlands of an England which still, to some extent, exists.

Lawrence predicted that his books would not be understood for three hundred years. Meanwhile, the critical activity continues. The enormous amount of Lawrence criticism now in existence has certainly convinced this biographer that any attempt at what is known as a 'critical' biography would be a dubious enterprise. Which does not mean, of course, that a biographic work should be anything other than objective and documented in the fullest sense.

I have also avoided the 'scientific' or deterministic approach to literary biography – which has its own pitfalls – and have deliberately kept the introduction of psychoanalytical theory to a minimum, tempting though it might be to turn the psychoanalysts loose on a man whose life and work seem to cry out for psycho-biography. My own feeling is that such an examination can be, finally, a reducer of genius, as can the insistence on getting 'behind' the writings in order to explain them.

My editors have urged me to put forward an explanation of my method, in the belief that the reader needs to be prepared for a book which is perhaps not quite what he will expect. Let me say, therefore, that any departure from the conventional has only been made in an effort to bring Lawrence more vividly to life: and to bring history alive is the aim of all good biography. The story of Lawrence's life, from the facts presented so faithfully in the biographies of Harry T. Moore and Edward Nehls, and from a perusal of his letters, reads like a novel; and as far as possible I have tried to let Lawrence be the author of it. But it is also the task of any serious biographer to interpret, and at the same time to include important new material as part of this fresh interpretation. The publication of the suppressed Prologue to *Women in Love*, for instance, made all previous biographical writing out of date; as did, to a lesser extent, the publication of Lawrence's letters to Louie Burrows. In addition, there are the valuable new facts provided by Emile Delavenay in his ambitious study of Lawrence's formative years, and by Robert Lucas' biography of Frieda Lawrence.

When we contemplate Lawrence's unceasing struggle to escape that post-Dostoevskian state which he delineated with such precision as a death in life, it is logical to assume that in a very real sense his efforts killed him. I happen to believe that his 'failure' to extricate himself fully from this universal death was in fact a kind of success, for without it we would never have had the astonishing drama of his life and work. One result of that drama is the intense preoccupation with his meaning and influence which I have mentioned already. To that extent, at least, his death has been the creative triumph he so desperately wanted it to be. His little 'ship of death' still rides the waters.

Many of us now find ourselves turning naturally to Lawrence whenever we make the attempt to understand what is happening to man in this age: and by man we do not mean social beings, but irreducible, Lawrentian men and women. If we suspect that the modern male is becoming increasingly emasculated, and the female in consequence seems impelled to take the initiative, the reasons for this must, we feel, be somewhere in Lawrence. If Western society is beginning to show ominous warning cracks and fissures, we are uneasily aware that a study of Lawrence could reveal the whole process of disintegration mapped out for us in precise language. Like him or not, he is undeniably seminal, and one expects him to grow rather than diminish in stature in the years to come. Even though the future may prove him utterly wrong, he was unerring in his assumption of another reality, far greater than the one we normally inhabit. And in his power to transmit it and establish it, to flesh it out and give it a metaphysic, is the source of his lasting appeal and fascination.

As I became steadily more absorbed by my journey through his world – until I began to wonder if I should ever emerge – it was inevitable that I should want to explore the complexities of a man as drastically split as Lawrence, to examine the fertile ambiguities, deep divisions and contradictory longings for unity which exist side by side in his art, as they did so bewilderingly in his life, and so confront, in the context of a biography, the paradox embedded in the work of this great writer.

PHILIP CALLOW
Haselbury, Somerset
August, 1974

SON AND LOVER

The Young D. H. Lawrence

1

Eastwood: The Heritage

There was always the countryside. 'Walk down the fields to the Breach [now it has a posh name, Garden Road] and in the corner house facing the stile I lived from 1 to 6. And walk up Engine Lane, over the level-crossing at Moorgreen pit, along till you come to the highway, Alfreton Road. Turn to the left, towards Underwood, and go till you come to the lodge gate by the reservoir – go through the gate, and up the drive to the next gate, and continue on the footpath just below the drive on the left – on through the wood to Felley Mill [the White Peacock Farm]. When you've crossed the brook, turn to the right through the Felley Mill gate, and go up the footpath to Annesley. Or better still, turn to the right, uphill, before you descend to the brook, and go on uphill, up through the rough deserted pasture – on past Annesley Kennels – long empty – on to Annesley again. That's the country of my heart.'[1]

In spite of everything, of vast jerry-building, re-housing, factories and huge council estates everywhere, the country is still there now, menaced by Nottingham to the south but still amazingly intact, though the M1 slices straight through between Alfreton and Annesley on its way up to Leeds. Stand on one of the concrete road bridges connecting the fields on either side, and the traffic pours underneath like a dream, without shattering the reality. The reality is still the earth. On Saturday nights if you go through the lanes to the north of Eastwood, just behind the shops in the drab Nottingham Road, you will most likely find all the field gateways blocked with the cars of colliers busy doing their courting. The Nottingham Road, with its Co-op, its pubs, its fish-and-chip shop on the corner by the cinema, its supermarket and chemist and ironmonger and all the rest, could be anywhere in England; but at night the fields around reverberate with the soft humming of machinery from the nearest pit, which glows phosphorescent with light and looks sinister. The rural and the industrial are still inextricably mixed, more now than ever. The countryside refuses to be killed off: somehow the two have come to terms, as have the urban and the country man. A middle-aged man pushing his bike past the sleek cars turns out to be a disabled miner with memories of swimming naked in the canal, but though his living has always been industrial he looks and sounds like a countryman. Vanishing now, but still there: a phenomenon of these parts.

'In Nottingham Road', Lawrence wrote towards the end of his life, 'I feel at once a devouring nostalgia and an infinite repulsion. Partly I want to get back to the place as it was when I was a boy, and I waited so long to be served at the Co-op. I remember our Co-op number, 1553A.L., better than the date of my birth – and when I came out hugging a string bag of groceries. There was a little hedge across the road from the Co-op then, and I used to pick the green buds which we called bread-and-cheese. And there were no houses in Gabes Lane. And at the corner of Queen Street, Butcher Bob was huge and fat and taciturn.'[2]

A. L. Rowse, on a pilgrimage to Lawrence's birthplace at the end of the forties, thought the rawness and ugliness of the place, and the windy ridges of Eastwood, resembled the china-clay district of Cornwall he knew as a boy. The chapels, the absence of culture, the relentlessness – it was all like St. Austell to him. He sought out Willie Hopkin, a man of eighty-seven and 'bright as a bird', twenty years older than Lawrence and still alive twenty years after his death: the only friend who stayed the course, perhaps because he was something of a saint.

Leaving, Rowse looked back for a last impression of Eastwood, touched by the spirit of the dead boy who once knew it: 'those raw streets and miners' terraces, the wind blowing gustily along the ridges and up Victoria Street from the Breach, the harsh corners and the sharp spire of the Congregational chapel pricking the sky from the places where he lived.'[3]

In 1885, when D. H. Lawrence was born, his village of Eastwood, about eight miles from Nottingham and only a mile from the Erewash, the borderline between Nottinghamshire and Derbyshire, had a population of about three and a half thousand. In 1801 there were 753 people living in Eastwood, in 1901 nearly five thousand. It was a mining village at the time of Lawrence's birth, and had been one for over a hundred years before that, a tiny collection of thatched cottages with bulging walls, and broken rows of more recent dwellings, where the old colliers of the eighteenth century lived, 'working in the little gin-pits two fields away. The brook ran under the alder trees, scarcely soiled by

these small mines, whose coal was drawn to the surface by donkeys that plodded wearily in a circle round a gin.'[4] These were the
days when a mine was something you walked into, no more than a
hole in a hillside. There were also windlass mines, where you
stood in a bucket and were wound up one at a time by a donkey.
The old windlass mines were still in operation during Lawrence's
father's boyhood. 'And all over the countryside were these same
pits, some of which had been worked in the time of Charles II, the
few colliers and the donkeys burrowing down like ants into the
earth, making queer mounds and little black places among the
corn-fields and the meadows.'[5] The homes of these primitive
coalminers formed most of the parish of Eastwood.

Then the revolution, tremendous excitement, the discovery of
a huge coal and iron field running under Nottinghamshire and
Derbyshire. The financiers appeared. In 1820, along came Barber,
Walker & Co., a company powerful enough to sink the first big
shaft and put in the first machinery. Industry had arrived at
Eastwood, and not only there, but at Underwood, Brinsley,
Greasley, and these were collieries proper, mixed in with the odd
farms and cottages and churches and the grand houses on the
hills, the hill villages of Derbyshire and Nottinghamshire.

The bringers of industry, the master builders of modern Eastwood, were the Barber and Walker families. During the eighteenth century they had already begun to get control of the
scattered mines in the area, some of them dating back to the
sixteenth century. Then in 1800 the firm of Barber, Walker and
Co. was officially registered. All this new ferment of activity was
consolidated by a meeting convened by Barber and Walker and
other coal-owners in the region north of Nottingham to discuss
the possibilities of a railway. There was the threat of another
railway in Leicestershire. 'Farm labourers swarmed in from Lincolnshire and other counties, attracted by the higher wages.'[6]
Now was the time to act. You can see a plaque on the outside wall
of the Sun Inn in the square of Eastwood noting this meeting of
1832, since because of it the Erewash Valley Railway, later the
famous Midland line, came into existence, and 'six mines like
black studs on the countryside, linked by a loop of fine chain, the
railway'.[7]

With its new importance, Eastwood became the market town of
the area. And when Lawrence began to make his youthful excursions into the country it was nearly always with his back to
Nottingham, mucky Nottingham with its hundreds of slum terraces and cobbled streets, its little back-street factories, great
markets, grimy stations – the pride of 'the black, fuming, labor-

ious Midlands' and gateway to the north-country. The country of his heart was always to the north of Eastwood, a landscape faced by his father as he tramped to work along the Mansfield Road to Brinsley colliery. A mile to the east was Greasley, with the remains of a fourteenth-century castle, and north again was Beauvale Priory, also a ruin, and the setting of one of Lawrence's first short stories, 'A Fragment of Stained Glass'.

2

Families: The Father

Although Lawrence's geography of youth was so emphatically North-orientated, the Lawrences came in fact from the South. Not long after that crucial first shaft was sunk in 1820, along came John Lawrence, 'my grandfather, a young man trained to be a tailor, drifting from the South of England, and got the job of company tailor for the Brinsley mine'.[1] John Lawrence may have come no further than Nottingham. Certainly he learnt his trade there and was brought up there – learning tailoring from his step-father George Dooley, who, according to family talk, had married John's mother after the death of her husband in France, at Waterloo. In spite of the big class 'gap' which yawns before us in *Sons and Lovers*, there was not so much difference in class between the families. Indeed, the two families were related by marriage: Arthur Lawrence's aunt was the wife of Lydia Beardsall's uncle.

This tailor, John Lawrence, who came 'drifting' in from the South and settled in a cottage down by the brook at Brinsley, close to the pit, was a giant of a man. On the Trent he excelled at rowing, but he was most famous for his fights in the boxing ring. Legend has it that he beat champion Ben Caut unofficially. Apparently John Lawrence's cottage was also a shop, and D. H. Lawrence remembers vividly the big rolls of coarse flannel and 'pit-cloth' in the corner of it, and the 'big, strange old sewing machine, like nothing else on earth',[2] for sewing the massive pit-trousers. In those days the colliery supplied the men with their pit clothes, the thick flannel vests and the moleskin trousers lined at the top with flannel. Later, during Lawrence's childhood, this practice was discontinued. Lawrence's sister Ada preferred to dwell on the 'gentlemen's livery' her grandfather also made, if this was true. She may have been compensating with her gentility for those great rolls of workmen's flannel propped in the corner.

What about the tailor's wife? Her name was Sarah, and she was the daughter of a Nottingham lace and silk manufacturer, Adam

21

Parsons. Presumably they were still in that quarry-bed cottage shop at Brinsley when Arthur John Lawrence – D. H. Lawrence's father – was born in 1846. He was eventually to marry Lydia Beardsall, and she too came from Nottingham. There was some bitterness in her family because her Beardsall grandfather, after migrating to Nottingham from Wirksworth when the lace industry began to boom, lost his fortune in the depression of 1837. So we can see that, so far, there was nothing to choose between the two families on the class level. George, Lydia's father, was an engineer – 'a large, handsome, haughty man, proud of his fair skin and blue eyes',[3] and was, according to *Sons and Lovers*, 'bitterly galled' by his poverty. Nevertheless, he ended up foreman of the engineers at the Sheerness dockyard. But before leaving to take up this foreman's job, he married Lydia Newton, whose grandfather on her mother's side was a famous hymn-writer. You can still hear his hymns sung in English chapels.

D. H. Lawrence's mother, Lydia, was George Beardsall's second daughter. He was fiercely religious and cantankerous. Lydia 'hated her father's overbearing manner towards her gentle, humorous, kindly-souled mother. She remembered running over the breakwater at Sheerness and finding the boat. She remembered too having been petted and flattered by all the men when she had gone to the dockyard, for she was a delicate, rather proud child.'[4] Her father became famous for his quarrels, notably with Jesse Boot over the governorship of a chapel, and there was another set-to with William Booth. Lawrence claimed that Booth was George Beardsall's associate in setting up the first Salvation Army organisation.

What kind of man was the young Arthur Lawrence, the tailor's son Lydia Beardsall was to meet and marry, the man she thought was a negro bursting into the house the first night he came home from the pit? If we are to believe *Sons and Lovers* – and according to Lawrence's sister Ada the account there is substantially true – she had become an assistant mistress in a private school, had met a 'refined' young man, called in the novel John Field, who was the son of a well-off tradesman, had been educated in London and was brimming with prospects. She used to walk home from chapel with him. He wanted to go into the ministry, but his father meant him to go into the family business, and poor John had no guts. Then, to make matters worse, John's father became bankrupt, and John ended up a teacher. Two years later Lydia made 'determined inquiry. He had married his landlady, a woman of forty, a widow with property.'[5] Lydia kept his bible all her life.

Presumably after this experience she was somewhat disillusioned with refined young men. Arthur Lawrence made a startling contrast. Arthur had come over one Christmas from Brinsley to help sink a mine shaft at Clifton, near Nottingham. He was twenty-seven. He met Lydia at his aunt's home, which happened to be also the home of Lydia's uncle. Lydia sat up and took notice: she had never met anyone quite like him before. 'He was well set-up, erect, and very smart. He had wavy black hair that shone, and a vigorous black beard that had never been shaved. His cheeks were ruddy, and his red, moist mouth was noticeable because he laughed so often and so heartily. He had that rare thing, a rich, ringing laugh.'[6] Lydia was fascinated. Her father had humour too, but of the satiric kind. 'This man's was different: soft, non-intellectual, warm, a kind of gambolling.'[7]

This of course is Lawrence's imaginative reconstruction of how he thought it had been. The important thing is that he was endeavouring here to give a true picture. How vivid it is, how different these two were! In fact, 'she herself was opposite. She had a curious, receptive mind, which found much pleasure and amusement in listening to other folk. She was clever in leading folk on to talk. She loved ideas, and was considered very intellectual. What she liked most of all was an argument on religion or philosophy or politics with some educated man.'[8] So what was the attraction here, why did she find this man so fascinating? And, if Lawrence is to be believed, why was Arthur Lawrence equally fascinated?

'In her person she was rather small and delicate, with a large brow, and dropping bunches of brown silk curls. Her blue eyes were very straight, honest and searching. She had the beautiful hands of the Coppards [Beardsalls] . . . She was still perfectly intact, deeply religious, and full of beautiful candour.'[9]

And Arthur Lawrence, the miner, was faced with that thing of infinite mystery and fascination, a lady. Even her pronunciation was a thrill to him. She watched him, he listened to her. She noticed that his movement had a 'subtle exultation', and she loved the way his face seemed the flower of his body, blossoming and ruddy; and the black ruffled hair; and that laugh. How different from her father, harsh and ironic and subduing in himself all sensuality. Lydia was very much her father's daughter. She held dancing in contempt, she was high-minded, inclined to be stern with herself. What was this, then, this man whose sensuousness was so natural, not gripped and held in, but flowing off him 'like the flame from a candle'? His way of talking amused her, and she cleverly drew him into talk, because of the warmth that radiated from him. For once she didn't care what they talked about, so long as she kept in contact. She was a puritan, and would never have admitted this desire to herself.

'But you musn't miss your dance,' she reproved.

'Nay, I don't want to dance that – it's not one as I care about.'

'Yet you invited me to it.'

He laughed very heartily at this.

'I never thought o' that. Tha'rt not long in taking the curl out of me.'

It was her turn to laugh quickly.

'You don't look as if you'd come much uncurled,' she said.

'I'm like a pig's tail, I curl because I canna help it,' he laughed, rather boisterously.

'And you are a miner!' she exclaimed in surprise.

'Yes. I went down when I was ten.'

She looked at him in wondering dismay.

'When you were ten! And wasn't it very hard?' she asked.

'You soon get used to it. You live like th' mice, an' you pop out at night to see what's going on.'

'It makes me feel blind,' she frowned.

'Like a moudiwarp!' he laughed. 'Yi, an' there's some chaps as does go round like moudiwarps.' He thrust his face forward in the blind, snout-like way of a mole, seeming to sniff and peer for direction. 'They dun though!' he protested naïvely.[10]

He was tender with her, he wasn't being sardonic. He was so different from her father, the only other man she had really known. 'She had never been "thee'd and thou'd" before', and she found it touching.

They were married on 27th December, 1875, at St. Stephen's, the Sneinton parish church, a year after their first meeting. He didn't take her straight back to Brinsley – as if the shock might be too much. Instead they lived first at Sutton-in-Ashfield and at Old Radford, now on the western outskirts of Nottingham. Then he had to go back to his old job at the pit at Brinsley, and they lived in a cottage near his parents, below Eastwood. 'For three months she was perfectly happy: for six months she was very happy.'[11]

Gradually she began to realise things. He had signed the pledge and joined the Band of Hope, presumably to please her, and wore the teetotaller's blue ribbon. This was a kind of showing-off. She believed they lived in a house which he owned, a small one, but nice enough, with solid furniture, and though she didn't care for her new relatives, fancying they sneered at her lady-like ways, she kept herself to herself. So long as she had him, what did it matter? He was good and affectionate to her, deferential when she tried to talk seriously to him. But she saw he didn't understand. 'This killed her efforts at a finer intimacy, and she had flashes of fear.'[12] She was quick to notice things, for instance that he was restless in the evenings, alone with her. Having her was not enough, she realised. He pottered about, set himself to do little jobs, and that was a relief. He was very clever with his hands. When he was busy, hammering away at something, she overlooked the mess because he was happy.

His unthinking carnality often shocked her. He sat before her, in his body, blocking her off from him. He made her feel invisible. His own flesh and heat seemed to satisfy him completely. It was curious how extraneous she felt. Soon his physical complacency began to enrage her, but he failed to notice: she beat against it in vain. He sat there like a savage, impassive.

He always had his dinner before he got up to wash himself. Why not? Down the pit he ate in his dirt – why not at his own table? After the meal he smoked his pipe, still in his pit-dirt, while his wife fetched the big earthenware pancheon from the scullery and filled it with hot water, then tempered it with cold.

Then he got up, careless as a lord. 'He wore no coat, and his arms were freckled black. He stripped to the waist, hitched his trousers into the strap, and kneeled on the rug to wash himself. There was a great splashing and sputtering. The red firelight shone on his cap of white soap, and on the muscles of his back, on the strange working of his red and white muscular arms, that flashed up and down like individual creatures.'[13]

Seven months after the wedding, Lydia came across some papers in her husband's Sunday clothes. They were unpaid furniture bills. She asked him why he hadn't settled the bills.

'I haven't had a chance.'

This offended her pride at once. She would go off to Nottingham on Saturday and settle the bills. 'I don't like sitting on another man's chairs and eating from an unpaid table.' When she asked for his bank book he was silent: then he said, 'Tha' can ha'e it, for what good it'll be to thee.'[14]

She realised the uselessness of further questions. She was still with anger and bitterness. She went straight round to see his mother. To her horror, she found that she was in debt to her mother-in-law for the wedding expenses, and that the house they lived in was her mother-in-law's too. Lydia sat there, numb with shock. 'She was her father now.'[15]

When her husband came in she said hardly anything, but her manner had altered. It was October, and two years ago, at

Christmas, they had first met. This Christmas she was going to have a baby.

She began to find out things that rankled. Arthur had run a dancing class in the Miners' Arms club room for five years, and there were 'carryings-on, according to all accounts'; so her nearest neighbour told her, to take her down a peg. They didn't like her superior ways.

Finally, before long, he broke his teetotaller's pledge, and began coming home late. The other women who had to put up with their men's drinking habits expected her to join in alliance with them against the men. But Lydia didn't; she kept rigidly to herself. She began to have pangs of real loneliness, realising she was a long way away from her own people. She was ill when the baby was born – a boy. Arthur was good to her, tender and considerate. It made no difference; she was still lonely. 'His presence only made it more intense.'[16]

Another source of resentment among her neighbours must have been her comparative affluence, in spite of those unpaid bills. The indications again are in *Sons and Lovers*, first in the revelation that her mother-in-law owned two houses, and then when she enquired about the fact that her husband was rather late coming home at night.

'They're working very late now, aren't they?' she said to her washer-woman.

Arthur Lawrence could afford such luxuries as a washer-woman, for he was a butty: in other words a sub-contractor who negotiated with the company and arranged to mine a certain area of coal, called a stall, for so much a ton. (According to Professor Chambers, when Lydia asked Arthur at her aunt's house what he did for a living, he said he was a contractor.) The stall would be marked out in chalk by an overseer. Then the butty would employ his own day-men, paying them a fixed day wage, regardless of what the stall actually produced. Arthur Lawrence was said to be skilled at the art of estimating the worth of a stall and thus ensuring a good profit for himself.

Each man, including the butty, would 'hole a stint'. Holing a stint meant that a man had to lie on his side and hack away at the rock until he had dug a cavity five or six feet underneath the coal, propping up the hole as he went. Dragging himself out again, he would carefully pull away the props as he emerged, then drive in wedges to bring the coal down. This jagged black harvest, reaped in killing heat, choking dust and darkness, would be loaded on trams and hauled away to the bottom of the shaft.

Arthur Lawrence's stall brought him in personally as much as five pounds a week – gold pounds – during the first years of his marriage. Later on he grew quarrelsome, less cooperative with the managers, and so had worse stalls allocated to him. But five pounds in those days, even allowing for the stoppages and the sick-club money to be paid from it, was real wealth. Admittedly this would be in the winter, the busiest time. In the summer the pits went slack, and often the men would be home again at midday, after only a morning's work. So as an average his wage throughout the year would be fifty or fifty-five shillings a week. Of this he was supposed to give Lydia thirty shillings, and out of this sum she paid the rent, food, clothes, clubs, insurance, doctors. It was sometimes thirty-five shillings, but more often twenty-five. The winters then were the flush times, and at the weekends his sovereign all went on drink, and Lydia used to complain that she would rather he were hard-up, for 'when he's flush, there isn't a minute of peace.' He didn't save, and his wife, out of her allowance, wasn't able to save either. Now and then she was forced to pay his debts, such as they were: not drinking debts, but foolish extravagances, such as a new walking-stick or a bird in a cage.

The bugbear was his hatred of authority. 'He was blab-mouthed, a tongue-wagger.'[17] His pals egged him on in the pubs, when he abused the pit-managers. None of this did him any good, and the stalls he was landed with had thin coal, hard to get out, unprofitable. He was forced to curb his tongue, at any rate till he got home.

Their first child was weakly, but he recovered, blossoming into a beautiful boy with dark golden curls. Lydia loved him passionately; he made up for so much. And all this outpouring of love made Arthur jealous.

They called the baby George Arthur. And from the first, Lydia turned to the children for consolation, keeping her thoughts to herself. Her husband, for all his dancing and boasting, was all show, she decided, with nothing at the back of him now that the novelty of his own home was gone. This was harsh criticism, and arose from the basic incompatibility of their characters. She was the moral, religious one, and he was basically carefree, enjoying his morning walks through the dewy fields to the pit-head, liking animals, getting on well with his mates, feeling free in the pubs of a weekend. The pit was his world, and everything radiated from that. Even his rows with the managers were part of the life, while her life was centred on the home and the children. She strove to force him to face up to what she considered were his responsibilities, and this only made him truculent, as it did in the pit. He was best when left alone.

Ada remembered that her mother would wait up for her father at night, seething with rage, and when he came in she let him have it, a flood of biting truths which made him lash out blindly and brutally, whereas he had arrived apologetic, if fuddled. The children lay in bed, listening to the bitter words.

Left alone, he was handy in the house, mending the boots and shoes, and Ada remembered him sitting tailor-wise on the rug like his father before him, busy with the hobbing iron, hammering away happily and singing at the top of his voice. Nothing was too difficult to tackle, whether it was leaking pans and kettles or the eight-day clock going wrong again. The children loved to watch him dismantle the clock, 'carefully putting the screws and spare parts in saucers and boiling the works in a big saucepan to clean them thoroughly.'[18]

Harry T. Moore tells us that 'early in her martyrdom' Lydia Lawrence moved with her husband into Eastwood from that quarry-bed cottage where George Arthur and probably the next two children, William Ernest and Emily, had been born. Why this move was necessary has not been made clear, but possibly the new house had more room for the growing family. Even so, it was small enough, on the down-sloping Victoria Street, close to the junction with Scargill Street. One reason may have been the large square front-room window on the street level – there was no front garden – because Mrs Lawrence set up a shop in that front room, selling linen and lace for the Victorian caps and aprons of that time. At any rate, it was here that David Herbert Lawrence was born, her youngest son. A small plaque fastened to the wall over the door commemorates the birth. D. H. Lawrence moved from that house when he was two, so he had no memory of it. But he had very vivid impressions of the next place they moved to, lower down still to the north, against the Greenhill Road. It was a part of Eastwood known as the Breach, and in medieval papers is recorded as *le Breche*.

Not long before the Lawrences moved there, the pit-owners had built at the Breach six tenement blocks for the colliers' families. For an extra sixpence a week rent the Lawrences were able to live at the end of one of these blocks, which meant a bit more garden. All the same, Mrs Lawrence hated it from the start, presumably because it was so communal. It was a working-class custom – it still is – to live at the back of the house, and these backs all looked out on a scrubby bit of garden, probably separated by wooden palings, and then beyond were the ash-pits. Between these long lines of ash-pits ran the alley, where the Breach had its real life, where the kids played and the women gossiped and the men stood and smoked. The front were very different, with little front gardens, sweet williams and pinks in the brighter top block, auriculas and saxifrage in the more shadowy bottom block. There were dormer windows, privet hedges neatly clipped, small porches and smart front windows. The rooms were kept spick and span for appearance's sake, but nobody really used them, except at Christmas, when the families overflowed with relatives and visitors and a stoked-up fire in the front kept the damp at bay.

But at least the Breach was a cut above the New Buildings, 'two great hollow squares of dwellings planked down on the rough slope of the hill, little four-room houses with the "front" looking outward into the grim, blank street, and the "back", with a tiny square brick yard, a low wall, and a w.c. and ash-pit, looking into the desert of the square, hard, uneven, jolting black earth tilting rather steeply down, with these little back yards all round, and openings at the corners. The squares were quite big, and absolutely desert, save for the posts for clothes lines, and people passing, children playing on the hard earth.'[19] Living there was 'common'. 'And it was most "common", most degraded of all to live in Dakins Row, two rows of the old dwellings, very old, black, four-roomed little places, that stood on the hill again, not far from the Square.'[20]

When Mrs Lawrence moved to the Breach, the houses were already twelve years old and beginning to look dilapidated. Still, it was the best she could do, and her end house with the extra strip of garden gave her a modicum of superiority, though probably by now she had lost her washer-woman. She was now several years married, but it made no difference; she still shrank back into herself and failed to make ordinary contact with the other women.

Lawrence remembered living in that house when he was small. He remembered that 'A field-path came down under a great hawthorn hedge. On the other side was the brook, with the old sheep-bridge going over into the meadows. The hawthorn hedge by the brook had grown tall as tall trees, and we used to bathe from there in the dipping-hole, where the sheep were dipped, just near the fall from the old mill-dam, where the water rushed.'[21]

After they had been in their new home for only three weeks, the 'wakes', or fair, began. Her husband, she knew, would go off early on the Monday morning, and he did. Ernest, now a boy of seven, disappeared as soon as he had had his breakfast, and this left Emily discontented and restless, grizzling all morning to be allowed to go too. But she was only five, and this meant that her mother would have to take her in the afternoon.

Mrs Lawrence looked a lady at the wakes, in her cloak and her black bonnet. She didn't like it: the din of the organs, grinding and screeching, the roundabouts, one worked by steam and the other dragged round by a donkey, the violent clacking of the coconut man's rattle, the strident yells of the peepshow lady. She saw her son before her. He was standing enthralled outside a sideshow, and before she went to him she bought Emily some toffee on a stick. She looked up and there was her son, very pleased she had come, excitedly wanting to show her everything. He had won two egg-cups in a marble game; they were decorated with pink moss-roses. He had spent his tuppence. She knew he wanted the egg-cups as a present for her.

'"H'm!" she said, pleased. "They *are* pretty!"'[22]

He wanted her to carry them; he was frightened of dropping and breaking them. He was proud to have her there, but she was tired after her morning's work and had to leave him there. He was miserable, letting her go, but the excitement was too much – he had to stay on as long as he could. As she went she smelled the beer in the pub she passed, and guessed her husband was in the bar.

At home, when it was too dark to sew, she got up and went outside, into the little side garden. She could almost smell the excitement and restlessness of the holiday in the air, and in spite of everything it affected her. Usually the women and their children came home alone, the men staying away in a bunch while they had the chance, though sometimes 'a good husband came along with his family', a peaceful unit. The mothers who had stayed at home stood for a gossip at the alley corners in the twilight, their arms folded belligerently under their stiff aprons. These were the ones Mrs Lawrence shrank from. With another child coming she felt suddenly pitiful, sorry for herself. She couldn't afford it, she didn't even want it. It was just one more heartache to be endured, more grinding struggle to make the money spin out, and the ugly existence of her life here dragging on as before.

For Arthur John Lawrence, life wasn't ugly or intolerable, it was a day-by-day existence. He didn't look to the future or save up for it, he was completely absorbed in his daily life, which was all of a piece, even now, with the discontent of his wife becoming more and more evident. He expected no change, wanted none, only to be left alone to live his day. And that went on as before, woman or no woman, family or no family. In the work mornings he got up early, sometimes earlier than five, and so had plenty of time. He liked that. Some miners dragged their wives out of bed bad-tempered, but he preferred to see to himself: it was more enjoyable. He got straight out of bed and went down in his shirt, fresh as an animal; then dragged on the cumbersome pit-trousers which were left in front of the heart in the winter to warm. The fire was kept in. Upstairs, they knew he was up by the sound of the fire being raked, the poker smashing the half-burnt slabs of coal into flame. They knew he was filling the kettle then and leaving it on the hob to boil. On the table, there would be his cup and knife and fork, with the newspaper spread to prevent a mess. He wasn't fussy. He stoked up the fire, shut out the draught under the doors with rugs, and sat down with pleasure. Life was still good! The bacon he toasted on a fork and let the drops of fat fall on his bread, grunting with satisfaction at the sight of it. The rasher went on his door-step slice of bread. He cut off pieces with a clasp-knife, poured tea into his saucer and supped it up under his straggle of moustache. This was joy. Nobody about, to interfere or criticise. In a self-conscious little note in *Sons and Lovers*, Lawrence, no doubt with his new London friends in mind, wrote that his father 'loathed a fork; it is a modern introduction which has still scarcely reached the common people.' His father would sit on a stool with his back to the fire, luxuriating, and read what he could of the last night's newspaper – he was always semi-literate. But he could spell it out laboriously, as much as he wanted. The strange thing was, even when it was light outside he would keep the blinds down and the candle burning, as if he were already down the mine.

Then it was time to go, to cut his snap and fill his tin bottle with the rest of the tea. It would be cold tea when he was down the pit, with no milk or sugar. These days, with his wife often ill and expecting, he took her a cup of tea before he left. No farewell kiss, no leave-taking of any sort. If she had put an apple or an orange out for him, this was an extra treat – all he took for himself were the two thick slices of bread and butter. He knotted his scarf, put on his clumping great boots, his coat, and was off into the morning. The freshness invigorated him, as did the walk across the fields. Often he would arrive at the pit-head with a stalk in his mouth from the hedge, chewing on it like a yokel. Down the mine he was as contented as when he was up above in the fields.

He was only really ill-tempered at home, or coming home drunk and knowing what was in store for him, when the guilt began to bite into him, the thought of his wife's displeasure. This

always made him worse. Before the birth of David Herbert Lawrence came the searing scene which the other children remembered, when he had been in the Nelson with his bosom pal,
playing skittles. It had been another wakes holiday, a Tuesday,
and the two men had been ten miles over the fields to Nottingham, pub-crawling on the way. Coming in with a bad conscience,
the father kicked the gate open and broke the latch. That was the
start of it. Entering the house, he lurched drunkenly against the
table, where his wife was pouring boiled herbs and hops out of the
saucepan into the great earthen pancheon. The liquor nearly
tipped out. His wife went for him, accusing him of spending
money to 'bezzle' with, which she badly needed for the house, and
when he denied it, goading him further by saying that the only
other way he could have got drunk as a lord was by sponging on
his pals.

'"It's a lie, it's a lie. Shut your face, woman."'[23]

Now there was nothing but hatred between them. She said the
house was filthy with him, and he told her to clear off then, get out
of it, the house was his anyway. Oh no, she said, she knew that was
what he wanted, but did he think she'd leave the children to his
tender mercies, did he imagine she'd let him have it *all* his own
way?

He was drunk, but she wasn't afraid. Instead she frightened
him with her white fury. He came blundering up to her, rage
masking his fear, bundled her out of the door and bolted it, then
staggered back into the kitchen and slumped down in an
armchair. She was locked out in her own back garden.

It was an August night, full moonlight. 'She stood for a few
moments helplessly staring at the glistening great rhubarb leaves
near the door,'[24] her youngest son later imagined. She was
trembling with shock and fear, and pregnant. She stood where
she was for about half an hour, gradually aware of the indifferent
beauty of the night. What could she do? He would be asleep now,
she knew, dead drunk. What if the neighbours saw her? She
wandered round the side to the front garden, where she would be
less likely to be seen, murmuring to herself what a nuisance it was,
half weeping. She was suddenly very cold. In the coal-house was
an old hearth rug, ready for the rag-and-bone man to collect on
his rounds. She put this round her shoulders, then went to the
window and began rapping on the glass. He gave a start and sat
up. She could see by the way he was glaring in front of himself
blindly that he didn't know where he was.

At last it dawned on him what had happened. He got up
sullenly and let her in. Then he almost ran upstairs, ripping off

1. The Lawrence family. *Standing:* Emily, George, Ernest.
Seated: Ada, Mrs. Lydia Lawrence, David Herbert, Arthur
John Lawrence. (*See page 52*)

3. Walker Street, Eastwood home of the
   Lawrence family, 1891–1902

2. The Breach (now 26 Garden Road),
   Eastwood home of the Lawrence family,
   1887–91

his collar as he went, in a hurry to be away from her. On the stairs, there was the collar 'with bursten button holes'.[25]

She went wearily to bed herself after getting his breakfast things ready as usual. Outside she had touched the tall, pallid lilies, hardly knowing what she was doing. Now, as she stood at the bedroom mirror, she could see that her face was smeared yellow in patches from the dust of the blooms.

The worst thing about it all from his point of view – which made him worse – was the way she had turned the children against him. She was to do the same with her fourth. Out of sheer perversity he acted more coarsely and brutally at these times than ever. If he was going to be cast as a villain, all right, he'd give them their money's worth and be a really black villain. Then afterwards for a day or two he went about quietly, ashamed of himself.

In his fashion he was proud of his family, his two sons and the little girl, Emily. George, the first son, though short, was now the most handsome, with his thick, brown, wavy hair and regular features. Eventually to be a textile engineer, he served an apprenticeship to a picture-framer in Nottingham who was a relative. Ernest, the next son, was by contrast a tall boy, strongly built, taking after his father with his twinkling eyes. Very clever at school, he was the one Bert would be urged to emulate. Ernest was obviously going places. First he was a clerk in Shipley colliery offices, then in the Co-op offices at Langley Mill, a mile or two to the west of Eastwood. In his spare time he went to night school to learn shorthand and typing. Aiming high, he applied for and obtained a responsible job with a London shipping firm when he was twenty-one. Not content with this, he taught himself French and German by correspondence.

3

The Skinned Rabbit

Now Bert, the youngest and the frailest son, was about to be born. When it was time for Mrs Lawrence to be confined to bed, she did the traditional thing: banged with the poker on the back of the fireplace, thud thud, to bring her neighbour in. The year was 1885. It was raining when her husband came home from work and found his wife in bed, the boy already born. He had come up from the pit in a bad temper, after bashing at a lump of rock that was in the way for the next day's hewing. He knew it was raining above ground, the news had come down to him. He had an old umbrella, and the sound of the water plopping on it gave him pleasure. He went walking down the wet road to Eastwood with a gang of men, black-faced and red-mouthed. Being in a bad mood, he resisted the temptation to call at the pub and quench his thirst. Even so, he had worked a bit late, and the child was born. He found another woman getting his evening meal for him. Mrs Lawrence was very ill upstairs, he was told: she always was when her children were born. Her husband didn't go straight up, probably because the disapproving woman made him feel the obligation. Instead, he asked for a drink. 'She set the mug, with a little, disgusted rap, on the table.'[1]

He didn't like having the woman about the house, and when his wife upstairs asked the neighbour, 'Was that the master?' she replied that yes, it was, and she'd given him his dinner. He sat down below them, tired and a bit resentful. For a start, the dinner plate she'd given him was smaller than his usual one. And the fire was not stoked up enough for his liking. He objected to these strangenesses, more than he did to the fact that upstairs was another boy, his youngest son, the 'skinned rabbit' who was to recreate all this in due course, who would fly into rages against authority just as his father did, as if he needed to create antagonisms. And though *Sons and Lovers* is on the whole a denunciation of the father, the man was given his due sometimes, in spite of the quarrels that the over-sensitive boy hated, that flayed him even more than they did the other children as they heard the angry voices below, one hotly objecting, the other coldly criticising, all mingled with the wind in the ash-tree outside their window.

For instance, he remembered his father's naked body, still young and muscular and smooth, except for the blue coal scars and the hairiness of the chest. He remembered, as his brothers and sisters did, the times when his father made fuses for taking down the pit, fetching first of all 'a sheaf of long sound wheat-straws from the attic. These he cleaned with his hand, till each one gleamed like a stalk of gold, after which he cut the straws into lengths of about six inches, leaving, if he could, a notch at the bottom of each piece. He always had a beautifully sharp knife that could cut a straw clean without hurting it. Then he set in the middle of the table a heap of gunpowder, a little pile of black grains upon the white scrubbed board. He made and trimmed the straws while Paul and Annie filled and plugged them. Paul loved to see the black grains trickle down a crack in his palm into the mouth of the straw, peppering jollily downwards till the straw was full. Then he bunged up the mouth with a bit of soap – which he got on his thumb-nail from a pat in a saucer – and the straw was finished.'[2]

At first glance this could be any sensitive writer's prose: close, good observation. But notice the details, the almost religious heightening of the homely scene, the straws gleaming like stalks of gold, and the masterly touch of that 'peppering jollily downwards', conveying all the children's fun and fascination. The authenticity, too, is remarkable, the whole description of the operation unquestionably accurate. We can always trust the truth of Lawrence at these moments. The doubts come later. For instance, though he certainly loathed the scenes of family discord he records with such anguish in his novel, we find him in *Fantasia of the Unconscious* advising married women that if 'a woman's husband gets on her nerves, she should fly at him. If she thinks him too sweet and smarmy with other people, she should let him have it on the nose, straight out. She should lead him a dog's life, and never swallow her bile.' This of course was consistent with his stance in the novel, but leaves out completely the suffering of the children. But he had ulterior motives for these snarling remarks, as we shall see.

Meanwhile, he was barely alive when his father looked at him for the first time, said, 'Bless him' mechanically – this was what he always said, for the sake of anything better – and hastily left the bedroom, leaving the smell of his pit-dirt behind. William Hopkin recalls the baby as looking like 'a skinned rabbit' when he met Mrs

Lawrence wheeling her newborn child down the main street in Eastwood. Lawrence himself maintained that he nearly died of bronchitis when he was only two. Mrs Lawrence had doubts about his survival, for she told Hopkin sadly that 'I'm afraid I s'll never rear him.'

While she was still struggling to rear this child which she had dreaded like a catastrophe, another scene occurred, as crucial as the one where she was locked out of her own house. She must have told it to Lawrence later, and for the same reason, to bring him into the battleground of the parents' war, as Harry T. Moore puts it, and to bring him in emphatically on her side. In *Sons and Lovers* the episode comes after the visit of the shy young Congregationalist minister who was Lawrence's godfather and afterwards gave him lessons in French and German. This again was either retailed later by Mrs Lawrence or remembered by the older children. The clergyman had come to tea, the cloth and the best cups were out, all was prim and proper. The atmosphere can easily be imagined. Then in comes 'the lord and master', scraping his pit-boots.

The minister rose, as was proper, to shake hands with the husband, who told him not to bother, there was too much dirt on his. Then, to crown his wife's humiliation, he told the wincing young man to feel the sweat of his singlet.

'Goodness!' cried Mrs Lawrence. 'He doesn't want to feel your nasty singlet.'

Next, Lawrence started complaining about his thirst, about how hard a life he suffered down the pit. He poured out his tea in a saucer as usual and sucked it up through his moustache, letting out a great sigh of pleasure. Then he started to whine about his hard life again, simply because he had an audience. Ernest was nursing the baby, and he felt a child's contempt for the falseness of it, the lack of consideration for his mother. Emily ignored her father: that was her way of showing her disapproval. Years later the miner revenged himself in his own style, when Lawrence and Frieda were ejected from Cornwall by the police and stayed for a while in Derbyshire near the old man, who was a widower then and living alone. Lawrence asked him to repair a pair of shoes, and they came back promptly, neatly soled in tin. Another time he lit a large bonfire in their garden when they were out for a walk, an action which might have led to serious trouble, as they were then under surveillance by the authorities and it could have been interpreted as signalling.

The incident of the kitchen-table drawer comes in *Sons and Lovers* soon after the disastrous visit of the clergyman. One or two telling passages linking the two scenes reveal the surge of hot love the mother has begun to feel for her delicate, unnamed baby. 'With all her force, with all her soul, she would make up to it for having brought it into the world unloved.'[3] Uncannily, the child seemed to know and understand, looking at her as if aware of the pain and suffering to come. There and then she gave the child a name: the father wasn't taken into account.

When he came in that evening he was late, and nearly drunk. This was his only means now of having some obscure revenge for what he felt to be the injustice and ignominy of his position. There was nothing to eat that he could see, and this inflamed him, together with a few curt answers from his tired wife. He jerked clumsily at the table drawer to get at the bread knife, and the drawer jammed because he had tugged it sideways. In a temper now, he used violence on it. Out it flew and so did the entire contents, spoons, forks, knives, all over the brick floor. The din made the baby jump in its mother's arms. As the father was trying in his fuddled fashion to fit the drawer back in, she called him a drunken, clumsy fool. In a blind rage he hurled the drawer at her.

The corner of it caught her forehead as it went smashing into the hearth. Instinctively she clung to the baby, which began to cry. The piteous crying brought her round, and now her forehead was bleeding freely, and some blood had dripped down on to the white shawl of her child. But the baby was unharmed. Her drunken husband came swaying forward, hiccuping. She told him to clear off, then went into the kitchen and bathed the cut over her eye, still clutching her child. Now the whole picture before his eyes sickened him with hopelessness. 'He was turning drearily away when he saw a drop of blood fall from the averted wound onto the baby's fragile, glistening hair. Fascinated, he watched the heavy dark drop hang in the glistening cloud, and pull down the gossamer. Another drop fell. It would soak through to the baby's scalp. He watched, fascinated, feeling it soak in; then, finally, his manhood broke.'[4] The symbolism of this blood-letting, blood-sharing, is obvious, and too explicit to be ignored. The stage is all set for what is to come.

In the descriptions of Lawrence's father there is always the swinging to and fro, even in this early book, between sympathy and alienation. From now on, his references to miners will always be ambiguous. Sometimes Lawrence gets under the very skin of the father with such extraordinary skill that it is as though he *is* the father. He understood the man so well, the life of activity that was characteristic of him, the brutal behaviour he indulged in when cornered into any self-examination, the need to be worse than he was when he sensed the whole family shrinking back as he entered the house, waiting for him to leave, relieved when he took himself off to the kitchen and soused his head in cold water, wetted his hair and combed it with his steel comb. Then they knew he was making for the pub, where the windows were steamed over, the passage swimming with wet from all the feet, the stale air warm and welcoming, the smell of ale and tobacco smoke. This was where he thawed out, where the men made room for him and 'took him in warmly'. He was 'clear as a bell' for the rest of the evening. To get himself down there, though, he wasn't above stealing some of the housekeeping money from his wife's purse. She caught him out in this several times, accused him to his face, and he denied it. She knew he was lying. Once, shamed to the very depths of him, he came blustering down from the bedroom with a big bundle, some belongings of his done up in an enormous checked handkerchief. He was leaving for good, he said.

Both the children, Ernest and Emily, broke down and wept when they heard their father had run away. Mrs Lawrence laughed, she couldn't help it. Then even she became a little anxious. He was such a helpless, stupid fool. Where would he go? Something prompted her to go down the garden to the coal-place, and there behind the door was his bundle. She just sat down on a piece of coal and laughed, it was too much. And secretly she was relieved. She knew too that he would come slinking in, sullen, and about nine o'clock he did. Somehow, without losing any more face, he had to retrieve the bundle from the coalhouse and get it away out of sight, for he didn't know his wife had already seen it. Mrs Lawrence let him go, because he looked a fool and after all he was her husband; she had loved him once. Her heart was bitter with the memory of it.

Ten years after he had completed *Sons and Lovers*, Lawrence was deeply uneasy about the injustice he felt he had done his father in the book, and told a friend that he felt like rewriting it. He appreciated anew the vulgar gusto of his father, which he felt his mother with her militant self-righteousness had spoiled, just as she had irretrievably damaged the children. 'Shaking his head at the memory of that beloved mother,' said Lawrence's friend, Mrs Achsah Brewster, 'he would add that the righteous woman martyred in her righteousness is a terrible thing and that all self-righteous women ought to be martyred.'⁵

The worst part, perhaps, was the unrelenting intolerance. If Arthur Lawrence had been accepted on his own level he might have made a good father. Instead, quite early, he was put aside because Mrs Lawrence insisted on trying to make a silk purse out of a sow's ear. He would never be that, but she undermined, in front of his own children, the authority and the physical gusto he did have in the beginning. That was always the crux of the battle. And he was always the loser in these verbal battles: his wife was a clever woman. He even wanted to be proud of her, and after her death, when asked why he didn't marry again, he said, according to his youngest daughter Ada Clarke, 'I've had one good woman – the finest in the world – and I don't want another.'[6]

Another factor in the struggle was the Women's Guild, a club affiliated to the Co-operative Wholesale Society. Their meetings were held in a long room over the grocery shop. This was more subtle undermining of his authority, and the hostile husbands nicknamed it the 'clat-fart' shop. The Guild gave the women an objective view of their predicament, their homes and conditions, and of course this made them critical. They had a common basis now from which to find fault. It was natural for Mrs Lawrence, a clever woman who had once been a teacher, to want an outlet for her talents. Social questions were discussed, and sometimes Mrs Lawrence contributed a paper, reading it aloud to members. So there she would be at home, sitting deep in thought, thumbing through reference books as she wrote her paper. The children were proud of her. Monday nights she attended the Guild, and eventually became secretary. On these nights, and Friday, which was market night, the children looked forward to having the house to themselves. That was when they ransacked the place and experimented with cooking. Ada Clarke says they loved to make toffee. There was one night in particular she remembers, when Bert, dressed in his mother's blue checked apron, got out the rolling pin and the flour and decided they should make potato cake. He was always the one in charge. No doubt his two brothers were out playing in the street, and Ada Clarke remembers that on this occasion two friends, Mabel and Emmie, were with them, and Bert set them and his sisters to work cooking the potatoes while he got busy with the flour. This time it wasn't a success, and though they daren't disagree with him when they tasted the india-rubber bits that should have been crisp and tasty and he said they were nice, they soon followed suit when he had a violent reaction, shouted 'They're awful!' and flung his into the fire. They made sure to open the door and windows to get rid of the smell before their mother came home.

Ada says that her mother brewed very good herb beer. The younger children collected the herbs for her on Saturdays, starting out soon after breakfast. Once again Bert was head of the expedition, and he took them down past their old house in the

Breach, through Engine Lane and out past the railway line in the direction of Watnall pit. To discover the first spring flowers, the brilliant celandine, the shy violet, these were thrilling adventures when you were with Bert. On the way back they could see their home, perched high on a hill, like so many of the surrounding colliery villages and settlements. 'No wonder my father's feet dragged up it,' said Ada, 'in heavy pit boots after a hard day's work.' Evidently she too was anxious to make up in her memoir for the attitude she had taken against her father, along with her brothers and sisters.

Emily King was another who had good words to say for her father in later life. She remembers him as being 'very good on wild life', knowing the names of birds and animals, and mentions the wild rabbit he brought home, that became the subject of 'Adolf' a story published posthumously in *Phoenix*.

With Lawrence the countryside was always passionately there, still wild, against which industry 'fumed'. It was an accident, the industrial growth, almost taken over and mastered by the rural setting. Yet the scars and the new gashes inflicted by industry had an ugliness and power that haunted him, and the land took on a deeper meaning for him because it was threatened, becoming the more poignant as he understood more fully the incurable nature of its disease. 'The air is dark with north and sulphur, the grass is a darker green,' he wrote in his poem 'The North Country'. And with his own father a representative of this industry which kept ripping and gobbling at the fair land, he was bound to be ambivalent in his deepest feelings.

Then there was the bewildering mixture of the region around Eastwood itself. 'North and south of Eastwood it is half town and half country,' writes Alan Sillitoe, 'slum and mansion, pitstock and folly, red brick and priory ruins, lime-kiln and green glen, farmhouse and ironworks. It is the mixture that makes a landscape seem so vast in small mileages, an exploring ground that baffles the mind but goes far towards opening it.'[7] The Eastwood locality had a significance for Lawrence out of all proportion to its scale. It was magical, the one enduring love of his life. Its fields and lanes and hedges and birds' nests made roots in his blood and curled round his veins. He carried it everywhere. His loyalty to it was indestructible. It was what he meant by England.

As well as trips to gather herbs, there was always the deserted quarry to be penetrated anew, either alone or with the other children. Often he liked to wander there by himself. In the autumn it was thick with blackberries, and it impressed him with its darkness and mystery. It was very old and deep, tangled with oak trees and guelder roses and the blackberry briars. The open parts were rich in daisies and dog-violets, deadly nightshade and honeysuckle. The walls were pitted with little caves where he imagined adders were lurking.

Lawrence's physical frailty was to be permanent. People in his childhood used to comment that he was the thinnest little boy they'd ever seen. His older brother George often carried him around on his shoulder and says that he was always delicate, and because of it he was petted and spoiled by everyone from the time he was born: and he himself adds, even more significantly, 'it was a source of grief to him that he wasn't able to enter the boys' games – he used to gather the girls together and go blackberry-ing.' But was the young Lawrence so very grief-stricken about this? Certainly he was soon to be made to feel very sensitive about it, and more than one person describes him as 'mardy' or a grizzler, which would indicate a spoiled child. He couldn't bear to be criticised, Willie Hopkin remarked. He used to help his mother doing many of the household jobs. A childhood friend, Mabel Collishaw, once passed by the Lawrence house with her sister and saw Mrs Lawrence hanging up new lace curtains, her son Bert standing proudly beside her, helping. Many times when they were playing, Mabel Collishaw says, she told him to stop snivelling – 'you *are* a baby.'

A source of grief? Clearly it was a torment when at the age of five he was transferred into Standard 1 from the infants'. By that time he had already been at school intermittently for two years, though he was often away ill. Towards the end of his life he describes himself then as 'a delicate pale brat with a snuffy nose, whom most people treated quite gently as just an ordinary delicate little lad.'[8] One of his schoolmates in Standard 1, Albert Limb, says that Bert Lawrence hated boys and always played with the girls. He goes further: 'Tall and thin, with ginger hair and a face like chalk, he was the most effeminate boy I ever knew.'[9] The other lads called him 'Bertie', which he came to loathe. They thought he was toffee-nosed. Then Albert Limb uses a phrase that conjures up a world of misery for this white-faced boy whose gentleness appealed so much to the girls. He says that 'any little boy could go and punch him, and he would not retaliate.' He was weak and puny, he goes on, and the most cowardly boy he ever knew. But the thing that most surprised him, looking back on this weakling who became so famous, was that he 'was innocent of the facts of life when he was fourteen or fifteen years old. Yet when he started writing at nineteen or twenty he knew more about sex

41

than any of us.'[10] The people of Eastwood, he adds righteously, 'do not make a fuss of him.'[11]

Another old schoolboy of those early days, J. E. Hobbs, affirms that Bert was delicate, with a thin face, and in the summertime wore a white collar outside his jacket. On the way to Beauvale School his sister Ada would be with him, and Addy Stapleton and 'two sisters named Limb', and with these girls Lawrence kept up a steady, bright, high-pitched chatter, his voice squeaky when he was excited. Again comes the observation that he shunned the other boys at playtime, leaning against the playground wall in the hope of being overlooked. But of course they taunted him with 'Th'art a mard-arsed kid.'

Mabel Collishaw must have been one of the first to notice his agonies of hypersensitivity. Every Boxing Day the miners' children from the area were invited to Lamb Close House (later to be the model for Gerald's home, Shortlands, in *Women in Love*, as well as Highclose in *The White Peacock*), the mansion of the colliery owner, Mr Barber. This was southwest of the reservoir at Moorgreen, which became Nethermore in *The White Peacock*, and the Willey Water in which Gerald's sister drowned in *Women in Love*. At Lamb Close on Boxing Day the boys and girls were given one new penny and a large orange each. Bert would hang back, hating the ritual, and his childhood sweetheart Mabel got his, saying to the butler, 'Please, I am not taking two pennies for myself. One is for Bertie Lawrence.'

One of Bert Lawrence's tasks at this time – and it terrified him – was going to the company offices at Nether Green to draw the money entitled to his father as a butty. The boy took a calico bag with him from school on Fridays, according to Mabel the most unhappy day of his week. She says that if she could escape from nursing a baby, and there was always one in the cradle in those days, she used to go with him to give him moral support. Then when she got home she'd be in trouble, her pinafore soiled from the dirt of the miners, for she had to push the flinching boy forward to the counter when his father's name was called out. Her mother would say, 'You have been with Mardy Lawrence again, *I* can see.'[12]

But there were always compensations. A treat was to go on Saturday afternoons to a nearby pottery, where children were allowed to make clay marbles and fire them. Bert Lawrence took along his paints and decorated the marbles prettily. Again this had its dark side. Once some boys crowded round the artistic boy, shouting, 'Dicky Dicky Denches plays with the wenches.' Willie Hopkin happened to be on his way past and advised Bert to 'Sock 'em, lad!' But it was left to Mabel to do the fighting, and run to retrieve his cap for him as usual.

By the time Lawrence was six he was in the new home at Walker Street, on the north edge of Eastwood and overlooking the Breach that his mother had hated so much because of that common alley running between and the dampness of the situation. Besides, the new house was roomier, with bay windows (the bay-window period only began when Lawrence was a boy) – a definite move up the social scale. Its view took in the whole valley, 'which spread out like a cockleshell before it.' In front of the house, opposite, was a big old ash tree. As the west wind, rushing in from Derbyshire, hit the house, the tree seemed to cry out. In *Sons and Lovers* the ash-tree is associated in the children's minds with the increasing violence of their parents' quarrels: they would lie in bed listening to the 'booming shouts of his father, come home nearly drunk, then the sharp replies of his mother, then the bang bang of his father's fist on the table, and the nasty snarling shout as the man's voice got higher. And then the whole was drowned in a piercing medley of shrieks and cries from the great, wind-swept ash tree.'[13]

This was the terrifying aspect of nature, confused with the ugliness of humanity in the terror of the night. But the boy already loved nature with an almost religious intensity that was at once his own and typical of the nineteenth century he sprang from, the century that produced Ruskin, Carlyle, Stevenson, William Morris, Whitman, and Whitman's English disciple, Edward Carpenter. Many of these men were later to be decisive influences, some of them acknowledged, some not. Edward Carpenter in particular he could have met in his youth, but if he did so he makes no mention of the fact. More curiously, in view of his admiration for Whitman, he makes no reference to Carpenter in any of his letters or papers.

The most thoroughly known stretch of ground in Lawrence's childhood must have been between Eastwood and nearby Brinsley. Nearly every Saturday he went to Brinsley to visit his grandparents, with his sisters Emily and Ada, taking the short cut over the fields. Later, he was to take himself away from these lanes and fields and flowers forever: but in a very real sense he never left. In *Lady Chatterley's Lover* he was digging back into this very landscape, reliving the geography of his childhood and youth, with Eastwood renamed Tevershall. Somehow, though, he had lost the clue to its topography: perhaps he had been away too long. He looked at it through horrified eyes and saw only the blight and the ruin, and his lady's lover enacts the pain he must have felt. But his childhood was capable, as is any child's, of pure acceptance: he hadn't yet become aware of the sooty drabness of Eastwood, the 'meanness and formless and ugly surroundings, ugly ideals, ugly religion, ugly hope, ugly love, ugly clothes, ugly furniture, ugly houses, ugly relationships between workers and employers.'[14] He wandered over the fields with his sisters and there was his grandfather, rooted in the land, a shambling, generous man in his eighties, the front of his waistcoat dusty with snuff. He didn't talk much, but if it was the apple season he invariably said, 'Would you like some apples, my duckies?' and then went pottering into his backyard to choose some ripe Keswicks from his old tree. The grandmother was a bit sharp and cantankerous with him, but the old man was deaf; much of her nagging went unheard.

Also at Brinsley were the children's three aunts. Two of them were their father's sisters and the third was the widow of his dead brother James. This was Aunt Polly, who, after her husband had been killed in a pit accident, had married James Allum. She had a leading role in an early Lawrence story, 'Odour of Chrysanthemums' – a story later to be recast in drama form and entitled *The Widowing of Mrs Holroyd*. Aunt Polly's daughter by her first marriage, Alvina, would one day marry one of Lawrence's most intimate male friends, Alan Chambers. But Alan was to come along much later, when Lawrence was fifteen and hiking out regularly to the farm of the Chambers family at The Haggs, north of Brinsley.

Near the church at New Brinsley, in a country lane called the Alley, lived their father's two sisters. Although in the same lane, they lived in separate establishments. Aunt Sally, the wife of the sexton, kept a spotless, far from welcoming house, and was visibly relieved when the children left to visit Aunt Emma. She went on endlessly about her ailments, then asked in a complaining voice about their mother and father and how their health was. Aunt Emma, in contrast, was all warmth and hospitality: even as they approached they could hear her exclaiming in delight that her darlings were coming. She didn't mind about the crumbs they dropped, she didn't point out that their boots were muddy, and she cooked delicious things they never had at home, apple dumplings with brown suet crust, and soda cake. But the biggest attraction was Jack, an old donkey she kept, who would bite you as soon as look at you, and if he tried, Aunt Emma would give him a whack with a special stick she kept ready. What a character she must have been, tramping along with her clumsy man's boots and wearing a cloth cap belonging to her dead husband, leading the old donkey down the lane. Her generous nature overflowed: she sent the children home with enormous bunches of flowers from her overgrown garden, and if she didn't have any she asked the old cobbler next door for some of his dahlias and tiger lilies. And her generosity was impulsive: once she looked out and saw a woman going past in the rain, rushed out and gave her an umbrella. That was the last she saw of it, but she never cared about possessions, any more than she cared about what other people said of her appearance.

In the fields and lanes and farms lived animals, many of them wild. Emily King has noted that her father was 'very good on wild life' and always sympathetic to animals, characteristics his youngest son inherited and developed with such force and subtlety later. These tendencies, especially the love of animals, Mrs Lawrence countered whenever she could: after all, it was the province of her savage of a husband, and she wanted as little of his influence as possible in her house. But the world of animals seduced all the children in turn, and at least twice she had to yield to their craving for pets. There was Adolf, the wild rabbit their father had brought home cheerfully in his pocket. Alas, he grew too wild, so the children accepted that he had to go. Back into their father's pocket he was popped, for him to let the animal go free in the woods on his way to work. Before he left, though, he had to have his joke. '"Best pop him i' the pot," said my father, who enjoyed raising the wind of indignation.' Many times in later life Bert Lawrence was to think of that wild rabbit, its cheeky tail as it skipped off in flight like a flag of defiance, a cry of *'Merde!'*

Another minor disaster was the gift of two tame white rats, given to Bert by a friend, Pussy Templeman. Reluctant as ever, his mother gave in and his father, always an ally in these matters, fixed up a big wooden box in the scullery. One morning there was consternation in the house: a large family of baby rats had arrived. Before this happened the rats had become very tame, and soon, says Ada Clarke, knew the children's voices. They loved to run amongst Ada's long hair and burrow under Bert's waist-coat – 'down his sleeves and into his pockets to sleep.' They caused a commotion one morning as the brother and sister played with them in the yard. An old Irishwoman came to the gate with a bucket of water. As she went by, one of the rats ran out of Ada's hair and the other appeared, head only, in Bert's shirt-front. The old woman dropped her bucket, lifted up her arms and ran for it, shrieking, 'Rots! Deary me, rots!'

Mr Lawrence had the unpleasant job of getting rid of the rats when they multiplied so alarmingly. But soon there arrived 'an adorable little black and white smooth-haired terrier', left to be looked after by an uncle in Nottingham. This was a puppy, irresistible to the children, so once more the poor mother capitulated. Like the rabbit, the dog was to be enshrined later in a sketch of Lawrence's. The first night there was a general appeal for the dog to be allowed upstairs, but it was resisted vigorously by Mrs Lawrence. No, she was adamant: it was in the house, that was more than enough. Giving in, they went to bed and then were tormented by the hideous whines and growls of the puppy below them. Bert was the most agonised, and, unable to stand it any longer, he had to act. 'I'm going to fetch him up here,' he whispered, tiptoed downstairs and came back with the animal cradled in his arms. The pup slept on his bed contentedly until morning, then they made haste to get him back downstairs on the sofa before their mother was about. The latter part of this story is contradicted by Emily, who says her mother looked everywhere for the dog next morning and couldn't find it, then went to the bottom of the stairs and heard Bert saying, 'Oh, you little beauty. Oh, you're a king among doggies. I shall call you "Rex". I shall call you "Rex", because you're really a king of doggies!'

That morning at breakfast a fierce argument developed over the naming of the dog. Ada and Emily wanted to call it Toby or Spot, but Bert stuck to his choice. In these matters he was always the most passionate, and so had his way. Rex it had to be, because, says Ada, the little terrier was already 'king of our hearts'. And the exasperated mother, though the frisky pup dragged at the cushions and tore the girls' stockings, began to feel an affection for him too, in spite of herself. When the uncle suddenly turned up to take the dog back, they were all heartbroken. As for the uncle, he was furious, as Lawrence tells in his sketch. He swore at them: 'Why, what ha' you done wi' the dog – you've made a fool of him. He's softer than grease.' The dog cried piteously as he was taken off, and the children were mortified. 'Black tears, and a little wound which is still alive in our hearts.'[15]

This Uncle Herbert was the black sheep of the Beardsalls, but for some reason Mrs Lawrence had a soft spot for him. He kept a pub in Nottingham called the Lord Belper, at Sneinton. It stood at the bottom of a hill and was the setting for some of the scenes in *Sons and Lovers*. Lawrence transformed his uncle into Daniel Sutton in a story, 'The Primrose Path', which tells of the man's unhappy marriage, of his trip to Australia with a woman he said tried to poison him. Daniel Sutton worked for a sporting paper in Nottingham and also ran a taxi service, all details which were true of the uncle.

*

George Neville, one year younger than Bert Lawrence and later to be one of the Eastwood circle of friends known as the 'Pagans' and a student teacher at Ilkeston with Lawrence, remembers him at eight at Beauvale Board School, his high voice rising in pitch whenever he was worked up, the girlish toss of his head reminiscent of his mother, the lock of hair drooping over his high forehead. Early on there was the problem of the Christian name of this boy who later preferred to sign himself DHL or Lawrence or Lorenzo. To begin with he was called Bert, or Bertie, but he liked neither. For some reason he also disliked his first name, David, and this enraged his first schoolmaster, 'an excellent, irascible old man', who raved at him that David was the name of a great and good man and he should be ashamed of himself for objecting to it. Later, Lawrence said humorously that his father didn't know the difference between David and Davy of the safety-lamp.

It is curious how, despite all the evidence to the contrary, he identifies himself with the other colliery lads in these early school years. There is no mention of a preference for books or the company of girls, standing in a quiet corner and shunning the boys' games. In his autobiographical essays, looking back, he ranges himself alongside the 'honest, decent lads' who had to be violently thrashed occasionally to be got under. These boys, he says, were the first generation to be really tamed: anyway the first products of the national education which became compulsory for all in England in 1870. The first day was bound to be an anguish, when they were 'roped in' like wild creatures, captured and corralled. They hated school because it was like prison and the masters were their warders. They hated being made to learn, waiting only to escape, which for them meant going down the pit. They would jump the insufferable constriction of the rails and run wild again underground, wild and free as rabbits. They dreamed of the freedom of their fathers.

But school didn't occupy the whole day or the whole week: there were all kinds of compensations and many other potent influences. Quite frequently the boy was able to see the performances of strolling theatrical troupes that visited the villages. Eastwood and district was good business, and Teddy Rayner's company in particular came often, acting under an enormous tent. It was as exciting as a circus, and sometimes they stayed in the area for months, playing repertory, everything from *Maria Marten, or Murder in the Red Barn* to *Sweeney Todd* and Shakespeare. *Hamlet* was a play that Lawrence saw at the tuppenny

47

travelling theatre, where he 'sat in pale transport' listening to the Ghost chanting "Amblet, 'Amblet, I *am* thy father's ghost.'

For a penny you could attend a reading at the British School in Albert Street, and these were nearly always crowded. Readings, often from Dickens, were by local people, and there were musical evenings, vocal or instrumental, all drawn from local talent. The Dickens readings were probably imitations of the performances Dickens himself gave during his famous tours.

An even more important influence than education on this essentially religious boy was the religion of his family. It was Congregationalist, a popular sect in which theological dogma took second place to zeal and emotionalism. By the time he was sixteen he had outgrown the dogma, and as an adult he detested the 'beggar's whine' of Christianity; but the powerful emotional charge he received in these impressionable years remained with him all his life. Three times a day every Sunday the children were sent to chapel – nicknamed the 'Congo' – and urged into the Band of Hope by their teetotal mother. Yet Lawrence liked the raucous tub-thumping call to God, especially the hymn-singing and shouting. He even sneaked into the revivalist meetings if he got the chance, though his mother disapproved of them because they were common. There, the denunciations of the wicked and rich and slothful were even more violent, the surge of power and darkness and self-glorification was intoxicating, the detestable God of pity satisfactorily absent. Towards the end of his life he testified to the lasting power of the Bible over him, due to that early exposure. 'Not only was the Bible in portions poured into the childish consciousness day in, day out, year in, year out, willy nilly, whether the consciousness could assimilate it or not, but also it was day in, day out, year in, year out, expounded dogmatically, and always morally expounded, whether it was in day-school or Sunday-school, at home or in Band of Hope or Christian Endeavour.'[16]

When he thought about it later, it was the crudity and the sheer aggression of this intolerant religion that he had approved of, because it managed to avoid 'the ghastly sentimentalism that came like a leprosy over religion.' That was soon to come, when a woman teacher in the Sunday School tried to wring tears out of them over the Crucifixion. She kept asking them if they were sorry for Jesus. 'Aren't you sorry?' Most of the children wept, and Lawrence did too, but with mental reservations. In his late essay, 'Hymns in a Man's Life', he states proudly that it was good in his opinion to have been brought up a Protestant – and gives such a ring to it that, as Richard Aldington says, you would think he was

4. Beauvale School, Eastwood, where Lawrence attended
classes for five years

6. Eastwood, shortcut to Walker Street from the Breach

5. Eastwood, behind Victoria Street

being called to sit at the right hand of Oliver Cromwell. Certainly the hymns, ordinary as they seem, sank deep into his consciousness, deeper, he believed, than 'all these lovely poems which after all give the ultimate shape to one's life' – Wordsworth's Immortality Ode, Keats' Odes, some of the lyrics of Goethe and Verlaine, some of Shakespeare. The hymns, in the end, meant most; in particular 'the rather banal Nonconformist hymns that penetrated through and through my childhood.' He made use of a line from a hymn of Sabine Baring-Gould's, 'Birds and beasts and flowers', for the title of one of his books of poems.

Jessie Chambers' earliest recollection of Lawrence is set in the Congregationalist Sunday School at Eastwood they both attended, in the days long before they became acquainted. Each month the school superintendent used to persuade children to give recitations in place of the lessons. These usually took the form of poems. The little girl would be bored by them, but on one occasion her attention was held by the fact that the slight boy of eleven on the platform had forgotten the beginning of his poem. From the whispers going round she understood that this was Bert Lawrence, and the girl sitting near the front giggling at his predicament was Emily, his elder sister. He kept trying to speak, but the words wouldn't come. The room was tense, waiting for developments, the white-haired superintendent nodding and smiling encouragement. The boy's sister giggled louder. The boy 'turned a tortured face to the superintendent and made a request, which was granted by a cordial nod. Lawrence thereupon drew a sheet of notepaper from the inside pocket of his coat, glanced at it, then recited it correctly and got down from the platform with a white face.'[17]

Sunday School was in a gloomy room at the British School, where the penny readings were held and where Lawrence was to begin his career as a pupil-teacher in 1902. The white-haired superintendent was a Mr. Rimmington, 'with his round white beard and his ferocity. He made us sing!' The old man led the hymn-singing, clapping his hands and adding his own harsh voice to the children's shrill ones:

> Sound the battle cry,
> See the foe is nigh,
> Raise the standard high
> For the Lord.

– a verse that Lawrence must have appreciated.

The Congregational chapel that both the Chambers and Lawrence families attended had been built as recently as 1868 with stone from Bulwell outside Nottingham: an imitation Gothic construction with a spire. The pew where Jessie Chambers and her family sat was in the same aisle as the Lawrences', just across the gangway, but years were to pass before the two mothers befriended each other. Old-fashioned people in Eastwood, says Jessie, referred to the chapel as 'Butty's Lump'. If you wanted a good stall at the pit, one sure way was by making a generous donation to the building fund, since the promoters of the building scheme were influential colliery-owners. Hence the nickname.

Lawrence liked it there: for him it was 'tall and full of light, and yet still; and colour-washed pale green and blue, with a bit of a lotus pattern. And over the organ-loft, "O worship the Lord in the beauty of holiness", in big letters.'[18] Jessie herself described it as having an air of elegance which was rare in nonconformist chapels.

Although the Chambers and Lawrence children weren't yet directly acquainted, Jessie Chambers heard references to the Lawrences now and then. One day her father came home in a temper because he had seen Emily walking in the mowing grass on his farm.

'That eldest lass of Lawrence's is brazen soft,' he said to mother. 'When I shouted to her to get out she just stood and sauced me. I s'll tell her mother.'[19]

4

The Rise of Ernest

The Chambers family had already heard of Ernest Lawrence: he was becoming a local legend, with his job in the shipping office in London and his big salary, the handsome gloves and boots it was rumoured he brought home for his mother. Once, marvel of marvels, Jessie's father had seen him walking down the main street in Eastwood in a top hat, frock coat and yellow kid gloves. This fairy prince of the Lawrences brought out Mr Chambers' derision and made Mrs Chambers laugh when she heard about it. 'How weak-minded,' she said sarcastically.

They had heard tales of Mr Lawrence too, of what a first-rate worker he was, when he wanted to be. Whenever there was a ticklish job to be done in the pit he was invariably called on. And they knew what an independent cuss he could be. There was a story in circulation of the time when he was once having a haircut, and the barber left him halfway through while he turned to attend to a customer who was waiting with his chin lathered for a shave. Mr Lawrence got up in a fit of pique and went stamping off to another barber to have his haircut finished.

But they knew little or nothing of the over-sensitive, moody child, Bert Lawrence. He seemed to be getting thinner and thinner, following his mother around like a shadow, and though he was usually bright and eager enough, there would be times when he was overcome with fits of depression. Then his mother would find him on the sofa in tears.

'What's the matter?' she asked, and got no answer.
'What's the matter?' she insisted, getting cross.
'I don't know,' sobbed the child.[1]

He was never to know. All his life his feelings swung him about wildly. He was full of doubt, unsure of himself, and his mother saw this – indeed, she had helped to create it – and bore down on him with her strength and self-confidence, willing him to be strong like her. Instead he became a lifelong waverer, and each

51

phase, each reaction, he stamped with a vehemence of dogmatic assertion that was often bullying, as he tried to compensate for his secret misgivings.

To begin with, she tried to talk him out of his moods, but the child would be sunk in a nameless misery, crying. His father would leap up and let out a yell:

'If he doesn't stop, I'll smack him till he does.'
'You'll do nothing of the sort,' said the mother coldly. And then she carried the child into the yard, plumped him into his little chair, and said: 'Now cry there, Misery!'[2]

This was when he was only three or four. Now he was at school, competing already for his mother's favours, unconsciously in rivalry with Ernest, the 'fairy prince' of the family. George was away living in Nottingham, apprenticed to the uncle who made picture frames. Born in 1876, he had already lived away from home in the household of his great-grandfather John Newton the hymn-writer, and like his grandfather was destined to become an engineer. There he is in the family portrait (opposite page 32), standing dead centre at the back, called by his sister Ada the most handsome member of the family. Only just in the picture is the youngest, Lettice Ada, her mouth a little open as if surprised, in her white dress with the pale sash, hair in ringlets to below the shoulders, looking very diminutive. Her mother sits beside her with her head to one side, hands nervously clasped, her face hollow and worn, looking much older than her forty years. She looks ill. To the right of her, with little Bert standing between, is the father with his black-bearded head, who dominates the photograph even though he is obviously uneasy, hands bunched into fists in his lap, watch-chain and handkerchief in evidence, a white flower jaunty in his buttonhole. Uneasy or not, his face has a proud expression. Undoubtedly, in his own eyes at this moment he is the undisputed head of his family. Bert has an unusually chubby appearance, his figure as tall as his mother because he is standing, with a high white collar and his fair hair shining and neat. Emily Una, standing behind little Lettice, has all the fascination of the bemused adolescent girl, hair thick and long like an Alice in Wonderland. In her childhood the family names for her were Injun Top-Knot, and later Pamela, or Virtue Rewarded. And there, standing heavy and assured behind his father like a deputy, is Ernest, the pride of the family, whom the mother had selected as first candidate for the husband-substitute she was forever seeking. Harry T. Moore describes him as 'an animal-looking young man'. Certainly he is physically a strong presence, powerful jaw and flat cheekbones, with a big knotted tie bunched rather carelessly at his throat. His thick brown hair, according to Ada, had reddish tints, and his eyes were blue and twinkling. He was a fine and confident athlete, he had won prizes in swimming, and he was a hurdler who would vault easily over a gate rather than climb it or open it.

Curiously, although his scholastic career at Beauvale had been impressive, he had had no higher education – probably the reasons were economic; the County Council had not in his day begun to offer scholarships – and gone to work as a clerk at the age of twelve. This was the brother, brilliant and quick and self-assured, seven years older than Bert, with whom the youngest son had to compete, both at school and at home, for his mother's affection. For Beauvale remembered Ernest's achievements and there were odious comparisons. The headmaster told Bert once that he wasn't fit to tie his brother's bootlaces. From the beginning he was put under this double strain. Schoolwork that he would otherwise have regarded more casually took on an extra importance, and the additional studying he had to do gave the sickly child headaches. As one of his first biographers, Aldington, wrote, 'It was surely an odd freak of Fate to throw into such an environment, with its ferocities, prejudices and conflicts, a child who in his very different way was as responsive and over-strung as Shelley himself. Each was thrown into hostile and incongruous surroundings, against which he struggled as well as he could. In Shelley's case the conflict led him into much early writing of a worthless kind and into doing numberless rash, unconventional acts which baffled and enraged people.'[3] The comparison with Shelley is a pertinent one – and so would have been a reference to Rimbaud, another angelic figure. 'In the ordinary sense, Shelley never lived,' wrote Lawrence in his 'Study of Thomas Hardy'. 'He transcended life.' And as though issuing a warning to himself, he added, 'But we do not want to transcend life, since we are life.' Yet from his youth onwards he would feel impelled to make this very effort of transcendence, 'to prolong the moment of consummation' and be 'like the angels'.

In the autobiographical first half of *Sons and Lovers* there is virtually no reference to Lawrence's schooldays, as if the truth about them was altogether too painful to face. But he dramatised at length what he called 'The Casting off of Morel – The Taking on of William' by his mother. Morel was of course his father, and William was the dazzling Ernest. In the novel it was the mother who arranged for the boy to work at the Co-operative Society office at Langley, a nearby village, and there was the inevitable preliminary tussle with her husband.

'What dost want ter ma'e a stool-harsed Jack on 'im for?' said Morel. 'All he'll do is to wear his britches behind out, an' earn nowt. What's e' startin' wi'?'

'It doesn't matter what he's starting with,' said Mrs Morel.

'It wouldna! Put 'im i' the pit wi' me, an' 'e'll earn a easy ten shillin' a wik from th' start. But six shillin' wearin' his truck-end out on a stool's better than ten shillin' i' th' pit wi' me, I know.'

'He is *not* going in the pit,' said Mrs Morel, 'and there's an end of it.'[4]

Ernest could run like the wind, wrote Lawrence. When he was twelve he won a glass inkstand as a prize. There it stood on the dresser, an anvil shape, and his mother exulted in it. She knew it was for her, her prize. He had come flying home with it breathlessly and given it straight to her. 'Look, mother!' And it was the same when he started work: he gave her all his wages and she returned two shillings for himself. But he never asked her for it. He didn't drink, and with his two shillings accumulating every week in his pocket he was rich. Soon he was mixing with the middle classes – the sons of professional people and the richer tradesmen. He went to the Mechanics Institute and played billiards – about all that Eastwood offered, apart from sports and local dances. He danced too, and this his mother did frown on: it was too reminiscent of his father. He went to the sixpenny hops in Church Street, and was popular.

Girl friends began to accumulate, blooming and fading like flowers. Bert Lawrence, watching and listening and admiring, was fascinated. One day he would cut a swathe too. His weakness and unpopularity with his schoolfellows had already begun to drive him into the arms of girls. Later, Willie Hopkin was to remark that he noticed Lawrence hadn't much use for the Plain Janes – his girl friends were pretty, warm and lively. But for the moment it was Ernest's turn, and when his old flames came looking for him at home, his mother was there to repel them. She had no time for these 'brazen baggages' he met at his dancing classes. Ernest would be briefly angry with her for interfering, walking in with long strides and frowning down at his mother, his cap pushed back on his head. More strife when he announced suddenly that he was going to a fancy-dress ball at a rather common place. He had arranged to hire a Highlander's costume, and the thought of it excited him. His mother was cold with him, and when the parcel came, she just left it unopened. On the night of the dance she was off somewhere else, in her coat and bonnet, and wouldn't wait to see her son dressed up.

When he got a job at Nottingham, she approved. This was advancement, he was fulfilling her. She had dreams of him helping her other sons, especially Bert, along the same road, but he was too busy. Apart from studying hard, he played hard, still going to dances and to river parties on the Trent. When he came in it was often late and he would sit up, studying. 'Don't try to do both,' his mother advised him anxiously, 'or you'll make yourself ill.' But the thought of the virile Ernest ill was difficult to entertain.

Then he applied for and got the situation in London. This was different, very different. London! The wage sounded fantastic – a hundred and twenty pounds a year. The whole family rejoiced except her. She was half ready to cry.

He was to begin in Lime Street in a week's time. He read the letter aloud: 'And you will reply by Thursday whether you accept. Yours faithfully – ' This was on qualifications alone, without even an interview. Ernest's eyes shone with triumph. He told his mother they would soon be rich.

' "We shall, my son," she answered sadly.' [5]

She saw that he was unaffected by the thought of the departure, completely unaware of how hurt she might be. She was nearly in tears at the thought of losing the things she took such keen pleasure in, from getting his meals to ironing his collars. He was going away and leaving nothing of himself for her to keep at all.

He had a bundle of love letters and before he left he made a clean sweep and burned them. He was twenty-one. He was full of the future, intoxicated with the life before him, hardly conscious of his mother's misery. Bert Lawrence watched him as he took the first letter off the pile and sniffed at it.

'Nice scent! Smell!'

He pushed the sheet of notepaper under his brother's nose. Then he read out the letters, or bits of it, mockingly. 'This girl's father,' he said, laughing, 'is as rich as Croesus.' And here was Ernest tossing her mauve-tinted letter into the flames. What did he care – he had the whole world to choose from: he was rich with expectations. Before he burned all the letters he snipped off the corners for his brother because they were pretty; there were coloured drawings of thistles, swallows, forget-me-nots, ivy sprays. Bert soon had a little collection of thirty or forty snippings. Then off went Ernest to London.

He was badly missed by everyone in the house, for he was always laughing, full of fun. The parties they had now and then weren't a success any longer, without him to play the fool. All the same they had his homecomings to look forward to, and his letters. He used the nicknames he had given them when he addressed their envelopes: Emily was 'Injun Top-Knot' on account of her red hair, her sister was 'Corkscrews', a reference to her dangling curls, and Bert, with his light-brown hair, was 'Billy White-nob'. Even before the letters were in their hands they knew by the postman's face if there was anything from Ernest.

Meanwhile they remembered things about him, crazy escapades, some tomfoolery, anything to console themselves. For instance, there was the time their two pet rabbits had accidentally suffocated in their hutch, and Bert and Ada decided on a proper burial. The boy coloured a shoe-box black and in it they laid the dead bodies reverently. For the top, Ada wove wreathes of daisies and buttercups. A small grave was dug at the bottom of the garden, and they were about to carry the coffin there solemnly when Ernest suddenly popped out of the house, on his head a black silk hat from somewhere, with long black streamers, in imitation of a real funeral. He hadn't forgotten to bring one of their father's enormous white handkerchiefs, and his grief was so loud and prolonged that it fetched the neighbours out in alarm. At first the children were genuinely upset, but the spectacle put an end to their grief and they soon doubled up in laughter at the faces their brother was pulling.

They remembered too how, when Ernest was working in Coventry, riding home all the way at weekends on his bicycle, a distance of some sixty miles, he told his mother proudly that some of his workmates thought he must pad his calves because they were so well-shaped.

When he did come home from London, what excitement! All his young brothers and sisters wanted to do was walk beside him down the main street in Eastwood, as he strode along negligently in his frock coat and silk hat, the very picture of prosperity. 'The feathers in mother's bonnets,' wrote Ada, 'seemed to nod triumphantly.'

Perhaps it was before Ernest left for London that the incident of the smashed doll occurred, related so vividly in *Sons and Lovers* that one feels it must have been true; yet neither of the sisters refers to it. Lawrence's *alter ego* Paul was practising jumping from the sofa arm – no doubt his mother was out – and he landed by accident on the face of Emily's big doll. Emily was a tomboy till she reached her teens, what her mother called a 'flybie-skybie' and her sister a 'wild harum-scarum'. Later she became rather sedate. But now her doll was broken to pieces and she set up a long, mournful wailing. The boy protested afterwards to his mother that the doll was covered with an antimaccassar and put to sleep on the floor, so that he couldn't tell it was there. But nothing would assuage Emily's grief: Arabella was broken.

Emily did forgive her brother in a day or two – he was so obviously upset. Then he made a suggestion which shocked and yet fascinated her.

' "Let's make a sacrifice of Arabella," he said. "Let's burn her." '

It seemed a horrible idea, yet she wanted to see what was going to happen. It was curious how methodically he went about it, piling up some bricks for an altar, dragging loose shavings out of the doll's body. He soaked the thing in paraffin and put a match to it. The waxy broken face melted first, dripping into the flames, as the strange boy 'watched with wicked satisfaction'. When the flames guttered out, he took a stick and poked about among the blackened remains, recovered the arms and legs and pounded them to pulp under a brick. Emily, watching, was strangely stirred without knowing why.

' "That's the sacrifice of Missis Arabella," he said. "An' I'm glad there's nothing left of her." ' [6]

Now, with George and Ernest away from home, all the burden of the mother's love was borne by the remaining son. Bert was turning into a stay-at-home: it had always been his inclination, though he loved the little expeditions with his sisters, going mushrooming for example in the early mornings when the larks were rising, searching carefully through the dew-soaked grass 'for the white-skinned, wonderful naked bodies crouched secretly in the green.' He loved to think he was contributing something, helping the household economically; his mother would be pleased. She soothed and encouraged him always. His morbidity from earliest childhood had made her heart ache, for she knew intuitively what was in store for him. How ridiculous his hypersensitivity seemed, yet what protectiveness it roused in her. He was becoming her favourite, he seemed to understand her so well.

Friday nights she sallied forth to the market in front of the Sun Inn, where four roads meet, from Mansfield, Ilkeston, Derby and Nottingham. It was also baking night, and as a general rule the boy stayed at home and did the baking – he was good at it. When he had finished, he drew or read. Often he had the house to himself – he enjoyed the feeling of being left in charge. Mrs Lawrence enjoyed herself too: she always looked forward to her marketing, to the brakes rumbling in, the naked flares on the stalls, and women and men everywhere in the streets like a carnival. She liked her encounters with the fruit man, the rogue of a fish man, the linoleum man, the crockery man with his stall littered with straw, and she darted about, a little determined woman in her black costume and bonnet, quite certain of herself and how to handle the fruit man with his cheek. Once she was drawn back to a dish, and the pot man stood waiting for her to make up her mind. The cornflowers on the little dish captivated her. Such a small extravagance, yet she could barely afford it this week. She hated the man's manner and was cold with him in anticipation, but she had to have that dish. He wanted fivepence for it, and she expected a jeering remark to go with it.

'I'll have it,' she said.

'Yer'll do me the favour like?' he said. 'Yer'd better spit in it, like yer do when y'ave something give yer.'

She paid him coldly not caring what he said: the dish was hers.

Her son waited impatiently for her, loving her to come in with her parcels. He would hear her footsteps in the entry and stop what he was doing, instinctively attentive to her, putting down his brush if he was painting, helping her unload her basket. She unveiled her find, wrapped in a bit of dirty newspaper, the boy clamouring to see. He approved at once, responding as she did to the flowers. 'I *love* cornflowers on things.' Then followed a rapid discussion as to what they could use the dish for. Stewed fruit, suggested the boy. Or custard, or a jelly, said the mother. What about radishes and lettuce? he asked. The ideas passed to and fro, it was like a game between two children. Then, while he peered into the oven at his new-baked loaf, she unwrapped some pansy and crimson-daisy roots. For fourpence, she told him, and her voice betrayed the remorse she felt. That's cheap, he told her indignantly, immediately taking her side – and now they were like two adults. The point was, cheap or not, it wasn't something she could really afford *this* week. She could have done without. But the boy laughed like a conspirator and ran into the kitchen for the flannel, to wash the mud off the faces of the pansies. The yellow one delighted his fancy, it had a face like an old man. When they were wet the flower-heads glistened, they were magnificent.[7]

Soon he was thirteen. On 14 September 1898 he enrolled at Nottingham High School, and a period of arduous study and daily travelling between Eastwood and Nottingham began. It is a time left out of *Sons and Lovers* completely. He had been five years at Beauvale Board School, and the coaching and bullying of bearded 'Gaffer' Whitehead had resulted in a scholarship. Professor David Chambers tells us that this was the first scholarship

Nottinghamshire County Council had ever given. The muttering it caused up and down the terraces of Eastwood can be imagined.

Lawrence had been unhappy at Beauvale. His elder brothers had been tougher and able to defend themselves: Ernest excelled at games as well as scholarship. Bert Lawrence was a frail Dicky Denches for the Breach boys to peck at every day. In the end he found out how to retaliate: with his sharp tongue, but this wasn't until he was fourteen. One of his old schoolmates said of him later, 'He wor a bit to blame, for he wor rayther stuck up, and when Gaffer gin him a bit o' praise we didn' like it.' But 'he began hittin' back wi' his tongue an' he could get at us wheer it hurt.'[8]

His County Council scholarship took him to an ancient Nottingham institution which had been the grammar school thirty years earlier, and dated back to 1289. Locally it almost had the status of a public school. Bert Lawrence nearly missed enrolment altogether, because the scholarship was worth only fifteen pounds a year. Most of this would be swallowed up in tuition fees and railway fare: where would the money come from for all the other things, clothes and food and so on? For Mrs Lawrence this was the kind of grim challenge she was always ready to face for the sake of her children. In *Sons and Lovers* there is some bitter dialogue, undoubtedly true, about the failure of Ernest to send her any money from London. Bert has filled in the form for his season ticket to Nottingham and his mother tightens her lips when he tells her it is going to cost one pound eleven – more than she expected. Then she tells him of Ernest's promise to send her a pound a month when he went to London to live and work. He had sent her two amounts, of ten shillings each, and he was getting well over a hundred pounds a year. 'But they're all alike. They're large in promises, but it's precious little fulfilment you get.'

Now he was travelling daily in his student clothes, his high socks and his Eton coat with the point at the back, Eton collar, little blue cap and knee-breeches. Later he was joined on the train by a younger Eastwood lad, George Neville, who remembers Bert's willingness to help him with homework problems while the train went clanking and grinding towards Newthorpe on the journey home. Even then, Neville says, Lawrence was bothered by a hard little cough that made him jerk his left hand up to his mouth – a sharp, characteristic gesture that people noticed for the rest of his life.

His new headmaster was the Reverend James Gow, an educator whose tolerance must have amazed the young Lawrence after five years of the 'get them under' policy of fierce old Whitehead, beating lessons into his savage colliery lads. In his last year Lawrence was placed only thirteenth out of twenty-one in English, but won a Mathematics prize. He did poorly in French and German too, but he was in competition with some very bright boys, most of them older than himself.

For extra tuition while in Eastwood he went to a governess, Miss Wright, a woman who becomes Miss Frost in *The Lost Girl*. The 'lost girl' herself, her father, and the chief assistant in her father's shop, Miss Pidsley, together with Miss Wright, were all depicted in the novel later, as indeed was Eastwood itself. Next to *Sons and Lovers* it is the most thoroughly local book of all the novels, in its first half at least.

Graham Hough, in his study, *The Dark Sun*, rejects as misconceived both the Eliot and the Leavis attitudes towards Lawrence's background and education. To imagine that he sprang from an ignorant barbarism is as false, says Hough, as to maintain that he was the product of a persistent cultural tradition. He goes on: 'The fact is that from Elizabethan times intellectual ability and education, however acquired, have been a passport to the central stream of English culture. The reason that the English provincial tradition is so weak is that hardly anyone of first-rate ability ever stays in it; and they do not stay in it because it is so easy to get out. England is the land of snobbery, but not of rigid snobbery: class boundaries are shifting and often transcended. The upper bourgeoisie remains culturally dominant because it makes itself so accessible to all who have anything to bring to it, and thus attracts to itself all real outside talent. The inspired barbarian is not likely to remain a barbarian for long: if he is really inspired someone will soon make it his (more probably her) business to civilise him; and the talented provincial is not likely to remain long in his province . . .'

Ernest was coming home for the Christmas holidays. There was great excitement: Christmas had never seemed so glamorous. He had been a good boy, writing regularly with all his news, telling them about his French lessons, his discovery of London. His mother wrote back, and she thought about him endlessly. He had not left after all.

As the great day approached the preparations increased. The children went out hunting for holly and mistletoe, and got coloured paper and flour-and-water paste on the kitchen table, working away busily at the manufacture of paper-chains long enough to stretch from corner to corner of the living room. Then the excitement mounted as their mother cooked one thing after another, with incredible extravagance – the larder was transformed. There was the centre-piece, the splendid plum cake, and all manner of tarts, lots of mince pies, then cheese-cakes and Spanish cakes. There was fresh fruit, more than they could remember. The whole thing came to a climax on Christmas Eve, the day of Ernest's arrival. 'Everywhere was decorated. . . . A great fire roared. There was a scent of cooked pastry.' The children went off to the station to meet their brother, due from London at seven, like a knight in armour. The husband and wife were left alone to wait. Arthur Lawrence was as affected as his wife, you could tell by the awkward way he sat in his armchair. As for her, the more tremulous she felt, the more deliberately she did things, moving about quietly in the kitchen.

Young Bert was longing for the railwayman in his peaked cap to know that it was the London train they were waiting for, as he describes the scene in *Sons and Lovers*: 'it sounded so grand'. Of course it was more than he dared do, with his morbid self-consciousness and his shrinking away from strangers. The train was late, and it was bitterly cold on the platform as they hung about, Bert and Emily and Ada, peering under the bridge at the shining red and green lights. It was unbelievable that London was down there, at the other end of that darkness. Suddenly there was a flurry of activity, a bell rang, a porter appeared. Then the huge train itself, glowing and steaming majestically, en route for Manchester. A door opened like magic and their Ernest stepped forth nonchalantly, armed with his parcels and his Gladstone bag. Now Bert could advertise his importance to the world. He stood by his brother, quietly and proudly, in the shadow of the great pulsing train.

Ernest was handsome, a big, eager youngster, unafraid. His presence in the house was all they had anticipated, setting the seal on their happiness. The next day they unwrapped all his presents, overwhelmed by his generosity and thoughtfulness. His mother treasured for the rest of her life the umbrella he had brought her, with the touch of gold on the slender handle. As for Bert, he remembered best the exotic sweets, crystallised fruits and Turkish delight – he would swank about these later among his friends. Over the holiday, visitors came in to have a look at Ernest, almost as if it was good luck to touch him. It was all perfect, until he went away. The following year he was offered a holiday abroad at negligible cost, as his firm of lawyers represented a big shipping agency. His mother urged him to go, but he came home again for his fortnight that summer. Her hold on him was still strong.

But she began to worry as she noticed a change in his letters to her – as if the flood of new impressions was too much for him and he was beginning to lose his grip. He had stopped sending her any money now, but it wasn't that. He was trying to keep up with his new friends, and she feared for him. He rhapsodised to her about a girl he had met, tall and slim, a beautiful dresser, in fact a lady. All the men were after her, in competition with him. He wanted his mother to congratulate him, but she couldn't help issuing warnings. For him, this only intensified the hunt. He kept after the girl: she was like a prize that was rightfully his.

He sent her photograph home. Her name was Gypsy Dennis (in *Sons and Lovers* 'Gypsy' is the pet name of Louisa Lily Denys Western). She worked as a stenographer, though in the novel she didn't condescend to do anything more than live on the money an old aunt gave her. There she was in the photo, her elegant profile and bare shoulders. Mrs Lawrence was shocked. When the father came in one night, he found the picture propped up on the sideboard. He took hold of it clumsily and carried it into the kitchen.

'Who dost reckon this is?' he asked his wife.

She told him.

'An' come again to-morrer!' exclaimed the miner. 'An' is 'er an actress?'[9]

Bert was very impressed. But his mother wrote and told Ernest that she didn't approve, and so to make amends he persuaded the girl to send a more 'prim and proper' portrait. It arrived with a note, and there was the young lady arrayed now in a lacy black evening dress, which poor Mrs Lawrence found equally shocking. Bert told his mother she was being silly. To him the girl looked like a princess, and in fact he liked the bare shoulders one better. His mother grimly disagreed.

The following Christmas she came with Ernest. He had been wanting to bring her for months: they were engaged now. According to Mrs Lawrence's later account, the engagement ring cost eight guineas, a revelation which flabbergasted the children. The father was derisive. The mother's heart ached at her son's foolishness and generosity.

He wanted to show her off, as he showed her off at the theatre in London. It was a very different holiday this time, no children waiting for the train, and when he arrived it was without presents. Beside him was Gypsy, resplendent in her costume and furs. She was undoubtedly pretty. Mrs Lawrence noticed at once that she was also more than a little pretentious. Arthur Lawrence came forward meekly to be introduced, a bit abject. When the children got over their shyness they took her out at the front of the house to show her the view, the Derbyshire hills far off to the west, the fume of Moorgreen and Underwood and Selston. They were proud of the openness up there, 'the great scallop of the world it had in view.'

Ada, two years younger than Bert and always closest of the children to him, took the important visitor upstairs to the front bedroom, leading the way with a candle. She was to share the room with Gypsy, since there was nowhere else for her to go, but already she was in a subservient role as the shy little servant, asking if there was anything else the girl wanted. It was icy in the bedroom, and downstairs a strained atmosphere lingered on account of the strangeness of the girl and her rather grand airs. Coming down with a changed dress, she spoke to Ernest with her lover's voice, and he squirmed for his family. All the special crockery and table linen, to say nothing of the father's good behaviour, was for her. It only created an unnatural tension. The girl's nervousness was obvious and she talked too fast. She was nothing grand, if the truth were known, but she felt a cut above this working-class home and she couldn't help patronising them. Ada trotted up and down the stairs, fetching a handkerchief and other things. Ernest frowned: he didn't care to see his sister as a maid. All his class loyalty reasserted itself.

Five minutes after they went up to bed, he came down again to speak to his mother. He was troubled, he wanted his mother's reactions. She realised he was critical of the girl and thought her superficial in some ways, and he didn't care for the impression she was making.

'When she seems shallow, you have to remember she's never had anybody to bring her deeper side out.'[10]

He was voicing his own uneasiness. Then in the morning he seemed to recover.

He came home again at Easter, this time alone. The whole time he talked about Gypsy with his mother. He was so much attached to her now, he said, that he couldn't bear to think of losing her. But he was puzzled and confused. When he was away from his sweetheart he forgot all about her, didn't care a damn about her. As soon as he saw her, he wanted her passionately again. His mother made suggestions, voiced doubts, but he hardly listened. Really he was talking to himself, thinking aloud. He no longer understood what was happening, except that he was irrationally in love. The girl burned in him, slowly burned him up; and she was expensive. On his holidays now, he had no money for anything.

5

Farm and Factory

In her memoir, *A Personal Record*, Jessie Chambers says that the friendship with Lawrence which so deeply affected her life would probably never have begun if his mother and hers had not suddenly become acquainted one Sunday evening in the Congregational chapel they both attended. Mrs Lawrence had now lived for twenty years in mining country, while Mrs Chambers was a comparative newcomer. Bert's mother poured out her resentments to this ready listener. This could have been before Jessie's father, Edmund Chambers, moved with his family to become a tenant farmer at Haggs Farm, three miles to the north of Eastwood. Chambers came originally from Brinsley: then he went off to get married and came back to live with his wife and family in a cottage in the Breach, earning his living from a milk round. He suffered badly from rheumatism, but you could see him about the district with his milk-float, rain or shine. When he moved out to the farm he was helped by his sons.

A later close friend of Lawrence, Willie Hopkin, who was at school with Chambers, remembered him in the playground and classroom as a quiet and earnest lad, a conscientious boy who didn't have to be caned, and, when he grew up, 'a steady, plodding, reliable man with a particularly nice disposition.' But Edmund's youngest son, Professor J. David Chambers, doesn't agree that he was as meek and mild as that. His father cuts a more dashing figure in his memory, with his reckless penny-farthing bike rides and his quick temper.

There are discrepancies too in the two accounts of Lawrence's first meeting with Jessie: the vivid and momentous encounter described in *Sons and Lovers* and the more matter-of-fact one in the reminiscence by 'E.T.'. But there is little doubt that it was a great event for the young High School boy: not so much the meeting with the girl herself – she was shadowy and unreal – as the impact of the farm and its life. This fascinating homestead on the edge of the wood was to mean so much to him. To Rolf

Gardiner in 1926 he wrote: 'From the hills, if you look across at Underwood wood, you'll see a tiny red farm on the edge of the wood. That was Miriam's farm – where I got my first incentive to write. I'll go there with you some day.'[1]

And to J. D. Chambers in 1928, near the end of his short life: 'Whatever I forget, I shall never forget The Haggs – I loved it so. I loved to come to you all, it really was a new life began in me there. The water-pippin by the door – those maiden-blush roses that Flower would lean over and eat and Trip floundering around. And stewed figs for tea in winter, and in August stewed green apples. Do you still have them? Tell your mother I never forget, no matter where life carries us. And does she still blush if somebody comes and finds her in a dirty white apron? Or doesn't she wear work-aprons any more? Oh, I'd love to be nineteen again, and coming through the Warren and catching the first glimpse of the buildings. Then I'd sit on the sofa under the window, and we'd crowd round the little table to tea, in that tiny kitchen I was so at home in.

'Son' tempi passati, cari miei quanto cari, no saprete mai! [sic] – I could never tell you in English how much it all meant to me, how I still feel about it.

'If there is anything I can ever do for you, do tell me. Because whatever else I am, I am somewhere still the same Bert who rushed with such joy to The Haggs.'[2]

Lawrence remembered every detail, and with the bitter-sweet memory of his boy-and-girl love affair behind him, he enhanced and dramatised it all. Nevertheless, it *was* a great event for him and his mother, whose lives were so circumscribed by grinding routine and everlasting duties that to go anywhere freely, unburdened, stepping out joyfully in the early summer air, was enough to make them tipsy with delight.

It was a world of wonder, set down in the open air and flowing with light, that the boy responded to with all his heart. And he was intensely conscious of his role, as he escorted his mother proudly, with a touch of manly sternness, across the fields. After all, it was to *him* that Mr Chambers had entrusted the information about the short cut to the farm across the fields, and how to find the path which was their right of way through the Warren, at the lower end of Willey Spring Wood.

The whole narrative that he wrote later, in England and Germany and Italy, came in jubilant strokes and flashes at this point, like the young summer sky, the fizzing green hedgerows, the wide fields and deep woods waiting like a vision. There was a tension of excitement too. They were going in the afternoon, and Bert had to clean his mother's cheap kid boots. He did it willingly, 'with as much reverence as if they had been flowers.'[3]

On the way at last, she carried the umbrella with the touch of gold, to keep off the sun if it was too strong. Her son strode along and 'fancied himself'; he was already taller than she. They were shy with each other, they gave each other glances, there was banter between them, as if they were lovers. They were in great form that day.

On the way they paused to look at the pit-head, standing on the road to watch as a man with his horse and truck laboured up the steep, curiously symmetrical slag-heap to the top, and tipped out his load. It went falling down the long slopes of the enormous cone. For a man who was to rage unequivocally later against the ugliness of industrialism, this was writing of remarkable detachment. He was trying to get inside the skin of an artistic boy who hadn't yet separated his world into ugly and beautiful, who could take out a sketch pad and tell his mother to look at the pit, there was something alive and creature-like about it.

His mother looked, dubiously. Yes, perhaps it was, she said indulgently.

The very trucks were interesting, he persisted, because they had the 'feel' of men's hands on them.

She agreed, to please him. She was happy in the sun.

Further on, Lawrence's hero replies to Clara Dawes, when she objects that a coal pit spoils a pretty scene: 'Do you think so? You see, I am so used to it I should miss it. No; and I like the pits here and there. I like the rows of trucks, and the headstocks, and the stream in the daytime, and the lights at night. When I was a boy, I always thought a pillar of cloud by day and a pillar of fire by night was a pit, with its steam, and its lights, and the burning bank, and I thought the Lord was always at the pit-top.'[4]

'For Lawrence as a boy', writes Graham Hough, 'there was nothing particularly constricting about Eastwood, It was a normal place to live. If his family were poor, so were most of the others they knew. There is no evidence that the ugliness and meanness of a mining district oppressed him; and it would be surprising if there were. They oppress people who have seen something else, not those who have lived there all their lives.'[5]

Young Bert and his mother skirted Moorgreen Reservoir, the sun dappling the water, and then they hesitated. It was one thing for the boy in his role of guide and escort to take the man's part when he knew he was safe, but when his mother walked up to a farm door and asked the way, he sheltered behind her, with his old fear of rejection. On they went again. By the time they reached a stile, and she dithered nervously on top of it, he had recovered sufficiently to mock her.

'The spinney opened out,' he wrote in his first, femininely tender novel, 'the ferns were serenely uncoiling, the bluebells stood grouped with blue curls mingled. In the freer spaces forget-me-nots flowered in nebulae, and dog-violets gave an undertone of dark purple, with primroses for planets in the night. There was a slight drift of woodruff, sweet new-mown hay, scenting the air under the boughs. On a wet bank was a design of golden saxifrage, glistening unholily as if varnished by its minister, the snail . . .

'The wood was high and warm. Along the ridings the forget-me-nots were knee deep, stretching, glimmering into the distance like the Milky Way through the night. They left the tall, flower-tangled paths to go in among the bluebells, breaking through the close-pressed flowers and ferns till they came to an oak which had fallen across the hazels, where they sat half screened. The hyacinths drooped magnificently with an over-weight of purple, or they stood pale and erect, like unripe ears of purple corn. Heavy bees swung down in a blunder of extravagance among the purple flowers. They were intoxicated even with the sight of so much blue. The sound of their hearty, wanton humming came clear upon the solemn boom of the wind over-head. The sight of their clinging, clambering riot gave satisfaction to the soul. A rosy campion flower caught the sun and shone out. An elm sent down a shower of flesh-tinted sheaths upon them.'[6]

They were within sight of The Haggs. The red farm was low, with its farm buildings attached to the house, a front garden between the house and a neighbour's yard wall. It was on the edge of the wood that shut the homestead in from the west. The mother and son were entranced by the stillness. All the wood-work, yard gate and window frames and garden gates, was painted 'Queen Anne's White'.

J. D. Chambers, in his memoir, described Lawrence as having a love affair 'with a little farm house clothed in Virginia creeper and honeysuckle, with the old mare, Flower, who leaned over the garden gate and nibbled the roses, the good-natured bull terrier Trip who lay across the hearth in front of the fire; and there were two massive old sows to whom he gave classical names: one, a cheerful chubby creature with twinkling blue eyes always ready to hold up her snout for an apple, he called Dido; the other, a long lean lugubrious creature, always complaining and never satisfied, he called Circe.'[7]

When Lawrence came to write *The White Peacock*, something

held him back from describing the farm itself. More time had to flow, the affair with Jessie was too painful and inconclusive, too close. But Moorgreen Water is there, Lamb Close House, the Ram Inn on the Moorgreen road, Felley Mill Farm, the keeper's lodge in the wood, and the countryside itself, like a map of love. Trip is there by name, and so is Circe:

'I snorted, and he laughed, and the old sow grunted with contempt, and her little eyes twisted towards us with a demoniac leer as she rolled past. . . .'

Circe has produced a litter of fourteen, but 'that damned she-devil' ate three of them before they could stop her. The description of the eleven survivors has all the young Lawrence's joy and fascination in the life of the farm:

'I met George tramping across the yard with a couple of buckets of swill, and eleven young pigs rushed squealing about his legs, shrieking in an agony of suspense. He poured the stuff into a trough with luscious gurgle, and instantly ten noses were dipped in, and ten little mouths began to slobber. Though there was plenty of room for ten, yet they shouldered and shoved and struggled to capture a larger space, and many little trotters dabbled and spilled the stuff, and the ten sucking, clapping snouts twitched fiercely, and twenty little eyes glared askance, like so many points of wrath. They gave uneasy, gasping grunts in their haste. The unhappy eleventh rushed from point to point trying to push in his snout, but for his pains he got rough squeezing, and sharp grabs on his ears. Then he lifted up his face and screamed screams of grief and wrath unto the evening sky.

'But the ten little gluttons only twitched their ears to make sure there was no danger in the noise, and they sucked harder, with much spilling and slobbing. George laughed like a sardonic Jove, but at last he gave ear, and kicked the ten gluttons from the trough, and allowed the residue to the eleventh. This one, poor wretch, almost wept with relief as he sucked and swallowed in sobs, casting his little eyes apprehensively upwards, though he did not lift his nose from the trough, as he heard the vindictive shrieks of ten little fiends kept at bay by George. The solitary feeder, shivering with apprehension, rubbed the wood bare with his snout, then, turning up to heaven his eyes of gratitude, he reluctantly left the trough. I expected to see the ten fall upon him and devour him, but they did not; they rushed upon the empty trough, and rubbed the wood still drier, shrieking with misery.'[8]

But this was in the future. Now 'the small vigorous woman and the slender boy' stood before the house, and they could see the way they had come. Looking back, they could see, beyond the

Warren with its young firs and spruces, the flash of water at
Moorgreen, where they had left the high road and entered the
meadow. They could see the roofs of Felley Mill, tucked away
below in its hollow, as the land dropped. Then the rough bulk of
Annesley Hills rose up boskily, and to the right of that, the hills
beyond the lake, crowned by High Park Wood, with the lodge
described in *The White Peacock* embedded there, just visible.

The farm had an apple orchard, a pointed plot of land chop-
ped out of the wood itself. As they stood in the farmyard in the
afternoon sun Mrs Chambers came out to them. In Lawrence's
version a girl showed herself first in the doorway 'in a dirty
apron'. She dodged back inside, like a shy animal, and her mother
appeared, quite small, with rosy cheeks and large dark eyes. Some
freshly-baked bread was cooling on the threshold. The scent of
the loaves mingled with the red gilly-flowers in the garden. Mrs
Lawrence was hot from the walk, and as the farmer's wife took
them into the quaintly low parlour, guelder roses in a big heap in
the fireplace, Bert's mother said bluntly that she was glad there
wasn't a fire. She had a sharp way of speaking, and she called her
son Bertie.

In *Sons and Lovers* are Lawrence's first impressions of Jessie,
the intense, dark, rather lonely girl who was to influence him so
deeply and bring him to more than one adolescent crisis. She was
fourteen, her black curly hair was short; there was something at
once curious and defensive about her. She was like a startled wild
thing, as if she really belonged in the wood and not in the house at
all. Lawrence creates a scene, a first encounter with the girl in the
garden, which doesn't tally with Jessie's memory of their meeting.
In the scene his hero leaves the mothers talking, as Jessie put it,
'the incomprehensible talk of adults', and as he stands looking
round the garden the girl comes out shyly to the pile of coal by the
fence. To impress his knowledge on her he asks her if the bushes
in front of them are cabbage roses.

'I don't know,' she faltered. 'They're white with pink
middles.'
'Then they're maiden-blush.'[9]

He looks round, with the sharp, intent manner of his mother,
so critically that the girl takes offence and goes back in.
In *A Personal Record*, the first encounter is shown as having
taken place in the kitchen, where Jessie had gone to boil eggs for
their visitors. To her consternation the tall boy followed her and
stood gazing around, 'taking everything in' keenly. The girl
became ashamed of the kitchen, with its funny bulges and alcoves,

and very uneasy because he simply stood there and didn't speak. His intentness unnerved her. Her family hadn't lived long at the place and she was sensitive to other people's opinions of it. She quickly noted a patronising tone in Mrs Lawrence's voice as she talked to her mother over tea, and imagined the indomitable little woman was feeling sorry for her mother with her large brood of children and animals, and looking with pitying town eyes at them all, stuck in such an isolated spot. None of these sentiments appears in the novel: on the contrary, the miner's wife exclaims on the way home, crying out with happiness and poignant regret, that if only *she* had a husband like that, how she would work and run things, and want to help – what a will to happiness she would bring to it.

Jessie Chambers remembered, long after the event, her initial feelings of hostility towards this rather aloof, self-absorbed boy. She was envious of his continuing education, the fact that he studied French and German: he was superior to her in all kinds of ways, he had the key to the things she wanted to unlock for herself. She was almost his age, yet here she was, living as a drudge around the farm, an unpaid housemaid, all her potential going to waste as she worked in the kitchen for her father and brothers, and fed the hens and the pigs. She burned with the injustice of it, and felt an urge to score off this boy in front of her, as if he were somehow to blame for it. She told him spitefully that she didn't care for his name, Bertie, it was girlish. But he didn't take offence. He said they called him Lawrence at school. Relenting, she said she liked that much better.

Still needing to assert herself, she went off, while he was still there, on a short visit to a friend who lived on the other side of the wood. He was more impressed by the thought of her journey through the trees than by her independence.

Again there is a discrepancy, for the novel has an incident, which could either have happened during that first visit, or later, where Jessie is afraid to let a hen peck corn from the palm of her hand. Bert has been on a conducted tour of the farm with Jessie's brothers, and it is time to feed the fowls. One of the brothers, as a dare, takes a handful of corn and holds it out for one hen. He asks Bert to do the same. The bird's fierce eye and jerky head movements are startling, but the peck when it comes doesn't really hurt. It makes him laugh, and excites him. Then the brothers challenge their sister to do the same, knowing she is afraid. She shakes her head and pulls back, and they jeer at her. A little later Bert notices her stooping by the coop with some maize in her hand, steeling herself to offer it. She cries out in fear, not realising she is being watched, and the boy comes forward and encourages her. She tries once more, and this time succeeds, flushing with excitement. It is a love scene, a foretaste of all the difficult, delicate love to come, and like so many future encounters it ends in misunderstanding and resentment.

When Jessie came back from visiting her friend she found her family and the Lawrences in the kitchen. Mrs Lawrence held the floor with her vigorous, forthright speech and her interest in everything. Jessie waited till the subject came round to books: now was the chance to show this privileged boy that she knew a thing or two and wasn't just a maid-of-all-work. The talk was on favourite authors, so she said that hers was Scott, and Mrs Lawrence applauded her choice. It was a happy moment.

The Haggs and its countryside soon became Lawrence's world of escape, not so much from the squalor of his colliery village as from the discord and tensions of his household. Here at The Haggs the atmosphere, in spite of Jessie's discontent, was so much more harmonious: the same inside as out. 'He came to the fields and woods at The Haggs,' wrote David Chambers, 'as into a new world, a species of fairyland, where the contact with nature was direct and free; where a robin building in an old kettle, a lark in a beast's hoofmark left in the stiff clay, and above all the white embroidery of lady smocks and the foam of bluebells over the wood in spring were a matter for perpetual wonder and genuine excitement. I have seen these things since, but never with the same thrill as when Bert was there to see them. He imparted some of his own intensity of living to the rest of us; later, when life became difficult for him, he imparted something of his own sense of the enigma of life. So great was the weight of gloom he cast over us of his own insoluble conflicts and in which he involved us that he contributed to an abiding apprehension of tragedy behind the gayest, brightest exterior which has stayed with me ever since.'[10]

At the outset, Lawrence was friendly with the two brothers nearest his own age at the farm, rather than with Jessie. She was overlooked, and perhaps because of her sense of inferiority she preferred it that way. She had her Walter Scott fantasies, where she could be left alone. They at least didn't disappoint her. At times she hated her brothers for being loutish. This new friend of theirs wasn't like that, but she was afraid of his knowledge, of what he might think of her. She loved her mother; they were similar in character.

For the rest of that summer Bert went to the farm every week. Before the brothers let him into their lives, he talked to Mr Chambers a great deal. He would bring a book or magazine for them, and the father took a fancy to this intelligent, well-mannered lad, talking to him as he would to an adult. Jessie remembered one discussion, about electricity and whether it was feasible to store it, which went right over her head.

And he made a palpable hit with the overworked mother of this family of seven, simply by helping her whenever he could. Her own sons did next to nothing around the house, so this was delightful for her. He would fetch water, clear out the ashes in the fireplace and build a fire in the parlour. He worked deftly, like a girl: he was used to doing things at home, where he would get the stiff brush and the tin of blacklead and attack the big iron range. 'Lawrence told me himself', wrote Jessie, 'that he never minded father seeing him with a coarse apron tied round his waist, but if he heard my brother's step in the entry he whipped it off on the instant, fearing he would despise him for doing the housework.'[11] In her memoir she spoke of an incident that must have impressed her greatly, growing up as she was in a rather overbearing male world, with its rigid taboos. A pile of onions had been left outside the back door for a long time, ready for peeling and pickling. It was a finicky task, the onions were so small. Suddenly they were gone, and Jessie's mother told her that Bert had sat down in a corner and peeled them, without any fuss. It was as interesting to him as anything else that went on there. Jessie's mother said to her once: 'I should like to be next to Bert in heaven.'[12]

That summer, Ernest brought his girl to Eastwood again. They went for walks in the lovely weather, and once or twice Bert went with them, chattering away happily. Ernest was looking a bit haggard in the face; he had lost weight. They all dropped on the grass in a field by Moorgreen Church. The meadow was smothered with daisies, and the boy picked the big ones, and when Gypsy took off her hat he arranged the flowers in her black hair. The white-starred yellow centres looked very dramatic.

At home in Walker Street the girl still put on airs. She unpacked a mass of dresses and blouses, and she patronised little Ada and used her, in a way that her brother found intolerable. Ernest was now hopelessly in love with Gypsy, but he also hated her. Basically, he didn't *like* the girl. Almost everything she did irritated him unbearably. He found her shallow and stupid and insensitive, and his enslavement only made him more critical. He couldn't help comparing her to his mother all the time, and the comparison was odious. To his mother he poured out all his doubts, attacked all the girl's values. She was a foolish creature twittering about *marrons glacés* and letting money run through her fingers and forgetting to buy proper underclothes for the cold weather. But when his mother shook her head, he set himself miserably against her advice. He couldn't give her up, he was too committed now. It was like saying he had sold his soul to the devil.

The holiday was made unpleasant by his savage moods and his outbursts against the girl in front of his mother. He didn't care, he had to attack her. If he couldn't escape from her, if he had to love her, at least he'd hate her virulently for it. Mrs Lawrence was shocked by his behaviour and told him to stop being so unmanly. She took the girl's part in spite of herself, for Gypsy was in tears and turning to her.

' "He's always saying these things!" cried the girl.'[13]

When they had gone back to London there was general relief, and Mrs Lawrence turned to Bert and confided her fears to him, as she always did now; never to her husband. She took comfort in the fact that Ernest's money was being spent by that 'rag doll' at such a rate that he'd be too poor to marry.

More and more she was drawing closer now to her youngest son. For all the worry that Ernest was to her, he was still an unqualified success in the world of work. He was 'getting on' so famously that she now wanted Bert to do the same. It was the summer of 1901, the end of his High School scholarship. The boy was ripe to be urged along the same commercial path to glory as his frock-coated brother. The father muttered impotently in the background, afraid of his wife's tongue unless he had a few pints under his belt.

Already the 'rather finely-made boy' felt guilty at being at home without a job. He knew he must look in the papers for a vacancy. The thought was abhorrent to him, obscurely degrading. Even worse was the actuality, slipping into the Public Reading Room with the feeling that everybody knew exactly what he was up to. Again he was suffering all the torments of acute self-consciousness. The episode in the novel shows him as a fore-doomed victim of industrialism, the iron biting into him as he ploughed drearily through the list of jobs. In there one morning, gazing out of the window, he saw a brewer's dray roll by, the carter swaying on his seat in the sun, a contented tub of a man in his coarse apron. The boy longed to be stupid and fat like that man, instead of crucified on this search for a suitable place in the world.

He found a clerkship advertised by a Nottingham firm of surgical goods manufacturers, and with Ernest at home to give valuable help he drafted a letter of application:

Gentlemen,

In reply to your advertisement in the *Nottingham Guardian* for a Junior Clerk, I beg to place my services at your disposal. I am sixteen years of age, and have just completed three years' course at the Nottingham High School. Although I have not had any business experience in accounts yet, I studied bookkeeping and obtained two prizes for mathematics, as well as one for French and German.

If desired, I shall be pleased to furnish you with the highest references as to character and ability, both from my late masters and the minister in this town.

Should you favour me with the appointment I would always endeavour to merit the confidence you place in me. Trusting to receive your favourable reply, I beg to remain, gentlemen, Yours obediently,

D. H. Lawrence.

Dominated by his mother, with Ernest shining before him as an example, he had turned his back on his father's stubborn pride and self-respect as a man and gone crawling, cap in hand, in a way he would never do again. He would have to furnish references for several years to come, but he would do it with increasing irritation. From a position of boundless admiration for his brother's achievement he swung to a contempt for the standards of his world, though for a long time he was far from dismissing Ernest himself. For behind Ernest stood his mother: to topple one would have been to indict the other.

Lawrence was called for interview at the offices of J. H. Haywood, 9 Castle Gate, Nottingham. The letter heading was embellished by a picture of a wooden leg dressed in an elastic stocking, and the hero of *Sons and Lovers* felt his guts tighten with foreboding. The business world, monstrously and symbolically crippled and supported, was closing in on him like a nightmare.

The ordeal of the interview was similar to that of the search for a vacancy. It was an exposure and a humiliation to be held up before the impersonal eyes of strangers for inspection. His mother accompanied him, and this was a mixed blessing. In the train he sat squirming because she drew attention to herself, he thought, pointing at things through the window. To her it was an outing and she was excited like a girl.

In Nottingham they lingered on the bridge over the canal, enjoying the sun. The long lines of shops were another pleasure. They were in good time. They passed St. Peter's church, near the square. The street they wanted was in a commercial quarter, up towards the Castle; ancient, overhung, cobbled, 'gloomy and old-fashioned, having low dark shops and dark green house doors with brass knockers.' Georgian doorways belonging to the offices of merchants and solicitors were mixed in with warehouses and backyard factories.

The owner interviewed the boy snappily, while the mother sat on a horse-hair chair and said nothing, 'with that peculiar shut-off look of the poor who have to depend on the favours of others.'[14]

Lawrence was not frightened now. The 'common little man' made him translate a note in French, corrected a mistake, and the tight-lipped, pale boy shivered with rage at being made to look a fool. But he was given the job, at thirteen shillings a week: eight in the morning till eight at night.

They came out into the sun, and wandered downwards, till they were in the Market Place and Long Row, where the horse trams crossed and the fruit was heaped in generous piles on the stalls. Their spirits rose, they forgot Haywood's; it wasn't every day they were in Nottingham together. In a fit of daring Mrs Lawrence took her son for a dinner; then they sat eating it guiltily, because of the cost.

There is more than a touch of the North about Nottingham, yet it calls itself proudly 'Queen of the Midlands'; a big, open city which is definitely going somewhere. Nottingham 'has the finest situation of any big town in the Midlands, almost of any English town, except Durham,' writes A. L. Rowse. 'One thinks of Edinburgh, when looking up at the Castle upon its great limestone rock rising sheer out of that industrial plain. Or one sees the shape of the old town more clearly as a Tudor galleon, high in the prow and stern, low in the waist: at one end of the Castle on its rock, at the other St. Mary's church on its hill, the line of the old ramparts sinking down to Low Pavement whence the road issues out to bridge the Trent.

'The oval shape of the old town can be followed very clearly along that line and round to Parliament Street and Upper and Lower Parliament Streets, which take the place of the town walls. . . . Outside, all is industrialism, factories, workshops sheds, endless railway lines, all smouldering and smoking in the murk and gloom. But within – what riches!'[15]

Of the three periods of his life in Nottingham, first as a High School boy, then a clerk, finally as a university student, the time Lawrence chose to depict in detail for his Eastwood novel was the factory one. As Bridget Pugh puts it in her guide to the Lawrence country, 'he arranges the events of his own life to make them more acceptable artistically.'[16] In *Sons and Lovers*, Paul Morel is seen as an autodidact who went straight from elementary school to his clerical job and stayed at the factory for several years. This makes the story of his rapidly developing mind and imagination more poignant and dramatic, without isolating him too much from his environment. What happened in reality was very different. 'After leaving school I was a clerk for three months,' wrote Lawrence, 'then had a very serious pneumonia illness, in my seventeenth year, that damaged my health for life.'[17]

He began work in the spiral department. Like a Dickensian clerk he sat perched on a high stool and translated incoming letters from the French and German, copying them tediously, together with the English ones, into a letter book. His other duties were checking and invoicing. He was on the second floor, the warehouse part. Above him was the factory machinery, below him the storage areas. There was a hole cut through the floors down which the daylight filtered from the skylights in the roof. The new boy was told to sit in a dark corner, against some doors. He was out in the open, in full view of the factory girls as they came in, staring boldly and curiously at the newcomer.

As well as his other duties, he had to get parcels ready for the post in the middle of the day, then weigh them and address them, and the same again at night, by gaslight. The whole routine would accelerate and reach a climax with the arrival of the postman. Then he could leave and start on the long journey home. It was a twelve-hour day.

After a few days he was finding his way around more easily, blushing less in front of the girls, getting the measure of his immediate superior, whose bark was worse than his bite. The rougher girls worked up at the top of the building, the more 'refined' machinists on the ground floor in a sort of annexe. These were clean, and a little élite to themselves, proud of working the spiral machines.

Just as at school, Lawrence gravitated to the girls, finding them more to his liking, less predictable than the men. He liked the peak times, when the whole place was united in a rush to be ready for the post. He noticed that the men became completely absorbed in their work in these climaxes, at one with it, whereas the girls didn't take it so seriously.

In his dinnertimes he sat downstairs in the storeroom, on one of the trestle tables, talking to some of the girls about himself. He was often shy and quiet, but if he sensed a sympathetic audience he responded at once. The girls hardly knew what to make of him; so frail and quick and funny, not at all like the men. One of his favourites was a hunchback girl, touchily defensive and often in tears. When she was happy she sang, in a beautiful contralto, the others coming in on the choruses.

Night after night, when he reached home at the end of the long day, he told his mother about Haywood's and all that had happened to him. He was beginning to store away details, and to rejoice in his achievement, coping so well with an alien world. He described it to his mother and it took on a glamour: 'The light was subdued, the glossy cream parcels seemed luminous, the counters were of dark brown wood.'

This is the picture in *Sons and Lovers*, and it is indisputably accurate as far as it goes. The girls' portraits are vivid and perceptive; yet an unpleasant element has been left out. Why Lawrence was not prepared to deal with it at that time has been made clear by his friend George Neville, who spoke in 1931 of an incident at the factory which had had a 'searing' effect on the virgin boy. Twenty years later Neville elaborated on it in a conversation with Harry T. Moore. Some of the girls, perhaps cruelly intent on lacerating the boy's femininity, would tell him dirty jokes, and one day they trapped him in a corner of a storeroom and tried to unbutton his trousers. He escaped, but the experience knocked the wind out of him and he was sick. It was this savage little attack on his innocence which Neville believed to be a cause of Lawrence's subsequent illness. But Moore mentions another possibility. The pneumonia could, he thinks, have been a kind of unconscious mimicry of his brother's illness, as he saw his mother slipping further and further away from him into grief.

6

The Invalid,
and Mother Love

The blow was still to fall. Ernest came home suddenly for Goose Fair at the beginning of October. He had lost yet more weight, but his mother was so overjoyed at having him home again that she hardly remarked on it. He spoke morbidly about dying, and how soon Gypsy would forget him if he did die. All the same he was working overtime and saving hard, so that he could marry.

On Sunday night, 6th October, 1901, George Lawrence saw him off at Victoria Station, Nottingham; Ernest had called in on his married brother. It was obvious to George that he was feverish, but Ernest said it was just a cold that kept dragging on.

On Tuesday morning the telegram came from Ernest's landlady in London. She had found him on the floor of his room, unconscious. He had turned up for work on the Monday, but his boss had taken one look at him and sent him home. Mrs Lawrence put her nightdress and her brush and comb in a bag and set off for London. In Nottingham there was a long wait for the express, and she went up and down the platform trying to find out how to get to her son's lodgings at the other end. When she reached King's Cross she did the same again. Nobody seemed to know. In the end she travelled underground most of the way.

As well as the pneumonia there was erysipelas. Ernest's face was half covered with it, horribly swollen and inflamed. He was in a coma. The doctor came. The mother sat at the bedside of her dying son, who failed to recognise her.

Another telegram arrived at the stricken Walker Street house, this time to say that Ernest was dead, and for the father to come. Arthur Lawrence was on shift, and Bert, waiting at home for news, had to go to the pit with the message. Ada was frightened and began to cry.

At the pit, 'the white steam melted slowly in the sunshine of a soft blue sky; the wheels of the headstocks twinkled high up; the screen, shuffling its coal into the trucks, made a busy noise.'[1]

It was hallucinating, everything going on as usual. How could his strong, ambitious brother with his thick brown hair and his quick walk be dead? And what was his mother doing in London? He couldn't grasp any of it. He stood waiting for the cage to come up, noticing everything in great detail. His father emerged and came towards him, limping a little. As they walked off, the man asked his son: ''E's niver gone, child?' Then, in the novel, occurs a curious and chilling observation, as the father stands against a truck and puts a hand to his face. The hero saw everything, 'except his father leaning against the truck as if he were tired.'[2] This man, obliterated now as a human being in the eyes of the boy, had to be denied his human grief.

Frightened, Arthur Lawrence journeyed to London for only the second time in his life. When he eventually found the place, he was in such a dazed state that he was useless and could do nothing to help. There was the registrar to see, the funeral director, and then the parents came trailing back to Eastwood, to be met by Bert. Mrs Lawrence was in a stupor, quite shrunken and white. The boy crept up to her and she hardly noticed him.

There was still the dreadful business of the coffin arriving at the house, a ritual which had to be observed. It was taken into the front parlour and supported on six chairs. Arthur and some fellow-miners carried it in. The mother watched, Ada whimpered and held up her brass candlestick as she was told. Bert stood close to his grieving mother.

'Oh, my son – my son!' she repeated.

Coming in with the shouldered coffin, the men staggered, and Arthur Lawrence cried out to them to be careful, 'as if in pain.'

After the funeral Mrs Lawrence was more withdrawn from life than ever. She kept saying over and over that she wished she had been the one who had died. Nothing could console or distract her. Bert came in every night from work as usual, to find his mother sitting blankly as though stunned, still in her soiled apron. He forced himself to tell her about the events in his day, when it was obvious she hardly listened.

Soon her neglect began to affect him physically. He dragged through the months to Christmas, while his mother brooded incessantly and ignored him. Then at last it was the holiday. He came through the door clutching his Christmas Box money, trembling and shivering with a fever. His mother was shocked into life by this new threat.

'What's the matter?' she asked.

'I'm poorly, mother!' he replied.[3]

Like a baby, he was undressed and put to bed. The doctor came and diagnosed pneumonia, a word that struck dread into the mother's heart.

He was dangerously ill for days and nights, but the crisis saved his mother. She lay in bed with him like a lover, she fought for him; Ernest was forgotten. It was the living that mattered now, not the dead. She nursed her sick son for seven weeks, thinking of nothing else. Their intimacy was wonderfully complete. Sitting around the house as he recovered, he received all her musings, all her thoughts, all her bitterness at the cruelty of Ernest's death. Gypsy wrote a fulsome letter, saying she would never marry anyone else.

'She's thinking of *that* already,'[4] said Mrs Lawrence caustically.

For a period, husband and wife were reconciled. The loss of their son had made them draw closer, even if it was only through pity. Something had broken in the man; the tragedy was still incomprehensible to him. He refused to go near the cemetery, or go past the colliery office where Ernest had once been a clerk. In a part of himself he denied it all, and the best place to do that was the pub. He went back to his old habits.

Looking back, Lawrence was convinced that his illness at sixteen impaired his health for the rest of his life. He wasn't necessarily talking about tuberculosis, which as long as he lived he denied having at all, referring instead to his 'bronchials', bronchitis, attacks of 'this beastly 'flu', lying in bed for weeks at a time because he felt 'seedy'. But he knew he had come dangerously near to death in 1901, 'when all the cells in the body seem in intense irritability to be breaking down, and consciousness makes a last flare of struggle, like madness.'[5]

The psychological damage inflicted on him by the abrupt withdrawal of his mother's intense love is another cost to be reckoned. He had come to depend on that love so hungrily. This was how he summed up his novel: 'It follows this idea: a woman of character and refinement goes into the lower class, and has no satisfaction in her life. She has had a passion for her husband, so the children are born of passion and have heaps of vitality. But as her sons grow up she selects them as lovers – first the eldest, then the second. These sons are urged into life by their reciprocal love of their mother – urged on and on. But when they come to manhood, they can't love, because their mother is the strongest power in their lives, and holds them. . . . As soon as the young men come into contact with women, there's a split. William gives his sex to a fribble, and his mother holds his soul. But the split kills him because he doesn't know where he is . . .'[6]

*

Lawrence was at home for months, slowly mending. Jessie Chambers' sister, May, went to see him, and said afterwards that he sat up in bed and couldn't sit still for the new life going through his bones like electricity. 'And then the next news', says J. D. Chambers, 'was that my father had seen Lawrence, actually downstairs and being nursed by his mother, actually on his mother's lap and his long emaciated legs stretching almost down to the floor . . .'[7]

He was frail and white when Mr Chambers took him in the milk-float, in a heavy dark overcoat and tucked round with a rug, out to the farm at The Haggs. It was a bright morning in early spring – the convalescent boy's first glimpse of the country since before Christmas. The world was enhanced by his brush with death, and again and again throughout his life he was to know this rapturous feeling of rebirth. In an ecstasy he sat on the jolting cart, noticing everything, while the kindly farmer shouted remarks at him. There was the astounding freshness of the new year, the stir of birds in the hedgerows, 'vivid as copper-green', the birds active. It was bliss to feel the same stirring and unfolding within himself that he saw all around him, as his soul broke through, surfaced and opened in renewal.

He climbed down carefully from the cart and went into the small, oddly-shaped farmhouse kitchen. He remembered it exactly. He loved everything in it – even the old sack that served as a hearth rug and the funny little window in the corner which you had to peer out of, stooping, as if looking out of a porthole. The farmer's wife greeted him warmly, fussing over him, making him take off his thick overcoat and then noticing with a pang how thin he was, and how he was growing out of his clothes. When she had heard of the boy's illness she had said, 'I don't know whatever Mrs Lawrence will do if that son's taken from her. She told me when she was here with him that however much she loved Ernest it was nothing to what she felt for the one she brought with her. He had always meant more to her than any of the others.'[8]

Now here he was, and the Chambers' welcome was as warm as if he belonged to them. He called them, affectionately, the Haggites. Already he had won their love. Jessie was unable to account for the effect he had on her, but the mother and daughter were much alike, and this quick, eager lad, who could see almost too much, touched them both in the same way. He told them rapidly what he had seen on the way up in the cart, the sloe-blossom out already, and a whole crop of celandines. Their daffodils were almost flowering too, he said, and they looked 'cold', nodding their stiff green buds.

Jessie got the dinner ready, the visitor's bright blue eyes taking everything in. His insight was almost too much: it was rather frightening. The girl objected to being seen into, and became bitterly self-conscious of her ragged clothes. She hated to have her inner world disturbed, to be made aware of herself as she was. For his part, he was amazed all over again, when the brothers and the father came in and sat down to their meal, at the difference between this family and his own. The Lawrence children were united as one person around the mother, while here there was a continual 'jangle and discord', and it fascinated him. It was disturbing, but alive, not logical like the ménage his mother ruled, not under control at all in fact, but freer. He wasn't sure whether he liked it or not: he sat there and tried to get the hang of it.

That afternoon Mrs Chambers took him and Jessie to look at a wren's nest she had discovered in the hedge down by the orchard. With great care the boy explored the interior of the round nest with his finger. He startled them by saying that it was like putting your finger inside the bird itself, because of the warmth and roundness, pressed into shape by the bird's breast. And he cried out at the celandines, with their petals flattened, he said, as if they were pushing up at the sun.

It was during this year of his convalescence that his sister Ada went to The Haggs and met the whole brood of Chambers – nine of them altogether. Later, she and Jessie and Bert were to be pupil teachers at the same centre in Ilkeston.

Ada's recollections of Jessie, when she came to write them down, were friendly enough, if a little beady-eyed. 'Jessie', she remembered, 'inherited her mother's large brown eyes. Her figure was a little ungainly as she walked with her head and shoulders bent forward, but her black silky hair had a natural wave and from her shoulders upwards she was beautiful.

'I think she first attracted Bert because she was so different from the gay thoughtless girls we knew in the district. She was always very much in earnest about something or other, either her school work or a book, or her failing to understand her younger brothers or be understood by them. They delighted to offend her with little vulgarities.

'Unlike us, she was not interested in new clothes or sweethearts, and until her meeting with my brother she had made no friend.

'To know someone ready to listen to his ideas and views and accept his theories and beliefs was a new experience for him. She shared his enthusiasm for the beauties of nature and poetry and he loved the life at the farm – the companionship of the lads and her father. She claimed him before all others and their friendship continued for several years. Although mother accused him of being in love he would not admit it. Sometimes he said he was tired of the farm and Jessie and then mother would be glad, thinking he was all hers again. But after a restless weekend the desire to see Jessie again would become too strong, and when mother saw him wheeling his bicycle down the garden path she would say bitterly, "So – he couldn't keep away after all his talk of not caring." [9]

Lawrence told them at The Haggs one day that his mother said he was spending so much time with them, he might as well move in with them and have done with it. But to begin with all was well. His year of recovery was quite guiltless, and one of the happiest years of his life.

His friendship with Jessie started with pity. He felt sorry for her. For a long time her unhappiness baffled him and perhaps put him off. This shy, intense, soulful girl was impossible to talk to, at any rate for more than a few minutes: it was all too much of a strain. He much preferred the company of her mother, who seemed to understand him and who gave him the sympathy he needed, and he soon came to like Alan and Hubert, the two oldest sons. Their youthful brashness was only a surface thing: underneath they were sensitive, rather tormented lads, shut-in on themselves and longing for friendship. Once they trusted him, they were ready to love him.

As for Jessie and him, they were most intimate when they were responding to nature. 'And then the celandines ever after drew her with a little spell. Anthropomorphic as she was, she stimulated him into appreciating things thus, and then they lived for her. She seemed to need things kindling in her imagination or in her soul before she felt she had them.' [10] So for many months, as he came and went happily through the short cut of the Warren, this was the one unspoken bond between them.

In *Sons and Lovers*, the delicate, frail shoots of their intimacy take on a new strength in the scene with the swing. Always in these early days the girl hung back from revealing her secrets, because he was male and an intimate of her brothers now, and they judged things of hers harshly and mocked her. She had to remind herself continually that he was different.

The swing she wanted him to see, in the cowshed, was no more than a great hank of shaggy rope dangling from a high beam, with sacks for a seat. The boy's mood was gay; he sent himself flying to and fro joyously in the gloomy shed, sending the hens squawking for cover and defying the drizzly day. She had made him go first, and for the first time had felt the subtle pleasure of pleasing a 'man'. When it came to her turn, she was both terrified and thrilled as he took her by the waist and pushed her out firmly into space. It was almost sexual.

He attached himself to Mrs Chambers, then Alan, and finally Jessie. Pity was still his overriding feeling for Jessie, and that meant they were not equals. With her brother it was different, working with him on the land or lying in the hay with him, high up, yarning to him about Nottingham, which the shy lad knew nothing about, and about his time at the factory: they became comrades. He probably made it all sound more grand and worldly than it really was, his plunge into the heart of industry. And the brothers for their part initiated him into the mysteries of their rural life, showing him how to do many jobs around the farm.

That summer they took him out to their hayfields at Greasley, four miles from the farm. 'Far away was the blue heap of Nottingham. Between, the country lay under a haze of heat, with here and there a flag of colliery smoke waving. But near at hand, at the foot of the hill, across the deep-hedged high road, was only the silence of the old church and the castle farm, among their trees.'[11]

His illness had left him with a voice pitched even higher than before, and if he was angry or agitated it became almost a squeal. Physically he was weak, his nature passive, his appearance colourless, his face in repose tending to be almost ugly and stupid. In a room of people he was liable to be overlooked. Yet one of the brothers, David Chambers, said he had never met a more exciting person. His eyes were so alive, he had such a zest for life, and this bracing, nervous energy he had could infect their activity and expand it, give it new significance, whether they were working or playing. It was a matter of mood. Sometimes he seemed to have the devil in him, and then the friends who thought they loved him shrank back and wondered what it was they were loving. He had outbursts of vile temper, though in the idyllic early days at The Haggs these were rare. But David Chambers remembers more than one occasion when Bert frightened him by a lack of control. Once, in a mad fit of daring, he leapt to and fro across a dangerous millrace at Felley Mill. The slippery steep sides of the chute made it treacherous and the gap was nearly five feet across. David Chambers watched open-mouthed with a small boy's fear. There was no telling what Bert Lawrence would do if he was in the mood.

At the farm it was Lawrence who organised the charades and the sing-songs. He was a poor singer himself and once when he tried to learn to play the piano he lost patience and flew into a temper, but that didn't stop him from taking charge and conducting the singers. He always knew exactly what he wanted. Leaving them at night for his long walk back across the fields he would hear the family at the door, long after he could see them, singing a chorus of *There is a Tavern in the Town* or *Larboard Watch*, to send him on his way.

Already he was an excellent mimic, delighting the Chambers family with this gift, which had more than a touch of cruelty in it. By the time he came to write novels and stories he was well on the way to being a master. Nobody was immune, even then, not even his parents. There was the classic story of the ham his father bought once and gave to Mrs Lawrence with a splendid gesture of magnanimity. Lawrence pinned down his father with such precision, stance and all, that the Chambers didn't know whether to laugh or applaud. But the ham wasn't a free gift, explained Bert, it had to be paid for, and his father took something off his mother's housekeeping every week until it was. Mrs Lawrence had plenty to say in protest, and each time more virulently. Finally the miner shouted out in exasperation, 'Woman – owd thee feace.'

The more he came to know the oldest brothers, Alan and Hubert, the more he admired them. He soon saw that their rough exterior masked a longing for something passionate and significant, a quality they shared with their mother. He spent more and more time with them, and Jessie found this a bitter thing. But her turn was soon to come. Meanwhile he continued to cultivate the love of her mother; he could appreciate her, and her sympathy was readily accessible. She was completely won over now by his impetuous acts of kindness and generosity. At home in Eastwood he showed the same willingness. 'Well, if I was at the mangle,' said Mrs Mary Brice, a neighbour, 'or if he knew it had been a washday, he'd say, "Are you mangling?"' ... Then 'he'd come through and mangle, or wipe the pots, and do any little job, carry the bread from the bakehouse and into the shop for me. Any little job that he could do to help me.'[12]

He went away to Skegness for a month, to stay with his mother's sister, Lettice, who kept a boarding house there, right on the sea front. While he was there he did sketches of the melancholy Lincolnshire coastline – the flat, wide landscape affected him. He wrote detailed letters to The Haggs, conscious of his newly-won place in the family and no doubt eager to maintain it. In one letter 'he said that he could stand in his aunt's drawing room and watch the tide rolling in through the window. My sister wrote back at once and said what an uncomfortable drawing room his aunt's must be, with the tide rolling in through the window!'[13]

It could be that he loved the Chambers boys so much because they were strong, robust lads with hard muscles, living manly lives in the open air, who to his delight accepted him exactly as he was. They even deferred to him a little, hesitating shyly before him, allowing him to dominate them. Each time he asserted himself they wavered, and he saw where his strength lay. His will was stronger. It was his first real triumph in the world of men. He had never been accepted before by males; he had been jeered at by schoolboys, and his father despised him, or so he thought. Only his mother had supported him with her total love. She allowed him to strut and be the male with her because she cherished him and saw his chronic inadequacy. Perhaps later he would grow strong enough to stand up without her. It was partly sincere, a true anxiety, but it was also a reason for keeping him close to her for as long as she could.

Now these healthy boys admired him, Alan particularly. Admiration was the air he needed, almost as much as he needed tenderness. Jessie was forgotten for the moment. He was leaving childhood and about to enter manhood. He saw how beautiful it was to be a man. He had been spoiled nearly to death and now he was full of adolescent arrogance, a little tyrant in embryo – all of which he restrained and disguised by sudden acts of darting generosity and love. He adored the blossoming manhood of the brothers with a female adoration. He longed to be masculine himself, but his passionate desiring of it placed him in the position of a girl desiring a lover. All this was inchoate so far in his feminine soul.

The farm and all it represented to the young Lawrence could be summed up in one word: escape. Escape from the constriction of his own family, escape from his mother, escape from the mine in the person of his father, and from the streets of miners' cottages in which his life was locked: most of all, escape from himself and his failure to confront the world.

It was a great irony that his mother had taken him there, and now he fled there gladly to escape the bondage of their mutual love. For his dependence was perhaps even greater than hers. In *Sons and Lovers*, the boy 'loved to sleep with his mother', and while Ernest had been alive he had been 'unconsciously jealous of his brother'. When, in the novel, the father has an accident and has to go to hospital, Paul is able to rule the roost, at any rate in his own eyes. So in life. George was a married man living in Nottingham, and with Ernest away in London, the remaining son could say to his mother with undisguised delight, as does Paul in the novel: 'I'm the man of the house now.'[14]

Even before he became conscious of Jessie and her yearning love for him, her willingness to learn, and by implication her readiness to be dominated, he was running off to The Haggs as fast as he could go. The Chambers family never saw Mrs Lawrence at the farm again. She came to see the influence of the parents as a threat, and as Bert told her with eager innocence of his growing attachment to the brothers, she transferred her disapproval to them, and in due course to Jessie herself.

He had escaped, too, because of his adventurousness, his passionate curiosity, his need to explore. In an essay years later he defined the Novel as 'a thought-adventure'. He loved to discover things for himself – it gave him a thrill. The dark underground life of the mine, on which the very existence of his home and family was built, would cast its spell on him for the whole of his life. His response to the English countryside was like that of a miner coming off shift, being hauled to the surface and jolted suddenly into the blinding light of day. The mornings were more than good, they were miraculous and astounding creations. With the poignancy of a man stepping out of his tomb and finding himself alive, he was able to know the extraordinary freshness and beauty of the earth. 'The metallurgists and mining folk', reflected Aldington in his biography, 'were always mysterious and terrifying to those who in ancient times wandered with their herds and flocks or dwelt silently among the fields they cultivated. The daunted imaginations of the dwellers in the sun who came in contact with them brought forth weird tales of cyclops and gnomes and kobolds. And the mining folk, in turn, told each other tales of the fairy folk who lived in the dewy fields.'[15]

The mine, dark and hidden, was always there and exerting itself powerfully, like the father, in spite of the triumph of the mother and her values in *Sons and Lovers*. Gradually over the years the emphasis was to shift, from mother love and womb love to a furious attempt to re-establish the male, his father. From the earth he turned to the sun, from the world of light to a world of darkness behind the sun where his father stood.

The deserted quarry he knew in childhood, described in *The White Peacock* and again in a strange futuristic story towards the end of his life – published in *Phoenix* as 'Autobiographical Fragment' – was in a sense the kind of link he always sought in his efforts to reconcile these two worlds. The place fascinated him as a boy, it had open spaces, it was sown with flowers, but it also had secret clefts, dark places, mystery, like a mine in miniature. 'I loved it because, in the open part, it seemed so sunny and dry and warm, the pale stone, the pale, slightly sandy bed, the dog violets and the early daisies. And then the old part, the deep part, was such a fearsome place. It was always dark – you had to crawl under bushes. And you came upon honeysuckle and nightshade, that no one ever looked upon. And at the dark sides were little, awful rocky caves, in which I imagined the adders lived.' The narrator of 'Autobiographical Fragment' found a tiny cave, 'which would just hold me. It seemed warm in there, as if the shiny rock were warm and alive, and it seemed to me there was a strange perfume, of rock, of living rock like hard, bright flesh, faintly perfumed with phlox. It was a subtle yet most fascinating perfume, an inward perfume. I crept right into the little cavity, into the narrow inner end where the vein of purple ran, and I curled up there, like an animal in its hole.'[16] There, in the story, he fell asleep. He slept for a thousand years, and woke into a strange gentle world, the Midlands of his childhood transformed by splendid hill towns and Etruscan-like people.

Out at The Haggs it was another such transformation. Still under the sway of his mother, he could only express the ecstasy of it, when he came to write his first novel, by a profusion of flowers and by an adoration of the 'noble, white fruitfulness' of one of the brothers that was far from discreet.

All through the pastoral of *The White Peacock* the figures move dimly in a rain, sometimes a storm, of flowers. The effect is florid, the detail often exquisite and precise. Even the skies are turned into enormous quivering blossoms, the trees stand up like the bluebells, with equal delicacy, the riot of spring has, already, the rigour of a new religion: 'The tender-budded trees shuddered and moaned; when the wind was dry, the young leaves flapped limp. The grass and corn grew lush, but the light of the dande-lions was quite extinguished, and it seemed that only a long time back had we made merry before the broad glare of these flowers. The bluebells lingered and lingered; they fringed the fields for weeks like purple fringes of morning. The pink campions came out only to hang heavy with rain; hawthorn buds remained tight and hard as pearls, shrinking into the brilliant green foliage; the forget-me-nots, the poor Pleiades of the wood, were ragged weeds. Often at the end of the day, the sky opened, and stately clouds hung over the horizon infinitely far away, glowing, through the yellow distance, with an amber lustre . . . Sometimes, towards sunset, a great shield stretched dark from west to the zenith, tangling the light along its edge. As the canopy rose higher, it broke, dispersed, and the sky was primrose coloured, high and pale above the crystal moon.'[17]

*

That summer was the first of many, but when he came to write later of helping out at Greasley with the hay harvest it was with all the throb and vividness of a first impression. A new sensuousness broke over him, the waves of flowers came and went, the air ached and teemed with fragrance. 'As I passed along the edge of the meadow the cow-parsley was as tall as I, frothing up to the top of the hedge, putting the faded hawthorn to a wan blush. Little, early birds – I had not heard the lark – fluttered in and out of the foamy meadow-sea, plunging under the surf of flowers washed high in one corner, swinging out again, dashing past the crimson sorrel cresset. Under the froth of flowers were the purple vetch-clumps, yellow milk-vetches, and the scattered pink of the wood-betony, and the floating stars of marguerites. There was a weight of honeysuckle on the hedges, where pink roses were waking up for their broad-spread flight through the day.'[18]

Mr Chambers, concerned for the health of young Bert, counselled him to take the short cut whenever he came to the farm, so that he inhaled the scent of the pines into his lungs. They were supposed to be good for chest ailments. Now he said it would be good for the boy to come out to the hay-fields with them if he took care not to strain himself. He was gentle and considerate, even with his sons. Bert was more than willing. He went out in the early mornings, when the willows 'glittered like hammered steel', to the two large hilly fields that faced south. The farmer had to re-strain him, he was so eager to help. The brothers were glad of his company, it gave a new impetus to the work. Laughter rang out, and the break times were as merry as picnics. He worked as long as they did, till sunset and even longer, and sometimes his sister Ada joined them. Soon Bert was able to lift forkfuls of hay with the best of them, though being slender he used to stagger, and he had a turn at driving the cutting machines, sharpening 'the bristling machine-knife under the hornbeam'. He rode high on the load, 'like a long mushroom in my felt hat, sweating, with my shirt neck open.'[19] The cropped, gold-green slopes shone in the sun, and they worked till they heard the knocking-off hooter from a nearby pit.

The father had brought food for the dinner and tea in his milk-float. Sometimes his wife was there too, presiding over the meal. It took a fortnight to gather the harvest, and because the Nottingham road passed at the bottom of the hill, and they were a good way from the farm, tools were left overnight and somebody volunteered to sleep in the hay to keep an eye on the equipment. Ada Lawrence remembered Bert and George, one of the brothers, staying behind one night and being visited by a tramp in the small hours. The intruder appeared in due course in print, in

'Love Among the Haystacks': 'He was a very seedy, slinking fellow, with a tang of horsey braggadocio about him. Small, thin, and ferrety, with a week's red beard bristling on his pointed chin, he came slouching forward.'[20]

If Mrs Chambers had anything to do with it there would be a sparkling white cloth to spread on the sward for the meal, to say nothing of cutlery and plates. The farmer would be pleased with the 'proper' look of things. They sat under a leafy tree against the hedge and near one of the stacks. From their area of shade, the greenish stubble stretched before them, shimmering in the heat and looking as if it was melting, about to run off the slope. The great ragged stack rising beside them had begun to dominate the field. Bert loved the feeling of suspension in the air at noon, as they chewed and drank and their sweat diminished in the cool shade. Nobody spoke much to begin with. Mr Chambers had brought his newspaper, leaning back and spreading it out as if he were in his parlour. Now and then he would ask Bert how he was feeling, if he was over-tired.

In the cool of the evening, after the sun had set, the farmer would harness the horse to his float and go off, followed by his sons on their bicycles. Bert would either go with them, or linger behind for a while with Alan or Hubert; he liked to be there when the twilight gathered and thickened to darkness in the valley bottom. From their vantage point they could see the lights coming on in the cottage windows, the lamps on the carts wavering along the road, crawling up the long hill. The scents of the flowers and trees were intensified, almost to a sickliness.

Sometimes he liked to be there alone. He had begun to discover a kind of voluptuousness in solitude: 'Heat came in wafts, in thick strands. The evening was a long time cooling. He thought he would go and wash himself. There was a trough of pure water in the hedge bottom . . . All round the trough, in the upper field, the land was marshy, and there the meadow-sweet stood like clots of mist, very sickly-smelling in the twilight . . . The purple bell-flowers in the hedge went black, the ragged robin turned its pink to a faded white, the meadow-sweet gathered light as if it were phosphorescent, and it made the air ache with sweat . . . As he dried himself, he discovered little wonderings in the air, felt on his sides soft touches and caresses that were particularly delicious: sometimes they startled him, and he laughed as if he were not alone: The flowers, the meadow-sweet particularly, haunted him. He reached to put a hand over their fleeciness. They touched his thighs. Laughing, he gathered them and dusted himself all over with their cream dust and fragrance.'[21]

Standing there under the night sky, lifted up on the brow of the hill, he looked out on the darkness and was exhilarated. There was a hushed, fairy quality to it, lights tossed and winking in little galaxies like stars, marking the cottages, the villages, collieries, and, more sinister, a glare of red flame and a distant thumping from an iron foundry. Nottingham could be seen glowing, far off, its crowds and houses contained dimly on the horizon. Even that was magical. The big lime trees shivered in the night breeze, brimming baskets of scent. You could see the huddle of Ilkeston, and the viaduct bridging the valley.

On the night they were disturbed by a tramp it was wet and miserable. Four of them were bedded down under the stack when somebody heard a noise and jumped up. In a letter to a girl-friend, Lawrence described the incident with a priggish emphasis on his superiority. 'Tell the poor devil to lie down, and shut up,' he had called to the others, irritated by the whining tramp.[22] The next morning, taking a better look at the member of the 'great fraternity', he saw how the man had dug a hole for himself in the wall of the stack, and Lawrence found his bald head with the fuzz of dirty grey hair distasteful to him. It was drizzling, after a night of rain. In a dry shed they brought bits of kindling and made a fire on the earth floor, adding hay to it until it glowed, dangling a milk-can of coffee over it, on the end of a pitchfork.

In the story, 'Love Among the Haystacks', the tramp is given the left-over piece of rabbit-pie, which he wolfs down as though he is famished. 'There was something debased, parasitic about him.' He jarred on the company, who wanted him gone, resenting the way he sat there as though it were his right. Because they had given him so much, he expected more. He began to look round insolently as if he owned the place. The father showed no hostility, but the sons did, and Lawrence shared their contempt. 'He tucked his tail between his legs . . . He was a mean crawl of a man.'[23]

And he remembered that morning, with its slow, sickly dawn, the light breaking with difficulty into whiteness because of the dense mist. When it was day, he noticed how shrunken things were, the soaring trees of the night, the towering wall of the stack, and in the thick damp atmosphere the light 'could scarcely breathe.' The hedges dripped like washing, the mist clung to the hillside like smoke, smudging outlines.

Writing to his friend Blanche Jennings about an early draft of *The White Peacock*, then called 'Laetitia', he began by telling her that he had been working in the hay-field and his face and hands were satisfactorily tanned and toughened. He was a few years on from his near-fatal illness, but he was surely remembering it as he boasted of his new health and strength, the hard muscles gained from the work and from dumb-bell exercises he had done. Then he slipped into the language of narcissism and sensuousness he was already using in the novel, as he admired himself for her eyes only, 'because I can talk to you like this.' But Miss Jennings, feminist though she was, must have been startled to open her letter and read that 'as I passed my hands over my sides where the muscles lie suave and secret, I did love myself. I am thin, but well skimmed over with muscle; my skin is very white and unblemished; soft, and dull with a fine pubescent bloom, not shiny like my friend's.'[24]

This friend was Alan Chambers, the original of George in *The White Peacock*. He told Miss Jennings how fond of Alan he was, and Alan of him, and that she was right to suggest that he put a higher value on his friendships with men than on those with women. He went on to say that his men friends were 'all alike', and seemed to be suggesting that to get a satisfactory friend it would be necessary to combine them all. In an effort to convey his meaning he plunged headlong into complexity, writing of chords of feeling vibrating in different frequencies, male and female, then dragging in discords, harmonies, the great composers, as he foundered and finally gave up, because 'you are sick of this; and so am I.'[25]

In an earlier letter he had more or less dismissed his unfinished book, defensively, and with telegraphic impatience: 'In the first place it is a novel of sentiment – may the devil fly away with it – what the critics would call, I believe, an "erotic novel" – the devil damn the whole race black – all about love – and rhapsodies on Spring scattered here and there – heroines galore – no plot – nine tenths adjectives – every colour in the spectrum descanted upon – a poem or two – scraps of Latin and French – altogether a sloppy, spicy mess.' He wanted to 'write the thing again and stop up the mouth of Cyril – I will kick him out – I hate the fellow.'[26]

But Cyril survived into the finished book, confessing his love and admiration for the good animal that George potentially was, and doing it with all the freedom and recklessness of Lawrence in his letters. It didn't matter really who did the admiring, and to begin with it was Lettie who watched him towelling himself vigorously as he came in unconcerned and stood beside her, his shirt gaping open nearly to the belly and his sleeves rolled, so that he was 'naked at breast and arms.' She watched as if mesmerised as he shoved the towel inside his shirt and she noticed how the burnt flesh of his face and neck was quenched suddenly at the throat, and saw 'the rise and fall of his breasts, wonderfully solid and white.'[27]

Later it was Cyril's turn, and mid-summer: the hay harvest about to start. George stripped off his clothes for a dip in the pond, the dog Trip leaping excitedly around the legs of the naked man as he waited for his friend to join him. While he waited he rolled on the grass with the joyful dog, tussling with it, laughing as it pushed its head towards his face, licking madly, pushing it away and laughing again as it came lunging forward in a fresh onslaught, barking and snapping in play.

In the water together, the two young men flung themselves along, cavorted, floated, with Trip, in a frenzy of anxiety and eagerness to reach them, floundering at the bank. Out again, Cyril stood drying himself, laughing breathlessly and looking with pleasure at his friend's body. 'He was well proportioned, and naturally of handsome physique, heavy-limbed. He laughed at me, telling me I was like one of Aubrey Beardsley's long, lean, ugly fellows. I referred him to many classic examples of slenderness, declaring myself more exquisite than his grossness, which amused him.'[28]

So it went, with the rather puny, wincing youth justifying himself determinedly in words, pressing literature into service at an early age to compensate for basic inadequacies of his own. But there was another, even better way to do it, and that was by admiration of the other's 'noble white fruitfulness'. By love, by the feminine game of submission, you gained the desired body for yourself.

In the novel, Cyril stared so long and lovingly that he forgot to dry himself, until his friend 'began to rub me briskly, as if I were a child, or rather, a woman he loved and did not fear. I felt myself quite limply in his hands, and, to get a better grip of me, he put his arm round me and pressed me against him, and the sweetness of the touch of our naked bodies one against the other was superb . . . and our love was perfect for a moment, more perfect than any love I have known since, either for man or woman.'[29]

7

Jessie

The idyllic spring and summer were too good to be true: there were ominous mutterings again at home; something had to be decided about young Bert's future. Going back to Haywood's now was out of the question, and it was a bitter thing for Lydia Lawrence to accept that Bert was not likely to succeed her dead son in a splendid business career. She had set her Victorian heart on it: money and position were what counted in the cruel world of her experience. There was also her virulently-maintained superiority, fought for over the years in this squalid mining community. Ernest had triumphantly vindicated it, and now it was to have been Bert's turn. (Lydia's first-born, George, had left home at the age of ten to live in Nottingham with relatives, and seemed destined to be a picture-framer, though in the end he became an engineer.)

With her grim acceptance of yet another of life's disappointments, Mrs Lawrence resigned herself. The Reverend Robert Reid came to see her and said that Mr Holderness, in charge of the British School in Albert Street, had a vacancy for a pupil-teacher. If she wished, he would recommend her boy. Mrs Lawrence bowed her head. Really, she had no choice: it was either that or the pit. Even her husband, whose opinion had ceased to count in any case, agreed that Bert was far from robust. So it was settled that he should start at Albert Street in the autumn term. Mrs Lawrence bleakly closed her mouth on the subject. There was no comparing the career of a village schoolteacher, its dedication and lack of material rewards, with the shining path her Ernest had been cutting for himself.

This autumn of 1902 saw another upheaval. The Lawrences had been at the Walker Street house for twelve years. Now they submitted once again to the will of the mother, who wanted to leave this house with its unhappy memories. And for Mrs Lawrence any move she made had of necessity to be a move upwards. Along the road and up the hill in Lynn Croft Road was a vacant house owned by Thomas Cooper, the father of two of Bert's friends, Frances and Gertrude. It was suitably up the social scale, towards the Hill Top district of Eastwood.

This house in Lynn Croft Road seems to be the one Lawrence is describing in the opening pages of *Aaron's Rod*: 'The street sloped down-hill, and the backs were open to the fields. So he saw a curious succession of lighted windows, between which jutted the intermediary back premises, scullery and outhouse, in dark little blocks. It was something like the keyboard of a piano: more still, like a succession of musical notes. For the rectangular planes of light were of different intensities, some bright and keen, some soft, warm, like candle-light, and there was one surface of pure red light . . . The hollow countryside lay beyond him. Sometimes in the windy darkness he could see the red burn of New Brunswick bank, or the brilliant jewels of light clustered at Bestwood Colliery. Away in the dark hollow, nearer, the glare of the electric power station disturbed the night.' In the house owned by Aaron Sisson in the novel it was draughty, 'because the settling of the mines under the house made the doors not fit.'[1]

Not long before the move to Lynn Croft Road, Jessie had made what was probably her one and only visit to the Lawrences when they lived in Walker Street. She took a good deal of persuading, and Lawrence thought it was on account of his father: he knew she was afraid of drunks. He told here there was no need to be nervous, his father was always out. The atmosphere of constraint she found when she did call she analysed later as being compounded of hostility, grief, and possessive love, all tensions exerted by Lawrence's mother. She was unnerved and at the same time keyed up to a pitch of excitement by this curious 'tightness in the air'. It was clear to her now that Bert's infectious high spirits whenever he came to The Haggs were a kind of rejoicing at his escape, like his outings in the countryside.

The experience at the British School was grim. Lawrence was unhappy at having to masquerade as a teacher on his own doorstep. Ada had also begun as a pupil-teacher. Then a year later there came a reprieve: a new education act reformed the teacher-training system and a centre was established at Ilkeston, four miles to the south of Eastwood, in Derbyshire. Jessie Chambers broke out of her rural fastness, her mother persuaded by Lawrence to let her daughter have her chance in further education, and joined the little group of travellers each morning, getting on the train and crossing the Nottingham Canal and the Erewash, which marked the border. In the afternoons they usually came back on foot. George Neville joined them, transferred from his teaching post at Greasley, and Jessie's brother, Alan, together with several girls, including later on Louie Burrows from Cossall, who was to usurp Jessie for a time in Lawrence's affections. The whole lively group coalesced over the next few years into the 'Pagans', all friends of Lawrence who were to be seen at various times at his house in Lynn Croft Road or out at The Haggs on picnics and helping with the harvest, taking part in the excursions he loved to organise.

Lawrence did well at Ilkeston, but he disliked Thomas Beacroft, the headmaster, more or less on sight. The man was generally disliked, according to Neville. When Lawrence came to write *The Rainbow* he used Beacroft as a model for Mr Harby, 'a short, sturdy man, with a fine head, and a heavy jowl . . . There was something insulting in the way he could be so actively unaware of another person, so occupied.' It was not so much what he did as what he was; the power behind everything: 'All the other teachers hated him, and fanned their hatred among themselves. For he was master of them and the children, he stood like a wheel to make absolute his authority over the herd. That seemed to be his one reason in life, to hold blind authority over the school. His teachers were his subjects as much as the scholars.'[2]

Through the person of Ursula in *The Rainbow*, the shrinking, hypersensitive girl who is yet so keenly aware of her own worth, Lawrence set down in a few rapid strokes his own first impressions of the Ilkeston Centre: 'The school squatted within its railed, asphalt yard, that shone black with rain. The building was grimy, and horrible, dry plants were shadowily looking through the windows.' Inside, 'she looked at the walls, colour washed, pale green and chocolate, at the large windows with frowsty geraniums against the pale glass, at the long rows of desks, arranged in a squadron, and dread filled her.'[3]

It was easy for Lawrence, drawn towards the girls as always, identified with them often, to feel immediate resentment for this crude headmaster who treated Jessie Chambers and Louie Burrows with contempt. Young Lawrence felt himself overruled in the same maddening fashion, until he learned later how to assert himself. Yet in *The Rainbow* he allows his heroine to show, in spite of herself, a sneaking regard for this man, even to admire his strength and admit that whatever else he was, he was not small. He had been forced into a false position, and the torture of it had turned him into a bully, all because he had to earn a living. 'It seemed such a miserable thing for him to be doing. He had a decent, powerful, rude soul.'[4]

When the youth of seventeen got into his stride and gained

confidence he became a good teacher. Even Beacroft appreciated him in the end for his quickness and intelligence, and when the other students exasperated him once, he pointed to some working on the blackboard that Lawrence had done and asked them why they couldn't do as well. This was music to the youngster whose alter ego in *Sons and Lovers* asked his mother, when he won a prize for one of his watercolours, 'Why don't you praise me up to the skies?'

As an apprentice teacher he was apt to lose his temper suddenly, especially if he felt he was being made to look a fool. The veracity of his portrait of Ursula in similar circumstances, the effort it cost her and her violent trembling afterwards, leaves no doubt that it was his own experience he was relating. Richard Pogmore, one of the Pagans, saw him leap across the room one afternoon at Ilkeston to catch a boy who was playing him up, and the stinging slap 'sounded all over the school.'

These were huge classes, never less than fifty, often with two such classes crowded into one room and not even a partition between. Looking across at him, Jessie saw him in a moment of love as 'totally different', and she winced to see his vulnerability, the ease with which he could be hurt, 'his finely-shaped head with small well-set ears, and his look of concentration, of being more intensely alive.' But it was more than a physical thing; it was a fragile and sensitive spirit she saw. There was a 'quality of lightness about him, something that seemed to shine from within'[5], and it went flickering through his deft hands and his blue eyes. This linking of love with pain was typical of Jessie, whom one of her brothers described later as being 'almost a devotee of suffering'.

She felt she owed him a great deal. It was partly his efforts that had got her away from the farm and alongside him as a student teacher. He not only convinced her mother, he helped Jessie to prepare for her examination. He was sorry for her, but teaching her French and algebra was also a good outlet for his bossiness. When he found out how discontented she was, he was surprised. Why couldn't she be satisfied with just being a girl, like Emily? Her restlessness and her fierce sense of injustice were altogether outside his experience. Though he was prepared to help her, he didn't exactly approve. Why should a woman want to ape a man? She burst out vehemently that she didn't want to be a man, she wanted a man's opportunities. Men had everything, women nothing. Learning, education, that was the key to the door for her. Otherwise she would be kicked about forever by her brothers, or some other man.

Lawrence agreed to help her, though she wasn't exactly sure of him as a teacher, and with good reason. His motives were ulterior, if he told the truth. The intimacy of it excited him, perhaps that was it. But he was naïve enough to tell his mother what he was doing. Her reply was caustic: 'I hope she'll get fat on it.'

He began to instruct her, vastly enjoying his feeling of authority, yet finding to his surprise that he had very little patience with the girl. She was so pathetically in earnest, for one thing. Algebra terrified her; it was worse than feeding the hens from her hand, though he told her airily, with the infinite superiority of the High School scholar, that there was nothing to it: all you had to do was substitute letters for figures. He went too rapidly, and interrogated her ruthlessly, until she was on the point of tears. This affected him strangely, stirring a kind of sadism in him, and instead of being ashamed of himself he bullied her more. She was such a victim that she provoked him. One day he lost his temper and chucked the pencil at her. He was ashamed then, for the moment.

Student days began, and the period of finding out, soon to develop into an orgy of reading. He was becoming more aware of his gifts, but they baffled him. What to do with them? He thought at first it was painting he should concentrate on. When he came to write his 'colliery novel', he made his hero a budding artist, not a writer. For years he had sketched and painted assiduously at home, copying illustrations in magazines, reproductions, even photographs. Later on he had some private tuition from a man in Eastwood who ran an art class, a relative of Lord Leighton. When he came back from his Skegness holiday he had some sketches to show. He took them to The Haggs for them to admire. He knew his mother didn't care about his things unless they fitted into some pattern of achievement she wanted for him, but the Chambers were different, they were simply interested in whatever he did for its own sake. Yet from his mother he drew his resolve, and a knowledge of his uniqueness that could be overbearing at times. Like her, he always had to be 'right'. He marvelled later at her hard, inflexible character. He could be like that himself, but he also wavered horribly, whereas she always acted as if she had no doubts whatsoever about anything. Again like her, he tended to fret at things, and couldn't be contented like other people. He could have great spurts of happiness, but he was never finally contented inside himself. Something was wrong – and it always would be.

Painting and sketching from nature interested him far less than copying did. Again it was a question of finding out. In *Women in*

Love, Hermione surprises Birkin copying a Chinese drawing of geese which he had found in a bedroom in her house, and she remarks on the beauty of his attempt. When she asks him why he copies instead of doing something of his own, he tells her that it is a marvellous drawing and he is copying it in order to know it. 'One gets more of China, copying this picture, than reading all the books.'

So in his youth he copied English water-colourists, from Girtin onwards, he copied Corot, Brangwyn, Greiffenhagen, and he found reproductions of the Italians he liked, such as Carpaccio, Piero di Cosimo, Fra Angelico. All his life it gave him pleasure, as a relief from words.

It was natural that as fellow-students he and Jessie should explore the world of literature together. They had the same set books to study, from which they branched out, always with Lawrence laying down the guidelines. He was fortunate in coming from a home which had books, mainly belonging to Ernest, and in having The Haggs for a second home. The Chambers liked to read, and they were familiar with literature from the *Nottingham Guardian*, which carried instalments of famous books of the time, such as Hardy's *Tess*. Jessie sat as a small girl and listened to Mr Chambers reading these instalments from the newspaper for her mother and anybody else who happened to be in the room. It was a simple matter for Lawrence, when he became accepted, to initiate play-readings in a family like this.

Though he took charge of Jessie's reading too, carrying her along with him easily enough, she had plenty of opinions of her own. In her own record of this thrilling time, when life expanded out of all recognition, she refers to more than a hundred authors they read and discussed together. The key to much of the poetry was a red-bound pocket edition of Palgrave's *Golden Treasury*. On lots of their walks Lawrence carried this book and read aloud from it. Always he wanted to know what she thought, and why, and how it affected her. As well as the *Treasury* they read the Lake Poets, the Victorians, the Pre-Raphaelites. Whitman they touched on. Baudelaire he liked, and Verlaine, but Jessie didn't care for them. At his instigation they studied them in the original. Miriam-Jessie in *Sons and Lovers* is set to work copying out Baudelaire's 'Le Balcon' and then her instructor read it aloud. He seemed to be taunting her with it as he read the lines throatily, with a suppressed sensuality she found brutal. She hated the sudden fury and frustrated passion of the youth. The meaning of such poetry was beyond her. Lawrence could be gentle and sweet, then his savage moods plunged her into misery and she feared him like a stranger. He was helping her to improve her French and during the week she filled a school exercise book with personal thoughts, a kind of intimate journal, writing it in French and passing it to him for correction. In spite of frequent misgivings, when she felt 'trampled' on, it was a measure of her trust in him. Horace and Virgil he also read in the original, surpassing her. At the other end of the scale, he brought her *Little Women* to read, without any condescension. It had his full approval, and so did the romances and adventure novels they devoured together, the latest Haggards, *The Prisoner of Zenda*, going on from there to *Lorna Doone*, the books of Cooper and Stevenson. Dickens was a favourite they had in common, but with others their tastes diverged. Jessie didn't like *Hiawatha* or *Evangeline* when he read them aloud to her, and *Launcelot and Elaine* she thought 'revolting'.

David Chambers remembered those years at The Haggs as including 'the liveliest discussions about books I have ever known. Lawrence invested books with the attributes of something alive; we lived in their world rather than our own.'[6] They peered out of the kitchen window and imagined Carver Doone riding up through their woods instead of in Devon, and from then onwards it was Bagworthy Forest to them.

Jessie, in her list of reading, included many of the standard English novelists, but left out the rumbustious ones, Defoe, Fielding, Smollett and Goldsmith. Lawrence may have ruled these out as too coarse for her eyes at that age, just as he expressly told her not to read *Wuthering Heights*. At one point in their relationship he told the protesting girl that she was like Emily Brontë: 'You *are* like her, you are intense and introspective like she was.'[7] This was at one of their crisis points, when he was continually finding fault with her, so she took it for criticism and objected bitterly. If she was like anyone, good or bad, it was only herself.

As the new books by writers of the day came out, the pair included them in their programme. George Moore, Wells, Bennett and Galsworthy alternated with the Russians, Flaubert, Cervantes. And it was not after all essential to transfer the Doones to the Midlands, for in George Eliot they had a novelist who located some of her stories in bordering Derbyshire. Lawrence was particularly fond of *The Mill on the Floss*.

His serious reading of philosophy did not begin until he was at university, though by then he was familiar with Carlyle and with Ruskin, like the later Lawrence an apostle of purity who hankered after a colony, a nucleus of friends who would initiate a completely new way of life. Even as a boy, dreaming of what he might do, Bert confided to his mother that if they could live in a big house one day, with all the people they liked in it, how fine that would be. It was a dream he only relinquished on his death-bed.

He was too poor as a student to devote all his free time to books. One of his ways of supplementing his meagre grant was by making out bills for Charles Barker, the pork butcher, at his shop in Nottingham Road. He only did this on Friday nights, but he hated it, and Jessie hated to see him there. When she did, it pained her so much that she turned her head away.

The spate of reading continued, and everything was related to it, evaluated, discussed. 'I have never known any young man', wrote Ford Madox Ford, 'who was so well read in all the dullnesses that spread between Milton and George Eliot. In himself alone he was the justification of the Education Act . . . he moved amongst the high things of culture with a tranquil assurance that no one trained like myself in the famous middle-class schools of the country ever either exhibited or desired.'[8]

It was a heady time. Ideas from dozens of sources whirled through his head, as he pored over books with this dark, intense girl who approached it all so very religiously. Passionate though he was, the quivering emotionalism of Jessie angered him for some reason and he wanted to attack her for being so soulful. He liked to think of himself as a bright blade of intellect to her groping feelings. She made everything a matter of earnestness, sincerity. How could you be *sincere* about algebra?

In literature they came closer. There were thrilling correspondences, intoxicating moments. It was a kind of unacknowledged love. But he was losing himself, he had to get back to earth again: he was not his mother's son for nothing. A man who helped to locate him anew in his own region and its realities at this time was William Hopkin. Hopkin and his wife, Sally, were an enlightened middle-aged couple who lived near St. Mary's Church in Devonshire Drive, off the Nottingham Road at the western end of Eastwood. Sally Hopkin befriended him first, as had Jessie's mother: he had an attraction for older women, who felt subtly appreciated by him.

William Hopkin was a shopkeeper who had once been a clerk at the pit, and after that a cobbler. Now he sold the boots and shoes he had previously mended. Mrs Hopkin was plump, with glossy brown hair, and her husband was a jaunty, good-looking little man, with a small Shakespearean beard and an air of idealistic goodness, which a touch of devilry about the eyes contradicted. He had made himself unpopular in his youth by his socialist politics, but had gradually earned the respect of the community by his selfless efforts and his obvious loyalty. He became a councillor, a local magistrate and eventually an alderman. But it was as an amateur antiquarian and a rambler that he was of most interest to the young Lawrence. He knew all there was to know about Eastwood's past: his memory was rich with anecdotes and odd characters. He knew about subsidences in the area, about the martyrdom of a man named Robert Lawrence who had been a prior of the little Carthusian priory at Beauvale and resisted Henry VIII. He had funny stories to tell of a local eccentric, Rodolphe von Hube, Vicar of Greasley, author of an antiquarian book, who claimed to be a Polish aristocrat. This foreigner had curious rules about burials, refusing to conduct a burial service after four in the afternoon. When a coffin arrived one day, a few minutes after the deadline because of some delay on the roads, the vicar was adamant. The bearers leaned on the corpse against his front door and said loudly, 'So we'll leave the old booger here till morning', and the vicar popped out hastily to call them back.

Another of his yarns concerning the vicar must have delighted Lawrence, who was becoming impatient with religion as he delved into such writers as Darwin, T. H. Huxley and Haeckel. Apparently the minister had been on his way back to Greasley from an evening with the Barbers at Lamb Close House. He had been drinking, and it was foggy. Suddenly he found himself wading in Moorgreen Reservoir. 'Lost, lost!' he shouted. Two miners on the road nearby heard him call for help and one said, 'Oh 'e's not wanted till Sunday.'

When Lawrence came to write *The Rainbow*, he had Tom Brangwen marry 'a Polish lady', thus glamorising his own meeting with Frieda and at the same time connecting her to his mother by calling the Polish widow 'Lydia'. Rodolphe von Hube was introduced into the novel as the widow's friend, one 'Rudolph, Baron Skrebensky, Vicar of Briswell'. Von Hube's work of local history became *The History of the Parish of Briswell*, 'a curious book, incoherent, full of interesting exhumations.' The little Baron was 'now quite white-haired, very brittle. He was wizened and wrinkled, yet fiery, unsubdued.'[9]

Jessie was much like her mother, whose sensitivity as a girl had been an agony to her. As Lawrence came to know Jessie better he realised this, and in spite of himself he resented it. She was too much like himself. Instead of freeing him, she threw him back on himself. All the same, because they were so alike, he knew instantly what she was thinking and feeling. It was impossible not to draw close to her. With a foreboding of the pain to come, he kept wanting to pull back, while she was full of fear. But there were almost perfect times, looks and silences that were like consummations, and the communion of books and flowers went on.

His mother became steadily more disagreeable, criticising him for coming in late at night. She would make little self-pitying remarks to torment him. It wasn't that he was seeing too much of Jessie, she protested, but taking the girl home at night and walking all the way back was too much, it was bad for his health, and anyway she was tired herself and he kept her up. When he challenged her directly, she said, 'I don't hold with children keeping company, and never did.' What about Ada and her boy-friend? he wanted to know. That was different – she wasn't a serious type like him. She might have added that Ada was a daughter, not a son.

He had to promise to come home earlier in future. He explained to Jessie, and she frowned and said nothing. The boy bit his lip: he was caught between two fires. He startled the girl at times with his angry, half-violent movements, as if he were struggling with something inside himself.

They were both slow developers, terrifyingly puritanical and flinching. As a youth, Lawrence suffered more than she did from this. At least she had the excuse of her girlhood, she could shelter within that. Even her brothers and her father recognised it and out of consideration for her went outside when they had anything 'unseemly' to discuss. All mention of mating and birth of animals was kept from her ears, otherwise she would be 'chastened almost to disgust'. It was the normal process of discrimination between the sexes which went on in 'refined' families everywhere, but nobody seemed to find it preposterous that it should happen on a farm. Lawrence was naturally sensitive to her feelings and accepted them unquestioningly: after all, he came from a similar household. In his case, the gross elements of life were all concentrated in his father.

One Easter Monday he organised a walk to Wingfield Manor in the Derbyshire hills near Matlock. Jessie would have liked to have gone alone with him, but it was out of the question. She hated to see the change in him when he was with others, chattering brightly but somehow superficial and without 'soul'. She felt hurt and abandoned, hardly alive. Already she had come to depend on him for her insights, to look on him as hers only. What right had these gay, inconsequential friends to him, how well did they know him really?

But he expanded among them, escaping her worshipful,

brooding intensity. Another part of his nature sprang to life; and anyway, he would come back to her, need her again. He responded spontaneously to company.

It was already warm in the Easter sun when they set out, a merry young group: Ada and Jessie, one other girl, and three youths of his own age. They took a train to Alfreton that was crowded with Bank Holiday trippers. There was an old church there and they should see it, Lawrence announced, leading the way along the main street and sniffing the atmosphere of this colliery village, a place curiously different from Eastwood, the miners in their best suits walking their dogs. When they reached the church entrance they were nervous and thought they might not be allowed in, with their packets of veal sandwiches and their hot cross buns. Lawrence hung back, afraid once more of being rebuffed.

Inside, it was a feast of blossom; daffodils, narcissi, lilies, primroses, they overflowed on the font, in the stone alcoves. The young visitors went tiptoeing about reverently in the waves of scent, the subtle light filtering through the stained glass. In charge again, Lawrence drew attention to the architecture. Before the party came out he made them sing a hymn, and it had to be done without a giggle.

Jessie was usually subdued on these outings, unless she found herself alone with him. Other boys would be embarrassed when they talked to her, without knowing why. She was only at ease with Lawrence.

The group pushed on, and it was past noon when they caught their first glimpse of the ruins, perched high on the long green slope. It was a tranced place, held in a pocket of past time, with nothing to disturb the atmosphere of the old walls. Gilly-flowers were growing in the crevices of the tower, the glossy ivy hardly stirring. There was an outer courtyard, and an entrance fee had to be paid before the crypt could be explored and before they could pace about excitedly on the paved floor of the inner court, enter the remains of rooms and finally climb to the top of one of the crumbling towers.

Years later, Jessie passed over to Lawrence her own notes on this visit for him to incorporate in the first draft of *Sons and Lovers*, and eventually he handed the manuscript over to her for her criticisms. In his narrative there occurs one incident, a true one, which called for tact and chivalry at the time it happened. As the lovers climbed the stone stairs in a spiral within the tower, a sudden violent gust of wind filled Miriam's skirts and sent them flying upwards, and Paul caught hold of her dress by the hem and held it down. He ended the passage with the phrase, 'chatting naturally all the time'. Jessie deleted this in the manuscript, adding the stern comment: 'There was no need to chat. It was an act of the purest intimacy. Do not degrade it.' The young author duly did as he was told, and the final version concludes the incident with: 'He did it perfectly simply, as he would have picked up her glove. She remembered this always.'[10]

The party went on to visit the village of Crich and climb to Crich Stand, a landmark for miles around. It was so high a hill, sliced in half by quarrying, with a tower on top, that the Lawrences could see it from their garden at Eastwood. At the peak it was like standing on the edge of a cliff, a sheer drop of raw limestone, the wind always blowing, with magnificent views of grey Derbyshire villages and the hills around, the Derwent Valley and the dreary plains of the Midlands spreading away to the south.

At Whatstandswell they were suddenly attacked by pangs of hunger. All their food was gone, and the money they had left they needed for the return fare when they reached the station at Ambergate. Ada remembered later that they pooled their resources and it came to sevenpence. Bert, for once finding the courage to approach strangers, marched up to a cottage and returned with a pile of bread-and-butter for them all.

But it was on another Easter outing, a few days before this, that something apparently trivial happened that was yet crucial enough to make Jessie see Lawrence in an entirely new light, and for Lawrence himself to write in *Sons and Lovers* that now for the first time 'she knew she must love him.' This excursion on the Good Friday to the mushroom-shaped Hemlock Stone at Bramcote was in one sense a disappointment; but the journey was worth it. Waiting for the train to Ilkeston, the small group was bright with laughter and expectation. They gazed in wonder at the miners on holiday, knots of men outside the pubs with hands in their pockets. It was a new, carefree world. They went from there to Trowell, and when they reached the field with its outcrop of ancient sandstone, almost within sight of the pits and foundries, they joined a large crowd of people from Nottingham drifting about.

On the way home, Jessie and Lawrence became separated. He had reverted to his expansive, jolly self, which alienated her as it always did. Leaving him to the others, she lagged further and further behind, luxuriating in her sad mood. Turning a corner she saw Lawrence alone in the middle of the road, stooped over an umbrella. Something about his figure, a concentration that had a kind of despair in it, touched her inexplicably. She knew then that she cared deeply about him.

'What is the matter?' I asked.

'It was Ern's umbrella, and mother will be wild if I take it home broken,' he replied.[11]

Another spring came and went; another hay harvest. The spring now made her nervous. Lawrence fell into ugly attitudes, mocking himself and others, lashing at the inept chapel services as he veered towards agnosticism, and his sarcasms cut into her cruelly: she wondered when it would be her turn. She went with him regularly now on Fridays to the literary society in Eastwood, and on Sunday evenings he walked her back home after chapel. They had dropped into a routine. Often he turned up at the farm on his bicycle, wheeling it into the yard. She had come to hope for the signs which meant all was well with him. If he was happy, he rang his bicycle bell and she looked out to see him pushing the gleaming machine towards the house, laughing as he came.

The farm still meant a great deal to him, even if the harmony was now impaired. It was still, he wrote in *Sons and Lovers*, 'the dearest place on earth to him. His home was not so lovable. It was his mother. But then he would have been just as happy with his mother anywhere. Whereas Willey Farm he loved passionately. He loved the poky little kitchen, where men's boots tramped, and the dog slept with one eye open for fear of being trodden on; where the lamp hung over the table at night, and everything was so silent. He loved Miriam's long, low parlour, with its atmosphere of romance, its flowers, its books, its high rosewood piano. He loved the gardens and the buildings that stood with their scarlet roofs on the naked edges of the fields, crept towards the wood as if for cosiness, the wild country scooping down a valley and up the uncultured hills on the other side. Only to be there was an exhilaration and a joy to him. He loved Mrs Leivers, with her unworldliness and her quaint cynicism; he loved Mr Leivers, so warm and young and lovable; he loved Edgar, who lit up when he came, and the boys and the children and Bill – even the sow Circe and the Indian game-cock called Tippoo.'[12]

For many reasons he was unable to stay away. The place was necessary to him. He and Jessie fled into books, flowers, nature, as they fled hand in hand from the terrors of unacknowledged sexuality, and for this headlong flight Lawrence half blamed the girl. He was now totally confused by the internecine battle with his mother, and the conflict within himself. His mother's dry, pungent comments, her rational attitude to life, were a wholesome thing, he decided at one point, compared with the chaste mysticism of Jessie and her mother. From being relieved to

escape the tensions of his family, he swung back to an appreciation of its normality, and to regard the 'unworldliness' of the
mother and daughter as abnormal. All the same, he could do no
more than fret against its negations; there was no question of him
ever challenging it. His spasms of cruelty and his wild outbursts
were only means of letting off steam. He lacked the strength to be
outright and confront the girl – and in any case he was too
divided. His cruelty only went so far. It was only later, when he
had cut himself clear, that he could look back and understand to
some extent what had been happening. And in order to get clear at
all, he had to wait for a woman to appear who was as strong as his
mother. The decisions he made with regard to Jessie were in reality
no decisions at all. When he wrote of it in *Sons and Lovers*, Jessie saw
his version of the affair as simply 'a slander – a fearful treachery.'

Meanwhile, he was in turn aloof, mocking, cold, and wistful. He
upbraided the girl for 'fondling' the flowers with a spirituality
that was an affront to him, accusing her of pulling the heart out of
them, just as his mother had said Jessie was pulling the heart out
of him. He resented her bitterly for restraining him, not letting
him be 'jolly' with people, and in the next breath said she should
not drool over the flowers so, it was virtually indecent. He
brought her to tears by his onslaughts, then hated himself bitterly
for his behaviour, hated her too for causing it, got on his bicycle
and went careering home dangerously in the dark, half hoping in
his misery that he would crash and break his neck.

In his more reflective moods he conducted a careful probing of
the wound, and she endured it with the submissive, Christian-like
turning of the other cheek that was in itself a form of accusation.
He would have preferred her to retaliate, rather than suffer in
silence so infuriatingly. If she did protest, it was usually mild and
murmuring.

He asked her:

'You're not really popular, are you?'
I laughed and said that probably I was not, but anyhow, what
did it matter? I was rather hurt when he went on:
'Very few people *like* you, do they?'
'I don't know *very* many people,' I replied.
'That doesn't matter,' he returned. 'The point is you don't
get on very well with people.' He seemed to be following a
preconceived train of thought.
'I get on well enough,' I replied, in vexation. 'Why should I
wish to be popular? People like me as well as I want them to.'
'That's just it,' he declared. 'At the bottom you don't really

care whether people like you or not.'

'Why should I care? I can't help it, either way.'

'No, but you see,' he said with sudden gentleness, 'there must be some fault in you if *nobody* likes you. The others can't *all* be wrong.'[13]

He went on to inform her, without a flicker of humour, that she lacked a sense of humour. This time she did retaliate: 'What comes next when you've finished taking me to pieces? Will you be able to put me together again?' And it must have given her some satisfaction to note that 'he looked startled.'

His cross-examinations were crude and relentless, but pathetically in earnest. And he could disarm her completely by ending wistfully: 'You'd be easier to understand, you know, if you would be a bit naughty sometimes.'[14]

He was nineteen and he had still not begun to write. For the past four years he had been absorbed by painting. Apart from teaching, that was his only real mode of expression. Now with Jessie a whole new experience was in spate within him, as they made one new discovery after another. For the moment, the very act of adventuring was sufficient. They went about glowing with inner life, no longer trivial persons buried alive in the dreary Midlands. Together 'they read Balzac, and did compositions, and felt highly cultured.' At such times their growing difficulties were forgotten and they loved to be in each other's company.

More than once, in *Sons and Lovers*, Lawrence indicates that the fault could have been his. One thing was certain: his mother could never be accused. Harry T. Moore has characterised Lawrence's work as being essentially kinetic, and it is by movements even more than through conversation that Paul and Miriam are most tellingly contrasted. The girl's clenched, over-intense nature causes her to be physically inhibited: 'Her body was not flexible and living. She walked with a swing, rather heavily, her head bowed forward, pondering. She was not clumsy, and yet none of her movements seemed quite *the* movement. Often, when wiping the dishes, she would stand in bewilderment and chagrin because she had pulled in two halves a cup or a tumbler. It was as if, in her fear and self-distrust, she put too much strength into the effort. There was no looseness or abandon about her.'[15] Here is the substance of much of the boy's complaint against her, as it began to dawn on him that his own manhood would have to be fought for. He needed an ally, and he felt he was being betrayed. Instead of helping him to achieve some abandon of his own, she held him back, chained him down with her own inadequacies. Often he pitied her and wanted to comfort her, but there was nothing he could do. Yet she had a hold on his soul. He complained bitterly and at times attacked her, and she looked at him reproachfully, not understanding.

Even when the couple in *Sons and Lovers* are seemingly harmonious, there is always some flaw. Miriam watches Paul one night out in the barn mending a puncture, turning the bike upside down and asking her for a bowl of water. Coming back with it, she is absorbed in looking at him: his movements are quick and sure, beautiful to watch. 'She loved to see his hands doing things. He was slim and vigorous, with a kind of easiness even in his most hasty movements. And busy at his work he seemed to forget her. She loved him absorbedly. She wanted to run her hands down his sides.'[16]

She does so, her innocent caress setting fire to him. 'He laughed, hating her voice', for it echoes the same non-sexual caress of the touch of her hands. She seems unaware of the confusion and torment she is causing.

There is burning truth in this picture of the young Lawrence in love for the first time. There is also special pleading, and the bending of facts by a writer who is already immensely accomplished, who is prepared to tell 'lies' in order to reveal another kind of truth. Life was being changed into art. Jessie was afraid of sex, as he was, and it must have been difficult to resist the temptation, when Lawrence came to a portrait of himself, to confuse his own fears with hers, and so disguise them. It would also have been shaming if he had owned up to other misgivings he was beginning to feel about Eastwood, as their relationship dragged on for year after year and refused to resolve itself. He had decided quite definitely that he was a young man who was going somewhere, 'he was going to alter the face of the earth in some way that mattered.' He must have asked himself more than once what his chances were if he settled for love and marriage and a little home somewhere with Jessie.

Yet, from the first, he thought of writing as a collaboration with her: After all, he came from a background where nothing was done in isolation. No one else he knew was remotely interested in writing. It was 1905 and they were walking through the fields when he asked her if she had ever thought of trying to write. She admitted she had, and asked him: 'Have you?'

'"Yes, I have," he said, "Well, let's make a start. I'm sure we could do something if we tried. Lots of the things we say, the things you say, would go ever so well in a book."'[17]

Yet in spite of Jessie's enthusiasm months passed before a start was made. Then one night Lawrence announced, 'It will be poetry.' She fully agreed, not understanding at first that he was still hanging back and in need of reassurance. There were difficulties she hadn't anticipated. He lived in a small world, known to everybody: what would people think of him, a miner's son, wanting to write poetry? Jessie told him firmly that his father's job had nothing to do with it, but he was unconvinced. He shook his head mournfully over her naïveté, her ignorance of class divisions. This was another reason for getting clear of the region: it was too inhibiting for a young man about to open his wings and dazzle them all. Sooner or later he would have to get away. And there was another factor: thanks to his mother, he was already a considerable snob, and when he described the encounter with the tramp in the hay-fields he could hardly contain his disgust. But that was in an early story, and by the time he came to write *Sons and Lovers* he could at least make a clean breast of his ambivalent feelings for his 'people':

'You know,' he said to his mother, 'I don't want to belong to the well-to-do middle class. I like my common people best. I belong to the common people.'

'But if anyone else said so, my son, wouldn't you be in a tear. *You* know you consider yourself equal to any gentleman.'

'In myself,' he answered, 'not in my class or my education or my manners. But in myself I am.'

'Very well, then. Then why talk about the common people?'

'Because – the differences between people isn't in their class, but in themselves. Only from the middle classes one gets ideas, and from the common people – life itself, warmth. You feel their hates and loves.'

'It's all very well, my boy. But then, why don't you go and talk to your father's pals?'[18]

His fear of ridicule, his extreme timidity, were one thing, his aspirations quite another. There was no point in not aiming high, and he informed Jessie on another occasion that their age would never breed a Shakespeare because 'things are split up now.' He would have to be a different kind of poet, perhaps a poet of disintegration. But he realised, even then, that he would need a woman behind him. 'Every great man – every man who achieves anything, I mean – is founded in some woman,' he told her. 'Why shouldn't *you* be the woman I am founded in?'[19]

So he began. He wrote rhyming verse in celebration of flowers, of nature, he dredged up painful memories of childhood, he addressed poems to Jessie, and to his own 'helplessly bound' sexuality. His first efforts were tentative and proper: they were 'To Guelder-Roses' and 'To Campions', composed appropriately and rather self-consciously on a Sunday afternoon in spring, and promptly handed over to Jessie for her approval. He wrote, quite early on, a long rich hymn to 'The Wild Common' sparking with gorse bushes and exploding with rabbits, verses aflame with youth, crackling in every line with energy and impatience:

> But how splendid it is to be substance, here!
> My shadow is neither here nor there; but I, I am
>   royally here!
> I am here! I am here! screams the peewit; the may-
>   blobs burst out in a laugh as they hear!
> Here! flick the rabbits. Here! pants the gorse. Here!
>   say the insects far and near.

Soon his words began to reveal more than he wanted, and he reverted to a 'half-furtive' activity which absorbed him, then made him want to 'run away from the act and the production as if it were a secret sin'. He never 'liked' these poems as he liked the lady-like ones, but he handed them over to Jessie just the same, and wrote nothing down permanently until he went to university the following year. The aching poem to his own baulked sex, 'Virgin Youth', was probably written soon after he had left Eastwood. In it he speaks to his lonely erect phallus as tenderly and admiringly as to a woman:

> How beautiful he is! without sound,
> Without eyes, without hands;
> Yet, flame of the living ground
> He stands, the column of fire by night.
> And he knows from the depths; he quite
> Alone understands.
>
> Quite alone, he alone
> Understands and knows.
> Lustrously sure, unknown
> Out of nowhere he rose.
>
> I tremble in his shadow, as he burns
> For the dark goal.
> He stands like a lighthouse, night churns
> Round his base, his dark night rolls
> Into darkness, and darkly returns.
>
> Is he calling, the lone one? Is his deep
> Silence full of summons?
> Is he moving invisibly? Does his steep
> Curve sweep towards a woman's?

By Whitsun, 1906, he was ready to attempt a story. All you needed to do to write a novel, he told Jessie with blithe self-confidence, was 'take two couples and develop their relationship. Most of George Eliot's are on that plan. Anyhow, I don't want a plot, I should be bored with it. I shall try two couples for a start.' He wanted her to keep him company with a book of her own: they could help each other.

'Laetitia', the first version of *The White Peacock*, started to grow, and soon Lawrence was pressing Jessie into service. His George was about to marry Lettie in Nottingham, and he wanted details of the register office there. As Jessie was going into town, would she take a tram out to Basford and find out exactly what it looked like? She returned with the information: the building was depressing. He went off smiling with her impressions, and when he showed her his next batch of manuscript it contained the wedding at the building she had visited for him.

Jessie was critical of this first effort; she thought it weak and unconvincing, in fact derived. Lawrence listened to her intently and was only too willing to agree. Long before it was finished he detested it. Doggedly he began all over again. The second version was more to Jessie's liking, except for the emergence of Annable, the gamekeeper. She reproached Lawrence for the brutalising effect this new character had on the story, as well as pointing out his irrelevance, but the young author held his ground. 'He *has* to be there,' he told her. 'Don't you see why? He makes a sort of balance. Otherwise it's too much one thing, too much me.'

She did not see at all. Lawrence was at this time kicking out at religion and embracing materialism for want of anything better, and Jessie thought Annable's presence somehow symbolised this dilemma. She was at a loss to understand Lawrence's interest in gamekeepers, and remembered one unpleasant encounter when a party of them, including Ada, wandered into the private part of Annesley Woods. The group were gathering primroses and having a sing-song when a red-headed gamekeeper surprised them. He took down names and ordered them off the estate. Lawrence, she recalled, was white in the face and silent.

Not long before this, on Easter Sunday and Monday, their slowly burgeoning friendship had nearly come to an abrupt end. The shock to Jessie was profound enough for her to write, long after the event: 'The world was spinning round me. I was conscious of a fierce pain, of the body as well as of the spirit. I tried not to let him see my tears. As clearly as if in actuality I saw the golden apple of life that had been lying at my fingertips recede irretrievably.'[20] Lawrence called it in a letter (afterwards destroyed by Jessie's husband) 'the slaughter of the foetus in the womb.'

There had been no warning for the girl. On Easter Sunday she walked down to the chapel service as usual, and then Lawrence took her back home. Jessie had learned by now to submit to a succession of tiny snubs from Lawrence's mother and from his married sister, Emily, if she happened to be there. She was present on this occasion. As soon as she saw Jessie, she asked her brother, possessively, when he was going to visit her. He made some non-committal reply, and left the house with Jessie. He took her to the gate where the short cut to The Haggs began, and told her, 'I shall come up tomorrow – early.' Her happiness was complete. Her sister would be away with her boy-friend and her brothers were off on a cycling trip, so she would be left at home with the small children.

He wasn't early, he was late. Something was wrong, she could tell at a glance. His lips were shut tight, his stance was aloof, his walk had something loutish about it. His cruelty was evident before he opened his mouth, and she flinched in anticipation.

They went in to tea with the family. He had been to chapel and was in a mood to mock the service. Mrs Chambers was a little shocked, but she laughed in spite of herself, and so did her husband, fuddled from his afternoon sleep. Jessie's brothers laughed loudly, especially Alan, who has now a rationalist.

Lawrence thought he and Jessie should do some French, and they took *Tartarin de Tarascon* and went out with it, to sit against the stack. The bull-terrier, Trip, came up in a rush, open-mouthed, prancing and licking and wanting to play, 'grinning all over'. He always made a tremendous fuss of Lawrence, and Jessie was shocked when he shoved the dog off.

He had no heart for French either. He had come with a mission. His eyes were so tormented, she could hardly bear to look at them. He began to speak painfully, telling her that he thought they might be getting too serious, that their friendship was in danger of overbalancing. Did she think so? He wanted desperately to have her admit he was right, to agree. But she only crouched there, not grasping anything properly. Why did he beat about the bush, why didn't he have the courage to say what he meant?

She said, stunned, that she had no idea what he was talking about. She was half angry, and she felt terribly sorry for him. He was pitiable, unable to come out with it. Then she knew that something must have happened.

At first he denied it, and blamed the season; they were often like this at Easter-time. It was a last attempt at trying to make her share the responsibility for it. Finally he came dragging out with it, as if loathing the sound of his own voice.

'Well, they were talking last night, mother and Emily. Emily asked mother if we were courting. They said we either ought to be engaged or else not go about together. It's the penalty of being nineteen and twenty instead of fifteen and sixteen,' he concluded bitterly.

'Ah – I always thought your mother didn't like me.'

'It isn't that, you mustn't think that; mother has *nothing* against you,' he urged. 'It's for your sake she spoke. She says it isn't fair to you . . . I may be keeping you from getting to like someone else. She says I ought to know how I feel,' he went on painfully. 'I've looked into my heart and I cannot find that I love you as a husband should love his wife. Perhaps I shall, in time. If ever I do, I'll tell you. What about you? If you think you love me, tell me, and we'll be engaged. What do you think?'[21]

Jessie stared at him aghast as he delivered this 'proposal': now it was her turn to writhe in humiliation. Where was his sensitivity, that she had loved so passionately? Didn't he see that to put their friendship in such terms was the last word in brutality?

Senselessly, in 'a lifeless voice', he struggled on, trying to make his feelings clearer to her and to himself, trying above all to justify himself. How could he explain to this virginal, shuddering girl that what she set aside by her very nature was absolutely vital to him? To her, sex was not only unmentionable, it was totally without importance. To him, it was the supreme test on his manhood, a manhood he would have the greatest difficulty in achieving. He stammered on about this, saying that physically he was unable to love her, even accepting the blame for it as 'a flaw in my make-up'. Listening drearily to him, she could only think how stupid he was. It was obvious to her that they belonged together. What else mattered? Men were such children.

In her misery she was unable to speak for some time. They sat in silence, in their smashed world. With a little shock she recovered enought to realise that he was talking again. He thought they should decide there and then what they ought to do.

She still had her pride. As firmly as she could, she said that an engagement was out of the question on those terms. It would be better if they stopped seeing one another from now on.

This revived him. He thought it would be foolish for them to throw away all they had. Then he infuriated her by invoking his mother's words. ' "Mother said we needn't give everything up, only we must know what footing we're on, that's all. Life isn't so rich in friendship that we can afford to throw it away. And this is the only friendship that's ripened," he ended pathetically.'

Then he came out with a preposterous plan of action, apparently worked out beforehand. ' "There's the question of writing, we want to talk about that. And there's the French, we can go on reading together, surely? Only we'll read in the house, or where they can see us. And chapel, that's important. You must keep on coming, and I'll ask Alan not to cycle, and then he can walk home with us. And when we go down the fields we'll take the youngsters with us. We needn't let people think we're on a different footing from what we are, that's all. Only we *must* go on talking to one another." '22

He had finished. The irreparable damage had been done. They fell into silence again, until he asked her miserably if she would tell her mother about the new arrangement. On the verge of tears, she said that if she did they might tell him not to come round any more. This hurt him visibly.

When they finally went indoors he looked so white and shaken that Mrs Chambers remarked on it. Was he feeling ill? He shook his head and tried to laugh. It was twilight and the air was chilly. That was it, her mother decided, fussing around him – they had been sitting out there too long and got cold. She turned on her daughter, saying she was thoughtless. Jessie bowed her head: it was too ironic.

He sat on the sofa like an invalid, saying nothing. On the table was the youngsters' paintbox. Lawrence picked it up and saw that refills were needed. He wrote on a sheet of paper: 'The children's painting-box needs replenishing. Who will subscribe? I open the list. D.H.L. 1s.'

Before nine, he got up to go. When Jessie's mother asked him why he was so early, he stammered some excuse and went out to get his bike. In the normal way, Jessie would have gone out with him to the barn to say goodbye. She sat where she was, pretending to nurse the children. 'At the window Lawrence turned and gave me an unforgettable look.'

A few days later a letter came from him, full of concern for her. 'A man can do so many things,' he wrote. 'He reads, he paints, he can get across his bicycle and go for a ride, but a woman sits at home and thinks.'23

The next time he came up to read French with her, they stayed near the house. They simply had to be more in the public eye, he told her. True to his word, he rounded up the two small children to come with them when they went off for a walk. There they were, two disconsolate lovers being chaperoned by a couple of kids and an excited puppy. Jessie looked at him, secretly scornful and hurt. What kind of poet was this?

That Sunday, on her way home from chapel alone, she heard Lawrence calling and rushing after her. He had a friend with him. Why was she hurrying off, instead of coming back with him as usual? He had a new painting of roses he wanted her to see. Reluctantly she let herself be persuaded. But she was wary now of any further hurt. There was no trust between them. At last she had got the measure of him and his instability.

Lawrence's own version of the split, in *Sons and Lovers*, is substantially the same as Jessie's, except that he has dramatised and extended it. In the novel it is enacted in two stages, with a week between, and a few of the humiliating consequence of the 'arrangement' are left out. But in the main it tallies remarkably with hers, and exposes him with complete honesty in the worst possible light.

After this crisis he swung over to Alan Chambers for a while, going for cycle rides with him, helping him in the loft with bits of carpentry, and Jessie waited moodily for him to come drifting back to her. He wrote to her constantly, and in the end he had to seek her out again. He saw them now as active collaborators in writing. There were so many things he wanted to ask her about. Novel-writing meant the creation of characters and their conversation, and the characters had to develop and their talk had to be natural. He would thrust his latest work at her and demand her opinion. Did people really say the sort of things he had put in their mouths? Writing dialogue he found devilishly easy – was that a danger, something to be watched? He realised he tended to be prolix in his prose. Should there be more condensing, as in poetry? They sat with their heads together and she pondered these thrilling problems and felt at one with him again, harmonious: the hateful, jangling discord of Easter sank into the past. He told her in a rush of gratitude that whatever writing he did, it was always for her.

'Every bit I do is for you,' he said. 'Whenever I've done a fresh bit I think to myself: "What will she say to this?"' And of his poetry he said, 'All my poetry belongs to you.'[24]

It was the same with his ideas, his beliefs, his questioning of religion, which had brought him to an agnosticism so equivocal that Jessie was not too much hurt. She gladly accepted that she 'was the threshing-floor on which he threshed out all his beliefs.

While he trampled his ideas upon her soul, the truth came out for him. She alone was his threshing-floor. She alone helped him towards realization. Almost impassive, she submitted to his argument and expounding. And somehow, because of her, he gradually realized where he was wrong. And what he realized, she realized. She felt he could not do without her.'[25]

It was all splendid and loving and devoted, it was love in the pure sense, with none of 'the inexplicable things of sex' to drag it down to the mundane level of the street, the farmyard. For a time she was intensely happy again.

One evening, Ada Lawrence came up to The Haggs, bursting with some juicy gossip that was circulating around Eastwood. A student-teacher friend of Bert's had got a girl 'in trouble'. At Lynn Croft Road the Lawrences had been buzzing with this 'disgrace', and the mother had seized the opportunity to drive home the moral of the unfortunate girl's predicament. Now her 'five minutes' self-forgetfulness' would have to be paid for, and for the rest of her life. Lawrence came up the next evening to discuss it all with Jessie. With hypocritical solemnity he endorsed his mother's sermon by implying that there, but for the grace of God, went both of them. It was a great triumph for his mother and her advice about them getting engaged, or staying well clear of each other. The Victorian horror of 'that' had never been closer.

Another sobering thought for Lawrence in years to come must have been 'George's final nabbing', as he described it six years later in a letter to his literary mentor, Edward Garnett. Writing from Croydon, he reported two shocks through the post that morning. One was that

> my very old friend, the Don Juanish fellow I told you of – went and got married three months back, without telling a soul, and now boasts a son: 'Jimmy, a very fine lad.' . . . The girl is living at home, with 'Jimmy' in Stourbridge. The managers asked George to resign his post, because of the blot on the scutcheon . . . In the end, he was removed to a little headship on the Stafford-Derby border – has been there six weeks – alone – doing fearfully hard work . . . This has upset me – one never knows what'll happen. You know George has already got one illegitimate child. It's a lovely story, the end of it: the beginning was damnable. She was only nineteen, and he only twenty. Her father, great Christian, turned her out. George wouldn't acknowledge the kid, but had to pay, whether or not. That's five years back. Last October, I am told, the girl got married.

Before the wedding – two days or so – she went to George's home with the child and showed it to George's father and mother.

'I've come, Mr — for you to own this child. Who's the father of that?' pushing forward the small girl.

'Eh, bless her, it's just like him, cries old Mrs —, and she kissed the kid with tears.

'Well, Lizzie,' said — to the girl, 'if our George-Henry says that isn't his'n he's a liar. It's the spit and image of him.'

Whereupon Lizzie went away satisfied, got married to a collier, and lives in Cordy Lane. She, with one or two others, will rejoice over George's final nabbing. Isn't it awful?[26]

In the same year as this letter he incorporated George's dreadful downfall in a skit, 'The Married Man', written 'as a sort of interlude' to *Paul Morel*. 'This comedy will amuse you fearfully,' he promised Garnett; 'much of it is word for word true – it will interest you. I think it's good. Frieda makes me send it you straight away. She says I have gilded myself beyond recognition, and put her in rags.'[27]

But in the spring of 1906, Lawrence, not yet twenty-one, was definitely not amused. Indeed, one never knew what might happen. Life was a grim struggle, in more ways than one. And he was in urgent need of money. In a conference with his mother it had been agreed that he would get nowhere in teaching unless he got himself to university. This meant more financial hardship for the mother, but she, 'her mouth always closed with disillusion', decided once again that the sacrifice must be made. He had already proved his worth academically: in the King's Scholarship, which he took at Ilkeston in 1904, he came first in all England and Wales. Sitting for the London Matriculation in Nottingham the following year, this time accompanied by his mother, he did not do nearly so well, but he got through.

To take advantage of his scholarship grant he needed twenty pounds for advance fees. At Lynn Croft Road there was a great scraping and saving of pennies during his last teaching year. He was no longer a pupil-teacher, but had taken a job as an uncertified teacher in the British School at Eastwood.

By the summer the goal was in sight; so much so that they could even afford a fortnight's holiday at the seaside. With Lawrence's and his father's money, together with that of a young friend of the Lawrences, they would rent a cottage at Mablethorpe. Ada was coming, with a friend or two, and Jessie had agreed to join them. She had never been to the coast before in her life. Lawrence as

usual was stimulated to excitement at the thought of a party. He
went about making endless plans, helping his mother compose
letters of inquiry as they searched for the furnished place they
wanted. 'He loved to think of his mother, and the other jolly
people.'[28]

The flatness of the land and the immense skies enchanted
them, and the cottage, isolated in a sea-meadow in solitary splen-
dour, sent Lawrence and Jessie into raptures of romanticism.
Windmills were still used on the farms; the sight of one in action
put them in mind of *The Cloister and the Hearth*. Lawrence's
father had come, a docile man away from home, who rose early
from force of habit and went off to explore the area. Jessie
afterwards had good memories of Lawrence gathering water-
cress with his father from a brook nearby, delighting in their find
and their contribution to the tea-table. When Lawrence came to
describe the holiday in *Sons and Lovers*, he remembered being
alone with Jessie while the others went off to minstrel shows in the
town. The 'Coon' songs were catchy and he wanted to join in the
sing-songs, but as Jessie looked down her nose, he preferred to
lecture his sister on her stupidity in liking the songs. Alone, he
sketched, and talked non-stop to Jessie as he had always done,
pouring out his ideas and latest theories on 'horizontals' and
'perpendiculars', making it alive and personal for her. She was
Gothic, he told her, she soared and yearned ecstatically, while he
went stubbornly leap-frogging forward into the future, which was
Norman. She listened and loved him, caring little about the sense of
what he said. She had him completely to herself at such moments.

The dissonances, too, were recorded in different ways. One
night, walking together among the dunes at the edge of the sea,
they were confronted by the newly-risen moon. 'The country was
black and still. From behind the sandhills came the whisper of the
sea. They walked in silence . . . Suddenly he started. The whole of
his blood seemed to burst into flame, and he could scarcely
breathe. An enormous orange moon was staring at them from the
rim of the sandhills. He stood still, looking at it . . . His blood was
concentrated like a flame in his chest. But he could not get across
to her. There were flashes in his blood. But somehow she ignored
them. She was expecting some religious state in him.'[29]

Instead, she was subjected to a bitter verbal attack, incomprehensible to her. 'I cannot remember now what he said, but his
words were wild, and he appeared to be in great distress of mind,
and possibly also of body . . . He upbraided me bitterly, and when
I protested he blamed himself, and poured himself out in a
torrent of passionate words.'[30]

In her memoir, Jessie tried to seek reasons for his grotesque behaviour in the strained atmosphere between him and his mother before they set out, when Mrs Lawrence showed obvious disapproval of the attention he was giving the girl. But the same thing happened again under the full moon, this time a year later at Robin Hood's Bay. 'He talked and behaved so wildly,' she wrote, 'that it is difficult to recall what he did actually say or do,' except that he rushed off and put a distance between them 'like a strange, wild creature, and kept up a stream of upbraiding.'[31] The third occurrence was at Flamborough, Yorkshire, in 1908, and this was the most violent of all. She was terrified as he went skipping 'from one white boulder to another' by the light of the full moon, so that she 'almost doubted whether he was indeed a human being.' He was possessed, she felt; he 'created an atmosphere not of death, which after all is part of mortality, but of an utter negation of life, as though he had become dehumanised.'[32] To her they were like seizures, quite irrational and frighteningly sinister.

In the novel, Miriam asks her strange, overwrought lover what is wrong.

'"It's the moon," he answered, frowning.'

Then Lawrence attempts to unburden himself to the reader, thrashing at the 'problem' for the hundredth time. 'He did not know himself what was the matter. He was naturally so young, and their intimacy so abstract, he did not know he wanted to crush her on his breast to ease the ache there. He was afraid of her. The fact that he might want her as a man wants a woman had in him been suppressed into a shame.'[33]

It reads like a confession of guilt. But Lawrence was capable by now of endless convolutions, evasions, flutterings back and forth. He hated himself, he hated Jessie for throwing him back on to himself, he was rubbed into unbearable irritation by his mother, he longed to be natural and 'jolly' like the others. But that would have meant being ordinary and normal. He was brilliantly observant and appreciative of the normal, but he could never stay long in that state. His very penetration isolated him. This tormenting duality was noticed very early on by Ford Madox Ford, who wrote: 'I mean that always, at first, for a second or two, he seemed like the reckless robber of hen-roosts with gleaming eyes and a mouth watering for adventure and then, with the suddenness of a switched-off light, he became the investigator into the bases of the normal that he essentially was.'[34]

The time had come for him to enter university, and escape again from Eastwood. And, from the evidence of *The Rainbow*, he arrived there with high expectations. It was September: he had just turned twenty-one.

At first he intended to take the degree course. The Teacher's Training Department had two categories: there were those reading for a degree, and those taking the shorter course which led to a Teacher's Certificate. Ursula, in *The Rainbow*, considered herself 'of the elect', worshipping at the shrine of pure education, whereas the student teachers, preoccupied with a 'mere' professional training, moved on a lower level of existence.

The University College was in a wide sloping street near the centre of Nottingham: an imposing, if rather lugubrious, gothicized stone building, certainly stylish, in the midst of industrial dirt and anonymity, with Victoria Station and its tall clock tower just around the corner. The place could have been absurd, but somehow it wasn't: big, quiet, 'with a rim of grass and lime trees', the hall with its balcony supported by Gothic arches was impressive, and with a little imagination it was possible to imagine monks and cloisters, to feel the lambent glow of education as it must have been in medieval times, when all learning was religious and dedicated to God. The harsh, scurrying streets, the vulgar factories, warehouses, canals and sidings were mysteriously cancelled and spirited away, just as their sounds were excluded by the lofty windows of the lecture rooms. This was surely a sacred and priestly place. There seemed endless time here for the soul to expand, nourished by pure knowledge.

By the end of his first term this noble edifice had come crashing down in his mind: reality had blasted his high hopes. This wasn't a temple, it was a miserable annexe to industry. All the brilliance this gifted lad from Eastwood had brought in was quenched in a matter of weeks by a handful of barren professors, ordinary men 'who ate bacon, and pulled on their boots'. Now his disgust was as extreme as his expectations had been. Later, remembering his first impression, he drew a nimbus of glamour around Ursula's university life in *The Rainbow*, then tore it into shreds after a page or two. 'The professors were not priests initiated into the deep mysteries of life and knowledge. After all, they were only middle-men handling wares they had become so accustomed to that they were oblivious of them. What was Latin? – so much dry goods of knowledge. What was the Latin class altogether but a sort of second-hand curio shop, where one bought curios and learned the market value of curios. . . . And not only Latin, but the whole thing seemed sham, spurious; spurious Gothic arches, spurious peace, spurious Latinity, spurious dignity of France, spurious naïveté of Chaucer. It was a second-hand dealer's shop, and one bought an equipment for an examination. This was only a little side-show to the factories of the town.'[35]

But he didn't walk out: with his mother's shrewdness he decided to get what he could out of it. He knew very well what the alternative was. Swallowing down 'the ash of disillusion', he transferred promptly from the degree course to the more mundane curriculum which would gain him a Teacher's Certificate and at the same time enable him to concentrate on his own writing. He was working on the second version of *The White Peacock*, now called 'Nethermere' with George married to Meg instead of Lettie. He set himself grimly against the disgustingly compromised and debased education and got down grimly to work. As late as 1928 he had his revenge, commemorating the newly-risen university at Beeston with a stinging little poem:

> In Nottingham, that dismal town
> where I went to school and college,
> they've built a new university
> for a new dispensation of knowledge.
>
> Built it most grand and cakeily
> out of the noble loot
> derived from shrewd cash-chemistry
> by good Sir Jesse Boot.[36]

George Neville and the other Pagans had seen enough evidence of Lawrence's talent by now to expect great things of him at university. Neville noticed that his friend's relationship with Jessie was very closely knit during these two years. On Saturday evenings he would call round at Lynn Croft Road to see if Lawrence was at home. If his writing was going well he would be there, grinding away. Otherwise he would stuff his papers into his pocket, snatch his cap and be out of the door and on his way to The Haggs before Neville arrived. His mother, whom he called 'Little Woman' or sometimes 'Little', would tell Neville ominously, 'He's gone up there again, George.' And if Neville went out to the farm after him, there would be Lawrence and his 'princess' with their heads together over Lawrence's writing, which quickly vanished as soon as they saw him.

As well as the writing, the enthusiastic reading went on in collaboration with Jessie. Lawrence now seemed to be trying to break down the girl's unworldliness by enlisting the help of French authors. They read Balzac, Loti and Flaubert in the original, and then one day he presented her with a translation of

Maupassant's *Tales*. He must have felt that this was too brutal a step, for after a day or two he scribbled a note to her: 'What am I doing to you? You used to be so vigorous, so full of interest in all sorts of things. Don't take too much notice of me. You musn't allow yourself to be hurt by Maupassant or me.'[37] Unsatisfactory and galling as the friendship was to him, to give it up was unthinkable. 'I went on imagining beautiful things to say to her, while she looked at me with her wonderful eyes from among the fir boughs in the woods.'[38]

Nor were the English authors neglected. Together they read Rutherford's *Autobiography* and *Clara Hapgood*, and something about this writer was, Lawrence thought, typical of Jessie. Meredith was another favourite, and Borrow's *Lavengro*. Perhaps because he regarded Nottingham now as 'his' town, he took Jessie to the Theatre Royal to see operas and plays. He went alone to see Sarah Bernhardt in *La Dame aux camélias* and explained to Jessie in a letter that he couldn't bear to sit through it to the end. The poor Armand's fate had terrified him: he thought he too might finish up 'enslaved by a woman' like that.

Every now and then he swung back remorsefully to his mother, as if to a faithful lover he was neglecting. She still tugged dreadfully at his heart, and never more than now, as he realised with a pang that she was getting old at last, worn down by her struggle to have life on her terms, to do her utmost for them all. He took her on an excursion to Lincoln, to look at the castle and the great cathedral, but the grieving son of *Sons and Lovers* seems to do little except watch his mother for signs of frailty and then rage wildly against it. With all the force of his youth he urges her to live. He tells her she is his girl, out on an outing; he buys her violets and pins them to her coat, and begs her to 'Strut! Be a fantail pigeon.' The defiance seems about to work, she brightens visibly and laughs, and all along the High Street she is her normal self, interested in everything; the Glory Hole, Stone Bow, the cathedral they have yet to see.

> But she could scarcely climb the cathedral hill. He did not notice. Then suddenly he found her unable to speak, He took her into a little public house, where she rested.
>
> 'It's nothing,' she said. 'My heart is only a bit old; one must expect it.'
>
> He did not answer, but looked at her. Again his heart was crushed in a hot grip, He wanted to cry, he wanted to smash things in fury.[39]

He couldn't bear her sudden timidity, as she hesitated before entering the cathedral. He saw he had surpassed her in pride. He hammered at all the doors of life that seemed closed to them, as he walked beside her. He had the strength, he had the right. Suddenly he burst out at her pathetically, like a spoiled child: 'What are you old for? *Why* can't you walk? Why can't you come with me to places?'[40] His impotence made him nearly ill with rage; the unfairness of life appalled him. All at once he had a dreadful vision of himself without a mother, literally unable to stand up.

By now he was sure enough of his gifts to declare his literary ambitions to his friend, Willie Hopkin. One Sunday evening he startled the older man by announcing firmly, 'Willie, I am going to be an author.' Hopkin told him to go ahead, with a few words of caution about the rejections he must face. Lawrence swept these aside. 'I have genius!' he said, flushing, 'I know I have.'

When Jessie came of age he sent her a long letter in which he made one more attempt to clarify the issue between them. 'The search for some basis for a relationship', wrote Jessie, 'went on like an undercurrent to all our activities.' He had already explained that he was 'two men', and though he couldn't do without her, the 'other side' of him needed something else. She refused to accept this idea of a dual nature, for it undermined everything she believed in. It was true, he insisted, he was 'two men inside one skin'.

Once, with shattering brutality, he told her that what it really amounted to was that she had no sexual attraction at all. Her answer was typical.

'Well, how can I help it?' she said. 'Is it my fault?'

'I don't suppose so. It simply is the fact. You are absolutely lacking in sexual attraction, and that's the truth of the matter.'[41]

But he was far too riddled with guilt to leave it at that. If they were in truth physically incompatible, and yet he still needed her, what did it mean? He sought for a means of justifying it philosophically. He was working round slowly to an idea which had been growing in his mind for some time. If he was indeed two men, then why shouldn't he have two women to satisfy them? 'I don't believe in the idea of one man one woman, do you?' he asked her. 'I mean, there isn't just one woman and one only that a man can marry. There might be half a dozen that would do equally well. What do you think? You're not the complement of me, you don't complement me in any way. Do you think you do?'[42]

The poor girl would rather have not discussed it. If she thought anything, it was that his mother had been giving him doubts about her again. But he kept pounding at her relentlessly, struggling to rationalize it, and the bitter fruits of it all were offered up to her as a twenty-first birthday present. The letter to Miriam in *Sons and Lovers* is painfully fulsome and stilted. According to Jessie, the actual epistle read as follows:

'When I look at you, what I see is not the kissable and embraceable part of you, although it is so fine to look at, with the silken toss of hair curling over your ears. What I see is the deep spirit within. That I love and can go on loving all my life . . . Look, you are a nun, I give what I would give a holy nun. So you must let me marry a woman I can kiss and embrace and make the mother of my children.' And he added a significant postscript: 'The anguish that impinges so cruelly upon you now comes only from your association with me. Once you have passed out of my orbit life holds nothing but sunshine for you, of that I am convinced.'[43]

As he began his second year at university, he came up with a scheme for making a bit of extra money that was as practical as any his mother could have devised. The *Nottinghamshire Guardian* was running a pre-Christmas short story competition, offering three prizes of three guineas each. Lawrence set to work at once writing the stories: he would send in one under his own name, and Jessie and another girl agreed to submit the other two. Only Jessie won a prize, with 'A Prelude to a Happy Christmas', published in the newspaper on 7th December, 1907. It was Lawrence's first appearance in print. The cheque arrived, made payable to Jessie, so her father paid it into his account and handed over the money to Lawrence. 'Well, Bert, it's the first,' he said, 'but I hope it won't be the last.'[44]

'A Prelude', set at The Haggs on Christmas Eve, has a sentimentality which Lawrence afterwards disowned, but it charmed the judges with its 'simple theme handled with freshness and simplicity altogether charming'. Three bucolic young brothers arrive at a neighbouring mill to do some 'guysering' for a lark (guysers were country amateurs who disguised themselves comically and acted out an old Christmas play, in the same yuletide tradition as carol singers). At the mill lives Nell, once the lady-love of one of them. Suddenly finding his situation intolerable, capering about in his absurd Bedouin costume as Nell watches gravely and then throws a coin, he rushes out. The girl feels a pang. A year before, they had become estranged. How she regrets it now! With a friend she goes in pursuit to make amends, sings carols outside his cottage and then slips away with him.

This story, which Lawrence cheerfully wished 'to glory in the absolute sense' and refused to collect later in volume form, was accompanied by 'Legend' and 'The White Stocking'. His first collection of short stories, *The Prussian Officer*, contained both 'The White Stocking' and a longer version of 'Legend' called 'A Fragment of Stained Glass'. Symbols had begun to obsess him: the peacock and the angel in the churchyard of his 'Nethermere', and now here were two more – a bit of stained glass he had picked up, and a white stocking his mother had once pulled out of her bag instead of a handkerchief, on her way to a girlhood dance at the Castle.

He was now in a state of acute indecision on a number of issues. Apart from Jessie, there were his religious uncertainties, and now the question mark over his future as a teacher. If only he could find a system of thought and bolt himself to it with the unquestioning assurance of the engineering students he admired now at university, swaggering about as if they owned the place. 'His mind thought in symbols, not in ideas,' wrote Aldington, 'dwelt on emotions and impressions and rejected abstractions and definitions.'[45] And the more uncertain he felt inwardly about his own direction, the more important it was for him to be 'right' at all costs. His dogmatic assertions struck many people as absurd and illogical, if not downright stupid. He could be abominably rude one minute and as tender as a girl the next. Willie Hopkin was often baffled and amazed as Lawrence, sometimes accompanied by girl-friends, came whirling furiously at the tolerant little socialist in an effort to demolish the man's lifelong values and beliefs with a virulent surprise attack. 'You, my boy, are dead,' he told him once, his hand up like a policeman to prevent interruption. 'You move and think mechanically and repeat the tricks you have been taught – at best you are an automaton.' Turning to Hopkin's wife, he added magnanimously: 'You, Sallie, have some glimmerings of life.' If Lawrence had one or more of his 'soulful females' in tow, Hopkin would politely offer his chair. Lawrence fumed: 'For goodness' sake don't be polite. Let 'em find their own. When you get to Heaven you'll get up for every blessed woman who enters until the last seat is gone, and then you'll fall backward into Hell and serve you jolly well right!' Hopkin was already impressed by this young man's apparent knowledge of women, but it must have made the deeply insecure Lawrence wince to hear the naïve compliment: 'Bert, you were a woman last time you were on earth.'[46]

He was in his second year at College, and plunging now into philosophy, searching for something corroborative which would at the same time make sense of these wild impulses and repudiations of his that had him swinging helplessly to and fro like a pendulum. For a time he thought he had found some of the answers in Schopenhauer. Turning as always to Jessie and to Alan Chambers, he talked her brother into giving her a translation of the *Essays* for her birthday in 1908. That way he could discuss Schopenhauer's ideas with them both. A chapter which struck him as particularly significant was 'The Metaphysics of Love', from *The World as Will and Idea*. He annotated her copy copiously and drew her attention to many statements with underlinings:

P.177: 'Because the kernel of passionate love turns on the anticipation of the child to be born and its nature it is quite possible for friendship, without any admixture of sexual love, to exist between two young, good-looking people of different sex, if there is perfect fitness of temperament and intellectual capacity. In fact aversion for each other may exist also.' (Lawrence: *'Qu'en pensez-vous?'*)

P.182: 'In the first place, a man in love is by nature inclined to be inconstant and a woman constant. A man's love perceptibly decreases after a certain period; almost every other woman charms him more than the one he already possesses; he longs for change: while a woman's love increases from the moment it is returned. This is because nature aims at as great an increase as possible . . . This is why a man is always desiring other women, while a woman clings to one man . . .'

P.188–189: 'While . . . two lovers are pathetically talking about the harmony of their souls, the kernel of the conversation is for the most part the harmony concerning the individual and its perfection, which obviously is of much more importance than the harmony of their souls – which frequently turns out to be a violent discord shortly after marriage.'

P.201. 'From this it is obvious why we often see very intelligent, nay, distinguished men married to dragons and she-devils, and why we cannot understand how it was possible for them to make such a choice.' (Lawrence commented in the margin: 'Never vice-versa?')

P.207: 'Why, then, is a lover so absolutely devoted to every look and turn of his beloved, and ready to make any kind of sacrifice for her? Because the *immortal* part of him is yearning for her; it is only the *mortal* part of him that longs for everything else. That keen and intense longing for a particular woman is accordingly a direct pledge of the immortality of the essence of our being and of its perpetuity in the species.'

P. 208: 'And yet, amid all this turmoil, we see a pair of lovers exchanging longing glances – yet why so secretly, timidly, and stealthily? Because these lovers are traitors secretly striving to perpetuate all this misery and turmoil that otherwise would come to an ultimate end.'[47]

Swerving away suddenly from this speculation, he brought Jessie his copy of *Anna Karenina* to read, telling her that without doubt it was the world's greatest novel. She and her family all read it in turn, enthralled by the farming chapters and identifying themselves readily with Levin and Kitty. But for Lawrence the whole crux of the book was Anna and what happened to her.

A photograph of Lawrence on his twenty-first birthday shows a bright-eyed, short-nosed boy with his throat encased in a high, stiff collar, as if he were being punished for being good. The picture of him only two years later (opposite page 128) is startlingly different: the shining scholarship boy has become a distinctly sardonic young man with gleaming animal eyes and a rather coarse-looking mouth under a thin droop of moustache. Something about the moustache, the ears flattened against the skull and the soft collar with its striped tie loosely knotted gives an impression of a virile young plumber on his way to a Saturday night dance at the Palais.

It was probably this second photograph he was describing when he wrote to Blanche Jennings, the girl in Liverpool who was a postal worker and belonged to the Hopkin circle in Eastwood: 'Do you like my photo? It is not bad. It represents me in gross; it has no subtlety; there is no insight in it; I like it exceedingly; I like myself bluff, rather ordinary, fat, a bit "manly".'[48]

In June, 1908, he reported to her: 'My exams are on – they continue till July 4th. Today and tomorrow, however, are holidays. I ought to be swotting, but I don't want, therefore I will not. I am scandalously unprepared, consequently; I cannot rouse myself to study things I am not interested in; I cannot have anything but a poor result. It does not trouble me – exams are among the grimaces that I will laugh at. I have not got a job. – I will not write for any more – I cannot bear to advertise myself.'[49]

To his disgust, he soon found that as a junior teacher in Nottinghamshire he could not hope to earn more than thirty shillings a week. He discovered too that there was a glut of certified teachers, who were 'a drug on the market'. Well, glut or not, they would not get him for less than ninety pounds a year. It didn't worry him either if he remained unemployed for the moment. It was summer, there was endless work waiting for him at The Haggs. 'I have written to Egypt for a job', he wrote airily to Blanche Jennings. Meanwhile, the hateful examinations were over and he had

7. D. H. Lawrence aged 23. (*See page 128*)

8. Louie Burrows

9. Jessie Chambers

done well enough. He was glad to leave. He regarded the university staff cynically, and he had quarrelled with at least two of the English faculty for having the audacity to mutilate his essays with red-ink corrections. Even a poem he sent in to the college magazine was turned down.

His teaching practice tutor, in his report, expressed doubts as to Lawrence's stamina: this new recruit out of the Nottinghamshire coalfield was found to have almost too much taste and refinement for the job:

'Well-read, scholarly and refined, Mr Lawrence will make an excellent teacher if he gets into the right place. His work at present is uneven according to the ordinary standard owing to his lack of experience of the elementary schoolboy and his management. He would be quite unsuitable for a large class of boys in a rough district; he would not have sufficient persistence and enthusiasm but would become disgusted.

'Mr Lawrence's strong bias is towards the humanistic subjects and at times boys' interest in such lessons is intense. Intelligence, however, is cultivated in lessons on all subjects by the treatment, especially the questions, the defect being a want of that persistent driving home and recapitulation which are necessary. Like many intelligent teachers, Mr Lawrence tends to teach the best pupils exclusively. Though very fluent, he sometimes has an obvious difficulty in finding words suitably simple. He is emphatically a teacher of upper classes.

'Mr Lawrence is fastidious in taste, and while working splendidly at anything that interests him would perhaps easily tire amid the tedium and discouragement of the average classroom. With an upper class in a good school or in a higher school he could do work quite unusually good, especially if allowed a very free hand.'[50]

But for the moment he was independent, deaf to their strictures and their execrable prose. The next three months were carefree, as he worked as an unpaid farm labourer at The Haggs, and continued with his rewriting of 'Nethermere'. Finally he was offered a job as junior master at Davidson Road School, Croydon, for ninety-five pounds a year, and this he accepted. In early October he was saying his farewells. Suddenly it seemed a dreadful thing, this uprooting of oneself.

He arrived to say goodbye to the Chambers family, looking pale and tense. The father, too upset to say very much, tried to pass it off with a casual remark, but only made it worse. Lawrence ate his supper with them and then started for home. Jessie went with him as far as the last gate. There he looked back at the farm and the wood. Jessie burst into tears, and then heard him whispering that he was sorry, as he stood consoling her with his arms around her. It was the final cruelty. It was as if he was not only saying goodbye to the farm and to her, but to their friendship. Once again she had woefully misunderstood him. The past seven years lay in ruins around them.

'I'm so sorry for this,' he said again in a deadened voice. 'But it can't be helped, it can't be helped.'

'Never mind,' I said. 'It doesn't matter.'

We stood for some minutes seeing the familiar outlines of the landscape in the dim October evening. It was all utterly hopeless, there was no use beginning the old argument again.[51]

8

The Teacher in London

Down the valley roars a townward train.
I hear it through the grass
Dragging the links of my shortening chain
Southwards, alas!¹

Before he even reached London, Lawrence had begun to suffer the anguish of exile. Arriving, he went wandering bleakly through the rawly new houses of Croydon, looking for his lodgings and aching hopelessly for bits of remembered path 'between the wood meadow and the brook'. Even before he had departed, his mother had wailed to Jessie, 'What shall *I* do when he's gone?'²

All the time he lived at Croydon, Lawrence stayed with the family of Mr Jones, who was School Attendance Officer at Davidson Road School. John William Jones, a Lancashire man, had a red-brick villa in Colworth Road. Lawrence settled in with them easily enough, liking their homeliness. The rooms were cramped, he said, and added proudly that at times he was the only one who was able to get the baby off to sleep. His mother approved of the baby in the house. 'It will keep him pure,'³ she told Jessie.

At first, though, he couldn't bear the awful pain of separation from 'the valley of home'. He had been there a day and a half when he wrote a letter to Jessie that was like a shriek of fear. He was terrified of the effect of it all on him. He spoke of the experience in terms of mutilation: he was amputated from his roots, he would become foul, black, deformed. It was all part of the terror of being outside, far from the good and the true, banished from paradise. He implored the girl not to show the letter to his mother: he wanted her to think everything was fine. Jessie dutifully burned the dreadful words.

Events soon rushed Lawrence through the worst of his homesickness, but the ache was to remain for months to come. It found expression in one grieving poem after another. The loneliness he felt then had its echo too in *The White Peacock*, as he sat in front of Mrs Jones' living-room fire in the evenings with a pad on his knee, working on the third version of his novel. The book was still called 'Laetitia', and it was still sticky with sentimentality. He sent versions of it travelling through the post now to Blanche Jennings in Liverpool for her opinion.

The young, rather self-opiniated young teacher from Eastwood got on well with his landlord, at any rate in the beginning. On Sundays they could be found painting together, and years after Lawrence's departure Mr Jones had a landscape of the younger man in his front room, the white paint of the clouds imprinted with Lawrence's impatient thumb.

Arguments between them on the subject of religion were apt to strain the friendship: Lawrence would become excited to the point of rudeness. Mr Jones was also shocked more than once by the hateful manner in which his lodger spoke of his father. Fortunately this was offset by his obvious devotion to his mother. When Lawrence began to go about with London writers, and visit them in their houses at weekends, the Lancashire man noticed that he would come back with a rather superior accent. He pointed this out one day, and Lawrence said coldly that he didn't understand what he meant.

On 12th October, 1908, he began what was to be a three-year stint of teaching at Davidson Road, a new school and considered to be one of the most up-to-date in the London area. It was a large, three-storied building of red brick, surrounded by the grey asphalt of playgrounds. The rooms had modern innovations, such as continuous blackboards fixed to the upper half of the walls.

The young provincial who reported to the headmaster on the first morning made a vivid impression. 'I noticed', remembered the headmaster, 'that his hands contrasted palpably with his general appearance. They were fragile, long-fingered, expressive, well-controlled. Lawrence was not a robust being. He made no pretences in the matter of dress. His expression always showed a kind of confident amusement. It was rarely serious. He did not appear to be perturbed with his new surroundings nor doubtful of his powers to succeed in his new duties. Circumstances permitted no gradual introduction to his work. A large class of boys, the regulation 60, awaited him, and he commenced at once.'[4]

This was coalface teaching with a vengeance, and one can imagine him rolling up his sleeves and mastering it, with a grim puritanical zeal worthy of his mother. He knew all about these harsh realities. He wasn't afraid of hard work, he could concentrate almost fanatically on the task in hand, and his obvious conscientiousness earned the respect of the rest of the staff, most of whom were young like himself. His main interests were Art, Biology and English. Because of his inner tensions and his inability to commit himself to a career he found more and more meaningless, teaching strained him to the limit. He lived continually and dangerously on his nerves. To his fellow-teacher, A. W. McLeod, he would burst out from time to time with such sentiments as: 'I'll not go on. The Committee has had blood and tears out of me for a hundred a year. I'll not endure it. I'd rather work on a farm. I know a farmer at Eastwood who would take me on tomorrow. Nay, I'd rather be a tramp.'[5] When, in his *Fantasia of the Unconscious*, he imagines himself with dictatorial powers, he issues a notice throughout the land to close down all the schools. 'Before the age of fourteen,' he rules, 'children should be taught only to move, to act, to *do*. And they should be taught as little as possible even of this. Adults simply cannot and do not know any more what the mode of childish intelligence is. Adults *always* interfere.'

All the same, there were moments when the whole class seemed to swing into unison with him. He could feel it now and then in the art period, when he got them drawing boldly, really enjoying themselves, magically absorbed; and in one or two of the nature-study lessons. And, luckily for him, in Philip Smith he had stumbled on a headmaster who was aware of his gifts and gave him, more or less, the freedom he wanted.

He writes of these 'best moments' in an early Croydon poem:

And very sweet it is, while the sunlight waves
In the ripening morning, to sit alone with the class
And feel the stream of awakening ripple and pass
From me to the boys, whose brightening soul it laves
For this little hour.

   This morning, sweet it is
To feel the lads' looks light on me,
Then back in a swift, bright flutter to work;
Each one darting away with his
Discovery, like birds that steal and flee.

Touch after touch I feel on me
As their eyes glance at me for the grain
Of rigour they taste delightedly.

As tendrils reach out yearningly,
Slowly rotate till they touch the tree
That they cleave unto, and up which they climb
Up to their lives – so they to me.[6]

So it was possible, then, to feel something other than futility. His gladness darts through the lines and touches the reader with its yearning wistfulness, its longing to be convinced that these tender shoots sprouting palely in the backyards of suburbs can actually be nurtured and brought on with loving care. More often, though, it was a feeling bitterly thwarted and betrayed, and then the sweet caring Lawrence vanished in a flash: he responded to rejection with a desk-banging exasperation and impatience:

My pack of unruly hounds! I cannot start
Them again on a quarry of knowledge they hate to hunt,
I can haul them and urge them no more.

No longer can I endure the brunt
Of the books that lie out on the desks;
  a full three-score
Of several insults of blotted pages, and scrawl
Of slovenly work that they have offered me.
I am sick, and what on earth is the good of it all?
What good to them or me, I cannot see!

  So, shall I take
My last dear fuel of life to heap on my soul
And kindle my will to a flame that shall consume
Their dross of indifference; and take the toll
Of their insults in punishment? – I will not![7]

When verses such as these appeared in the evening newspaper, some of the boys retaliated with lines of their own and pinned them to his desk-lid. Then they waited for him to discover them and react. Instead of the rage they expected, Lawrence crowed with delight and set the class to considering how the verses could have been made more effective. What did it matter how you got a response? Anything was better than pushing against the old dreary inertness, and feeling at the end of the day that all your efforts had gone down the drain, and saying grimly to yourself: 'Why should we beat our heads against the wall/Of each other? I shall sit and wait for the bell.'[8]

On the days when there was no reprieve, and he turned for his lodging in disgust at the stupidity of it, sick of shoving in endlessly and getting nothing back, his *White Peacock* manuscript drew him more strongly than ever as a means of justifying his very existence as a man. Or he would pick up the Jones baby, asleep after sobbing fitfully, and feel a strange, voluptuous comfort in the touch of it. To hold the sleeping baby and inhale the curious milky smell, to cradle a creature so utterly drenched in sleep, with its wet eyelashes and drooping legs, was like coming to terms with one's weariness and defeat.

So there were compensations. At times he could write quite jauntily to Louie Burrows, one of the original Pagans, that he was really lucky to be with such jolly people as the Jones family, lucky to have landed at such a handsome-looking school – and he endeavoured to make its dreary setting against the railway yards sound glamorous. The school, he reported, looked over 'great stacks of timber, over two railways to Norwood where the music-hall folk live in big houses among the trees, and to Sydenham, where the round blue curves of the Crystal Palace swell out into view on fairly clear days.'⁹ In truth, there was little that was glamorous about it: what he was conveying was his tingling excitement at being there in London, and surviving his first despair. He told Louie gaily about Winnie, a little girl of five, who was, according to Mr Jones, infatuated with him, adding wickedly that Mr Jones pronounced the word 'infatuated' by 'manipulating the syllables of the big word cautiously'. He said that he sometimes had a room to himself, when Winnie and her father were out, and there was an abundance of good food, all for eighteen shillings per week. As for the school, it was a fine, up-to-date one, with wood block floors everywhere and dual desks. Then came some carping, and a swift, furious attack on the head, for being 'a weak-kneed windy fool' who was afraid to punish anybody, so that when he, Lawrence, wanted to cane a boy he had to send for the regulation cane and write up every scrap of detail in the punishment book. Because of the virtual absence of discipline he found teaching a constant battle for order. But by 28th February, 1909, he was able to announce firmly: 'School is really very pleasant here. I have tamed my wild beasts – I have conquered my turbulent subjects, and can teach in ease and comfort.'¹⁰ What he still desperately missed, though, was his own country, and above all his own people. The people around him in London weren't frank enough. They were smooth, untrustworthy. Instead of having the warmth he craved, they were merely polite. Nothing bound them together: they hadn't known the hardships of the North, they hadn't been tested, tempered. Once he dipped his toe into the polite, buzzing water of a literary society meeting, and the temperature was icy. How could he take to these cold fish, what were they to him?

Then there was the country, or rather, its aching absence. To compensate for that, he went on trips to Wimbledon and over to Richmond Park, where he discovered oaks that were 'great and twisted like Norwegian tales, like the Vikings; the beeches are tremendous, black like steel.'[11]

He kept up a sporadic correspondence with Louie, this dark, handsome girl from college who had gone straight to her first job at Leicester in June, 1908, and now was unhappy in it. Writing to her helped to relieve the agony of his isolation from the few people who meant something to him, and with her he was free of the tension that always tormented him in his friendship with Jessie. Also, he was beginning to enjoy the piquancy of flirtations, and would continue to do so. He compounded his pleasure by confiding to Blanche Jennings that Louie, whom he had known for a good many years, 'has black hair, and wonderful eyes, big and very dark, and very vulnerable.'[12] But this open admiration came later; for the moment he was content to stay in touch, keeping her abreast of his news with small bursts of information about himself and his new world.

Of course there was still Jessie, and in his way he kept faith with her, even feeling the bond between them stronger than ever, more poignant, now they were forced to be separate. In a poem-letter he addressed her with a breathtaking new gentleness and a delicacy that must have made her tremble with love for him again, in spite of all her misgivings:

You promised to send me some violets. Did you forget?
  White ones and blue ones from under the orchard hedge?
  Sweet dark purple, and white ones mixed for a pledge
Of our early love that hardly has opened yet.[13]

He was reading voraciously again, ransacking the second-hand bookstalls and barrows he had discovered in Surrey Street, Croydon. The moment he came across something exciting he wanted to share it with Jessie, as he had done for so many years. Books began to arrive at The Haggs by post, or else he would bring them with him on holidays. Always they were accompanied by little notes, urging her to concentrate on this or that, or give him her opinion. Sometimes he sent a copy of a new poem he had written, and as *Leaves of Grass* was now one of his models, he would refer to these new poems as 'Whitmanesque'. Now and then the accompanying note would be urgent, telling her to drop everything and read the book he had sent. Doughty's *Adam Cast Forth* had such an instruction, as did Francis Thompson's essay on Shelley. A great find in Surrey Street was a tattered copy of *The Playboy of the Western World*, which he took to have bound before passing it on to Jessie. He was in the habit of copying verses from Baudelaire or Verlaine on the fly-leaf of a book he wanted her to have, and into *The Playboy* went Baudelaire's *Sonnet d'Automne*. One book he brought home with him was Samuel Butler's *Erewhon*, and on their walk to the Warren he talked to her excitedly about it, giving her a complete summary of the story. 'It begins like a book of travel,' he said. 'You'd never dream it was satire. It's so fresh and romantic, such a sense of a new country. And then he just turns all our ideas of society upside down, but with the greatest seriousness . . .'[14]

The moderns interested him: he was reading the latest Wells and Galsworthy, Conrad and George Moore, almost as soon as they were published. Turgenev he loved, but he had reservations about Gorky. The greatness of Dostoevsky's *Crime and Punishment* certainly had to be acknowledged, but all the same 'I don't like it. I don't quite understand it. I must read it again.'[15] Olive Schreiner's *Story of an African Farm* was passed on with approval: so was *The Trojan Women*, a favourite Gilbert Murray translation. From the library he had got Nietzsche, but he only referred to this obliquely.

As soon as he felt tolerably happy in Croydon, he got down to giving *The White Peacock* its final shaping. Just as in the old days, he needed her seal of approval on new developments. In a letter he asked her about the marriage of Emily and Tom, and if she minded. Jessie replied that she didn't, and that she thought the book much stronger and better now than the first version she had seen. When she wasn't personally involved, at any rate directly, she could be an excellent critic, as Lawrence knew very well. It must have been about this time that the book changed its name to 'Nethermere'. It would only be reborn as *The White Peacock* in a publisher's office.

A canny Scot, Stewart Robertson, a school inspector who called at Davidson Road School, was alerted one day by a piece of verse in the *Western Gazette* in which a teacher spoke of looking out of the classroom window towards Norwood. He knew all the schools in the area, and the only one facing in that direction was Davidson Road. He called on the headmaster, asked to be introduced to his poetry-writing assistant master, and in the fourth-form classroom met a man with 'a pale face, stooping shoulders, a narrow chest, febrile hands, and a voice which I can only describe as contralto. He coughed occasionally. . .'[16] Later, he took this unusual member of staff to a literary society, and remembered that Lawrence chose to speak on Rachel Annand Taylor. He introduced his talk by saying that Miss Taylor had squirrel-red hair, a sentence Mr Robertson described long afterwards as characteristic of a man who was so obsessed by the physical. From this he went on to say that Lawrence was 'abnormal' and therefore not interested in normal human beings, and this was why he didn't like teaching. He once told Lawrence to his face that he might have been more normal and less morbidly sensitive if he had been a Boy Scout. According to him, Lawrence retorted that Scotsmen want the whole world to be like themselves: which at least was civil.

If the pictures of Lawrence at the Croydon school provided by colleagues and former pupils give us the facts, his own school poems, and the slight sketches from that period – when, after all, he was still casting about and making false starts – give us the sensations. Take, for example, a Dickensian sketch called 'Lessford's Rabbits':

'On Tuesday mornings I have to be at school at halfpast eight to administer the free breakfasts. Dinners are given in the canteen in one of the mean streets, where the children feed in a Church Mission room appropriately adorned by Sunday School cartoons showing the blessing of the little ones, and the feeding of the five thousand. We serve breakfasts, however, in school, in the wood-work room high up under the roof.

'Tuesday morning sees me rushing up the six short flights of stone stairs, at twenty-five minutes to nine. It is my disposition to be late. I generally find a little crowd of children waiting in the 'art' room – so-called because it is surrounded with a strip of blackboard too high for the tallest boy to reach – which is a sort of ante-room to the workshop where breakfast is being prepared. I hasten through the little throng to see if things are ready. There are two big girls putting out the basins, and another one looking in the pan to see if the milk is boiling . . . When the boys' basins are placed along the outer edge of the bench, the girls' on the inner, and the infants' on the lockers against the wall, we are ready. I look at the two rows of assorted basins, and think of the three bears. Then I admit the thirty, who bundle to their places and stand in position, girls on the inside facing boys on the outside, and quaint little infants with their toes kicking the lockers along the walls . . .

'. . . I looked at the boys, dressed in mouldering garments of remote men, at the girls with their rat-tailed hair, and the infants, quaint little mites on whom I wished, but could not bring myself, to expend my handkerchief, and I wondered what I should say. The only other grace I knew was "For these and for all good things may the Lord make us truly thankful." But I wondered whom we should thank for the bad things . . .'

As writing this is youthfully awkward, as well as being a product of the suffocating class atmosphere of Edwardian England.

Impressionistic pieces like this are difficult for a young man to pull off, especially one so uncertain of his social position. He would do this sort of thing brilliantly later, when he had outlawed himself from society and his hand was sure. For the present, he needed a story to tell and characters to focus on. 'Lessford's Rabbits' only jumps with life when the author is confronted by Lessford himself, stuffing lumps of bread under his jersey to take home to his pet rabbits, 'glancing furtively with a little quiver of apprehension up at me.'

Though his touch was still uncertain, when it came to a critical examination of the faults of others, he knew exactly what was wanted. The pedagogue in him delighted to advise and correct, to hammer home points, and the hammer hit the nail unerringly. To Louie Burrows, who had let him see one of her short stories, he wrote severely, and with great thoroughness: 'I have read your tale; it is very jolly. I'm sure it will take if you write it out again once or twice. The great thing to do in a short story is to select the salient details – a few striking details to make a sudden swift impression. Try to use words vivid and emotion-quickening; give as little information as possible; make some parts swifter; avoid bits of romantic sentimentality like Crusaders and too much Wishing Well; select some young fellow of your acquaintance as a type for your lover, and think what he would probably do – Bonnie and the girl are good, but the young keeper is not well-defined; be *very careful* of slang; a little is as much as most folks can stand . . .'[17]

In another letter to Louie, after he had been away in the South for several months and was beginning to find his feet, he speculated on the threesome they made, Louie, Jessie and he, and whether it was a happy triangle. Was he perhaps considering a 'triangular' solution to his old dilemma, bearing in mind that he was, as he had confessed to Jessie, two men in one skin? Or was it merely, as he said in his letter, that the devilry and perversity in him became more pronounced when he was rootless? He put forward the suggestion to her and then promptly dropped it. He was already adept at these flirtations by correspondence that left him quite free. It was a kind of literary strumming. All the time he was getting ready. Soon he would refer to a demon in him that had to be let out. There was also a vivisector in him, as Willie Hopkin had already noted: 'My wife one day said she very much objected to him putting a woman on his operating table for dissection and then saying in a sneering tone: "There you are! That is a woman, body and soul." He turned round and said: "If I need any woman for my purpose – you included – I shall use you.

Why the devil should you or any other woman come between me
and the flowering of my genius?" He almost made me believe in
the theory of reincarnation, for he had a most uncanny knowledge of women.'[18] Another Eastwood acquaintance, F. D.
Chambers, remarked: 'As a matter of fact Lawrence was a woman
in a man's skin and only women had much sympathy with him.'[19]

Back again for his first Christmas holidays amongst his own
people, he enjoyed some mild flirting 'in the flesh' for a change,
and no doubt enjoyed even more his descriptions and hints of it in
a letter from his old Lynn Croft address to Blanche Jennings in
Liverpool. Calling her playfully 'Sweet Bee', he thanked her for
her gift of *The Shropshire Lad*, then ungraciously attacked it and
the author for being gloomily death-obsessed. Housman wasn't a
poet: or rather, if he was, he was a poet of one song and that was
bankruptcy, death-in-life. It was one of Lawrence's lifelong horrors, the idea of the living dead. The book wouldn't have been
bound in red if he had had his way, he told Miss Jennings: it ought
to be dressed in grey, or black and white. Suddenly he reined
himself in, and thanked the girl for the gift. With one of his swift
transitions he went on to hint darkly at his irresponsible flirtations
over Christmas, in particular with a 'certain girl' whom he kissed
until she hid her head in shame. It was time he got back to
Croydon and out of mischief. Then comes one of his direct,
startling questions: should a girl be passive in love, or a bit of
a devil, like a Carmen? What does she think? He confesses that
most of the girls he has anything to do with are the passive
type, and indeed, men seem to like them that way. But not
him . . .

The passive girl who had prompted this reflection was waiting
for him at The Haggs with her usual intense fearfulness. Would it
be more cruel passion, the old mixture as before? Or might the
enforced absence have somehow changed things for the better
between them? When Lawrence came, it was with the same quick,
eager step that the whole family delighted in, and he brought with
him a copy of the *English Review* for December, 1908. Jessie's
father, as hungry for literature as she was, gazed at the 'fine blue
cover and handsome black type' and there and then decided to
take out a subscription. It looked so splendid and it seemed to
promise so much, shining from the world of literature direct
into their fastness.

Jessie noticed that the editor, Ford Madox Hueffer, was not
only asking for contributions but extended a welcome to previously unpublished writers. She mentioned this to Lawrence, urg-

ing him to send in some of his work, but he wouldn't consider it. Possibly he was afraid of being rebuffed. He had submitted things before, and Jessie hadn't known of this until one evening in the spring of 1908, when he started telling her, in a 'deliberately unexpressive voice', that he had sent some of his stuff to an author who wrote regularly for the *Daily News*, asking him what he thought. After a month or two the manuscripts came back, returned by the author's wife, with a note to say that her husband had no time to read Lawrence's work. To Lawrence, this off-hand treatment was the worst kind of rejection. 'I've tried, and been turned down,' he said flatly, 'and I shall try no more. And I don't care if I never have a line published.'[20]

His tone then had been so dismissive that she hadn't had the nerve to raise the issue again until now. When he said no again, she pointed out that if he didn't submit anything, then his writing would just be wasted and unread. Lawrence shook his head stubbornly and repeated that he didn't care what happened to it; he wasn't dying to get into print anyhow, and he was damned if he was going to send stuff in and have it thrown back in his face. Jessie persisted. How did he know what would happen unless he tried?

Relenting, he told her that if she wanted she could send in some of his poems for him: it didn't matter which ones. Then, realising she meant it, he added, 'Give me a nom de plume, though; I don't want folk in Croydon to know I write poetry.'[21]

Afterwards Lawrence told the story differently. A school-teacher friend had copied out a batch of his poems and sent them in to the *English Review* without telling him, he said.

It wasn't until June, 1909, that Jessie sorted through the poems sent to her from Croydon, selected the most suitable and copied them carefully. Those she remembered sending were 'Discipline', 'Dreams Old and Dreams Nascent', and 'Baby Movements'. In her covering letter she gave the poet's name, but provided a pseudonym to be used in the event of publication. Lawrence's parish was called Greasley, so she decided on Richard Greasley.

Ford Madox Hueffer later chose to remember that, with his talent for instant genius-spotting, he was able to proclaim the discovery of a new star in the literary firmament on the very day that he first read something by Lawrence. The first words he read were, he declared, from a story called 'Odour of Chrysanthemums', and he proceeded to explain exactly how he recognised the power and authority of the talent that had so miraculously appeared under his nose:

'The small locomotive engine, Number 4, came clanking, stumbling down from Selston', and at once you know that this fellow with the power of observation is going to write of whatever he writes about from the inside. The 'Number 4' shows that. He will be the sort of fellow who knows that for the sort of people who work about engines, engines have a sort of individuality. He had to give the engine the personality of a number . . . 'With seven full waggons' . . . The 'seven' is good. The ordinary careless writer would say 'some small waggons'. This man knows what he wants. He sees the scene of the story exactly . . .

'The gorse still flickered indistinctly in the raw afternoon' . . . Good too, distinctly good. This is the just-sufficient observation of nature that gives you, in a single phrase, landscape, time of day, weather, season . . .

That same day he was at a dinner party at the Pall Mall Restaurant, surrounded by celebrities, H. G. Wells, Hilaire Belloc, Maurice Baring, Chesterton, among many others. To interrupt an incipient debate on Jesus Christ, Hueffer told Wells casually that another genius, named D. H. Lawrence, had strayed into his net. At this, Wells promptly shrilled over in the direction of Lady Londonderry: 'Hooray, Fordie's discovered another genius!'[22]

Later, Hueffer maintained that Jessie had written him a note of inquiry first, asking if she could send anything by Lawrence, and he had told her to send both prose and poetry, if she had both. According to him, three poems about Lawrence's life as a schoolmaster arrived, together with 'Odour of Chrysanthemums'. The poems were 'nice', he says, but didn't have the force of the story. As if to authenticate his reminiscences, Hueffer said that he could still recall the look of the handwriting in Jessie's letter – 'as if drawn 'with sepia rather than written in ink, on grey-blue notepaper.'

Violet Hunt's memories of this same launching of a genius went as follows: 'The moment the *Review* was started the usual concourse of friends, contributors and would-be contributors attended the editor's levées. Ford was out for new blood – for talent if not for genius. He printed, so I believe, the first articles of Norman Douglas, Gilbert Cannan, Wyndham Lewis and D. H. Lawrence.

'That *was* a Moment! The first blush – the blowing – of Mr Lawrence's flower of genius. I was, at that time, reader. The editor handed me some manuscript poems written in pencil

and very close, which had come to him from a young schoolmistress in the Midlands. She said her sweetheart was schoolmaster in the same school. He was the son of a miner, and not very
strong, but she had copied out some of his poems, and would the
editor give them a glance?

'They were perfectly wonderful. The editor was beside himself
with pleasure at his discovery . . .'[23]

These arch, amusing, cosmopolitan people were not exactly
dying to meet the obscure young teacher from Eastwood, but they
were waiting, with that curious blend of the genuine and the
spurious which Lawrence captured so accurately later, in his
novels and stories. They wanted to help him, and at the same time
be diverted by him. For his part, Lawrence prepared to enter
their dazzling new world with a mixture of countrified awkward-
ness and provincial defiance.

Meanwhile he continued to consolidate his position in
Croydon. A colleague introduced him to her close friend, Helen
Corke, a woman of Lawrence's age who had once taught at
Davidson Road. She was attractive, independent, and like himself
an aspiring writer. Their friendship rapidly flourished, as Lawrence first showed her his manuscript of *The White Peacock* and
then urged her to deliver judgement on it. She liked to walk, as he
did, and sometimes they took a train and then rambled together
over the North Downs. She was to inspire a whole cycle of 'Helen'
poems, though as a woman she baulked him endlessly, shrinking
from him physically and emotionally, as he accused her in poems.
Could it have been that, like Jessie, she was unable to initiate him,
and so received, like her, the fury of his frustrations? At any rate,
when she eventually met Jessie, they found they had a great deal
in common. Both had the same instincts of sympathy for Lawrence as a developing artist. As he walked with Helen, he talked
out his problems and found that she could listen with great
intelligence and insight. She was small, quick-tempered, and their
meetings were sometimes stormy.

Another girl with whom he was able to talk freely was Agnes
Holt, a fellow-teacher whose chief virtue seemed to be that she
'takes me seriously'. Once he toyed with the idea of marrying her
– when he felt he had to marry *somebody* and get it over with – but
he speedily abandoned the idea.

He still enjoyed being alone, utterly free, tossed about on the
winds of life. It was worth something, after all, to be young and
unattached in London. In the spring of 1909 he would get on a
bike and head for the sea, over the Downs to Brighton, rushing
down lanes frothing with primroses, past bluebells among the

hazel copses, in deep, still pools of colour. He would stretch out on Brighton beach and look at the 'sea like pale green jewels', and then slowly allow himself to be repelled by the magnificence of the town and push on to Rottingdean, watching his hands redden on the handlebars in the sun and wind. On the Downs he thought the land was like an unevenly shaken cloth; he noticed the cowslips peeping out in the sun, then had to stop and get off to push a sheep's head back through the rails of the fence where it had foolishly got itself stuck. Looking across, 'Brighton in the red fusing light looked like a wonderful imagined place,'[24] and up on the cliff-top he watched a man sitting still with his arm around his sweetheart's waist. Yes, it was good to see it all, describe it, toss it to and fro in his mind as the Downs had tossed him all day in the shaking cloth of their folds. What did it mean, other than that? He wrote to Blanche Jennings from Rottingdean, using the playful tone he often put on for her benefit. You don't take me seriously, he seemed to be saying, so I'm damned if I'm going to reveal my seriousness to you. I can be as amusing as the next fellow. His letters to her are always half sincere, half disingenuous.

In the summer of 1909 he went home as usual, but this time it was to help organise a visit to the Isle of Wight. For some reason, Jessie didn't go. Among the party were George Neville, Alice Hall, Lawrence's sister, Ada, his mother, and Gertrude and Frances Cooper. They clubbed together to share the expenses of a cottage at Shanklin, spent their time hiking and bathing, and were chaperoned by Mrs Lawrence and Alice Hall's mother. It was while this holiday was being taken that Jessie had an exciting letter from Hueffer, saying that he certainly liked the work she had sent him and asking her to ask her friend to call on him when he had the opportunity. 'I appear to have said that I thought Lawrence had great gifts, but that a literary career depended enormously on chance, and that if Lawrence had a good job in a school he had better stick to it for the present.'[25]

A long, newsy letter came from Lawrence, bursting with life and gaiety, full of descriptions of the island. He was happy and carefree; his mother was with him, and his friends, and there was no emotional disruption. Perhaps it was resentment that made Jessie hold back the good tidings from the *English Review* until he came back to her. When she told him, his excitement was barely suppressed. '*You* are my luck,' he murmured.[26] Quickly he took the letter to show his mother, and that was the last Jessie saw of it.

The rest of the holiday was a time of discord and misery for her: the mixture as before. It began with Lawrence telling her

144

11. Moorgreen Colliery, Eastwood

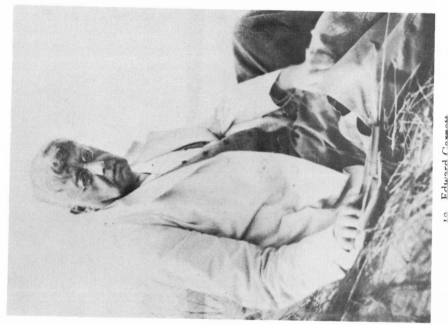

12. Edward Carpenter

that Ada and his mother were finding fault with him because he had come back from London 'different'. He was embittered by their narrowness. Pouring out his feelings to Jessie, he said that surely they could accept the inevitability of change in him, for now he was living away from home it had to happen. It didn't mean he had abandoned them, or grown superior, or cold: why should they insist it did?

The moment Jessie entered the house at Lynn Croft Road she sensed by the hostile atmosphere that the blame for Lawrence's change was somehow attached to her, and decided that his mother resented her action in sending his poems to the *English Review*. They set off, she and Lawrence, on an excursion to the old quarter of Nottingham. She was thankful to escape, the house was oppressive. But her heart sank as she saw the effect on Lawrence. He spoke sharply to her, he was cold and aloof. Once again she felt wretchedly that she was the scapegoat for his own unhappiness.

After buying postcards of Greek sculpture in an antiquarian shop near the Castle, he presented her with one of them. It was called 'Amor et Psyche'. Jessie knew him well enough to realise that there had to be some significance in it for her, and before he left her he said, with an agonised expression, that she was Psyche, nothing but soul. She went home completely crushed.

Two days later she decided on a course of action: anything to wrench herself back to life. She rode on her bicycle into Nottingham and applied for a teaching job in the city. That way she would be able to take evening courses at the University, and continue her education. If she didn't have something to occupy her, she knew she would fall into endless morbid brooding.

She saw Lawrence once more before he returned to Croydon for the autumn term. During the evening, as she walked part of the way home with him, he went on talking obsessively again about marriage, how it was to be achieved, and with whom. He seemed brutally indifferent to the devastation he was causing her. Finally he blurted out in a kind of despair, like a drowning man, that he would marry straight away if he could find someone suitable. There was nobody, so he would have to go from woman to woman. He made it sound as if the need crucified him. When Jessie left him and trailed back through the Warren it was very late, and she was oppressed by a feeling of horror. Above all, she pitied him. It tormented her that she could do absolutely nothing to help him.

Back in Croydon, Lawrence lost no time in going to meet Hueffer at the *English Review* office, which turned out to be

Hueffer's flat in Holland Park. Writing a report on the confrontation to Jessie, he told her that the editor was 'fairish, fat, about forty, and the kindest man on earth.' When Hueffer came to write down his own recollections of that meeting he expanded it to several pages, and because he had, years later, read Lawrence's story 'The Fox', he couldn't help picturing the young author leaning on his doorpost and peering in alertly, his head cocked, as a fox. Even his hair and moustache, and appraising glance, were fox-like. The 'reckless robber of hen-roosts' had arrived.

From the outset, apparently, Lawrence was critical of Hueffer's office. Unnerved a little, but intrigued by such directness, the kindly editor asked him what was wrong with the room, adding that he personally found it immensely satisfying. But for Lawrence, whom Hueffer was now shrewdly regarding as a strange blend of poet and North country puritanical businessman, the room, with its Chippendale, its pictures, its windows at either end and glimpses of trees beyond, was altogether too elegant. Lawrence told the paunchy man, with his deceptive softness and keen gaze, that it didn't look the kind of place in which money was made. Hueffer put on an airy manner and said, to amuse, that money wasn't made here, it was spent. It was an unfortunate remark, and Lawrence's suspicions of the metropolitan type were at once confirmed. London folk were a bit degenerate, not to say stupid. His severity hardening, he spoke to Hueffer with an odd combination of superiority and deference, insisting on called him 'Sir'. When the older man protested, Lawrence came out with the blithe remark: 'But you are, aren't you, everybody's blessed Uncle and Headmaster?'[27]

Hueffer's first impressions contain some unintentionally comical asides, and to the end of his days he never got over his astonishment at his protégé's origins. In his rambling account of that first meeting he assumed Lawrence's knowledge of the world to be so restricted that the only kind of office he could possibly imagine was a replica of the office at the colliery where his father worked, 'with counters and swing-doors and brass and the clink of coins unceasing on the air'.[28] From the beginning he saw Lawrence as an exciting, slightly dangerous, fundamentally incomprehensible intruder from that other England north of the Trent he had heard rumours about.

But whatever his shortcomings, Hueffer was a sharp, kind and generous man who knew the value of what he had found, and in the November issue of the *English Review* he gave Lawrence a real splash. His sequence of poems, entitled 'A Still Afternoon', occupied the front of the magazine, followed by Galsworthy,

Lowes Dickinson, Cunningham Graham, J. A. Hobson, Henry Nevinson, G. P. Gooch, and Hueffer himself. Lawrence seems to have been caught unawares, blossoming like this so rapidly as a poet. In a whirl, he made haste to complete the final version of *The White Peacock* so that he could show it to Hueffer. He was launched. At home in September he had rushed round to the Hopkin family with his exciting news that some poems of his were probably going to be published. Calming down, he told Hopkin that Jessie had sent them in, and it was a complete surprise to him. Hopkin said, 'Bert, fancy owing your entry into the world of literature to your sweetheart!'[29] Lawrence didn't bother to answer.

He was spending more time with Agnes Holt, and told Jessie in a letter that he had more or less decided to marry her, but needed to get some money together first. His sister kept having digs at him, he added, because he wasn't sending money to his mother.

After he had met Hueffer he began to lay siege to Jessie, saying she must come to London to read a play he had written, as well as more poems. Then there was this girl he thought of marrying: Jessie should meet her. At the end of November, a Saturday, after a full week of teaching, she left The Haggs at six in the morning and got on a train to London. Lawrence was there waiting for her at King's Cross. Whisking her off to see the sights, he shocked her by saying they were both going to see Hueffer the next day, followed by a lunch with Violet Hunt. She shrank almost visibly at the thought of facing these grand people. Lawrence quickly disarmed her by telling her he had already mentioned to Hueffer that she would be shy, and that the only way to get her there was by springing it on her as a surprise when she reached London.

Over lunch at Selfridges he said he would take her round to meet Agnes Holt on Sunday morning. She listened in a kind of daze. London was like an Aladdin's Cave, it left her breathless. Lawrence showed her the shops. To the wide-eyed farm girl, everything was dripping with wealth. They visited the National Gallery, and as the light failed they saw the bridges lighting up with traffic, trams reflected in the river. Derelicts were bedding down for the night along the Embankment. Lawrence pointed them out conscientiously, like a tourist guide. To round off the evening he took her to see a play, *The Making of a Gentleman*. Afterwards he told her solemnly that it was worthless, but that wasn't the point: the theatre was really a fashion show. London society went to the theatre chiefly to admire the dresses of the leading ladies.

He carried her off to his digs in Croydon. It was late, and the

Jones family were in bed. The young couple let themselves in quietly. Glowing with pleasure, Lawrence made her sit down while he warmed some macaroni for supper. Then he spread papers over the table for her to read, poems and also a play based on his life in Eastwood. Tired out by her long day, the girl asked if she could take the play back with her. He agreed, but still wanted badly to talk. He was tense, concentrating on her, watching her intently. At one in the morning he began to put questions to her about the future and what her expectations were, waiting for replies as if his life depended on the answers she gave. She was exhausted, felt overwhelmed by the old hopelessness, and found herself weeping silently. Recovering a little, she said: 'I don't hope for anything much. But I shall get along somehow. I'm not afraid.'[30]

Preoccupied with his own affairs, he scarcely heeded her words. She listened to him bleakly as he talked, as if to himself, about the great strain he was under, and how necessary it was for him to have a companion, to cope with the constant excitement and newness of it all. He ought to be married. He went on, battering away at this insoluble problem, and it slowly sank into her like a stone, what he was suggesting. He was saying that he couldn't marry because he had no money: all the same, he couldn't wait either, he had to have 'that'. Did she understand? Would a girl give him 'that', did she think?

With as much sympathy and fortitude as she could dredge up, she gave the stock answer, that if a girl did, he would rather despise her.

He turned the question cruelly, aiming it at her. If he asked *her*, would she say it was wrong? No, she answered, not so much wrong as hard, very hard.

He gave up then, after murmuring that he thought he'd have to ask Agnes if she would. Released at last, Jessie crawled off to bed, numbed by 'the inscrutable ruling of fate.'[31]

The next morning, true to his word, he took her round to meet Agnes Holt. She was a schoolteacher, like Jessie. But unlike the Eastwood girl, there was something very self-possessed about her. Jessie thought her a bit patronising when she spoke to Lawrence. She had grey eyes and brown hair and she was tall. Lawrence put on a jaunty manner for her benefit, Jessie noticed, the sort of thing he did if he were unsure of himself. Agnes Holt was pleasant to her: she picked up a spray of berries and fastened it to her coat; and that was that.

They were on their way to Holland Park Avenue, where Jessie was to meet the great magician, Hueffer, for the first time. The inexhaustible riches of London around them caused Lawrence to cry out exultantly: 'I'll make two thousand a year!' Jessie treated this to a sniff of northern disdain. She knew his hard-headed mother would approve, but she hated the thought of him making money when he was so obviously cut out for something 'finer and more original'.[32]

Ushered into the large flat and office by a servant, she noticed heaps of *English Review* copies on the window seat and around the black polished floor. Over the fireplace was a framed photograph – of Violet Hunt, so Lawrence told her in a whisper. He had most likely said already that Violet Hunt was a rich novelist who, according to rumour, had taken Hueffer for her lover. Later he divorced his wife and married Violet.

Jessie was shy, but eager to meet the person who had the power to open up a new world for Lawrence. This fat, yet delicate man captivated her at once with his attentiveness. It was a totally new experience for her, having someone of his stature listening to her so carefully. There was some desultory conversation about the Suffragette movement, then he said to her that he assumed she was a sort of socialist. She wasn't in the least interested in politics, but the notion pleased her, and his manner of putting it was so vague that she decided on the spot to be one. It sounded an interesting thing to be, yet gave her plenty of room for man-oeuvre.

Walking along between the editor and Lawrence, on the way now to Violet Hunt's house in Kensington, she found to her surprise that she was enjoying it all, especially Hueffer's company. In her mind she ticked off his virtues: they all added up to a considerable kindness. The maidservant let them in and showed them to the drawing-room, then got Jessie's name wrong when she announced her. Violet Hunt shook her hand warmly, seeing 'a brown bird, bright-eyed, her little head covered with curling russet locks like feathers.'[33] She introduced the girl to the others, including a strange American poet who moved in jerks like a piece of mechanism, and turned out to be Ezra Pound. Jessie coped with everything nervously, only panicking a little at lunch: she asked the maid serving the potatoes if she should take off her hat and gloves. Lawrence, with more defiance, wanted to know 'what knives he was expected to use with fish or asparagus.'[34]

Jessie watched with an expert eye as Violet Hunt carved the massive joint of meat, and the gravy went oozing into the dish. Young Ezra Pound kept firing questions that were like fireworks zipping into the air and exploding, and after lunch added to his tomfoolery by demonstrating the American way to eat an apple.

Also at the table was a subdued man named Byles, who smiled at Jessie in a charming way. Apparently he had once lived on a small farm. The man was too polished to be a genuine toiler in the fields, Jessie thought.

After the meal, Pound continued to behave alarmingly, with no regard for English decorum. Dead-pan, he demanded to know how Hueffer would talk to a working man if he had to: the same as to anyone else, or not? This was brutally direct, and Jessie held her breath as Hueffer paused and considered before he answered. Yes, in exactly the same way, he said urbanely, because the man would be essentially the same as himself, or anyone else he might be speaking to. Jessie decided, glowing, that this was sincere.

But gradually a reaction set in, as she felt herself to be in an invidious position, regarded by both Hueffer and Violet Hunt as Lawrence's fiancée. Nothing could have been crueller, nothing further from the truth: she had the spray of berries on her coat to remind her of her complete rejection. Glancing across at Lawrence 'sitting so straight and alert', it depressed her horribly to think that this scene could mark the end of their long friendship. What had she gained from it all, finally? Some bright chatter in a fashionable Kensington drawing-room – a collection of strangers who meant absolutely nothing to her. 'The conversation pattered around me like raindrops, and at last the interminable meal came to an end.'[35]

It was a relief to be heading for King's Cross and the four o'clock train. Hueffer came with them part of the way, talking easily about this and that, Lawrence struggling to curb his nervous energy and the speed of his walk. After Hueffer had gone, he burst out: 'Isn't he fat, and doesn't he walk *slow*!'[36] Jessie said loyally that she had never met a kinder man. That was true, admitted Lawrence, as if it was something hardly worth mentioning. He wanted to know what she thought of the champagne, and indeed the whole glittering show. It impressed him, he told her, and then looked almost guilty.

Seeing her off, he asked her to go to his mother and describe everything; she would enjoy that.

The time came for her to go to a Nottingham school to teach, and her family left The Haggs and moved to a farm nearer the city. Jessie felt glad to be uprooted so decisively from her past. It had brought her much pain, and sometimes she nearly hated the thought of the old days. She still waited numbly for Lawrence's news, telling herself that he would soon be married. Then she could forget him, cease to care, abandon him to his fate as she had abandoned The Haggs, and begin to live again. After reporting on their Kensington visit to Louie Burrows, Lawrence went on to tell her about a subsequent visit to H. G. Wells in Hampstead: 'He is a funny little chap: his conversation is a continual squirting of thin jets of weak acid: amusing, but not expansive. There is no glow about him.' He was more favourable to Pound, who was twenty-four, like himself, 'but his god is beauty, mine, life. . . . He lives in an attic, like a traditional poet – but the attic is a comfortable well furnished one.' The American poet had just been kicked out of a teaching post at Wabash College, Indiana, and after wandering around Europe for a while had landed up in London. His *Personae and Exultations* came out during this year.

There is another picture of Lawrence and Pound together, at a soirée organised by Ernest Rhys at his home in Hermitage Lane, Hampstead. Yeats was present, talking at length on a favourite subject of his, the marriage of poetry and music. As his monologue kept endlessly unwinding, Ezra Pound, who perhaps felt disgruntled at not getting his share of the limelight, created a diversion by munching at one of the red tulips in the vases on the supper table. Yeats was too far gone in his trance to be aware of him, and the others showed their good manners by pretending that it wasn't happening at all. Pound just went on chewing the flowers.

After a few readings, and a performance on the psaltery by Winifred Emery – a wailing recitation of Yeats' 'The Man Who Dreamed of Fairyland' – the hostess passed around the claret cup. Then at last it was Lawrence's turn. The quiet young teacher with the reddish moustache got up from his corner, crossed the room and sat down with his back to everyone, without saying a word. His voice was too low to be heard properly, and after he had gone on for at least half an hour without showing signs of flagging the company grew restless. There were nudges and murmurings, and it was left to Rhys to go up to Lawrence and suggest tactfully that maybe he needed a rest. Hueffer, who had brought his protégé along, took him off again.

Now he had status as a contributor to the *English Review*, Lawrence went back to the Midlands – during school breaks and some weekends – with renewed zest and a certain man-about-town recklessness. He had heard from Hueffer and Violet Hunt about *The White Peacock*, and their reactions were definitely positive. He wrote immediately to Heinemann, with suitable humility:

'I have just received the accompanying letter from Mr Ford Madox Hueffer. I hasten to forward it to you, and in doing so to offer you the novel of which he speaks.

'It is my first. I have as yet published nothing but a scrap of verse. At the moment I feel a trifle startled and somewhat elated by Mr Hueffer's letter, but already a grain of doubt is germinating in me.'[37]

This was on 15th December, 1909. It would soon be Christmas again, and Eastwood was waiting to receive him. His love affairs were still unresolved, in fact distinctly chaotic, with two or three on the boil in London, and at least another two he could resume in Nottinghamshire. In some elation, he returned to the country and people he still loved with passion and increasing exasperation, and plunged into the activities of the Hopkin circle, with its local intelligentsia and visiting luminaries, such as Philip Snowden, Charlotte Despard, the Webbs, Edward Carpenter. Among the women of interest there, he was friendly with Hopkin's first wife, Sallie, and with Alice Dax, friend of Blanche Jennings, a married woman of strong character and definite views of an 'advanced' nature. As for love, he was still attempting an unlikely fusion of Louie Burrows' sexuality and Jessie's soulfulness, still at the rather desperate game of shuttling to and fro between one and the other. And of course, there was his mother. While she lived, none of these affairs would come to fruition.

Back again in Croydon the following January, he repudiated his 'latest love', presumably Agnes Holt, in a deadly and detailed account which he rendered to Blanche Jennings, who was far away in Liverpool and therefore sufficiently removed from both his stamping grounds to be relatively safe. He had been considering marriage, but now suddenly 'I don't like her. She's rather a striking girl with much auburn hair. At first, she seems a person of great capacity, being alert, prompt, smart with her tongue, and independent in her manner. She is very popular with men, and goes out a good bit. She's going for 27. I have been out with her a good bit. Now I'm tired of her. Why? She's so utterly ignorant and old-fashioned, really, though she has been to college and has taught in London some years. I have enlightened her, and now she has no courage. She still judges by mid-Victorian standards, and covers herself with a woolly fluff of romance that the years will wear sickly. She refuses to see that a man is a male, that kisses are the merest preludes and anticipations, that love is largely a physical sympathy that is soon satisfied and satiated. She believes men worship their mistresses; she is all sham and superficial in her outlook, and I can't change her. She's frightened. Now I'm sick of her. She pretends to be very fond of me; she isn't really; even if she were, what do I care!'[38]

In other words, it was the old stumbling block. After this savage demolition work, he went on to say that over Christmas an old flame had burned up again, mad, passionate, hinted at 'fine, mad little scenes' and concluded proudly with a boast: 'She is coming to me for a weekend soon; we shall not stay here in Croydon, but in London.' It is a skilfully worded bit of wickedness, to compensate for the London collapse and set Blanche Jennings marvelling at the life he was leading now. To round it off, he throws in a final titbit about a new girl – Helen Corke – who 'interests' him. The black-haired girl who set fire to his Christmas was evidently Louie Burrows.

Helen Corke and her lover had been staying on the South Coast in the summer of 1909, not very far from Lawrence and his friends on the Isle of Wight. Lawrence did not know her very well at that time. Meeting her again in the autumn, he found her devastated by a personal experience which at first she was unable to talk about. Much later, she wrote about it in a novel, *Neutral Ground*: the heroine, Ellis, has an affair with a married music teacher, and goes away with him one summer for a holiday which is disastrous. The man returns home to his family in London and then commits suicide.

Lawrence saw that Helen Corke's state of shock was serious, and his attempts to bring her back to life resulted in her showing him some of her own writing. In response, he asked her to read a story of his own that was in progress. Lawrence appears in *Neutral Ground* as Derrick Hamilton, who asks Ellis to read a short story of his and be quite ruthless with any unnecessary sentences she finds there. When she baulks at showing him her own writing, saying she only writes for herself, Derrick corrects her with Lawrence-like severity: 'That is not true! You may imagine it is, but it is not. One wouldn't write at all if one hadn't, though subconsciously, the presupposition of a reader. You can despise your public as much as you like, but to deny it is absurd.'[39]

This produces the protest that she isn't writing a story, but setting down an experience: but she admits that she wants to do more than simply record it. 'There you are, then,' he cries, pouncing, 'you're an artist! You know that it's not just for you, it's for humanity.'

After hesitating for some time, she gave Lawrence her 'record' of the experience which had ended in tragedy and reduced her to a kind of emotional paralysis. Lawrence read her diary rapidly, absorbing the situation of the locked lovers to such an extent that within two months he was writing a tale of the two protagonists, Siegmund and Helena, who stay on the Isle of Wight and can only torment each other, until Siegmund tears himself away and goes home to kill himself. As well as the story gleaned from Helen Corke's notes, he had inserted himself into the narrative as a character named Cecil Byrne, who consoles Helena after the death of her lover, hurting her in spite of himself by his irony and involuntary bitterness. He knows she is caught in the past and not really aware of him at all.

The story was Wagnerian, turgid in the extreme, and as soon as Hueffer was shown the first half of it he shied away violently. The book was far too erotic; in fact, it was 'a rotten work of genius', and no doubt he was shrewd enough at the time to see that it was also, as he said later, 'a thoroughly bad hybrid book'. He recognised too that Lawrence had now got away from him, 'and the rest of his gift was outside my reach.' Lawrence at his best, he concluded later, was unique, 'rich and coloured and startling like a medieval manuscript.'[40]

As Lawrence set to work to transform her disconnected notes into what he called at first a long poem, under the title of *The Saga of Siegmund*, Helen Corke found out more about him. He worked in the evening, she discovered, after a day's hard teaching, and wrote rapidly, with extraordinary concentration. He was, or seemed to be, quite indifferent to his surroundings. He was capable of writing while the landlady's baby sat on his knee.

In some curious way, which Helen Corke only half understood, Lawrence suppressed his own personality, and even, she thought, tried to assume the identity of her dead lover in his efforts to make her turn back into life again. But she remembers at least one occasion when his normal self broke through savagely. They had gone into London together one Saturday in May to see some opera. They arrived too late. Lawrence wanted to take her on to a music-hall; he thought the carefree noise of it would do her good. Feeling jangly and irritable, she said no: he could go if he wished. She would make her own way home. He flew into a temper, pulled her into a bus and then off again when they reached Hyde Park. He gripped her arm and walked her up and down in the dense crowd, against the background of traffic. She almost hated him, he was so brutally insistent. Again she told him she was going home, her nerves couldn't bear to be exposed to such ugliness. She felt sick. Angry still, he marched in front of her to the station. Getting out at Croydon, after standing all the way in the crowded train, she burst into tears and ran off.

In more tolerant mood, as they were strolling one weekend through the Surrey hills, he said to her gravely, 'When I'm middle-aged, I shall probably be married and settled, and take my family to church every Sunday . . .'

Negotiating with Heinemann in the spring of 1910 for the publication of *The White Peacock*, he mentioned that he was at work on a second book: 'I have written about half of another novel. I wonder what you would think of it.'[41] In June, revolted by the whole business of getting books published, he wrote to Helen Corke expressing his loathing: ' . . . Heinemann was very nice; doesn't want me to alter anything; will publish in September or October, the best season; we have signed agreements concerning royalties, and I have agreed to give him the next novel. Will he want it? This transacting of literary business makes me sick. I have no faith in myself in the end, and I simply loathe writing. You do not know how repugnant to me was the sight of that 'Nethermere' MS. By the way, I have got to find a new title. I wish, from the bottom of my heart, the fates had not stigmatised me "writer". It is a sickening business . . .

'I assure you I am not weeping into my register. It is only that the literary world seems a particularly hateful yet powerful one. The literary element, like a disagreeable substratum under a fair country, spreads under every inch of life, sticking to the roots of the growing things. Ugh, this is hateful!'[42]

Already he was good at loathing. To his antiquarian and socialist friend, Willie Hopkin, he wrote to say, 'I seem to have lost touch altogether with the old "progressive" clique: in Croydon the Socialists are so stupid, and the Fabians so flat.'[43] In this same August letter, he passed on, as his reason for not turning up for 'tea and talk' with the Hopkins, the ominous news that his mother had been taken ill at Leicester. Probably because his mother had never in her life allowed herself to be ill, he told his friend without alarm that 'a tumour or something has developed in her abdomen.'[44] The doctor had said it was serious, but Lawrence was not yet convinced. Her will had always triumphed, in spite of doctors.

William and Sallie Hopkin had open-house gathering in their home at Eastwood on Sunday evenings. If Lawrence happened to be on vacation, or at Lynn Croft Road for the weekend, he would invariably call in. Sometimes he would meet distinguished visitors there. Always they had music, readings, and the talk flowed freely. Enid Hilton, the Hopkins' daughter, remembers a young Lawrence whose 'face was always pale and thin under a mop of blond-to-brown hair, and there were those deep, intense eyes. When talking vehemently he would, in those days, use his hands a great deal, and I remember one old trick of his of hitting the palm of the left hand violently with the doubled fist of the right hand.'[45]

A frequent visitor to these Sunday evening soirées of good talk and good food was Alice Dax, an intimate friend of Sallie Hopkin. She was small, blonde, a socialist and a suffragette. Her husband, Henry Dax, was a chemist in Eastwood. Alice Dax was exceptional enough, as far as Lawrence was concerned, to provide inspiration for the portrait of Clara Dawes in *Sons and Lovers*. Jessie Chambers says that it was Alice who introduced her and Lawrence to the journal *New Age*, edited by A. R. Orage. Her memory of Lawrence at a gathering of the Hopkin circle has him ensconced in front of the fire, 'full length on the hearthrug', reading out shyly but firmly an essay he had written, called 'Art and the Individual'.

Henry Dax's sole claim to local fame seems to have been his stock of leeches, which he kept wriggling horribly in a big glass jar near the door of his shop. The village children came to peer at them in horror and fascination, but some of the miners still wanted them for blood-letting remedies. Eventually his wife, who had already persuaded her husband to sell feminine goods in addition to his pills and medicines, got him to hide the leeches under the counter.

Alice Dax was an advanced woman who had daring ideas about dress, decor, and, of course, the role of women in a modern society. She was widely read. If she didn't look like Clara Dawes, she certainly sounded like her. Sallie Hopkin's daughter would go into Nottingham and hear Alice haranguing the ignorant from her platform; she helped to wave the flags, green, white and purple, and remembered the awesome visitors, the Pankhursts, Annie Kennie and others, the intense talk going on into the small hours at her home, and Eastwood's violent reactions to this formidable woman who insisted on taking things to extremes. Her home, which Lawrence visited, reflected her views. The knick-knacks, antimacassars and little mats beloved of the Victorians were swept away, and the resultant interior was spare, uncompromising, even a trifle harsh. Books were everywhere, but ranked neatly in rows.

It was this remarkable woman – who made the gentle Hopkin nervous, for all his sympathising in theory with the emancipation of women – whose influence was probably responsible for bringing Edward Carpenter's books to the attention of Lawrence. She lent Jessie *Love's Coming of Age,* and doubtless Jessie discussed it with Lawrence afterwards.

Edward Carpenter was a gentlemanly homosexual who wanted to simplify life, a man inclined to sainthood and asceticism, in full revolt against his Victorian upbringing. A close friend of Havelock Ellis, he was a pioneer in sexual frankness, an advocate of nudity and a devotee of Whitman. In practice this didn't seem to amount to much more than the wearing of open-necked shirts and rope sandals. He had been to India and Ceylon in 1890, absorbed 'pre-civilisation man' in his ancient surroundings, and then gone on to meet Whitman, that 'amazing representative of the same spirit in all its voluminous modern environment.' Two years previously he had abandoned his market-gardening activities at Millthorpe and become a writer and lecturer. His most successful book is probably *Love's Coming of Age* (1896). Irene Clephane wrote in 1935 that this book was, 'for the day in which it appeared, startlingly frank. It entered a world ashamed to discuss the intimacies of sex relationships, either verbally or in print. It went through one edition after another, and for twenty years after its appearance it revealed a new outlook on sex as something to be accepted and enjoyed instead of repressed and feared, to the impressionable young who read it.'[46]

Carpenter's connections with Fabian socialism led him to preach socialism in industrial centres such as Bradford, Halifax, Liverpool and Nottingham. He was in the forefront of the development of the intellectual side of the Labour movement in the North, attacking capitalism as a failure and calling for a complete reorganisation of resources and attitudes in the future. Included in this package was his set of proposals for sexual reform and for the fair treatment of homosexuals, which he elaborated guardedly in a cloud of mystical poeticising in his books. As a figure he was not so much exceptional as typical of the strange ferment of ideas bubbling richly in the Midlands and the North, 'in that time before the great strikes and the labour troubles, and after the worst of the Victorian era and the Boer War.'[47] He wrote a lush, weak, sentimental prose, and his poetry was Whitman-and-water. His influence failed to survive his time; yet in his day the centre he established at his home in Millthorpe in Derbyshire became a focal point for men and women from all classes of society, who mixed together with idealistic fervour for arguments and discussions. His teachings, though vapidly expressed, could well have sown seeds in a receptive Lawrence, who was ranging widely and voraciously through a whole sea of ideas at the time of his contact with Carpenter's books.

Did Lawrence and Carpenter ever meet? If they did, why is it that Lawrence made no reference to the fact? Emile Delavenay, in his book, *D. H. Lawrence and Edward Carpenter*, seeks to establish that they must have done. Sallie Hopkin's daughter went to Millthorpe several times with her parents, and once she and her father went alone – an exciting experience because her mother

157

wasn't there to steer her into another room while the daring talk flowed. Long afterwards, she said that 'unless memory fails, I think that Lawrence was with us on one of these visits. I have a mental picture of the two of them standing in the cottage doorway, under the arch of "climbers" over the door. The picture includes George [Carpenter's friend] in the background. Carpenter wore a beard but in those days Lawrence had only a moustache. Lawrence wore immensely high collars, stiff and awkward. He reminded me of the mad hatter in Alice . . .'[48]

The high collar and moustache, says Delavenay, establish the visit as being just after Lawrence left Eastwood for Croydon. And it was at about this time that the sexual initiation of Lawrence took place. A married woman in Eastwood, who must have been as uninhibited and 'high-minded' as Alice Dax, took him upstairs and 'gave Bert sex',[49] and then explained to Mrs Hopkin that if she hadn't done so, he would never have finished a poem he was struggling with. The whole incident is shrouded in mystery, but there seems little doubt that it happened, and during this period of his worst frustration.

Still under Hueffer's tutelage – although Hueffer had now been succeeded as editor by Austin Harrison – Lawrence published a short story, 'Goose Fair', in the February, 1910 issue of the *English Review*. It was his first short story in the magazine. Here without doubt was the same promise of great things to come which had caused Hueffer to snatch him out of the murky Midlands with such alacrity after reading, and buying, 'Odour of Chrysanthemums' though it did not appear until June, 1911. The goose girl of the new story's opening, instead of being an inert literary device, comes smouldering alive under the telling strokes of observation. 'She needed chiselling down, her contours were brutal. Perhaps it was weariness that hung her eyelids a little lower than was pleasant.' Even the picturesque geese are suddenly real, 'lifting their poor feet that had been dipped in tar for shoes, and trailing them along the cobblestones into the town.' But what makes the story flare up, like the torches of the fair, is the author's acute class-consciousness, together with his astonishing mobility and adroitness, and the delicacy with which he touches in, so lightly, the social and psychological subtleties of his characters. In this early story it is as if he is showing, within a few pages, in a kind of flourish of power, just what he can do. Here is a goose girl, eyelids a bit unpleasant, and then for complete contrast 'a girl of superior culture', who 'very carefully preserved the appearance of having come quite casually to the door.' Here too is Will, her lover, humiliated in front of her, shuffling his feet, but still 'they walked side by side as if they belonged to each other. . . . She was far from forgiving him, but she was still further from letting him go.' And he hangs his head like a boy before her, but with 'a genuine bitter contempt in the curl of his lip'.[50] The exactness hurts, it has the acrid taste on the tongue of the Midlands itself; yet because Lawrence is out to conquer and triumph, and provide a showcase for all his qualities at once, the self-consciousness between the lines makes the reader wriggle uncomfortably at times. But the mastery is everywhere in evidence in this accomplished early work.

In August, 1910, as his mother's fatal illness began, Lawrence tried to break finally with Jessie Chambers. He had written the first draft of *The Trespasser* at speed between Whitsun and August. Involved now with Helen Corke, and still keeping in touch with Louie Burrows, he arranged to stay with the Chambers family for a few days in August at their Mapperley farm on the outskirts of Nottingham. He had warned Jessie by letter not to try to hold him. As she had put up with years of his vacillating, she wasn't to know that this time he had steeled himself to 'finally and definitely part', as he wrote to Helen Corke. And this time he managed it, even though the actual words were forced from him by Jessie's refusal to compromise further. Instead of going to the farm, he met her at home and talked vaguely again about leaving her free to look elsewhere. Jessie, unable to take any more, said that it must either be complete union or a complete break. Lawrence shook his head and said it would have to be nothing.

They decided to stop writing to each other. After a week, he sent her a note: 'Do read Barrie's *Sentimental Tommy* and *Tommy and Grizel*. I've just had them out of the library here. They'll help you to understand how it is with me. I'm in exactly the same predicament.'[51] The first book concerns a boy who is unable to love any girl except his sister. In the second, Tommy's sister gets married, but Tommy's marriage to Grizel is a failure because he can't love his wife.

By October, he knew that nothing was going to save his mother. She was dying of cancer. He wrote to Heinemann to ask for an advance copy of *The White Peacock,* so that he could let her see it before she died. 'She looked at the outside, and then at the title-page, and then at me, with darkening eyes. And though she loved me so much, I think she doubted whether it could be much of a book, since no one more important had written it. . . . It was put aside, and I never wanted to see it again. She never saw it again.' His father's reaction was typical, and crushing:

'And what dun they gi'e thee for that, lad?'
'Fifty pounds, father.'
'Fifty pounds!' He was dumbfounded, and looked at me with shrewd eyes, as if I were a swindler. 'Fifty pounds! An' tha's niver done a day's hard work in thy life.'[52]

For Jessie, the ultimate cruelty was that Lawrence's release, when it came with his mother's death, shattered them both. It sundered him from the past, but what it delivered up to her, to claim if she dared, was a mere husk of a man. By the time he came to write *Sons and Lovers,* the story of his mother's dying had become for him the account of a bleeding, slowly-expiring love affair. It was terrible to read because the description of the death of the small, indomitable woman, unforgettably clenching her mouth in the lonely, stubborn way she had, implied in every word the destruction of her son. And in the aftermath, when Miriam came to comfort and to claim him, the sight of his thin, dark-clothed body strewn in the chair like a single stroke of life thrown down, defeated her. She stood before him, shuddering, her paralysis complete. She knew the moment for what it was, one of utter breakdown. 'She was not to have him, then!'[53]

In his poem, 'Last Words to Miriam', Lawrence sought to explain this catastrophe in terms of a lack of cruelty, which must have been irony indeed for Jessie. In the poem, she needed 'the last fine torture', but his nerve broke at the task. In these few lines he compressed the hate and misery of a whole series of failures with her, struggling desperately all through to extract some crumb of comfort, to justify his behaviour to himself in some way. He begins:

> Yours is the sullen sorrow,
>   The disgrace is also mine;
> Your love was intense and thorough,
> Mine was the love of a growing flower
>   For the sunshine.

But by the last verse he is no further on. The sense of bafflement and acute frustration will haunt him for years, as it will her. He is left with the disgrace, ashes in the mouth, the feeling of shame as he remembers her face:

> A mute, nearly beautiful thing
>   Is your face, that fills me with shame
> As I see it hardening;
> I should have been cruel enough to bring
>   You through the flame.

But the flame of sex, mingled always in his mind with the fire of his mother's reproof, meant nothing now, as he witnessed the rapid, dreadful burning of the cancer within her, shrivelling her to a cinder almost as he watched. 'She had a way of curling and lying on her side, like a child. . . . And he sat by the bedside, slowly, rhythmically stroking her brows with his finger-tips, stroking her eyes shut, soothing her, holding her fingers in his free hand.'[54]

Two weeks before her death, he wrote to Rachel Annand Taylor from Lynn Croft Road: 'My sister and I do all the nursing. My sister is only 22. I sit upstairs hours and hours till I wonder if ever it were true that I was at London. I seem to have died since, and that is an old life, dreamy.

'I will tell you. My mother was a clever, ironical delicately moulded woman of good, old burgher descent. She married below her. My father was dark, ruddy, with a fine laugh. He is a coal miner. He was one of the sanguine temperament, warm and hearty, but unstable: he lacked principle, as my mother would have said. He deceived her and lied to her. She despised him – he drank.

'Their marriage has been one carnal, bloody fight. I was born hating my father: as early as I can remember, I shivered with horror when he touched me. He was very bad before I was born.

'This has been a kind of bond between me and my mother. We have loved each other, almost with a husband and wife love, as well as filial and maternal. We knew each other by instinct. . . . We have been like one, so sensitive to each other that we never needed words. It has been rather terrible and has made me, in some respects, abnormal.'[55]

He was hacking out, like a miner, the first notes for his 'colliery novel'. He had the restraint now: there was nothing headlong about this remarkable confession. All he needed was the strength, the fire. But first he had to die, and drift, alone in the vast dark. To avoid this fate he began to plunge about in a kind of inner terror. In the same letter, he announced: 'I have been to Leicester today, I have met a girl who has always been warm for me – like a sunny happy day – and I've gone and asked her to marry me: in the train, quite unpremeditated, between Rothley and Quorn – she lives at Quorn. When I think of her I feel happy with a sort of warm radiation – she is big and dark and handsome.' It was Louie Burrows. He continued: 'Muriel [another name for Jessie] is the girl I have broken with. She loves me to madness, and demands the soul of me. I have been cruel to her, and wronged her, but I did not know.' He was sounding the themes, one after the other, of *Sons and Lovers*. He went on: 'Nobody can have the soul of me.

My mother has had it, and nobody can have it again.' And then back to Louie, who 'loves me, but it is a fine, warm, healthy, natural love – not like Jane Eyre, who is Muriel, but like, say, Rhoda Fleming or a commoner Anna Karenina. She will never plunge her hands through my blood and feel for my soul, and make me set my teeth and shiver and fight away.' And he ended, with a quiver of horror: 'Ugh – I have done well – and cruelly – tonight.'[56]

Jessie, when she heard of the engagement, told him he should not have implicated Louie in their affairs, since she was ignorant of the real position. It was the day before the funeral, and they were walking aimlessly through the lanes. Near the pits, he told her in cold arrogance that the words *should* and *ought* didn't concern him. It was a snub, not only to her, but to the world they had grown up in together. A miner went by, a billycan bulging in his jacket pocket, a red scarf round his neck. It was getting dark. Lawrence said, 'There you are, a story by Chekhov – "The Man in the Red Muffler".'[57]

Before they parted he gave her a poem he had just written, called 'The Virgin Mother', as well as two others on the same theme. He made no comment: there was no need. 'The Virgin Mother' ends with:

> Is the last word now uttered?
> Is the farewell said?
> Spare me the strength to leave you
> Now you are dead.
> I must go, but my soul lies helpless
> Beside your bed.

It was the first of many laments. Back again in Croydon, coping mechanically with his sullen classes, the grief broke from him in poem after poem. Everything brought her swirling back, and the bitter tears fell into the abyss of his loss. Again and again he sounded the note of remorse. In some inexplicable way he felt he had failed her too. He wrote in his poem, 'Sorrow':

> Why does the thin grey strand
> Floating up from the forgotten
> Cigarette between my fingers,
> Why does it trouble me?
>
> Ah, you will understand;
> When I carried my mother downstairs,
> A few times only, at the beginning
> Of her soft-foot malady,

162

I should find, for a reprimand
To my gaiety, a few long grey hairs
On the breast of my coat; and one by one
I watched them float up the dark chimney.

9

Collapse and Recovery

The new year (1911) began with the launching of his first book, *The White Peacock*. Looking back, he came to see it as his 'sick year'. Jessie Chambers called it 'perhaps the most arid year of his life'.[1] He was rudderless, isolated, he drove himself into work pointlessly, like a man getting drunk in order to blot out reality. He took a morbid delight in dwelling on the dark side of life, pressing authors like Maupassant and Baudelaire on Mrs Hopkin, urging her to read *Oedipus Rex*, 'the finest drama of *all* times. It is terrible in its accumulation – like a great big wave coming up – and then crash!'[2] The wave had mounted and crashed last December: now he was fighting to stay alive in the midst of it. Often he felt he was losing, drowning. And his engagement couldn't save him; he knew that only too well. Louie Burrows only rubbed her cheek against him like a big cat, as if that was sufficient. For real succour he turned to his sister, Ada, and, as always, to Jessie. 'I am not strong like you,' he wrote to her, early in the year. 'You can fight your battle and have done with it, but I *have* to run away, or I couldn't bear things. I have to fight a bit, and then run away, and fight a bit more. So I really do go on fighting, only it has to be at intervals . . . At times I am afflicted by a perversity amounting to minor insanity.'[3] But the fighting talk was mere bravado now, no more than a howling in the storm. The perversity, though, was only too real. In company with Helen Corke, he was by turns crass and derisive about the people round him, stamping them as types and refusing to acknowledge their individuality. He and Helen went to see Strauss's *Electra*, and when she resisted the savage mood of it he laughed at her, telling her the cruelty had to be accepted. If he went to a literary party, she was treated to a merciless caricature of it afterwards. In 1911, he said later, 'everything collapsed, save the mystery of death, and the haunting of death in life. I was twenty-five, and from the death of my mother, the world began to dissolve around me, beautiful, iridescent, but passing away substanceless. Till I almost dissolved away myself . . .'[4]

The White Peacock came out, and was called by the London journals 'feminine', 'cinematographic', and 'a modern study of nerves'. More than one reviewer commented that the book went nowhere and was puzzling, though there were plenty of compliments and some encouragement. Two critics actually thought the author was a woman. The most enthusiastic words, not surprisingly, were in the *English Review*: there was mention of 'flashes of genius', but this had to be qualified with complaints about the author's limitations, together with sly digs at his parochialism.

Reactions in America were along the same lines, though if anything more tepid. To Lawrence in his bitter, dark mood, it must have seemed that nothing whatever had changed for him. He still faced a full weekly syllabus of grinding school work, and now he could barely find the energy, let alone the inclination, to write. He wrote bleakly to Jessie in the spring: 'I've got a grinning skull-and-crossbones headache. The amount of energy required to live is – how many volts a second?'[5]

Desperate, he turned to painting some small pictures as presents for Ada and Louie. He hung on grimly, waiting for the Easter break. Even the impulse to write letters had left him – 'I have to fairly kick myself towards a sheet of notepaper' – and he had begun to talk of the necessity of living alone and keeping to oneself. The great religion now, the one salvation, was work. 'Heavens, how I do but slog! It gets the days over, at any rate.' Friends were of no help; in fact, they made things worse. 'I am as much alone with the friends here as if I were solitary. But how one gets used to a lonely life. I'm sure I've now no intimate friends here, and I don't want any. I am sufficient unto myself, and prefer to be left alone.'[6] Thus to Ada, at the beginning of March. At the end of the month he was still sunk in the same morbid isolation: 'In the things that matter one has to be alone in this life, or nearly alone. I never say anything to anybody but sometimes I can hardly swallow the meals. And there is no refuge from one's own thoughts day after day.' Pathetically, he tried to end this letter on a more cheerful note: 'It's no good writing in this strain, however. Bear a thing as if it weren't there – that's the only way. Folk hate you to be miserable, and to make them a bit miserable . . . School goes quietly. I often go to the boss for an evening.'[7]

He ground away at teaching, worked fitfully at his Eastwood novel, called at first 'Paul Morel', and struggled to keep going by sheer force of will. Nothing had changed, now that he was a published author – or had it? Surely it meant something, made some difference? With as much brightness as he could muster he tried to whip up some interest in himself for his new role, telling

Ada in a letter that George, his married brother, had written to say that the *Nottinghamshire Guardian* was hailing him as an author of note. In March *The White Peacock* was reprinted by Heinemann, though this meant little enough in terms of money. To Willie Hopkin at Eastwood he wrote: 'The book's going moderately, but the shekels are not deluging me yet. Alas, no!'[8] And in April he was telling Louie wryly not to 'worry about my fame: it'll certainly not trouble you too deeply during my lifetime, I think.'[9] He could see no possibility of abandoning the security of teaching; nor did he see how he could afford to marry. There was a ray of hope in June, however, when he received a letter from a publisher, Martin Secker, who asked whether he had sufficient short stories in hand for a volume. Lawrence perked up at once, rapping out a reply that was brisk and professional, with a spice of irony at the end to show them how aware he was – a kind of mock ingenuousness: 'My second novel is promised to William Heinemann. It is written, but I will not publish it, because it is erotic: in spite of which Mr Heinemann would take it. But I am afraid for my tender reputation. Therefore, I stick at my third book like a broody hen at her eggs, lest my chickens hatch out in a winter of public forgetfulness.' Nor did he forget the obligatory final note: 'Of course I am sensible to the honour you do me.'[10]

He had in fact been thrown into doubt and confusion over *The Trespasser*, first of all by Hueffer calling it 'a rotten work of genius', and, even more frighteningly, 'an erotic work'. If he was going to be confined to the classroom for years to come, and it looked like it, then the last thing he wanted was to be stuck with such a label. There was also his 'churchy' girl, Louie, whose parents already disapproved of him. Heinemann said they would bring it out, but he had found their attitude offensive. Later in the year he told his new friend, Edward Garnett, that a man named Atkinson at Heinemann's had told him, with 'a sweet smile', that after fifteen months he hadn't managed to finish the manuscript because of the handwriting, which was 'perfectly legible, but so *tedious*'.[11] That, said Lawrence tartly, was all the criticism the man ever offered.

From the start he was characteristically clear-minded about publishing and the way it should go. Of *The White Peacock*, he said to Jessie Chambers, its 'nurse', that the fate of it was really unimportant because publishers 'know that nearly anybody can write one novel, if he can write at all . . . A second novel's a step further. It's the third that counts, though. That's the *pons asinorum* of the novelist. If he can get over that ass's bridge he's a writer, he can go on.'[12]

When he sent Jessie the unfinished first draft of 'Paul Morel' in October, 1911, her reaction was unfavourable. She told him why in a letter, and he must have read her uncompromising words with care. He always took her opinions seriously. He had been labouring at this third book for a whole year now and had ground to a halt. Jessie thought the theme of it could make a superb story, but what he had produced was curiously dispirited, inert, contrived stuff. How could he have had such a failure of nerve, how could he have been so disastrously unfaithful to his material? The whole thing she found inadequate, and presumably she was now in the right mood of disenchantment with him and said she felt he ought to start all over again, this time 'with both hands earnestly'. His response was typical: he agreed with her completely and invited her collaboration. But before anything more could be done, he was ill.

The White Peacock, nursed into being by Jessie, was now in the world, circulating among her friends and acquaintances in the North, but giving her a good deal more pain than pleasure. It was like having salt rubbed in her wounds to be told by one of these friends that Louie Burrows was blithely handing round copies in her new role as the fiancée of 'the clever young author'. Many years later, Jessie wrote with careful dignity that the situation was 'literally too funny for words.'[13]

While she suffered this humiliation, Lawrence in Croydon tried vainly to convince himself that he was indeed an author. Increasingly morose, he sought solace in the company of his landlady's two children, larking in the garden with them, participating in the romp of bath night. 'I really think Mary is the prettiest youngster in England,' he wrote to Louie in April. 'And she's such a rascal. When she's bathed, her hair comes out in full blossom like a double flower, and her face is like apple blossom buds. She insists on sitting on my head, and kicking her heels against my neck. Then she sneaks off and drinks my beer.'[14] Watching the other child, Winnie, getting undressed, was another source of pleasure; 'When I turn round to look at her she croodles down to hide her dishabilly state. She always looks so funny in her combins: like, I say, a puffin or a penguin or a deacon in his shorts. She's very tubby.'[15] He liked to show Mary the stars and the moon. The stars, he told her, were like little girls going to bed with their candles.

Soon he put Mary into a short story, 'The Old Adam', faithfully setting the scene in a London suburban house with a high railway embankment behind, shutting in the garden above its row of poplars. 'And over the spires of the trees, high up, slid by the golden-lighted trains, with the soft movement of caterpillars and a hoarse, subtle noise.' As for the little girl, she was a 'bacchanal with her wild, dull-gold hair tossing about like a loose chaplet, her hazel eyes shining daringly, her small, spaced teeth glistening in little passions of laughter within her red, small mouth. The young man loved her. She was such a little bright wave of wilfulness, so abandoned to her impulses, so white and smooth as she lay at rest, so startling as she flashed her naked limbs about.' How simple and direct she made life seem, how he envied her! 'She sat on his knee in her high-waisted nightgown, eating her piece of bread-and-butter with savage little bites of resentment.'

To Ada at this time, who was undergoing the 'torment of religious unbelief' and doing her best to cope with a difficult father, a bewildered, cowed, shell of a man, he wrote exhorting her to remember that 'tragedy is beautiful also.' It was an attempt to convince himself, as much as her, of the truth of his new creed. He had sent Mrs Hopkin some books, great tragedies, and he wanted Ada to read them too. As for him, she mustn't judge him harshly if all she could see was mere 'rattle, like dead leaves blown along the road.' He had been doing some painting recently, all he was capable of. 'I've not written much. I find I can't.' Then he confessed to her that Louie would never take over the part of him which belonged to his sister. 'You and I – there are some things which we shall share, we alone, all our lives.' Louie knew nothing of the 'horror of life', she had no understanding of tragedy, her gawkishness irked him. It was her birthday on Monday and he had forgotten it, he told Ada consolingly. So 'don't be jealous of her.'[16]

Somehow he reached the summer, and went trailing back to Eastwood – though he loathed it there now – to spend some time with his other sister, Emily. Unable to stay anywhere long, he went with a party of local friends to North Wales, and then on to Louie Burrows and her parents, who lived now in Leicestershire. It didn't seem to matter where he was, but he had to keep moving. Then out of the blue came a letter from Edward Garnett, then editor at Duckworth's, and a little flurry of correspondence started up: his dormant literary aspirations revived. Hueffer had gone off to Germany and was soon to marry Violet Hunt: in any case, it was no good looking to him now for support. He had left the *English Review*, and Lawrence's second novel wasn't to his liking. Garnett wrote to ask if Lawrence had stories he could place with an American magazine with whom he was connected. By the autumn, Lawrence had cast him in the role of personal benefactor, earnestly seeking his advice on his literary future. Edward Garnett and his family lived near Edenbridge in Kent. After visiting him there, Lawrence wrote excitedly to Ada: 'I had such a ripping time at Garnett's. The Cearne is a big cottage built in the 15th century style, and you'd think it was a fine old farmhouse. Everything old, thick blue earthenware, stone jugs for the beer, a great wood fire in the open hearth in the inglenook and all buried in the middle of a wood, hard to find. I like Garnett ever so much.'[17] What a contrast this was to the countryside he knew, sown with pits and threaded with smoke and the throb of engines, desecrated with miners' dwellings and their squalid, poultry-run backyards, ash-tips, brawling kids, the hooters sounding from the ironworks, the colliery blowers and their whirring headstocks, the miners calling to each other as they gathered in gangs and went tramping off to work. The Cearne could have been on another planet. He sat there and basked gratefully, yet with pride. He might have been born to it. He went as often as he could.

Garnett, a friend of Hueffer's, was influential – and as generous with his influence and advice as Hueffer had been. At The Cearne, Lawrence was introduced to Scott James of the *Daily News*, and Garnett saw to it that his poems were given a showing in the *Nation*. Until Garnett's intervention, two stories in the *English Review* were all he had managed to place in journals this year. It was cheering, even though he was writing little that was new. From time to time he tussled away at 'Paul Morel', but it gave him no satisfaction, coming as it did in 'inchoate bits', like the first novel. He told nobody about it. He did tell Garnett though about the 'erotic' manuscript which Heinemann still hung on to, and his new friend asked to see it in his capacity as editor for Duckworth. It took Lawrence until the end of November to 'extort' the novel from Heinemann and send it to The Cearne, and by then he was ill.

7th November, 1911 – the date is a turning point. According to the school records, he did no more teaching after that date, complaining that he was feeling rotten and blaming it on the dry heat in the classrooms. Yet he wrote fairly brightly a week later to Louie, mentioning that he had been to Covent Garden to hear Wagner, and was due to go to spend the weekend again with Edward Garnett in Kent. What should they do about Christmas? he asked her.

Returning to Croydon from the Garnetts, he got wet as he stood around waiting for trains on cold platforms. His chill rapidly became pneumonia. Philip Smith, his headmaster, said Lawrence had been in poor health and under obvious strain for the whole of that year. Alarmed, the Joneses informed his relatives, and Ada hurried down from Eastwood to nurse him. On 4th

December she was able to report to Louie that her seriously ill brother could now read his own letters, but was still unable to sit up. He was going to have an egg and toast for dinner, she added. Lawrence scrawled a note on the bottom of this letter, thanking Louie for the roses she had sent him. They were still alive. And so was he: but so frailly. It was a bitter repetition of his illness in youth, following the death of Ernest. The flowers, as always, beckoned to him poignantly and with intolerable freshness from the land of the living.

He hated to lie there, the invalid, receiving visitors in his bedroom, but he had no choice. Edward Garnett came to see him. 'Take the Addiscombe car at East Croydon,' wrote Lawrence from his bed, 'and come to the terminus, then you are here.'[18] After his visit he sent a parcel of books, and then a cheque, which Lawrence insisted must be a loan. Thanking him, he told Garnett, on 17th December, that he was at last sitting up to tea, but didn't like it much: it made him feel 'like the seated statues of kings in Egypt.'[19] He went on to say, ominously, that his doctor had warned him against any more teaching if he wanted to avoid being consumptive. All very well, but how then could he live? Instead of sending in his notice, he decided to ask for long leave of absence, so that 'I can go back if I get broke.'

Lying in bed hour after hour, he wondered impatiently if Garnett had read his second novel, confessing in the same letter that he winced away from it now, just as he imagined Richard Jefferies must have shrank from his too emotional 'The Story of My Heart'.

He lay chafing, but had to wait until the end of December before he could escape from his bedroom and go hobbling about outside. His left leg bothered him.

At the beginning of the new year (1912) he was installed in a boarding house in Bournemouth for his convalescence. Before that, he had been visited, over the Christmas holidays, by Louie Burrows, by Jessie Chambers, who stayed with Helen Corke in London, and by his sister, Emily. When Jessie called to see him, he was 'sitting by the fire in his bedroom, grievously thin, but yet somehow so vital.' She had been writing down the details of their early days, for him to use in 'Paul Morel', when she heard how ill he was. Then came a scrap of paper with a message in pencil saying, 'Did I frighten you at all? I'm sorry. Never mind, I'm soon going to be all right.' It was at times like these, as his life fluttered, sank down, then spurted up bravely like a candle in the wind, that her sorely tested love for him returned. And she had never taken his engagement to Louie seriously, much as it had wounded her.

Travelling once with Lawrence's brother, George, she had asked him if he thought Lawrence and Louie would soon marry. George looked at her in amazement and said he *knew* they wouldn't. 'Why, how d'you suppose he let me know about his engagement?' he went on scornfully. 'On a blooming postcard.'[20]

At Compton House, Bournemouth, Lawrence was soon on the mend. The inmates, ranging between forty-five and eighty, interested him. 'A fellow is giving physical demonstrations, very weird, to a little Finnish chap.'[21] He reacted favourably at first to Bournemouth, seeing it as a big, interesting town set among pine trees, the sandstone cliffs looking fine with the sun on them. The wintry sea had waves rolling in majestically and smashing and leaping all over the front. Interesting! The sea fascinated him, it had such moods, he could watch it forever: it was like milk, then steel, then 'like silvery grey silk – lovely.'

But soon it disgusted him. It was a good sign; his old impatience and exasperation and his eagerness to live had returned. 'I advise you', he lectured Jessie in a letter, 'never to come here for a holiday. The place exists for the sick. They hide the fact as far as possible, but it's like a huge hospital. At every turn you come across invalids being pushed and pulled along. Quite a nice place of course, everything arranged for the comfort of the invalid, sunny sheltered corners and the like, but pah – I shall be glad when I get away.'[22]

Edward Garnett had reacted favourably to *The Trespasser*, and now Lawrence was eager to rewrite it. He thought it needed 'wringing out', and appealed to Garnett for another title – at present it was still called 'The Saga of Siegmund'. Did he think 'Trespassers in Cythera' would do? On 19th January he had done the first 135 pages of a new version, moving with extraordinary speed for a convalescent whose energy was still at a low ebb. He spoke of the book with a new detachment, saying frankly that he didn't like it particularly. Nevertheless, it had a certain inevitability in the telling, a development, and he thought it maintained the standard he had set for himself in *The White Peacock*. What he disliked most of all was its stickiness: it was too 'florid'. And in fact, none of his writing pleased him at the moment. 'Harrison is putting in next month's *English* a story ['Second Best'] I do not care for. Altogether, I am out of sorts in my literary self just now.'[23]

He was deriving a good deal more pleasure from the people around him, and from the fact that his legs were getting fatter. Apart from the three big meals a day at the house, he had tea when he went into the town. 'It is the fashion here. The house tea is a bit dreary, and there are some lovely restaurants.'[24] In the house, besides the main meals, there were always quantities of butter and toast and biscuits to be consumed.

As well as writing steadily at the new *Trespasser*, his thoughts were leaping ahead now to the spring. He had an aunt whose sister-in-law, Hannah Krenkow, lived in Germany. Hannah had invited him, and he thought he would go in April or May. He was toying with the idea of landing a post as *Lektor* in a German university, to improve his knowledge of German and French. This would stand him in good stead for secondary teaching if his literary career foundered, as it might.

There was no doubt that the communal nature of his new life at Compton House suited him. The others were nice to him and deferred to him as an author, and it was good to luxuriate, if only temporarily, with no burdensome responsibilities, no timetables apart from meals, and plenty of distractions. Reporting on these distractions to Louie, he told her about Scheinen, the 'little fellow from Finland' who particularly amused him. It was the man's twenty-first birthday, with 'a sort of bun fight' in the recreation room to celebrate. Some of the details of his activities Lawrence thought it wise to withhold from Louie, for obvious reasons. But he poured them out without restraint when writing to his old colleague, Mac – A. W. McLeod – in Croydon. The little Finn was playing billiards with an elderly boarder from South Africa as Lawrence wrote his letter, so that 'I live in constant dread of a cue in my ear and a ball in my eye'. The night before, Lawrence had been drinking Scotch with a man named Scriven 'till the small hours'. The old ladies of the place mothered him and the younger ones continued to 'sister' him. Then followed an account Louie would have surely found disagreeable: 'There was one chap here last week, with whom I had fine sport. He [Jenkinson] was mad with his wife on Friday, so he went out with me to Poole Harbour. There he went on the razzle. I had a fiendish time. He kept it up when we got back here: walked away with a baby in a pram in Christchurch Road – tried to board and drive off with a private motor car – nearly had a fight in the Central Hotel, and got us turned out. We were four, arm in arm, swaying up the main street here, people dodging out of the way like hares. It was hot. In the end, I had to throw all the drinks they kept forcing on me to the floor, lest I got as drunk as they. Then, when at last, after superhuman struggles, I got him home . . . *I* – *I* had to stand the racket from Mrs Jenkinson, whom I like, who is young and pretty and has travelled a good bit – and who sits at my table.'[25]

172

It is an account by a man suddenly liberated, and delighted in a body that was getting steadily better every day. It evidently gave him mischievous pleasure to present this 'fiendish' picture of riotous living to the quiet and amiable McLeod, and perhaps rouse him to envy. Although Lawrence could never penetrate the other's reserve, he wrote some of his most expansive letters to Mac, and was always urging him to make the effort to visit him. He was obviously fond of him, confided in him repeatedly, and regarded him as his best friend in Croydon. The portrait of him – as Mr McWhirter – in *The Trespasser* is an affectionate one.

With his friend Jenkinson departed from Compton House, life became tame again for Lawrence. He put on more weight. Garnett kept him fed with letters and books, and was thanked graciously for his trouble. Already Lawrence had 180 pages of *The Trespasser* completed. On 21st January he sent them on for Garnett's inspection. He hoped the writing was now 'knitted firm', though he was basically unsatisfied, and would remain so. The thing was just too literary. Worse, it exposed his naked feelings, and that was why he loathed the book, because 'it will betray me to a parcel of fools'. Surely Stendhal must have squirmed at the thought of his *Le Rouge et le Noir* being published? Lawrence was here protesting, not for the first time, at the inevitable crucifixion every personal writer must endure when he puts his work on public show. But what was the alternative?

Pleasant though his life was, he hungered more and more for news from the outside world. He even had spasms of nostalgia for Davidson Road School. True, he was getting letters from the headmaster, from Agnes Mason and his old friend, McLeod, but, curse them, they told him so little, they were such cagey, 'stumpy' correspondents! He hadn't finally decided yet about leaving Davidson for good. It was a gamble. All depended on his literary luck. But he had had enough of Bournemouth now. By the end of January he would have the rest of *The Trespasser* done, if he kept up his present pace and the weather stayed dirty. Garnett's suggestion of a May publication by Duckworth gave him all the inclination he needed. He decided to make straight for Edenbridge and stay a day or two, so that he and Garnett could go over the manuscript together. Then he would go on to his married sister at Queen's Square, Eastwood, for a while. There were plenty of exciting things in store for him, and he was gleeful at the thought of turning his back on the hated classroom, perhaps for good. Yet he fell back into nameless misery from time to time, for no apparent reason. He didn't know what it was. 'It is very queer,' he wrote to Garnett on the eve of his departure from

Bournemouth. 'But my dreams make conclusions for me. They decide things finally. I dream a decision . . . It is a horrid feeling, not to be able to escape from one's own – what? – self-daemon – fate, or something.'[26]

To Helen Corke, who had been expressing some concern at the way her intimate experiences were being pressed into the service of art, he wrote a letter which began with words of reassurance and ended in squawks of exasperation and reproof. She had read the first draft of his saga and been satisfied. What alterations was he making now? He reminded her sternly in the name of art that he was not falsifying her 'truth', he was erecting a work of fiction on a frame of actual experience. 'It is my presentation, and therefore necessarily false sometimes to your view. The necessity is not that our two views should coincide, but that the work should be a work of art.' This was satisfactorily crushing and austere, but he must have read her forebodings again and found hints of an attack on his character. He flew at her: 'How am I one thing today, and another tomorrow? It is an absurdity . . . You never believe that I have any real unity of character.' If this was her charge, it was unpleasantly reminiscent of the kind of thing Jessie would say. He was of course aware that the two women were now good friends and saw each other frequently, with ample opportunity for comparing notes. He lashed around a bit more, then simmered down and managed to end philosophically: 'An illness changed me a good deal – like winter on the face of the earth: but that does not mean I am shook about like a kaleidoscope.'[27]

This was to be virtually the last word in their friendship, which had been stormy almost from the start. He met her at Victoria Station, en route to the Garnetts. She travelled part of the way with him and they parted amicably, having said nothing vital to each other. It was their final meeting.

After conferring with Garnett, Lawrence went on to Eastwood. He had given up his Croydon digs now. Queen's Square would be his address for the next three months, but in truth he had no home. What a mixture of relief and trepidation he must have felt at this reunion on his native ground. Was he on the threshold of something totally new, or was it all a dreadful falling back, a retrograde step? At any rate, he had no choice: for the moment, he literally had nowhere else to go. He was homeless. He sought out Jessie again, taking her a box of chocolates as a peace offering. While at the Garnetts he had written a brief letter to Louie breaking off his engagement: Jessie was right. His excuse to Louie was that the doctors had advised him against marriage. Also, it looked as if he wouldn't be able to teach any more, so his prospects were hopeless. He stumbled on for a few more lines, then blurted it out, the truth: 'I am afraid we are not well suited . . . It's a miserable business, and the fault is all mine.'[28]

So at least he was free to see Jessie again. He handed over his chocolates almost mutely. She looked at him, surprised. She felt her cold feelings of sorrow and regret. How strange it all was! She asked him in, she picked up her knitting. 'There's nothing I admire like industry,' Lawrence said sarcastically.[29]

He told her he planned to go to Cologne in the spring, and probably he would live abroad for a year. He spoke without conviction. She watched him gravely, noticing his restlessness, his air of loneliness. To her, he was just 'not well adapted to fit into the rather grim Midlands life now that he had no mother to make a home for him. In company he would maintain his jaunty exterior, but under the surface was a hopelessness hardly to be distinguished from despair. He seemed like a man with a broken mainspring.'

She gave him the notes she had written for 'Paul Morel', to use as he thought fit. He sat on for a while, and she looked at him with helpless pity, thinking: 'It was the familiar spectacle; Lawrence in the grip of forces that pulled him with equal power in opposite directions.'[30]

Lawrence was finding Garnett altogether more solid and dependable than Hueffer had been. Their friendship rapidly burgeoned. Nevertheless, he didn't forget that it was Hueffer who had brought him to the attention of the other man. He made a quick raid on London and renewed contact with his first mentor, who had come back from Germany with Violet Hunt. Back in Eastwood again, he wrote Garnett a description of the encounter that was all hard brilliance, yet bubbling with fun and malice. Hueffer now was 'very fat', and Lawrence decided that this was Violet Hunt's doing. 'Do you know,' he began innocently, 'I rather like her – she's such a real assassin. I evoked the memory of various friends that were her friends twelve months ago. Behold, she nicely showed me the effigies of these folk in her heart, each of their blemishes marked with a red asterisk like a dagger hole. I saluted her, she did the business so artistically: there was no loathsome gore spilt over the murdered friends.' Then he tempered the wickedness with some affection: 'She looked old, yet she was gay – she was gay, she laughed, she bent and fluttered in the wind of joy. She coquetted and played beautifully with Hueffer: she loves him distractedly – she was charming, and I loved her. But my God, she looked old.' Why? 'Perhaps because she

wore – she was going to some afternoon affair of swell suffraget-
tes – a gaudy witch-cap stitched with beads of scarlet and a delicate
ravel of green and blue. It was a cap like a flat, square bag . . .' And
he provided a sketch of it for good measure, adding that 'I think
Fordy liked it – but was rather scared. He feels, poor fish, the
hooks are through his gills this time – and they *are*.'[31]

The sudden confidence, the satirical stance, were significant:
Lawrence was a professional writer now, the equal of these
privileged members of metropolitan literary life. It was important to let someone like Garnett know this. In his letter he scaled
them down by finding them amusing, and at the same time
distanced himself. He knew, none better, that there was no real
love between them and him. They were too discreet to admit that
they didn't like him much, but it was true: as Hueffer admitted
later, 'He remained too disturbing even when I got to know him
well.' And he was still on his guard, still smarting from the off-
hand treatment meted out by Heinemann and Co. 'Publishing
people are more sickly than lepers,' he told Garnet. 'I am thankful
to be out of London.'[32] Sickly or not, he had to deal with them,
come to terms with them. He had more or less decided to finish
with teaching and take his chance. Heinemann had just paid his
royalty account of £49 15 10, which represented his total capital.
The seven guineas' loan he had had from Garnett would have to
remain unpaid for the moment, because 'I've got to pay the
doctor and my sister and so on. But I'll square up as soon as I
can.'[33]

He had fallen between two worlds. Eastwood depressed him
now, with its strike ballots and relief tickets, its men and women
bitterly divided against each other. It made him feel physically ill.
The men 'seem such big, helpless, hopeless children, and the
women are impersonal – little atlases under a load that they know
will crush them out at last, but it doesn't matter.'[34]

He may have thought he had finished with Louie Burrows, too,
but she still clung. He took her to an art exhibition at Nottingham
Castle and she was rather haughty, no doubt in revenge for his
unpardonable behaviour. 'She had decided beforehand that she
had made herself too cheap to me, therefore she thought she
would become all at once expensive and desirable.' She insisted
on goggling unashamedly at the paintings and sculptures of
'naked men' until poor Lawrence wanted to sink out of sight.
Outside, he stood with her at the parapet looking over the town,
and thanked God she was being offensive to him. That made it
easier to finish. In the café over tea and toast she was still impossible. She 'sarked' him, she cried, then laughed, then cried again,

while he sat there coolly with 'a sort of cloud over my mind'.[35] She went off in an angry huff, to his great relief.

He seldom went to the farm now to see Jessie, preferring to meet her at her married sister's cottage. But he did turn up one Sunday. Jessie's mother welcomed him as warmly as ever, but the father's attitude had changed subtly. As if anticipating this, Lawrence had adopted a jaunty manner, which made things worse. He had always loved talking to the quiet farmer who had looked on him as one of his own family. It had been a wordless, palpable affection. Now it was gone.

As for him and Jessie, they were together again, but she knew perfectly well that 'his mother's ban was more powerful now than in her lifetime.' This may have been a simplification. Lawrence's desire to continue his endless post-mortem on their affair seemed now to be the only bond between them. Leaving the farm that Sunday, he said to her when they were alone that she never thought about sex 'except in relation to beauty or passion.'[36] It was the old reproach, and there was no answer to it.

His short story of this period, 'The Old Adam', is strung unbearably tight with the tensions of unsatisfied sex. A young man and his landlady sit in a room in a London suburb, enduring a thunderstorm. The suspense crackles with the dangerous lightening of suppressed sexuality. Violence hangs in the air. The young man, 'half suffocated by the beating of the heart', feels it 'thud to a crisis'. The woman has just lowered her baby for him to kiss the child goodnight, knowing as she does so that 'he was aware of her heavy woman's breasts approaching down to him.' The thundery atmosphere of the narrative grows more and more oppressive, until the young author bursts suddenly into the open with the naïve blurting confession that his hero is twenty-seven and yet 'quite chaste. Being highly civilised, he prized women for their intuition, and because of the delicacy with which he could transfer to them his thoughts and feelings, without cumbrous argument. From this to a state of passion he could only proceed by fine gradations, and such a procedure he had never begun.'

Sex was a crucifixion. Its awful complexities occupied his thoughts obsessively, in a kind of loathing. As a young man of innate puritanism who had been loved to excess by his mother, he needed help just as desperately as the spiritualised girls and women of his day. Yet he was attractive to women, they felt his appreciation of them and responded: he could not avoid entanglements. It was disastrous. Books like Havelock Ellis' *Studies in the Psychology of Sex* and Wells' *Ann Veronica*, just out, were no good: the emphasis was all wrong somehow. Neither could he help, with

177

his quivering soul that was so like a woman's, putting himself in the girl's place when he tried to make love to her, identifying with her feelings of dread and revulsion. These endlessly torturing frustrations filled his poems and stories and haunted page after page of *The Trespasser* and *Sons and Lovers*. After one agonising attempt at lovemaking in *The Trespasser*, Helena's sobbing 'was like the chattering of dry leaves. She grew frantic to be free. Stifled in that prison any longer, she would choke and go mad. His coat chafed her face; as she struggled she could see the strong working of his throat. She fought against him; she struggled in panic to be free.' Afterwards, afraid that she might have lost him, she tried to make amends. 'She gave a little sob, pressed her face into his chest, wishing she had helped it. Then, with Madonna love, she clasped his head upon her shoulder, covering her hands over his hair. Twice she kissed him softly in the nape of the neck, with fond, reassuring kisses.'[37]

Duckworth had *The Trespasser* under consideration now. Taking their continuing silence as a bad sign, Lawrence dug away with renewed determination at his Eastwood novel. It was going well, and he wanted to finish it before he went to Germany. He concentrated all his powers. He would stand or fall by this book, instead of wavering in the balance as he had done before. As he worked, he passed the completed sheets of manuscript over to Jessie. It was like *The White Peacock* days again, except for the furious pace.

Writing this third novel must have thrown him afresh into all the sensations of his boyhood and youth. He was there, on site, as if he had never left. Perhaps it was the force of these recreated emotions which impelled him to go out and immerse himself in the local life from time to time. He wrote chatty letters to Garnett, projecting himself as a denizen of the rip-roaring Midlands scene, emphasising the crude vitality 'up here', as though he wanted to swagger a bit before the cloistered man of letters: it was the emergence of the other Lawrence, the one Jessie had observed, who would jauntily present a tough exterior. He reported: 'My sister and I were at a bit of a dance last night at Jacksdale – mining village four miles out. It was most howling good fun. My sister found me kissing one of her friends goodbye – such a ripping little girl – and we were kissing like nuts – enter my sister – great shocks all round, and much indignation. But – life is awfully fast down here.'[38] In his next letter he dropped the flirtatious image and concentrated on the man's world: 'Here, in this ugly hell, the men are *most* happy. They sing, they drink, they rejoice in the land. There were more "drunks" run-in from the Crown and the

Drum here last weekend than ever since Shirebrook was Shirebrook. Yesterday I was in Worksop. It is simply snyed with pals. Every blessed place was full of men, in the larkiest of spirits. I went in the Golden Crown and a couple of other places. They were betting like steam on skittles – the "seconds" had capfuls of money.'[39]

By now he was getting in a tangle between Heinemann and Duckworth: the latter now definitely wanted *The Trespasser*. Also there was Martin Secker, hovering interestedly for stories. Lawrence asked Garnett what he should do. Would he like to see the manuscript of the Eastwood novel before he sent it to Heinemann? He was past the halfway mark now. He asked to be remembered kindly to the cook-housemaid, Miss Whale, who had thought him rather wicked when he was last at The Cearne. He told Garnett to tell her that he was only wicked on the surface: 'The inside is pure white sugar.' This may have been the occasion when Garnett plied him with wine 'to make me talk, but I always knew what I was saying. He thinks I told him everything, but I didn't. I told him nearly everything.'[40]

At the end of March he went to Leek, on the Staffordshire–Derbyshire border, to stay for a week with George Neville, his old schoolteacher friend of the Pagan days. Neville had a post at the rural school, so that Lawrence was left during the day to potter about by himself. He liked the country, its grey stone, dark green fields and steep hills, finding it 'Switzerlandish'. In the evenings they hiked around and talked. Neville expressed some reservations about the wisdom of using thinly disguised incidents from real life in books. This was too near the bone for Lawrence, and long afterwards his friend remembered the fury of his reply. 'You always were such a sentimental devil – more's the pity,' Lawrence told him. 'Think of the stories you could write if only you would let yourself go. Don't you see that we must each of us be prepared to take the responsibility for our own actions? How can anyone complain so long as the narrator tells the truth? And suppose their puny feelings are hurt, or what is probably nearer the mark, they get a pain in their pride, what does it matter that their lesson is given to the world and they shall have taught others to avoid the mistakes they made?'[41]

10

Frieda

In the spring of 1912 Jessie Chambers had an experience that she would remember for the rest of her life. Lawrence had been passing the manuscript sheets of 'Paul Morel' over to her as he worked on 'at a white heat of concentration'. At first she was full of admiration for the family scenes, the loving exactness, the glow of inner warmth. Everything seemed raised up, reconciled, restored in mystery and truth, from the mother spitting on her iron to the miner, his face smeared with sweat and dirt, unlacing his great boots: nothing was too insignificant. The concern for everyday things and the insight into the lives of the working people thrilled her deeply: the interpretation was so faithful, yet so brilliant.

Then she came to the Miriam theme, clutching at her in person, whirling her into the vortex of a conflict which she saw as 'fundamentally a terrific fight for a bursting of the tension.'[1] The climax was reached for her with the defeat of the girl and the subsequent glorification of the mother. As she read on, in growing dismay, the words of Lawrence's letter from Croydon the previous spring must have sunk into her as if she had read them yesterday: 'You say you died a death of me, but the death you died of me I must have died also, or you wouldn't have gone on caring about me . . . They tore me from you, the love of my life . . . It was the slaughter of the foetus in the womb.'[2] Now she was being made to live through that slaughter all over again, relive that anguish – and then asked for her opinion! How could he do such a thing? Did he actually know what he was doing? It was unbelievable, utterly brutal. How could he continue to talk blithely of a bond between them? She felt wounded beyond measure. She shrank from contact with him. As if sensing this, he stopped calling to see her and sent the remainder of the manuscript through the post. He dropped her a note to say that he would like to know what she thought of the book and would call at her sister's place in Shirebrook on his way back from George Neville.

On the Sunday of his arrival he was delayed by slow trains and bad connections, and appeared at twilight, lugging a heavy suit-case and looking pale with exhaustion. Over tea he recovered a little, telling stories about his adventures with some 'theatricals' he had met on the train. George Neville had a baby son, he went on acidly. In the savage mood he was in, paterfamilias was as good a convention as any to swipe at. Mary Holbrook and her husband listened patiently as he declared that the family man was nothing but a cart-horse dragging its load through life, 'and I'm not going to be a cart-horse.'³

Bill Holbrook needled him gently. They all knew Bert Law-rence and what a rake he was! Lawrence shook his head, lapsing into comic dialect to deny it.

He went home to Eastwood and came again next day, knowing Jessie would still be there. They went for a walk, turning into the fields near Greasley Church where he had helped Mr Chambers and his sons at harvest times so often in the past. Lawrence had seen young miners coming home with bunches of violets, so he watched the bottoms of the hedges as they walked, to see if he could spot any. He asked her, suddenly shy and wistful, if she had anything to say about his book. All she could answer was that her notes were in the parcel with the manuscript. He said no more. After she had gone, he questioned her sister closely, wanting to know if Jessie was angry with him.

Jessie saw him on another two occasions, both by chance: once at the Midland Station in Nottingham, and once more at the Holbrooks. Her father had taken her to her sister's in the trap. Lawrence happened to be staying there for the weekend. He had nothing to say. He sat on the garden wall outside the cottage and stared at the ground, as if he only had to concentrate hard enough for some answer to spring out of it. There was an atmos-phere of strain. Jessie was not sorry to leave. As a gesture of friendship, Lawrence climbed into the trap and went part of the way home with her and her father. She felt he was steeling himself to suffer her father's changed attitude towards him, chattering 'with a forced brightness' about his forthcoming trip to Germany. They climbed Watnall Hill and he got down to shake hands with them almost formally. Turning to look at him for the last time as they rolled away, she saw him lift his hat in the air and wave goodbye. The passionate friendship with the sad girl he called his 'Lady of Shalott' was over.

Back again at the cottage with his friends, he seemed strangely abstracted. The Holbrooks were used to these swift changes of mood, so they left him alone. He liked them for that. Mary was sympathetic – she had her sister's quick intelligence – and Bill

Holbrook's calm, amiable nature created an atmosphere in which Lawrence could be himself. He carved the joint for them, and afterwards they took some rugs and sprawled out in the field. Then Lawrence startled them by saying that what he liked was a *gushing* woman. He had met Frieda Weekley.

One day in early April, Lawrence had called on his old professor of French at his home in Victoria Crescent, Nottingham. He had got on reasonably well with Professor Weekley at University: now he remembered that Weekley had connections in Germany, having lectured at Freiberg. Also, he had a German wife. Lawrence's relatives in Cologne were still pressing him to come: it seemed a good idea to ask Professor Weekley's advice on the possibility of a German lectureship before he went out there. Professor Weekley invited him to lunch.

It was a fresh spring day, warm enough for the French windows to be open and the curtains fluttering. The three children, two girls and a boy, were outside playing on the lawn. The house in Mapperley was elegant. Lawrence knew the area quite well: his brother George lived not far away, and so did the Chambers family on their Arno Vale farm.

As soon as Frieda Weekley set eyes on Lawrence she was intrigued. He was slight and quick, touchingly sincere, yet something about him eluded her. 'What kind of bird was this?'⁴ she thought to herself. Then he amazed her by plunging, without preliminaries, into an attack on women. For years he had worn himself out in struggles with them, trying to know them. Now he'd had enough, he was finished. To hear this kind of harangue from a total stranger, and before they had even gone in to lunch, was disturbing. Frieda laughed: but in some uncanny fashion she felt they understood each other at once. She could have clapped her hands with pleasure at his intensity – it was so unexpected in an Englishman.

There was nothing ordinary about her either. With all her indolence, she seemed to blaze with life. Her voice was husky, glamorously accented. She had a Continental sophistication, yet she could be almost childishly direct. Physically she was most impressive, with her strong body and shoulders and a regal way of holding herself. Her high cheekbones and tawny lioness eyes, green flecked with yellow, fairly sparked vitality. Lawrence forgot all about his mission: he couldn't take his eyes off her. Tearing himself away that night, he walked all the way home to Eastwood, his thoughts in chaos. Soon an ecstatic little note came from him: 'You are the most wonderful woman in all England.' She wrote back caustically to ask him if he knew all the others.

*

Frieda, as the daughter of a German aristocrat, was automatically a baroness. The von Richthofens were a Silesian family who had been impoverished by a series of economic disasters. Because of this, Frieda was not an heiress, which meant that she was unable to marry one of the dashing young officers who came courting. Her home near Metz, where her father had a civil service post, held many memories of parties: during one of them, to celebrate the award of the Iron Cross to the baron in the Franco-Prussian war of 1870, soldiers of her father's old regiment filled the house, carrying him around on their shoulders. From that moment onwards, Frieda saw him in a glow of pride as a national hero.

All his children were girls. Frieda and the youngest, Johanna, grew up together and were inseparable. Often the two sisters were invited into the barracks of the garrison town close by.

One young soldier who fell in love with Frieda was Ensign Kurt von Richthofen, a distant cousin. His head was as sleek as a seal's and his figure so slim that his sword seemed about to slip over his hips. He was twenty-one. Frieda, fresh from her finishing school in the Black Forest, was about to spend a year in Berlin at her uncle's grand house in the Tiergarten. Now there was Kurt, spending all his free Sundays at her home and throwing her into a state of bliss, with his gentle butterfly kisses and his sunny, trusting love for her. She was intoxicated by the nights, the stars, the fragrance of the summer flowers. Alas, the idyll ended as abruptly as it had begun: he was posted elsewhere. She went to Berlin, where the bustling thoroughfares and restaurants, operas and balls soon distracted her. Once, at the Royal Palace, she was noticed by the Kaiser.

Home again, she struck up fresh acquaintances among the new cadets, who rode out from the barracks towards the forest and called gaily to her as she passed by on horseback. She blushed and laughed, remembering Kurt, who had driven her home more than once in a landau. Even though she was only a schoolgirl she felt dreadfully adult and important. But how could she have married him? An enchanting princess she might be, but no young officer burdened with his army expenses would be able to afford her. Her father couldn't give her a bigger allowance: she had heard about his gambling debts and other extravagances. It didn't matter, she loved him. She liked men and their activities, and feared women.

Ernest Weekley was a sort of solution. She met him when she was nineteen, and this rather stiff and responsible English professor of languages, fifteen years her senior, fell passionately in love with her. He asked her to marry him and she consented in a daze. He was quiet, greying already, with sombre, drooping moustaches, a man proud of his academic achievement. At seventeen he had been a schoolmaster, studying in the evenings and eventually winning a scholarship to Cambridge. That impressed her: his strong will. Obviously he loved her. Her very nearness made him tremble, her laughter gave him back his youth. And how different he was from her fierce, irresponsible father who had always indulged his daughters. Now she was being offered a security she had never known before. She bowed before the solidity and importance of it.

Yet it was dream-like, hardly real. He wanted to take her back to England, where she had never been, to a background of solid family unity, which she had never known: her own home was flawed by cynicism, a father who had lost faith in himself, a mother walled up in disapproving coldness. This man, Ernest Weekley, whose parents were devoted to him, was all of a piece, strong and simple. She decided to love him, be a good wife to him. His life had been such a grind of duties and struggles: she would lighten it. Only she wished he did not idealise her so much – it gave her a very uneasy feeling. Now and then he stooped down and kissed her feet, that were booted none too elegantly, as if he worshipped her. At such moments his emotion half strangled him. She noticed her effect on him, and his helplessness before her: she became conscious of her power. It was flattering, thrilling even, but not what she deeply wanted. It was him as a man she needed. She didn't want to be an ideal, a reverenced thing.

Before her marriage, he took her on a first visit to England, with her mother. The foreignness depressed her so much that she wanted to cry. Her mother whispered to her not to be such a silly goose. And the countryside, how small it was, green and soft, a place for cows and frogs to live in, surely, not people! Then there was the shock of the towns, spreading and ugly, all iron power and teeming, gritty lives.

They were married in Freiberg, where there was an English church. In the train afterwards, being whisked away to Lucerne, her anticipations of happiness were endless. But why did her husband sit so miserably in the corner of the compartment? His hands were beautiful, slender, his body hardly existed. For most of his life he had suppressed it mercilessly. Now he suffered because he was about to deliver it up to this lovely girl, and the thought terrified him. She read it in his face and was frightened herself.[5]

Their rooms overlooked the lake; the night was beautiful and warm. Ernest took her on his knee and told her what he thought she didn't know, that she wasn't yet his wife. She could feel him trembling beneath her. Then he fled, leaving her to go to bed, while she sat there despondently, wondering why he didn't kiss her toes, her real toes, instead of just her boots. Instead of climbing into bed and waiting, as he had told her to, she became a child again and clambered on to the top of the carved cupboard in the corner. She had taken off some clothes and now she sat there, swinging her legs and flapping the frills of her knickers. When her husband came in, he looked so scared that she got down quickly. Getting into the great bed was like being buried alive.

They arrived in England and went straight to Nottingham. Ernest Weekley was eager to resume his duties. It was November, damp and grey. Grey houses, grey streets, grey people. Frieda struggled to accept it. She was completely ignorant of her new role of *hausfrau*: housekeeping was a new word in her vocabulary. She grappled with the strange routine of the English bourgeois wife. She had a cook and a maid, but it was necessary to do the shopping, and in England this happened only in the mornings. Then in the afternoon you visited friends, or other friends called, and you offered them tea, in a kind of ceremony of cakes and small talk. After that came dinner. Then more loneliness. If her husband wasn't giving his evening lectures to workers, he came in to eat, and then promptly disappeared into his study to work. At first the dreariness and rigidity of it all nearly drove her mad, but somehow she adapted herself. She even managed to draw comfort from the thought of his 'rock of ages' spirit. God, but she was bored! And now and then overwhelmed by a mad desire to run, run anywhere. She would put on a hat and slip out of the house and tear off up the hill towards Mapperly Plain like a fugitive, till she reached the top and could feel the wind. The movement of the trees up there consoled her, and she felt more sane.[6]

Her sister, Johanna, came to see her. Married to an officer in one of the crack regiments, she had changed out of all recognition. They had been so close, so fond of each other. Now she was elegantly dressed, she came forward to meet her sister with swaying hips, and when she spoke it was with a new, hard voice that had an edge of experience to it. She talked cynically about the fine life she was leading, the men, flowers, admiration, the jealousy of the other women. Frieda listened. It was a shock to realise that her sister pitied her. She felt drab and unutterably pathetic.

Johanna left, appalled by her sister's life in England. But Frieda hadn't told her everything; not quite. There was a dear friend who owned a car, one of the first in England, and he would drive her into Sherwood Forest, between glimmering pools of bluebells. This was Will Dowson, a lace manufacturer in Nottingham, who was married to a suffragette. The affair, such as it was, revived her, and she shed some of the beastliness of the grimy town, the damp smell of the house, the rigid straitjacket of routine. But always she longed to get back, because of the children. She had a boy now, and a baby girl who delighted her, drinking voraciously from her breasts, as if she were the source of all nourishment. She adored the boy so extravagantly that she kept her love a secret.

Then came the Austrian she called Octavio in her memoirs, a young disciple of Freud named Otto Gross, who quietly and inexorably broke down the walls of her world. Because of him, she began to question everything: she was alive and brimming with hope again. She wanted fun and adventure and mystery; not for herself, like her sister, but for everybody. The possibilities of life were endless. She began to read avidly, finding confirmation everywhere.[7]

Otto lived in Munich. Frieda had gone there for a holiday, staying with an old friend who took her to breakfast one morning at the *Kaffeehaus*. It was a meeting place for intellectuals, individualists, eccentrics. She met a liberated countess, and rubbed shoulders with impoverished poets, painters, socialists, all of them talking like mad. Frieda just sat and listened, loving their eagerness. They were alive, and their appetite for more life excited her. She had met Otto there, and he had talked to her about Freud, of whom she had never heard. Otto came from the mountains: he had the lithe physique of a climber. He didn't drink, he refused to eat meat.

His letters had reached her in England, making a bridge of words between them; but it wasn't enough: she had to see him again. Soon he was her lover, urging her impatiently to leave everything and join him in creating an entirely new future. Frieda's inner world was in chaos. She wanted him and his brightness more than she had ever wanted anything, but it was impossible to leave the children. Sorrowfully she let him go. To her brother-in-law in Munich, Edgar Jaffe, she wrote in 1907: 'I had promised to burn all my letters from Munich, but I cannot do it; relieve me of my promise, I must still have something. I am nevertheless *very* careful.'[8]

That was five years ago. Since then she had never resigned herself, waiting in a long dream. Now it had happened: this trespasser had appeared out of nowhere, a native son of the very

Midlands she had always found repugnant. He sat in her drawing-room and she looked at him in wonder. Lawrence didn't seem to belong anywhere. She sensed the magical quality, exciting to women, that he had, the curiously bright, intent look of a man who has had more than one brush with death. He wasn't tall, but his thinness made him seem so. She was aware of his bones. He looked dreadfully frail, yet not in the least pitiful. She was fascinated by his swift changes of mood, and by the smile that transformed his rough, almost ugly features. His blue eyes flared at her warmly, or ignored her in cold insolence. He startled her continually, like an animal. She had become so accustomed to the predictability of her husband that this struck her as something entirely new. She paid attention.

Her next encounter with him was on Easter Sunday. The sun shone. As before, the children were playing in the garden. Because the maid was off for the afternoon, and Frieda wanted to make tea for her guest, she had to cope with the kitchen herself. The awful truth came out – she didn't know how to turn on the gas. Lawrence, very shocked, was scornful. As for Frieda, she had never been reprimanded by a man before. 'It was something my High and Mightiness was very little accustomed to.'[9]

It didn't take her long to decide then she loved him. She took her two small girls and they met at a country station in Derbyshire. With the children running ahead freely, they walked through the spring woods. Lawrence stopped by the flowing water of a brook, knelt down and made paper boats for the children, putting matches in them carefully for cargo before letting them sail away. He plucked some daisies and placed them with the same careful movements in the brook, 'and they floated down with their upturned faces. Crouched by the brook, playing there with the children, Lawrence forgot about me completely.'[10]

She knew then. Her tenderness awoke and flowed towards him, as inevitably as the water flowing in the brook. It was like the first intimations of love in *Lady Chatterley's Lover*, only with the roles reversed.

When he came to see her again, one Sunday, her husband was away on a journey. With her usual directness, Frieda asked Lawrence to spend the night with her. He said no. If he was shocked at her suggestion, it was nothing to the shock she received when he told her what he wanted. She was to tell her husband the truth, which was that he loved her, and then they would go away together.

She was frightened. Her husband would be totally unprepared, and she knew what such a blow would do to him. Nevertheless, this was her chance, and she acted. Was she obeying Lawrence, or 'a force stronger than myself'?

Ernest Weekley collapsed. Suffering hideously, he wrote a demented letter to his father-in-law in Germany. The following day he wrote again to say that 'I was insane for ten days. Yesterday was the climax and I was not really responsible. You see, I had to bear it all alone, and the mind is as though gone. Tonight I finally slept, the pressure is somewhat gone from my head, and I am again a human being.'[11] But alas, not for long. Two days later he implored his mother-in-law: 'Dear Mama, please make her understand what a state I am in: I cannot see her handwriting without trembling like an old cripple – to see her again would be my death. I would kill myself and the children too.'[12]

If Lawrence had known of this insanity his mind would have reeled in horror. Still very much in ignorance of the consequences of his actions, he made plans to leave for Germany with Frieda on 4th May, and, with luck, spend a week with her somewhere. The arrangement did not commit them to anything more than that: Frieda was supposed to attend a jubilee at her old home in commemoration of her father's long service in the army, another boisterous regimental affair. After that, neither she nor Lawrence could foresee what might happen. 'There's nothing to do', he wrote to her from Eastwood, 'but shut one's teeth and look at the wall and wait.'[13] It might have been his mother speaking.

Lawrence was behaving now as if he were already on the run, moving erratically between Eastwood and Leicester, making hectic visits to London, keeping always in close touch with Edward Garnett as his literary affairs quickened. He had finished the first draft of his 'colliery' novel. Now he put this aside and concentrated on the proofs of *The Trespasser*, which had just reached him. After 'waging war' on the adjectives, he wrote again to Garnett, thanking him once more for all his efforts. Suddenly he erupted joyously, unable to contain himself: 'Mrs Weekley is perfectly unconventional, but really good – in the best sense. I'll bet you've never met anybody like her, by a long chalk. You *must* see her next week. I wonder if she'd come to The Cearne, if you asked us. Oh, but she is the woman of a lifetime.'

So far, Garnett was the only one who knew about Frieda. He was a good friend, but not close, and far enough from Eastwood to be safe. To him, too, Lawrence could boast without restraint: 'She is the daughter of Baron von Richthofen, of the ancient and famous house of Richthofen . . .'[14] The others would only be told later, when they were both safely out of the country. May Holbrook knew a little, but only Garnett was getting the blow-by-blow account. At the end of April, after taking Frieda with him to The Cearne, Lawrence wrote to ask for the return of his 'scrubby gloves' and the first chapters of 'Paul Morel', and to say that he was going back to Eastwood before leaving for Germany on 4th May. Then came some painfully glib words that betrayed his appalling ignorance of Ernest Weekley's continuing anguish of mind: he described Weekley as 'a middle class, gentlemanly man, in whom the brute can leap up. He is forty-six, and has been handsome, is usually ironic, pessimistic and cynical, nice, I like him. He will hate me, but really he likes me at the bottom.'[15]

Final hasty letters went between him and Frieda. As late as 30th April he was still unsure of her plans, imploring her to tell him about times of trains, ending almost incoherently: 'For goodness' sake tell me something, and something definite. I would do anything on earth for you, and can do nothing . . . I am afraid of something low, like an eel which bites out of the mud, and hangs on with its teeth.'[16] So much for his friendly feelings towards Weekley of a few days before!

The dreadful day arrived: Frieda left her son behind in Nottingham and went with her two daughters to Weekley's parents in London. The old people would have to look after them. In tears, wondering if she would ever see them again, she said goodbye on Hampstead Heath and hurried to meet Lawrence. He had written: 'I shall get in King's Cross tomorrow at 1.25. Will that do? You see I couldn't come today because I was waiting for the laundry and for some stuff from the tailor's'. The laundry! He went on, in a last desperate attempt to be practical: 'I hope you've got some money for yourself. I can muster only eleven pounds.' The precariousness of it all comes across with force in this detail. He must have asked himself how in God's name he could survive, and for how long, in Germany – even on his own. But he was in love, things were moving with terrifying speed. All he could really think about was her, and getting to her again. Once in Metz – if that was where they were heading – he would rack his brains, work something out. 'Till tomorrow, till tomorrow, till tomorrow,'[17] he ended, as if the train wheels were already beating out their rhythm in his blood, rushing him towards her. They had known each other for six weeks.

From Charing Cross they made for the Channel and Ostend. It was Friday, 3rd May, cold, with a grey, lowering sky. They sat on piles of ropes and looked at each other blankly, afraid to think, 'full of hope and agony'. What they had done was already irreversible, though neither was yet prepared to admit it: reality was too awful to contemplate.

Because of the celebrations at her old home, Frieda was able to use the overcrowded house as an excuse, and stay at the same small hotel in Metz with Lawrence. This was the Hotel Deutscher Hof, and they lived there separately. Johanna, the younger sister, was staying there too, and Dr Else Jaffe, the eldest, called in from time to time. Both were let in to the secret. There was a fair going on in Metz, blocking the streets with stalls full of pots and pans, Turkish delight, sideshows. Johanna, now a sophisticated beauty married to 'a brute of a swanky officer in Berlin'[18], was walking with Frieda through the fair when she met Lawrence for the first time. Slipping up quietly out of nowhere, he looked a curious apparition in his cloth cap and raincoat, unmistakably English, giving an odd impression of self-reliance. He spoke to them briefly and then left. Johanna decided at once that he could be trusted.

Though Frieda was calling frequently to see her parents, she told them nothing about the presence – or even the existence – of Lawrence. She confirmed however that she did want to leave her husband, and of course they knew this already. Ernest's frantic letters and telegrams kept arriving, while bands played incongruously in the garden. Now the battle was really joined, with her mother urging her to stay with her for a while, her father telling her in shocked tones that she should come to her senses, she did not know the world, and her own remorse and longing for her children tugging at her to return to England.

Sitting there alone in the small hotel, hating the town already because of its soldiers everywhere and its 'ghastly medley' of old and new, Lawrence felt that now his whole future was being decided. Worst of all, it was out of his hands almost entirely. He pounded at Frieda with daily letters, the only way now he could exert any influence, with no idea of the effect he was having. He told her ungraciously, honest as ever: 'I love you – but I always have to bite my tongue before I can say it. It's only my Englishness.'[19] It was also the distance he was from her: the enforced separation was driving him mad. 'Now I can't stand it any longer, I can't. For two hours I haven't moved a muscle – just sat and thought. I have written a letter to Ernest.' The situation tortured him, not least because he was rendered helpless by it. He urged her to tell the truth, to Ernest if not to her parents. 'No more dishonour, no more lies . . . no more subterfuge, lying, dirt, fear. I feel as if it would strangle me.'[20]

The letter to Ernest Weekley was dispatched, and Frieda heard from him by return: 'I had a letter from Lawrence this morning. I bear him no ill-will and hope you will be happy with him. But have some pity on me. Do you want to drive me to suicide to simplify things?' On the subject of the children he was horribly explicit and uncompromising. 'The children will go to school in London and form new friendships and there will be a family home. It is the best thing. All compromises are unthinkable. We are not rabbits. Do not let all generosity be on my side. Have some remorse for all your deception of a loving man.'[21]

A grotesque little incident brought things suddenly into the open. Lawrence and Frieda were on the outskirts of Metz near some fortifications. They were lying on the sloping grass, talking, Lawrence abstractedly twisting the old emerald ring on Frieda's finger, when a German policeman came up, arrested him and insisted on taking him into custody. They had been overheard speaking English: he was under suspicion of being a disguised British officer. The charge was espionage. Frieda flew to her father and told him everything, then begged him to get her lover out of this ridiculous mess. The old baron had plenty of influence in the town, and Lawrence was soon free again, but under one condition: he would have to leave Metz at once. Before he did so, Frieda took him home, and over tea and stilted conversation the fierce old aristocrat and the miner's son confronted each other. The old man, bristling, courteously offered Lawrence a cigarette. The scene was sufficiently traumatic to give Frieda a nightmare in which the two men fought each other. Lawrence won.

Lawrence, too, thrashed about in nightmares. 'I dreamed Ernest was frantically furiously wild with me – I won't tell you the details – and then he calmed down, and I had to comfort him.' This was less satisfyingly symbolic, and in any case Lawrence was hardly the person to attach undue importance to something as involuntary as a dream. 'It's because I get up so late,' he told her soberly. 'One always dreams after seven a.m.'[22]

He took himself off to nearby Trier, thankful to escape from the garrison town and its soldiers, which he now had good cause to loathe. Everything at Trier suited him better. Writing to Frieda, he said that the hotel was much nicer, and no more expensive, only two marks fifty per day with breakfast for a bedroom containing (he added hopefully) two beds. And the old town itself was attractive, the streets lined with trees. In a few words, flung down at random, he brought the short journey to Trier marvellously alive: 'The valley all along coming is full of apple trees in blossom, pink puffs like the smoke of an explosion, and then bristling vine sticks, so that the hills are angry hedgehogs.' He told her that they were all men in the hotel, adding, with a touch of retaliatory teasing, that he knew she didn't object to a masculine atmosphere. He was uneasily conscious of the men coming and going at her father's house, and she had begun to tease him gaily with news of her old lovers. He sat there, a man of the world now, waiting for another man's wife to come to him. He ought to feel wicked, he told her, but he didn't, because 'in heaven there is no marriage nor giving in marriage.'[23]

He continued to marvel, and exult, at the thought of her extraordinary family, now he had actually seen it at close quarters. Even though temporarily banished – he would never, in fact, meet the baron again – he was proud of them, and wrote descriptions to Garnett that showed all his amazement. Wandering aimlessly about the little town he noted the 'crazy' cathedral, and the plentiful supply of priests. He preferred them to the soldiers. One day, finding himself without matches and unable to remember the German word for them, he asked a young priest for a light, 'and he held me the red end of his cigar'. It was pleasant, yes, but when would she come? He began to address her possessively now in his letters, reminding her that she was in fact his wife, and any letters from England should come through him. He was still unsure of her, and only too aware that these were the most critical days and he had no more cards to play. Frieda's letters were abbreviated, telegraphic, and they maddened him with their uncertainty. Under constant pressure, she had begun to waver now, half convinced by her own family that the price was too much to pay. Lawrence's extreme poverty must have been discussed at length with her parents, as well as the burning question: what would become of her children? Flying bravely in the face of these practicalities, Lawrence told her that he kept seeing her chin, he loved her chin, and wasn't that ridiculous? Then the gaiety flagged and he ended plaintively: 'You *will* come on Saturday?'[24] The nagging doubt implied by that question never left him.

He worked in spasms at 'Paul Morel', but sustained work of any kind was impossible in these circumstances. All his energy went into his longing for Frieda, and the exertion of his will against the others. She came to him at Trier for a day or two, then he went up the Rhine to his cousins at Waldbröl. It was useless hanging about any longer for developments that refused to happen, and he couldn't bear to merely sit still and wait. He travelled along the Mosel Valley, a seven-hour journey involving four changes. At the last changing place, Hennef, he sat in the twilight with an hour to pass before his train came, and he wrote her a note. The

FRIEDA

place, and the poem which grew out of it, 'Bei Hennef', he regarded later as a turning point in his life: 'And at last I know my love for you is here;/I can see it all, it is whole like the twilight,/It is large, so large, I could not see it before'. It was 8.30 in the evening, the river was 'twittering' in the silence and all the pain and anxiety of the past few days seemed to be folded quietly away into the pale sky. The perfect peace overwhelmed him: the rest was nothing.

At Waldbröl in the Rhineland, installed with his relatives, the Krenkows, he sat himself down to work sanely in the mornings at the novel that was on his conscience. Waldbröl made him feel healthy, it was invigorating, whereas Trier had been 'like a perpetual Turkish bath'. To give Frieda something to think about – he hadn't forgotten those besieging lovers of hers – he told her about Hannah Krenkow, who was getting fond of him already. Hannah had married an uninspiring, good man, not from love but because she was nearly thirty and time was running out for her. But there was no need to worry, she was perfectly proper. He went to one of the villages nearby where there was a festival, and saw a great heart-shaped cake decorated with sugar birds and flowers and fruit – and three poems! He wrote humorously, and sounded calm and rested, but Frieda was writing wildly that she should go to England, and it worried him. A cry of panic broke from him: 'Don't leave me stranded in some unearthly German town.'[25]

His letters to her lengthened and became intricate with strategy, financial worries, doubts of all kinds, and the reiterated need for solemnity, dignity and even religiousness in their love from now on. God knows what she must have made of this mixture, as he showered her with questions and then switched bewilderingly to an eloquent call for slow motion and stateliness. He exhorted her to be clear, exact, efficient. Like a general he demanded more accurate information from the front, so that he could change his tactics if necessary. But he thought things were drawing to a conclusion now, and the 'tragedy' would soon begin to wane. If only he could *see* into her mind. 'Is the divorce coming off? *Are* you going to England at all? Are we finally to pitch our camp in Munich? Are we going to have enough money to get along with? Have you settled anything definite with Ernest?' Then after this maelstrom, followed the extraordinary statement: 'One *must* be detached, impersonal, cold, and logical, when one is arranging *affairs*.'[26] What frightened him was the thought of their extreme vulnerability if a surprise attack came when they were at last together, floating precariously with no possessions and next to no money. All the money he had in the world was a

193

few pounds. He would write to the publishers for a loan, to be set against future royalties. Somebody owed him £25, and there was £24 due to him in August.

Again and again he tried to combat her uncertainty with an unshakable insistence on their getting things on a sound basis at the very beginning of their life together, so that, even if he had to wait for a year for her, their relationship would be 'welded firm'. He was penniless, but he knew that Frieda's interest in money matters was nil. He knew too that she admired strength and integrity. It was a good attitude to adopt, but a devilishly hard one to maintain. The next day he attacked again, armed with letters from England which she had sent him. Ernest Weekley was now asking for a divorce, and Lawrence saw this as the direct result of his letter to him. 'We are coming on quickly now,' he wrote to Frieda, and told her primly that he wasn't going to tell his people at Eastwood anything till she had her divorce. As for finance, it would be necessary to live very frugally for the first three months, but he thought they could manage. If they had a child they would provide for it somehow. He was startled to find himself *wanting* her to have his children: he had never felt that desire before. Stubbornly, feeling he was winning now, he stuck to his guns: they would join up in Munich soon, but not till things were really 'solid'. She ought to think of this waiting as a kind of preparation: 'Do you know, like the old knights, I seem to want a certain time to prepare myself – a sort of vigil with myself.'[27] She must have accused him of hanging back out of fear and reluctance, for he refuted this emphatically. On the contrary, it was because he wanted her so much, above all because it was such a great, august thing, this new life, that he refused to hurry. Torn so many ways, accused by her father of being a loose woman, Frieda must have thought these fine points indeed.

The next day he wrote to urge her not to fall ill, telling her stalwartly that he was 'always well'. For a man never far from death, this was a remarkable stance. But a fight, especially if there was a chance of winning, always put new heart in him. He had been working on his novel again, and also watching an Ascension Day procession, which ended in a hailstorm, some of the stones 'as big as walnuts'. The ground looked as if it was covered with lumps of sugar.

Frieda was openly taunting him now with talk of an old flame, no doubt in an attempt to put an end to this unnatural procrastination, as it seemed to her. With amazing new confidence he told her that she was only using her friend H— like a drug, but if she wanted him she should have him. 'But I don't want anybody, till I see you.' Now he was gloriously strong and in the right. Without much conviction he threw in the observation: 'I also am a carcass without you.'[28] He was undeniably in charge again; this waiting game was a success. From this pinnacle, he ordered her to be well and sane.

One can imagine the reactions of this mature, impetuous woman to her monkish lover. In her reply she let him have it: her letter fairly exploded in his face with fury. What a tyrant he was, what rats men were! She reminded him again of her ex-lover, H— , and he counter-attacked with more news of Hannah, who was getting steadily fonder of him. 'So there!' he wrote, good-humouredly, and the whole tone of his reply was mild and conciliatory. Soon they would be together again: they were to meet in Munich in a few days. Frieda was already there, staying with friends. He hoped she didn't still want to die: he certainly didn't. As for his being a tyrant, that didn't amount to much, since she would never give in to him. She had accused him of leaving her in the lurch, and he promised to keep count of the number of times he did that, starting with this first time. It was the letter of a man calmly poised to claim the fruits of victory.

But he still had a small purgatory of days to get through. By 21st May he was ready to tell Edward Garnett that the soles of his feet burned with impatience as he waited to join her. The slow movements of the massive oxen, heads swaying as if they were half asleep, drove him into a frenzy of restlessness as they passed down the street, pulling the rumbling wagons. More suited to his mood was the sight of the dog in the milk cart, stepping along daintily.

Then on 24th May he travelled to Munich, stayed a night there with Frieda and went on with her to Beuerberg, forty kilometres away. There they had eight days together, all the honeymoon they could afford, putting up at the Gasthaus zur Post. Beuerberg is in the Bavarian Tyrol. To Lawrence, with his memories of Eastwood and Croydon, and after his spell at tame Waldbröl, it must have seemed a wildly romantic place. He wrote long, rapturous accounts to Garnett and to Mrs Hopkin in Eastwood, whom he let into his burning secret for the first time. He described their idyllic mornings, breakfast out of doors on the ledge of a garden high above the jade-green river, the Loisach, where they sat under the chestnut trees 'and the red and white flowers fell on us.' The Bavarians were strange, and opposite the Gasthaus were a convent and a church, the convent sunk to the eaves in peace, white-washed, the church wearing 'a black hat'. And the abundance and variety of Alpine flowers! He burst into a rhapsody at the thought of them by the swift glacial river, the 'great hosts of globe flowers, that we call bachelor's buttons – pale gold great bubbles – then primulas, like mauve cowslips, somewhat – and queer marsh violets, and orchids, and lots of bell-flowers, like large, tangled, dark-purple harebells, and stuff like larkspur, very rich, and lucerne, so pink, and in the woods, lilies of the valley – oh flowers, great wild mad profusion of them, everywhere.'[29]

They went to see a quaint peasant play: they were in Oberammergau country. Down the Isar valley lived Frieda's sister, Else, in a chalet-like house. It was the next village to theirs, and they walked there, past the baroque churches with their minarets, stopping by the greenish water of a lake to bathe their feet. They put Frieda's rings on their toes to see how they looked under the water. The whole world had become magical, transformed, a fierce and beautiful place. Love had done it: 'I never knew what love was before,' he wrote humbly to Sallie Hopkin. He wanted her to know, but not to tell anybody else. He was overjoyed, but also a little fearful. Perhaps something – someone – could still snatch it all away. 'Life *can* be great – quite godlike,' he affirmed. 'It *can* be so. God be thanked I have proved it.'[30]

It was at Beuerberg that he began an entirely new cycle of poems, to be called 'Look! We Have Come Through'. One poem confessed that their first night was a failure, and 'our love was a confusion, there was a horror, you recoiled away from me.' But the morning brought the same sunlight, the mountains balanced 'proud and blithe' on their love. They were godlike again, the source of all things. What did one failure matter? A few days later he wrote his 'Lot's wife' poem, wildly and bitterly upbraiding Frieda for looking back and insisting on her motherhood, grieving for her children and weeping, 'white sharp brine making hideous your eyes.' He railed on at her insanely, burning with a jealousy which made him feel he had been 'thrust into white, sharp crystals,/Writhing, twisting, superpenetrated.' Her motherhood would torment him for years to come; and as if rehearsing the agony, he cursed not only her, but all motherhood. This 'curse against all mothers' was not just aimed at her, it was a malediction torn from him in the night as he fought to free himself from the past, from his mother, even from himself. So they shared horror as well as ecstasy, and often Frieda would shrink away from a man who seemed at times perversely cruel to her, forcing his ghosts and his darkness on to her. There was something destructive about him.

Yet it was often marvellously good, this new life. Lawrence gave her the pure gift of himself, without stint, and as simply as he would give her a bunch of flowers or a bird's feather, coming in quickly and lightly from one of his walks. She loved the generosity of these moods, which left her free as never before to be herself, so that she could 'flourish like a trout in the stream or a daisy in the sun.'[31]

When he sat down to write in her presence, the absolute concentration he brought to it amazed her. He just transferred himself, he was gone. It was as rapid and unanswerable as his sudden changes of mood, when he would contradict something he had said a week or perhaps only a day before. It puzzled and fascinated her.

She thought there was something ethereal about him that had nothing to do with his frail physique. He had a habit of slipping out of sight sometimes without warning, frightening her. She called it his 'moonshine' quality, and told him so. That made him scowl.

Once, when they were in Munich, rubbing shoulders with well-dressed city people, she went into a shop and bought handkerchiefs that were embroidered in the corners with her initial and a small crown; very aristocratic. She came back with them, childishly pleased, and Lawrence snatched up a piece of paper and drew what he called *his* coat-of-arms: a pickaxe, a blackboard, a fountain pen and two rampant lions. Then he asked her if she would like him to be a lord, or the King of England. He was joking, she thought, but it upset her. She felt sure that he could get what he wanted, whatever it was: all she hoped was that he wouldn't ever want to be anything as dull as a king.[32]

This was grand talk indeed for a man who stood before her without three pounds to his name. He had written to Garnett to ask if Duckworth, who had just brought out *The Trespasser*, would advance him ten pounds. Now he wrote again and told his friend proudly that he didn't want a loan from the publisher: they would 'scramble along' somehow. With a woman behind him at last, he felt rich and strong. And what a woman she was! 'She's got a figure like a fine Rubens woman, but her face is almost Greek,' he crowed. 'If you say a word about her, I hate you.' To add to his riches, he had completed the second version of his Eastwood novel and was about to despatch it to Heinemann. Could Garnett send him the reviews of *The Trespasser*? Frieda had just told him she was so happy that she didn't even want to be kissed. 'So there, you see. Love is a much bigger thing than passion, and a woman *much* more than sex.'[33] For the moment his innate puritanism was supremely satisfied.

They had moved now from Beuerberg to Icking, a few miles to
the north. Icking was on the Isar. Frieda's sister, Else, had
arranged for her lover, Professor Alfred Weber, to let them have
his flat there for a couple of months. In this new enchantment
they began housekeeping for the first time. They had four small
rooms in the upper part of the building, and a balcony with a
glorious view of sky and mountains. By living frugally – and none
knew better than Lawrence how to do it – they could manage on
about fifteen shillings a week, eating fresh fruit and eggs and rye
bread, and the occasional cutlet. Lawrence was in charge of everything, including the cooking. Frieda's natural disorderliness
offended the working man in him, the need to have things neat
and ship-shape. Like a teacher, he took her over to the chest of
drawers and told her: 'Look, put your woollen things in this
drawer, in this one your silk clothes, and here your cotton ones.'
Frieda thought it funny, but she did it, murmuring slyly that she
was like the lilies in the field, happy to exist. The remark brought
down another lecture on her head. It was nonsense to say that
lilies didn't work: how did she think they sucked up nourishment,
brought up sap, put forth leaves, flowers, seeds, if not by working?[34]

She amused him, she delighted him, but she couldn't help
shocking him – simply by being herself. One day they were out
walking by the Isar and the heel of her shoe broke on the rough
ground. She promptly took off the other shoe and flung them
both into the river. Now she would have to walk back to Icking
barefoot. She didn't care – but Lawrence did. And she mistook his
shocked look: it wasn't the fact that she was barefooted, it was her
extravagance that appalled him. How could she have such little
respect for the man who had laboured over the making of those
shoes of hers?

She shocked him too with her aristocratic disdain for convention, sitting out on the balcony in the late mornings in her nightgown. For him to be in his dressing-gown was 'respectable', he
told her tartly, but not for her. He was only half joking. It didn't
matter if there was only 'the great blue wall of mountains' glittering in the sun, to see her: there were certain things you didn't do.
She laughed, and he looked with her into the distance, at the
peaks far off, 'pale gold with snow'. Directly below them was the
white village and the road, a bullock wagon creaking by, and on
the other side of the road you could see peasant women working
in the wheatfields. It was a vast and magnificent landscape, veined
with milky green rivers and swift streams, black cloud over the
hills, and great shadows of woods. Yes, they were happy, beyond

anything he had dreamed possible, in spite of their quarrels and his occasional bitter lapses into jealousy and destructiveness. Nothing could blot out for long the beauty on earth he had inherited, as if for ever; more than that, there was the amazing liberation he had achieved, in one giant stride. Where was his English timidity now, his 'little pathetic sadness and softness'? He felt 'barbaric' with love. It frightened him sometimes, the immense change in him. Why in God's name were the English so afraid to let out the 'big wild scope of their natures'? [35]

He never ceased to marvel at her, the swaying of her full breasts like 'Gloire de Dijon roses' as she washed herself, and he glowed all over in his newly-achieved body, like a risen Christ. When she looked at his naked body and told him that he, too, was beautiful, he believed her: he was a rose himself. Poems about roses kept blossoming and blowing from him, one after another: 'River Roses', 'Gloire de Dijon', 'Roses on the Breakfast Table', 'I am like a Rose', 'Rose of all the World'; as if, through their symbolism, he could express everything he wanted. They seeded out in his imagination, they swayed and smoked like his 'fine desire', they singled him out and perfected him, until he stood up, in his manhood, 'whirling in blossom and flame'. He had cut the cord and was clear of his mother now, clear of all the aching failure of the past. He was new: 'I am myself at last.'

In this transcendental mood, what did it matter that the *Nottinghamshire Guardian* called his *Trespasser* 'a reprehensible jaunt'? It was so irrelevant and ridiculous that he enjoyed it, and stuck out his chest at the thought, while Frieda laughed. There were other, more important things to think about and do, now that the awful 'cyclone of letters' had diminished and they were emerging at long last from the 'alleys and avenues of tragedy'. They went swimming in the Isar, naked, Frieda cavorting like a dolphin and looking 'fearfully voluptuous, rolling in the pale green water.' [36]

A letter came from Garnett, enclosing a cutting from the *Westminster Gazette*. It was moderate, like the others: the usual mixture of compliments and reservations. The *Daily News* advised him to 'cultivate an intenser vision', which for some reason sent Frieda into more fits of laughter. In his reply, Lawrence, anxious to correct the other man's picture of the lovely time he seemed to be having with Frieda, the 'billing and cooing, and nibbling grapes and white sugar', told him that the warfare still went on –and *that* was what real tragedy meant: not death, or unrequited love, or any of that *Tristan* stuff. But he was 'on the preach again'. [37] He just wanted Garnett to understand that he was paying for his paradise. The old Eastwood Lawrence, the man who insisted on paying his way, always chipped in realistically at these moments.

He heard from Helen Corke, to whom he had sent a copy of *The Trespasser*. He thought the letter 'fearfully affected', especially the conclusion, and decided she was angling after him. Frieda tore up the letter, and then proceeded to fling the contents at him for days afterwards. He reported this mildly, aware that she was looking over his shoulder as he wrote. Love suited him so well that he was 'getting fat'. His huge happiness and contentment kept breaking through, in spite of efforts to suppress it, and his tit-bits of information to convey the flavour of their battles were often humorous. 'F. raves over glow-worms, I over fire-flies, and we nearly murder each other.'

His blithe ignorance of the outside world showed itself in quaint little asides: 'What's the Parliamentary Reform Bill?'[38] What indeed, when the days and nights melted together and they lost touch with ordinary time, Frieda luxuriating magnificently in 'a dream of well-being', Lawrence making the breakfast and bringing it in to her – not forgetting the bunch of flowers left by the milk jug each morning. If Frieda spilt coffee on her pillow, she turned the pillow over; but she did it now when Lawrence wasn't looking, for fear of a scolding.

In those early days, England sank almost out of sight for them both. Then came set-backs, and they would feel their paradise heave under them. There was a sudden slap in the face from Heinemann, who rejected 'Paul Morel', presumably for business reasons. Lawrence, however, suspected that it was because Heinemann himself thought the book was 'dirty'. This enraged him, and he hurled a venomous tirade at the English, the whole race, which poor Garnett had to receive as their representative: 'Curse the blasted, jelly-boned swines, the slimy, the belly-wriggling invertebrates, the miserable sodding rotters, the flaming sods, the snivelling, dribbling, dithering palsied pulse-less lot that make up England today. They've got white of egg in their veins, and their spunk is that watery it's a marvel they can breed. They *can* nothing but frogspawn – the gibberers!'[39] As well as the unspeakable Heinemann, there was Ernest Weekley, trying all over again to get Frieda back, begging and pleading, sending 'storms of letters' and driving Frieda frantic with renewed love for her children. In paroxysms of grief she lay on the floor, while Lawrence hammered her with abuse. Instead of sympathising, he gave her an ultimatum: either her children or him. She must decide for herself. Either security and a doting, forgiving husband and her damn brood, or share his 'rotten chances'. Her answer was blind anger and hatred, for days at a time, taking herself off to her sister in Wolfratschausen and leaving him to stew with his vile ultimatum and his refusal to admit love for her.

Left alone, he was immediately afraid, and so frustrated by everything that he wanted to hit his head on the wall. God, yes, he did love her. If he thought of life without her now, his heart nearly stopped beating. If she left him and went back, he would be dead within six months, he knew it. The bother with Heinemann faded into insignificance, and in any case there was a way out of that: Edward Garnett had offered to read the manuscript for Duckworth. That was the least of his troubles. Whatever happened, he meant to hang on to this woman. 'I feel I've got a mate and I'll fight tooth and claw to keep her.'[40] One day, when he was alone, the Baroness von Richthofen came 'whirling' in on him, breaking her journey from the Tyrol to Constance to make this surprise attack. She gave it him hot and strong for an hour, pouring out abuse 'like a washerwoman'. For once, Lawrence was speechless, though when she demanded to know who he thought he was, expecting the daughter of a gentleman to 'clean my boots and empty my slops', he felt like saying, 'I don't think!' But instead he kept wisely quiet and accompanied the fuming lady to the station with his head meekly bent in submission.[41]

Only a week or two before this alarming interview, Lawrence and Frieda had entertained their first guest. He was David, the son of Edward Garnett, and his visit put an end to their isolation of two months in 'this tiny savage little place', where he and Frieda had 'got awfully wild.' He had heard from Duckworth about 'Paul Morel': in fact they had returned the manuscript, together with a long list of comments by Garnett. Now he intended to roll up his sleeves and 'slave like a Turk' at the book, starting again at the beginning. Getting down to it the next day, true to his word, he must have had thoughts of Jessie Chambers. In May he had written a note to her on the back of a postcard of Trier Cathedral: 'I am going through "Paul Morel". I'm sorry it turned out as it has. You'll have to go on forgiving me.'[42] He had followed this up a few weeks later with a letter explaining about Frieda, urging her to keep the news absolutely secret. What she called this 'hysterical announcement' went on to say: 'Don't tell M., don't tell N.C., don't tell *anybody*. Only A. knows . . .'[43] Presumably A. was Ada, and the other initials stood for May [Chambers] and Nell Corke.

David Garnett had been in Munich on holiday, and was delighted to have his solitary existence ended by an invitation to stay with Lawrence and Frieda. In his note to the young man,

Lawrence gave him directions with characteristic thoroughness, then explained quaintly that 'I am living with a lady who is not my wife, but who goes as my wife down here in Bavaria.' He added that he looked so 'fearfully English' that he didn't think either of them would need Union Jacks.

Reporting on the visit of 'Bunny' later to David's father, Lawrence said they found him adorable. His youth and energy, above all his gaiety, took their minds off Frieda's insoluble problems. The young Garnett swam in the rushing water of the Isar, watched by an admiring Frieda and an envious Lawrence. In the evenings he danced and threw himself about, acting the fool 'with great orange and yellow and red and dark green scarves of F's, and his legs and arms bare', brandishing a knife and frightening the life out of Frieda, kicking up such a din on the floor that somebody yelled up from underneath in German: 'Go and trample somewhere else.'[44]

Lawrence might have been less amused if he could have looked inside this young man of twenty and seen the first impression of himself forming there. David Garnett, after travelling to Icking on the small railway that wound along the valley, past sloping corn-fields and dusty July roads fringed with Canterbury bells, had got out at the station and looked for the author of *The White Peacock*. As the little crowd of trippers and sombre peasant women in black dispersed, he saw his man: a bare-headed, thin figure, obviously English. Above the moustache 'the most beautiful, lively blue eyes' scrutinised him.

As they set off for the house where Lawrence was living, David Garnett was able to look at his host more closely. He noticed his frailty, as everyone did, and the lightness of his movements. What he saw after that was not so much a man as a symbol of the bitter class struggle then getting under way in the England he had just left. Even the hair had to be of a special, underdog kind. 'His hair was of a colour,' he wrote later, 'and grew in a particular way, which I have never seen except in English working men. It was bright mud-colour, with a streak of red in it, a thick mat, parted on one side. Somehow, it was incredibly plebeian, mongrel and underbred. His forehead was broad, but not high, his nose too short and lumpy, his face colourless, like a red-haired man's, his chin altogether too large, and round like a hairpin – rather a Philip IV sort of chin – and the lower lip, rather red and moist, under the scrubby toothbrush moustache . . . He was the type of the plumber's mate who goes back to fetch the tools. He was the weedy runt you find in every gang of workmen; the one who keeps the other men laughing all the time; who makes trouble with the boss and is saucy to the foreman; who gets the sack; who is "victimised" the cause of a strike; the man for whom trade unions exist; who lives on the dole; who hangs round the pubs; who bets on football and is always cheeky, cocky, and in trouble.'[45]

This was wide of the mark, but there was worse to come. Lawrence reminded him of a mongrel terrier, cheekily inviting him, the well-behaved spaniel, to join him in some fun and games. Frieda came off much better: she was handsome, her head and 'the whole carriage of her body were noble', and there was an animal's power in the way she leapt up from her hammock. Above all, he adored them for being such obviously happy lovers. They were great fun to be with, and he enjoyed the flattery they heaped on him.

11

Wandervögel

As soon as David Garnett returned to Munich, Lawrence and Frieda set out to walk across the Alps to Italy, making first for Mayrhofen. Garnett hoped to join up with them there. Neither Lawrence nor Frieda had been to Italy, and the prospect thrilled them. They had twenty-three pounds between them. They carried rucksacks, with food and methylated spirit for the stove on which they did their cooking, camping out by streams and sheltering in hay-huts. It was the adventure of Frieda's life.

In a letter to David's father announcing these plans, he also outlined some literary projects. It was essential now for him to make some 'running money'. *The Trespasser* had been published in America – wouldn't his short stories go there? He intended to write six short stories as soon as possible, as well as rewriting 'Paul Morel', which would take him three months. As if all this wasn't enough, he had ideas for a new novel, 'purely of the common people'.

They reached Mayrhofen without mishap, and he settled down to some work while they waited for David Garnett to arrive. They were lodging beside a rushing stream, in a farmhouse. But it was August, and most of the day they spent out of doors, lighting small fires to cook on, eating boiled eggs and the local gruyère cheese. Wherever they went, icy mountain water was flowing, falling. The cows sounded their bells in the high summer meadows. They bathed together, and Frieda lay naked in the sun. Flowers were in abundance: 'tiny harebells, big, black-purple mountain harebells, pale blue, hairy, strange creatures, blue and white Canterbury bells – then there's a great blue gentian, and flowers like monkey-musk. The Alpine roses are just over – and I believe we could find the eidelweiss if we tried. Sometimes we drink with the mountain peasants in the Gasthaus, and dance a little.'[1]

While at Mayrhofen he wrote a long epistle to Sallie Hopkin at Eastwood, explaining more fully about him and Frieda, and their long walk across the mountains. His stories, 'A Chapel Among the Mountains' and 'A Hay Hut Among the Mountains', describe their setting out and subsequent adventures and minor misfortunes with wry good humour. Heading southwards from the Isar on that first morning, at daybreak, they felt brave enough. A few hours later they were floundering half drowned in a storm and sheepishly taking refuge in an inn, where seven 'joyous peasants' made eyes at Frieda as Lawrence sat dripping in a corner. The next day was better, and they began to make progress. They took a mountain path to Glashütte, three hours away, scrambling down the gloomy slopes of pine woods until they were lost and exhausted. Then, climbing high again, they stumbled on a wooden chapel in the twilight. Inside, it was 'all close and snug as a box', with candles on the altar, four tiny pews, and the walls covered with naïve little votive pictures painted by the peasants 'for God, because horses and cows and men and women and mountains, they are his own language.' Lawrence lit the candles. Suddenly he felt perfectly happy and at home here. It was dark now, they were tired, outside it was wet and cold: this was a good place to stay the night. Frieda objected to the hard wooden floor and wanted to push on a little further till they came to a hay-hut, but Lawrence was now in love with his shrine. He climbed up on one of the pews, with a candle, for a closer look at the pictures. The tiny domestic scenes, the cattle arranged like toys on the meadows, in strange perspective, were curiously touching. He looked higher, wanting to read the inscriptions. When he turned round, Frieda had disappeared. Soon she came back, excited as a child, to say she had found a hay-hut. Resentfully he followed her, sarcastic when she told him how lovely the chapel had looked in the dark, 'its row of candles shining, and all the inside warm!' Why the devil did they have to leave it, then? No, she said obstinately, a hay-hut would be so much warmer and more comfortable. He trudged behind, moaning fretfully at her, and she called him 'a damp match'. When he came to write his account he revenged himself joyfully. The hut was badly made, rain had leaked in: they clambered into the upper part and had to take care to avoid the soggy places. Outside it was raining and blowing, and inside 'a hundred horse-power draught' blew across the floor. Finally, the hay made him itch all over, he kept wanting to scratch his neck and there were seeds in his eye. He had been right, they should have stayed put. He squirmed and suffered all night, and Frieda laughed. His skin was more sensitive than hers, he shouted, and she laughed louder. But when the dawn came and he dragged on his boots and emerged blinking from the square window-hole, it was tremendous: the snow had fallen thickly higher up, but on their grass shelf it was still clear and green. They were surrounded by a ring of bristling pine woods, then the great peaks floating in the air of the sky. The whiteness, with those mountains smudged into the dawn, was hallucinatory. He felt that if he charged full tilt into the trees and kept going he could 'walk up the sky'. They talked in hushed voices, as if they were the only two people left alive.[2]

Now they paused for breath in Mayrhofen, waiting for young Garnett, but with their sights still set on Lake Garda and winter in Italy. Before long, he felt twinges of guilt: he should be settling down to some real work soon. A selection of new poems came back from Heinemann with a terse rejection note – and this after they had been recommended warmly by Walter De La Mare, who read for the firm. Lawrence now had a further reason for detesting 'his Jew-ship', William Heinemann. He thought longingly of a book of his verses coming out 'in hard, rough covers, on white, rough paper'. Maybe Duckworth would be interested? David Garnett, when he arrived, sat with Lawrence and Frieda as they thought of suitable titles for the volume. David suggested 'Asphodels', Frieda came up with 'Cabbage Roses', so Lawrence put the two together to make 'Asphodels Among the Cabbages'. Frieda became inspired, took a sheet of paper and drew a design of fat cabbages interspersed with tall, elegant asphodels.

Lawrence's letter to Sallie Hopkin was in part a confidential report. He wanted her to know about the 'wonderful naked intimacy' he had now reached with Frieda, for she was one of the few people back there whom he could trust with such details. His sister, Ada, had turned 'respectable' on him: she was soon to marry, and she preferred not to be associated with his reprehensible goings-on. Jessie had been told something, but no details; and the same with Mrs Dax. To Sallie Hopkin he laid down the foundations of his new faith. 'I have given and I have taken,' he wrote, 'and that is eternal. Oh, if only people could marry properly; I believe in marriage.'[3]

The stages of the journey to Italy were marked by poems. At Glashütte, swallowed up by the immensity of the landscape, and after some strife between him and Frieda, he wrote, in 'Song of a Man Who Is Not Loved':

If I turn quickly, I am terrified, feeling space
    surround me;
Like a man in a boat on very clear, deep water, space
    frightens and confounds me.

Reduced to a speck of dust, blown hither and thither by the big shouldering wind, did he count for anything really? These setbacks, like maladies of the spirit, still overwhelmed him at moments, betraying him back to the hopelessness and longing for oblivion he had experienced after his mother's death. He was happier than he had ever been – then a swirling black misery dragged him back by the heels. It happened again just before they reached Sterzen, after getting lost and finally taking refuge, depressed by the cold, in a freezing hut. The poem commemorating it he called, appropriately, 'Misery'.

David Garnett and a friend, Harold Hobson, accompanied Lawrence and Frieda as far as Sterzing, then caught a train to Verona. Before leaving Mayrhofen the lovers had sent their two suitcases – all they owned in the world – ahead to Riva.

They were a gay party. Lawrence and Garnett scrambled happily among the rocks on wild excursions, looking for plants to add to the younger man's collection. Garnett found it hard to believe that Lawrence had been critically ill only a few months before: he looked amazingly fit and overflowing with energy. At Mayrhofen, if he wasn't working away in a corner of the room at 'Paul Morel', or at new stories and poems, he would be darting about to see to the cooking, and in the evenings his high spirits dominated them all. Any self-pity would be pounced on and mocked, and it was difficult to complain, since his mockery of himself was so merciless. He acted out deadly caricatures of himself in impromptu sketches, 'of a shy and gawky Lawrence being patronised by literary lions, of a winsome Lawrence charming his landlady, a sentimental Lawrence being put in his place by his landlady's daughter, of a bad-tempered, whining Lawrence picking a quarrel with Frieda over nothing.' These hilarious cameos were sometimes the prelude to the complicated charades he organised whenever there was company. The only thing that diminished his gaiety while he was at Mayrhofen was the arrival of the post from England.

As soon as their young friends left them at Sterzing, Lawrence and Frieda 'quarrelled like nuts'. The old issue of the children came boiling to the surface, and their strong wills clashed continually. All the same, it was Lawrence's will which saved them from an icy fate above Merano, when a 'filthy and black' night threatened to engulf them and the wind battered them almost to a standstill. Straggling at last into Bozen, dead on their feet from exhaustion and looking like scarecrows, they stayed for the night in a room over a pigsty. The next day, recovered a little, they went on to Trent, where their inexperience and shortage of money landed them in a poky hotel with primitive toilets, dubious sheets and sinister marks on the bedroom walls. This was too much for Frieda's nerves. It had taken them six weeks of hard travel to reach here. The wet and cold and hunger she could bear, but not this squalor. She rushed off to be alone with her misery, and Lawrence found her on a bench under Dante's statue, sobbing quietly to herself. That decided him; they would finish the journey to Riva by train. 'This, of course,' he wrote to 'Mac' McLeod at Croydon, 'is the highroad from Germany to Italy, and one sees all sorts of queer cubs, from lords of England to Italian tramps.'4 They were beginning to look like tramps themselves.

So they got on the train to Riva, Lawrence still wearing the shapeless straw hat he had worn in the Tyrol, Frieda in her peasant sack. Riva belonged to Austria, but it was 'as Italian as an ice-cream man'. Austrian officers and their elegant women sauntered through the streets: this was a garrison town. Neither of them could speak Italian, and it was perhaps this handicap that caused them to rent a room in a residential hotel that was beyond their means. At the Villa Leonardi, though the room was beautiful, with a view of the lake from the windows, roses and grapes and oleanders in the garden, they had to eat frugally and hide their cooking stove and food under the sofa whenever the Italian maid came in to clean. As Richard Aldington says, 'They were genuine travellers, not ignorant tourists. But in that autumn of 1912 the inexperience which led them to choose a place as far north and as exposed as Lake Garda for the winter was matched by their total ignorance of Italian. Added to that was Lawrence's still acute shyness and fear of ridicule and rebuff which made him afraid even to ask the inhabitants about rooms and prices. Getting angry with him, Frieda went up to a man in one of the lake villages and stammered: "Prego – quartiere – d'affitare", only to have him insist on putting them in a bus which went back to Riva!'5

Lawrence's poverty was now so serious that they found the room at the Villa Leonardi too dear at 2/6 for the day for the two of them. He wrote urgently to Garnett for his £50 from Duckworths, asking for it to be sent in notes if possible, since a cheque in these circumstances would be difficult to cash. Duckworth had promised to pay him a little ahead of time, so in his letter he sounded suitably grateful. By 16th September he was joyfully acknowledging receipt of the little wad of banknotes. They had already cheered up considerably, for their suitcases had arrived, together with a trunk of Parisian clothes and hats from Frieda's wealthy sister, Johanna. Now Lawrence could change his frayed trousers – called 'Miriam' trousers as a joke, since he had been

208

14. *Left*
Frieda von Richthofen

15. *Below*
Frieda and Ernest Weekley

16. John Middleton Murry, Frieda and D. H. Lawrence

with Jessie Chambers when he bought them – and Frieda sail down the street in a soft blue dress that was in the latest fashion. They had been almost penniless, until the Duckworth money came, but now at least the two ex-tramps could strut like peacocks with the peacocky officers in beige trousers and pale blue jackets.

And their luck held. Screwing up their courage, they had told the hotel lady they wanted to stay on the lake for the winter and were looking for something more suitable. She put them on to Pietro di Paoli, 'a grey old Italian with grand manners and a jaw like a dog'. He had a villa in one of the lake villages, with the bottom flat to let, furnished. The place was at Gargano. They hurried off to view it. Because of the steep hills behind the village, the only way to it was across the lake by steamer. When they saw the village they were excited by its primitive appearance, everything crumbling and dilapidated. The hills rising steeply at the back were covered in vineyards and lemon gardens. The village square delighted them, with its gossiping Italians, and nearby the fishermen's boats pulled out of the water. It was twenty kilometres from Riva, but much nicer. The sun shone, the figs and peaches hung ripe for picking. And the Villa Igea was perfect. For just over £3 a month, everything supplied, they could have their own living-room, kitchen, and two bedrooms, 'big pretty rooms looking over the road on to the lake.' The garden behind the villa had peaches and bamboos. The living-room had 'three windows', exclaimed Lawrence, as childishly delighted as Frieda must have been, and he added happily in his letter to Garnett that the whole place was 'clean as a flower' – an important factor for both of them. They rushed back to clinch the deal with their new landlord. 'Frieda adores Pietro,' Lawrence reported, in great good humour, 'and I the wife.'[6] The thought of a ménage of their own at last and a kitchen to themselves, with 'gorgeous copper pans' hanging in a row, thrilled them. For Lawrence, this was a perfect place for him to sit correcting the proofs of his 'Love Poems' which had just come.

In this paradise, he settled down to work with a will on 'Paul Morel'. A man named Edward Marsh had written from England to say that he was editing an anthology of verse by the 'new men' and could he include Lawrence's poem 'Snapdragon'? The volume was to be representative of the Georgians, a rather tepid poetry movement then forming around Marsh as editor.

Just before moving to Gargano, Lawrence had written to his friend McLeod, asking for books. All he had read in English in the past five months had been *Under Western Eyes*, which he thought a bore. He was curious about the new novels by Bennett and Wells – what were they up to? Impelled by the same curiosity, he asked Edward Garnett too for reading matter.

When the books came, however, they only fed his loathing for England. He couldn't bear to be reminded now that he was English too: he felt 'soiled'. Here in Gargano the people *sang* in spite of their poverty, they looked healthy, they adored their children, and their women were calm and straight-backed and beautiful. Why couldn't England be like that, instead of grubby and shabby and resigned? The diatribe was prompted by a reading of *Anna of the Five Towns*, which McLeod had sent him. Bennett's Hanley characters, and their dialect, so like Lawrence's people, were weird creatures to read about in Italy. He felt confused, slightly sick: he didn't like it at all. Garnett had sent him Strindberg, and he too went down badly: 'I hate Strindberg – he seems unnatural, forced, a bit indecent – a bit wooden, like Ibsen, a bit skin-erupty.'[7] As for Conrad, his sadness and resignation were loathsome, good though he was. Why did he have to write as though sitting in the ruins? It was like Bennett, like 'all the modern stuff since Flaubert'. If only he could wash England from his skin for ever.

Let them wait: he would show them all. He wanted to take 'a great kick at misery'. Meanwhile, this primitive living in beautiful surroundings was surely as important as anything in books. He ploughed on steadily with his novel, breaking off from time to time to rescue Frieda, when her attempts at housekeeping ended in disaster. She would wail from the kitchen that the pigeons were burning, come quickly, what should she do? And she washed the sheets for the first time, with dreadful consequences. The things were totally unmanageable when they were wet, 'their wetness was overwhelming', the water ran over the kitchen floor and flooded it and she stood there dripping, adding to it with her tears. Lawrence sprang to bail her out, laughing at the mess she was in, and before she had time to feel sorry for herself he had dried her off, restored the kitchen and hung out the sheets in the garden. 'The One and Only is drowning, oh dear!' he had mocked, but she was too wet to care.[8]

Lawrence's fulminations against England's industrialised misery and squalor were a measure of his constant preoccupation with it, and of course he was immersed daily in the reality of it, as he wrote away at his Eastwood novel. Even here in Gargano, many things reminded him of his life at home when he was a boy. One of his favourite walks was to the next village on the Garda, Bogliaco, where he would sit among the Bersaglieri, in their red fez caps, drinking wine and eating chestnuts. Sometimes he would be with Frieda and sometimes alone. The place where you drank was a living-room of the house, the family sitting unconcerned on the other side, having their meal. There would be the grandfather with his white moustache, eclipsed by the sturdy father. The mother sat feeding the baby with soup, the grandmother sat by the slow fire. The father looked puzzled as Lawrence gave him thirty centesimi for the quarter litre of red wine; the price was only fifteen centesimi (1¼d.) 'He doesn't understand tips.'⁹

Winter seemed a long way off. Then in early October the long summer weather broke. It became stormy, the lake darkened, 'with white lambs all over it', the steamer went rocking by. But there was still beauty in abundance, and colour: the yellow and red vines, the flame of the fig trees behind them on the rocky hills. As though in defiance, he and Frieda went for a swim, in a thunderstorm, 'a great black cloud trailing over the lake.'¹⁰

Although he was working well, his working-man instincts gave him uncomfortable twinges of guilt when he thought of his routine – not getting up till eight, taking breakfast to her ladyship, who remained in bed, and then jawing away at her there until dinnertime. Always he was conscious of the world of work, the necessity to do one's share of it, and not indulge in the cardinal sin of loafing. By the end of October he could tell Garnett that he had completed four hundred manuscript pages of 'Paul Morel'. He wondered if *Sons and Lovers* might be a better title. In addition to this progress, and 'living hard', he had done, in three days, a play, putting himself and Frieda into it as characters. It was a comedy, done 'as a sort of interlude' to the novel.

In the same letter he asked for books for Frieda, to keep her amused – she was such a 'cormorant of novels'. He thought his 'fuliginous' novel was going well. He had pumped fresh blood and warmth into it, and Frieda maintained that this was on account of her. Certainly he was turning to her, as he had always done to the women in his life, for her reactions, wanting to know from her how a mother felt, how Miriam might have felt, and so on. He became so identified with his material that the writing about his mother's death visibly affected him. He would notice women in the village and on the steamer who reminded him of her. His distress at these moments was painful to Frieda: his courage in facing the darkness inside himself both impressed and scared her. And his attitude to women, so changeable, continued to baffle her. 'In his heart of hearts', she wrote in her memoirs, 'I think he always dreaded women, felt they were in the end more powerful than men. Woman is so absolute and undeniable. Man moves, his spirit flies here and there, but you can't go beyond a woman. From her man is born and to her he returns for his ultimate need of body and soul. She is like earth and death to which all return.'[11]

If Frieda could express herself nobly on occasions, she could also act as though the rest of the world were no concern of hers. Throwing water out of the bedroom one day, she half drowned an old lady who happened to be scuttling past against the wall of the house outside. After this incident, Lawrence thought it wise to keep the doors locked for a while; there were no police in the village.

In spite of everything – including vile news from England – he was irrepressibly chirpy. A new moon sailed up in the pink light of evening over the lake, wild cyclamens were in blossom all over the hills – and wine was 5d. a litre. The upstairs flat now contained a middle-aged artist, a hunchback, who spoke 'weird glutinous French', with his mother and a maid. Lawrence and Frieda now had company of a sort.

He had now reached the nub of his book: the final 'defeat' of Miriam and the awful death of his mother. As he worked, he dug into his recently buried grief and resurrected it. It went on so long that Frieda got sick of it, and in a kind of jealousy lashed out at him, calling him a mother's darling, still tied to her apron strings. Instead of retaliating, he accepted the insult as meekly as he had the angry words of her mother. These days he was being showered with abuse: Ernest Weekley had referred to him in letters as 'common', 'a lout', 'a clodhopper'. In the skit Lawrence wrote in three days and sent to Garnett, called 'The Fight for Barbara', some of the runaway couple's daily exchanges must have gone almost verbatim into these hasty scenes between Wesson, a young man of twenty-seven living in Italy, and his mistress, Barbara. The play has the crude immediacy of something transferred too soon from the raw material of life, but as autobiography it is fascinating. The young hero's name is Italianized by the woman, just as Lawrence was called Lorenzo by Frieda. The opening scene has Wesson, in charge of the cooking, reprimanding the high-born Barbara for calling his father a mere coalminer:

WESSON: A butty collier – and I wish yours had been ditto – you'd ha' been more use. Think of me, Lord of Creation, getting the breakfast ready. (*She takes his head between her hands, and ruffles his hair*). While you stand messing about.
BARBARA: Oh, your lovely hair! – it makes waves just like the Apollo Belvedere.

WESSON: And come again tomorrer.

BARBARA:Don't – don't laugh at yourself – or at me when I say it's nice hair. It is, Giacomo, it's really beautiful.

WESSON: I know; it's the Apollo Belvedere, and my beautiful nose is Antinous, and my lovely chin is Endymion. Clear out.

BARBARA: You are horrid to yourself! Why won't you let me say you're nice?

WESSON: Because the water's boiling.

BARBARA: You're not a bit nice.

WESSON: Mind! – my water's boiling! (*Breaks away – making coffee in a brass jug.*) If this was Pimlico or Bloomsbury, and this was a London kitchen, you wouldn't love me, would you?

BARBARA: If you do anything so horrid as to stifle me in a poor part of London, I would *not* love you – I would hate you for ever. Think of me!

WESSON: But because we come careering to Italy, and the pans are made of copper and brass, you adore me, don't you?

BARBARA: Yes – on the whole.

WESSON: That is, for the first month or two. We've been here six weeks.

BARBARA: Think of it – Giacomo mio, it seems like six minutes – it frightens me.

Lawrence was still unsure of Frieda. After all, she might run back, scared, to England: she was still under heavy pressure. Writing this short play, his anxieties ran into the dialogue, often turning to resentment in the process. He hated her for wavering, not totally committing herself to him. He even pitied her husband. When Barbara exclaims over the love of her husband for her, wondering why he always hid it from her until now, her lover replies cruelly: 'He didn't. You merely never saw it.'

This was treacherous. And there was more to come:

WESSON: You made him suffer worse underneath, twisting your spear in his secret wound, before you left him, than you do now that it's open. He can doctor an open wound. A secret one drives him mad.

BARBARA: But I didn't torture him. I was a joy to him. And think of it, Giacomo, I was the only joy he'd ever had in his life.

WESSON: And the only sorrow.

BARBARA: Why do you want to say horrid things about me?

WESSON: I don't.

BARBARA: But you do! Look, you say I tortured Frederick.

WESSON: So you did. So you torture me.

At the end of this scene the comedy turns ugly, with Barbara kneeling at her lover's feet in mock subjection, until in fury he grasps her arms and drags her to her feet:

WESSON (seizing her by the arm): Get up, you lunatic.
BARBARA: But don't you like to be worshipped?

Standing there face to face with her, he digs his fingers into her, wanting to punish her:

BARBARA (subduedly): You hurt my arms.
WESSON (through his teeth): And why shouldn't I?
BARBARA: Don't be horrid.
    (*Wesson puts arms round her, fastens her close*)
WESSON: Oh, you're not faithful to me! (*His voice is like a cry. He
    reaches forward, his mouth to her throat*)
BARBARA (thickly): I am.

The misogyny is almost Strindbergian, and one doesn't have to look far for confirmation of Frieda's view that Lawrence often dreaded and suspected women. Garnett didn't like the play, and Frieda was dissatisfied with her portrait: she thought Lawrence came out of it far better than she did. As well as 'The Fight', he had rushed off two other impromptus, 'The Merry Go Round' and 'The Married Man'. Sending off his novel, now called *Sons and Lovers*, to Garnett in mid-November, he asked for the plays to be returned so that he could recast them before plunging into another novel. He had been 'resisting' poems, more or less, until his novel was done, but more poems had been added to the *Look! We Have Come Through* sequence, and he had even written some preliminary chapters of a travel book, *Twilight in Italy*. This first six months in Italy would be one of the most creative periods of his life.

As well as all this intense activity, he was painting pictures. By Christmas he had done four: he liked to give them away as gifts to friends. And he wanted to do a copy of Maurice Greiffenhagen's *An Idyll*, the painting that had sexually aroused George in *The White Peacock*. 'In this painting', writes Jeffrey Meyers, 'a swarthy Pan figure, of great vigour and vitality, bare-chested and clothed in animal skins, seems rooted in a meadow where the grazing sheep and olive trees are lit up by a setting sun. He is lifting a pale, pre-Raphaelite young woman off her feet, which are covered with bright poppies and daisies. He presses her half-naked bosom against his own body, entwines his fingers in the thick auburn hair cascading down her blue garment to her buttocks, and kisses her cheek as she turns away and swoons limply in his muscular arms, half afraid of passion.'[12] In the novel, George and Lettie talked nervously about the painting, skirting the sexual implications until, 'it was torture to each of them to look thus nakedly at the other . . .' No doubt Lawrence had been reminded of the picture by these Italians all around him, climbing ladders so gracefully to gather in the olive harvest. They had 'such good figures and lovely movements', he wrote admiringly to David Garnett. And he went on to amuse his young friend with a description of the Italian lessons he and Frieda were now having from a punctual schoolmistress, Signorina Feltrelline, who came wearing black gloves and proceeded to keep the two foreigners in order: so much so that Lawrence would resort to the wine bottle 'to assert my masculine and marital independence'. Though the woman thought him a swell, she nevertheless put him firmly in his place and favoured Frieda. 'Of course,' Lawrence added, 'I am much quicker than F.'[13]

From time to time he tried to entice his few friends to visit them, luring them with descriptions of 'one of the most beautiful countries in the world'. The wild Christmas roses were out everywhere, 'under the hedges and rocks and by the streams . . . They rise from their budded, intact humbleness near the ground, they rise up, they throw up their crystal, they become handsome, they are heaps of confident, mysterious whiteness in the shadow of a rocky stream. It is almost uncanny to see them. They are the flowers of darkness, white and wonderful beyond belief.'[14]

He had got the manuscript of *Sons and Lovers* off to Edward Garnett in mid-November, right on schedule. He sent the package registered, then followed it next day with a letter firmly establishing his defence of the book. Garnett's previous criticisms had given him the measure of the man, and he knew more or less what to expect. He had gone through the whole thing again, 'patiently and laboriously', from start to finish, and now he loved it: he felt that this time he had a great book. He also suspected that Garnett would want to tamper with it. To head him off, he set out a powerful summary of the novel, with the theme stated starkly, in almost Freudian terms. Frieda, who called herself 'a great Freudian admirer', had alerted him to Freud, but he was a poet and therefore wary of the Freudian doctrine as it stood: it was altogether too medical, and didn't go nearly deep enough for him. He and Frieda argued for hours about it. But he made no mention of Freud in his letter to Garnett. As he understood it, he had written a tragedy, and it was 'the tragedy of thousands of young men in England – it may even be Bunny's tragedy. I think it was Ruskin's, and men like him.' It had *form*, he insisted, and it had development. Anticipating timidity over the love scenes, he asked, 'Have I made those naked scenes in *Paul Morel* tame enough?'[15]

Waiting impatiently for a reaction, he was heartened by a gay letter from the editor's son, and responded with a joyous account of their daily life that must have had the young man in England yearning to pack a suitcase and begin travelling. At his most charming, Lawrence beguiled him with words ('The place is lovely as a dream'), ending with a vivacious postscript: 'We cook over a charcoal brazier – *fornello* – we eat macaroni and Maggi and I grate pounds of cheese. I cart a fowl from Brescia (three hours' journey) and we fry it in olive oil. Oh it's great! The weird fish we get – the poor little thrushes and blackcaps they bring to the door, on strings – oh, Italy, Italy! But I want a cloak, that I can fling over my nose. You should see 'em! But come!'[16]

These high spirits were dashed by the news that his book of poems had sold barely a hundred copies to date, and by Garnett's verdict on the rewritten *Sons and Lovers*. The novel would have to be pruned. Resigning himself with difficulty, Lawrence replied that he sat 'in sadness and grief after your letter.' It was painful beyond words to think of his beloved book being edited in the name of decency, when he knew it was so clean and beautiful; but at least he was to get a hundred pounds on account from Duckworth. 'I feel quite a thief,' he confessed to his old friend, McLeod.

After the long haul on his novel, he had fully intended to take a rest for a while. Being Lawrence, however, he couldn't be idle. Neither could he settle to writing poetry in the midst of 'tragedy', by which he meant the joint onslaughts by correspondence of Ernest Weekley and the Richthofens. He was heartily sick of Weekley's 'bloody gushings', his wild threats, his insults – his latest was 'that filthy hound' – and resisting these attacks week after week put an intolerable strain on him. He felt more like a business man, who 'stands firm and keeps his eye open', than an artist. How on earth could he write poetry? Yet he badly needed to occupy himself, so as not to brood. He began turning over in his mind an idea for a new novel based on the life of Robert Burns. But he didn't know Scotland, and he wanted to take liberties with the facts. To do this, he would transfer Burns to the Midlands and make him a Derbyshire man. A colleague at Croydon, Agnes Mason, had sent him Lockhart's *Life,* and he now wrote to McLeod to ask him to search out anything of interest in the library. He had always been fond of Burns, he told Garnett, 'as a sort of brother'.

Before he could get started, they had a surprise visitor from England, Harold Hobson, son of the economist J. A. Hobson. They had got on well with him in the summer, and now they did so again. It was good to have some company and it reduced the pressure somewhat. Then, just before Christmas, Lawrence went down with a 'venomous cold', feeling so 'seedy' that he took to his bed. It was the bitter wind, he said, that was making him feel 'beastly'. These were all euphemisms for his incipient tuberculosis, which always struck in the winter months. It was a grim reminder of the essential precariousness of his life. Compensating furiously, he wrote to a young English artist named Ernest Collings, a new correspondent, with as much fire and aggression as he could muster, lashing out at the Garnetts of the world: 'These damned old stagers want to train up a child in the way it should grow, whereas if it's destined to have a snub nose, it's sheer waste of time to harass the poor brat into Roman-nosedness.' Then he came out with what was really rankling in him: 'They want me to have form: that means, they want me to have *their* pernicious ossiferous skin-and-grief form, and I won't.'[17] In a gentler, more humorous vein, he asked Collings to spread the word around in England that he was a great writer, and as pure and sweet as a Sunday school. He voiced the fear that often nagged at him, of having to retreat into teaching again. Early in the new year (1913), though, he had recovered enough to tell Garnett defiantly that he would never go into a school again: at any rate, he added, not a big one. He'd rather starve in a garret, detestable as that fate was. 'I've no sympathy with starvers, Gissings or Chattertons.' He thought he *might* be able to tolerate life in a country school, if it came to it, but Frieda would feel buried alive. She reminded him frequently that he was common, and it was true that he could rub along with anybody. Not Frieda: she was 'a lady'. His attitude to this fact was a curious mixture of pride and irritation. When she spoke to ordinary people, his discomfort was acute. 'She is not a bit stuck-up,' he tried to explain to Garnett, 'really more humble than I am, but she makes the *de haut en bas* of class distinction felt – even with my sister.'[18] He might have added that she encouraged, simply by being herself, his own latent snobbery.

The faithful McLeod, 'the decentest man in England', sent him a 'pack of books', which kept Frieda amused and him absorbed. One he singled out for comment was Rutherford's *Revolution in Tanner's Lane*. Now he was 'fearfully fond' of this rather dull, but 'just and plucky and sound' writer. He was even grateful for the dullness, with all the thunder and lightning of melodrama whirling round his own head at the moment.

Suddenly a confession of love arrived from Alice Dax and must have startled them both, though it was addressed to Frieda. Mrs Dax told her: 'I had always been glad that he met you, even from the day after the event, when he told me about you, and I knew that he would leave me . . . I loved him. But now I think you will understand why I was glad that you loved him too – you who could give him so much, but my cup was bitter when he wrote from the Garda in the richness of fulfilment. How bitterly I envied you that day! How I resented his snobbery and his happiness whilst I was suffering in body and sick in soul, carrying an unwanted child which would never have been conceived but for an unendurable passion which only *he* had roused and my husband had slaked. So – life! And with its irony that same unwanted child is the most enduring and precious joy of all my years.'[19]

Possibly it was her preoccupation with Mrs Dax's words that caused Frieda to leave a letter from her old flame, Will Dowson, in the copy of *Anna Karenina* she now posted to Ernest Weekley. The letter contained Dowson's reactions to her flight from England, and said: 'If you had to run away, why did you not do it with me?' She may have sent Weekley the book in a forlorn attempt to persuade him to see ʌer affair more objectively, but the discovery of Dowson's letter would hardly have had a calming effect. He reacted at once, and maliciously, sending the letter back to Lawrence direct.[20]

As soon as Hobson departed, Lawrence had a go at the new novel based on Burns' life. He sped along quite happily for about eighty pages and then got stuck. Two fragments of this abandoned manuscript survive, neither of them having much to do with Burns.[21] The prose can be regarded as a sort of trial run for the expression of a half-wordless world of sensuality and growth and darkness, centred on woman, that he wanted to forge into shape soon – and would eventually call *The Rainbow*:

'There was scarce a sound anywhere. And yet the night seemed to breathe. He felt his breast burning. Again he went forward down the hedge. Suddenly he started. There was a rush and a flurry down in the hedge. It was a rabbit in one of his snares. He bent down over it. The creature spurted away, to be choked back. The wire ring that throttled it was lightly pegged. He put out his hand to get hold of it. Like a bullet it bounded the other way. But it could not escape. He pulled up the pegs and took the rabbit up in his hands. Suddenly, in its black eye, he saw a point of light glitter with fear and agony. The thing was afraid of him. It gave his heart a shock. There alone in the darkness with the rabbit, that crouched now still, too terrified to move, feeling its little heart quivering, his wrists went weak and his heart melted like fire in him.' The clarity belongs to *Sons and Lovers*, but the gravity and the living, breathing darkness are hints of the later Lawrence, though the stylistic splendours have still to emerge.

This novel came to nothing, but it didn't matter. He was 'simmering' all the time now with new work and felt he had to go on letting the stuff come. He worked at the *Twilight in Italy* sketches, at small poems that came spurting up, sharp with colour and life, like the crocuses, and at something else, a novel probably, which he refused to tell Garnett about: it was too early. 'But the thought of it fills me with a curious pleasure – venomous, almost. I want to get it off my chest.'[22]

Their life of loneliness went on. Now they were really cut off at Gargano, a winter fastness where the wind howled viciously and brought the snow nearer, only a few yards above them. Lawrence objected to that. Italy meant warmth and sunshine, and that was what he had come for. Trying to peer into the future sometimes gave him the blues, so to cheer himself up he scrubbed the floors of his flat, 'acres' of it, or made marmalade.

On 19th November he had delivered a shamefaced *coup de grace* to Louie Burrows. 'I am living here', he wrote, 'with a lady whom I love, and whom I shall marry when I come to England, if it is possible. We have been living together as man and wife for six months nearly now, and I hope we shall always remain man and wife. . . I feel a beast writing this. . . I have nothing to be proud of . . . The best thing you can do is to hate me . . . I loathe signing my name to this.'

They were enlivened by a visit to the village theatre: their landlord gave them the key to his box, and they sat there feeling very grand. The play was an Italianized *Hamlet*. Amletto, a short, stout, bull-necked, middle-aged man, acted especially for them, as important persons. They watched in amazement, struggling not to laugh. All this was elaborated later for inclusion in *Twilight in Italy*. Lawrence saw a farcical *Ghosts* also, and some D'Annunzio.

In this 'pretty hole', in solitude, among these careless peasants, he began to work up, in the *Twilight in Italy* chapters, a virulent hatred of all the manifestations of modern life, yet tempering it with a recognition of the inevitability of 'progress'. England was a fact, America an even greater fact: what could be done? He had met a young Italian, Giovanni, who had emigrated to Pennsylvania with a few other youths, drifting about aimlessly and then getting a job in a dry goods store. There he had been bullied abominably and called 'damn Dago' and spat upon, but he was favoured by the ladies who came to be served by him, for they appreciated his sensitive nature. He went to night school and learned English, lived frugally and earned a hundred dollars a month. By Italian standards, he was rich. What had brought him home was a desire to see his father again before the old man died. He had married, done his military service, and now hankered to go back to the New World again. The past was Gargano, the future was America. He was young, he belonged to the future. In the spring, Lawrence and Frieda saw him off on the lake steamer. 'He was tall and thin and somewhat German-looking, wearing shabby American clothes and a very high double collar and a small American crush hat . . . There was a strange, almost frightening destiny upon him, which seemed to take him away, always away from home, from the past, to that great, raw America. He seemed scarcely like a person with individual choice, more like a creature under the influence of fate which was disintegrating the old life and precipitating him, a fragment inconclusive, into the new chaos.'[23]

Pondering on enigmas like Giovanni, as well as on his own fate, Lawrence went on walks along the lake, if the wind was not too 'beastly', sometimes stopping at the tavern in Bogliaco, sitting in the great open fireplace which was raised up level with your' knees, where the girl came to revive the fire with a long iron blowpipe. He learned to play cards the Neapolitan way, and chatted with the gentle peasants, and the draper, and a man who had been to South America. He loved these people, loved Italy, but he had no intention of settling; anyway Frieda longed to see her children, and for that they would have to go to England.

Poems came quite freely now out of his moods, his dilemma, the regular fights with Frieda and the reconciliations: they were like a map of his progress towards a manhood that was being slowly but surely achieved, despite many setbacks. But sometimes his dead mother would claim him again with her love, when he and Frieda were at loggerheads and what bound them together seemed more like hate than love:

> And because you love me,
> think you you do not hate me?
> Ha, since you love me
> to ecstasy
> it follows you hate me to ecstasy.[24]

Then the 'little woman' would rise from the grave and he would long to have her there with him, in Italy, to show her the loveliness

of the lake and the flowery hills, gather them up and bring them
to her:

> To you, my little darling,
> To you, out of Italy.
> For what is loveliness, my love,
> Save you have it with me![25]

And there was Frieda, damn her, crying over her children.
Why shouldn't he be enough for her? He abused her, until he saw
it was no use; they would have to return to England soon. Then he
gave in, was gentle:

> Hush then
> why do you cry?
> It's you and me
> the same as before.[26]

The weeds grew on his mother's grave. There was only Frieda:
it was undeniable. But now and then he would be torn horribly by
remorse, at the thought of what he had done:

> I forgot you, have forgotten you.
> I am busy only at my burning,
> I am busy only at my life.
> But my feet are on your grave, planted . . .
> I am a naked candle burning on your grave.[27]

Then the spring burst upon them, whirling, the sky came in
glorious flashes, pink and blue, the almond flowers were out. He
watched a sparrow, who 'clouts the tufts of flowers/In his impu-
dence', cheeky enough to think that his 'bit of blue egg' was more
important than the whole blue sky. The spring poems unfurled
like the blossoms:

> Ah, through the open door
> Is there an almond-tree
> Aflame with blossom!
> —Let us fight no more.[28]

For there was always the marvellous newness of Frieda, her
splendid shoulders and breasts and 'bruised throat', above all her
nourishing and fiery love, which he needed so much; and his
grateful tenderness overflowed: 'My little one, my big one,/My
bird, my brown sparrow in my breast . . .'
What more did he want?

Deeply influenced by his new life-in-the-flesh with Frieda, Lawrence now made his first deliberate attempt at the formulation of a doctrine for himself – for a doctrine of some kind was as essential as it had been for Blake. This was the 'Foreword to *Sons and Lovers*', which, Lawrence emphasised to Garnett, was not for publication. Using the language of Christian dogma – he would eliminate this later – he managed to envisage a gospel for man and woman that took full account of the modern 'tragedy'.

At the centre of this doctrine is Woman. Beyond is God, 'the Inscrutable, the Unknowable', and a man can only know God through the flesh of a woman. Thus he is the 'Go-between'. If he fails the woman, he also fails himself, and neither will know God. Then she must find another man, for she is like a queen-bee in the hive, and 'in her all things are born'. 'She is the door for our in-going and our out-coming. In her we go back to the Father: but like the witnesses of the Transfiguration, blind and unconscious.'

Finally there comes the terrible statement: 'And if that Woman be his mother, then is he her lover in part only; he carries for her, but is never received into her for his confirmation and renewal, and so wastes himself in the flesh. The old son-lover was Oedipus. The name of the new one is legion. And if a son-lover takes a wife, then she is not his wife, she is only his bed. And his life will be torn in twain, and his wife in her despair shall hope for sons, that she may have her lover in her hour.'

In January, 1913, Lawrence wrote the now famous letter to Ernest Collings about his new 'belief in the blood, the flesh, as being wiser than the intellect.' He began disarmingly, saying that he was 'a great bosher, and full of fancies that interest me.' In the drawings of the young Collings he detected what he called a 'celibate' element. With Frieda strongly behind him, here was his chance to pontificate on Collings' apparent fear of the female. He was honest enough, though, to own up to his own dependence on Frieda. After speculating briefly on the two drawings Collings had sent him, he outlined a concept which he would keep at the core of all his thinking, all his novels and poems and stories, and elaborate in essay after essay, to the end of his life. 'What do I care about knowledge?' he wrote. 'All I want is to answer to my blood, direct, without fribbling intervention of mind, or moral, or what-not. I conceive a man's body as a kind of flame, like a candle flame, forever upright and yet flowing: and the intellect is just the light that is shed on the things around. And I am not so much concerned with the things around – which is really mind – but with the mystery of the flame forever flowing, coming God knows how from out of practically nowhere, and being *itself*, whatever there is around it, that it lights up.' He went on to develop this into an attack on 'Humanitarianism' and a belief in the truth of one's impulses, whatever they happened to be. This dangerously attractive idea had a desperado ring to it, for it enabled him to shed all his guilt and justify the taking of Frieda. As he put it to Collings, 'The real way of living is to answer one's wants,' to say 'For the living of my full flame – I want that liberty, I want that woman, I want that pound of peaches, I want to go to sleep, I want to go to the pub and have a good time, I want to look a beastly swell today, I want to kiss that girl, I want to insult that man.'[29]

Soon after this, he heard from a Katherine Mansfield in England, who asked for a story for a new magazine, *Rhythm*. Lawrence, in a friendly reply, referred her to Edward Garnett, and said that he might be in London by the spring. Frieda, desperate now to see her children, was determined to be there by Easter. She kept waiting anxiously for news from England which didn't come. She was afraid that if she waited much longer, her children would become estranged from her. Meanwhile, her divorce was at last under way.

Lawrence had begun a new novel, 'The Sisters', which was 'quite different in manner from my other stuff'. Because it was so different, he gave Garnett no details. He took it for granted that he would disapprove: that was no longer important. His early remarks on the subject were distinctly messianic: 'I think, do you know, I have inside me a sort of answer to the *want* of today: to the real, deep want of the English people, not to just what they fancy they want. And gradually', he added ominously, 'I shall get my hold on them.'[30]

One Sunday he and Frieda went on a trip to Campione, ten miles away. The jaunt had a terrifying sequel. Climbing a steep path to get out of the gorge and start back, they were guided, after a fashion, by a 'fearfully drunk' Italian who kept winking at Frieda over Lawrence's shoulder, then grew aggressive and threatened to throw Lawrence over the sheer drop to the water rushing below. Luckily some youths got hold of the man while the two foreigners escaped.

During February, Lawrence was hard at work correcting the proofs of *Sons and Lovers*. There was no doubt in his mind that this book was the best thing he had done, yet he would soon refer to it as the culmination of his youthful period. Working on the proofs must have revived his feelings of allegiance to the past, and that meant to Jessie. He sent his own copy of the proofs in a bulky parcel to her at Nottingham, and wrote: 'I think you ought to see it before it's published. I heard from A. [Ada] that you were in digs again. Send the novel on to her when you've done with it.' In conclusion, he extended a curiously inept, off-hand invitation, which to Jessie was as painful as the sight of those by now hateful pages: 'Frieda and I discuss you endlessly. We should like you to come to us sometime, if you would care to. But we are leaving here in about a week, it's getting too hot for us, I mean the weather, not the place. I must leave off now, they're waiting for me . . .'[31]

Still upset when her sister called, Jessie showed her Lawrence's letter. 'Send it back to him – send it back,' May Holbrook said angrily. At first this seemed an excessively mean thing to do. 'But I turned the idea over in my mind, and the more I looked at it, the better I liked it.' As she copied out the foreign address and slipped the letter in the envelope, she had second thoughts; it would give him so much pain. But she posted it, and immediately felt relief. 'No words', she wrote in her memoir, 'could have produced such a cleansing effect. In a favourite phrase of Lawrence's, it drew the line under the finished sum.'[32]

Lawrence told Garnett about the return of his letter and admitted that it had hurt him, adding ruefully: 'And look, she is bitterly ashamed of having had me – as if I had dragged her spiritual plumage in the mud. Call that love!'[33]

Frieda, after she had read the manuscript of Jessie's autobiographical novel, *The Rathe Primrose*, was more condescending. She thought it 'very lovable, I think, and one does feel sorry for her, but it's a faded photograph of *Sons and Lovers*, she has never understood anything out of herself, no inner activity, but she does make one ache!'[34] And she told Lawrence's biographer, Harry T. Moore, with devastating brevity: 'She tries to defend her position by insisting on the "purity", which gives the show away. She bored me in the end.'[35] She was by now heartily sick of Miriam and the endless discussions about her. Lawrence's first book of poems, just out, was crammed with poems addressed to her and to his other loves. Frieda was out of patience with them all.

The time had come to move. They went first to Verona, stayed a day or two and then continued to Munich. Once in Bavaria, they settled in a Bauerhaus in Irschenhausen which belonged to Frieda's brother-in-law, Professor Jaffe. Though it was their intention to stay for a week, they remained there until September, except for a flying visit to England in the summer. 'I am here,' he wrote to Helen Corke, 'in a little house made of wood, standing in the corner of a hilly meadow against a big pinewood, and looking over at the Alps. Sometimes a deer steps out into the wheat, sometimes a hare lobs among the grass.'[36] They were quite alone,

17. Cossall Church.
Cossall is the village known as Cossethay in *The Rainbow*

18. Church Cottage. Cossall.
The Yew Cottage of *The Rainbow*

and it was beautiful, but almost at once he was missing Italy badly. Going north was an admission of defeat, a come-down somehow. 'If one turns northward or eastward,' he wrote in *Twilight in Italy*, 'it is like walking down a cul-de-sac, to the blind end.' The weather in Bavaria was wrong, the landscape was wrong, 'too green and lush', and the mountains were so stupidly 'there'. All you could do was look at the damned things 'and write bloody rot'. The oxen plodded, the paths were all so definitely going somewhere.

In fact, he was now writing to greater effect than ever before, keeping two novels on the boil simultaneously, as well as short stories – including 'Honour and Arms' and 'Vin Ordinaire'. One of the novels, provisionally entitled 'The Insurrection of Miss Houghton', later on *The Lost Girl*, reached two hundred pages before he decided to set it aside and concentrate on 'The Sisters'. In *The Lost Girl*, one finds Lawrence's ambivalence towards miners and his growing need for hierarchy and subordination all expressed in the same passage:

'The miners seemed to her to loom tall and grey, in their enslaved magic. Slaves who would cause the superimposed day-order to fall. Not because, individually, they wanted to. But because, collectively, something bubbled up in them, the force of darkness which had no master and no control. It would bubble and stir in them as earthquakes stir the earth. It would be simply disastrous, because it had no master. There was no dark master in the world. The puerile world went on crying out for a new Jesus, another Saviour from the sky, another heavenly super-man. When what was wanted was a Dark Master from the Underworld.'[37]

Lawrence envisaged 'The Sisters' as a short novel. And a queer piece of writing it was turning out to be. He had no idea where he was going with it: he tried to let it 'come by itself'. And surprisingly, this 'first crude fermenting' of the book was in the first person. He would re-cast it into the third person later, he told Garnett tensely, and at the same time 'make it into art.' With 256 pages done, he still couldn't see where it was going. At this early stage it was very much Frieda's book, the heroine, Ella Templeman–forerunner of Ursula Brangwen–clearly modelled on her.

Lawrence's old friend and colleague, McLeod, continued to feed books into the post for him. *Medea* came, and Wells' *The New Machiavelli*, and a novel called *The Gadfly*, which left a bad taste with its flavour of sadism. As for Wells, Lawrence had mixed feelings about him: 'He always seems to be looking at life as a cold and hungry little boy in the street stares at a shop where there is hot pork.'

Now he positively hated Germany, so gloomy and moral, pressing down on one's head like a dark cloud. To think of Italy was heartbreaking; he would get back there one day. There was no judging and condemning there. 'It leaves the soul so free.'[38]

By June they were in England: Frieda could wait no longer. Edward Garnett had kindly offered them his house at Edenbridge for a fortnight, and then they were going to sit by the seaside somewhere, probably at Kingsgate, if they could find a flat.

Frieda, burning to see her children again, immediately rushed out to Chiswick, where she believed the family was now living. Not knowing the address, she simply trailed up and down the streets at random, in the hope of catching a glimpse of one of them. After a few days of this, she suddenly spotted a pair of familiar curtains, bought long ago in Nottingham. Without even thinking, she tore into the house and up the stairs. 'We children had been told', Barbara Barr recalls, 'that our mother had brought shame and misery on our family. And suddenly there she stood in the doorway of the nursery where we were having supper with our grandmother and aunt. She appeared to us children like a terrifying apparition, while granny and aunt jumped up in great excitement and hurled abuse at her, as if she were the embodiment of evil. I am sorry to say that we children joined in. Frieda fled, shocked and humiliated.'[39]

She made various attempts, sometimes accompanied by David Garnett, hanging around St. Paul's School in the hope of seeing her son, Monty. Lawrence usually went too, watching from a distance and cursing Frieda from the depths of his heart.

Finally her vigils were rewarded: she saw Monty among a group of boys leaving the school building. Montague Weekley remembers it well: 'A fascinating young lady with a charming and rather mysterious smile came with her. That was Katherine Mansfield.' The two women, one very excited and the other restrained, took him off to a teashop and bought him sweets.[40]

In much the same fashion, Frieda managed to waylay the two girls, Elsa and Barbara. This time they were alone, and jumped around her as joyfully as puppies. But they must have mentioned the encounter when they got home, for the next time they hurried on without speaking, and 'only little white faces looked at me as if I were an evil ghost.'[41]

At The Cearne Lawrence found a pile of reviews of *Sons and Lovers* waiting for him, and a cheque for fifty pounds from his publisher. It was a good welcome. The general tone of the reviews was respectful: he was now a novelist of 'great promise'. He had brought with him the 'Honour and Arms' story about a German officer and his orderly, and one or two others, which he hoped to place in magazines with Garnett's help.

It was idyllic at The Cearne. Mrs Garnett and her son David were there too, and Lawrence and Frieda got on well with them. At Kingsgate, near Broadstairs, they moved into a flat and felt equally cheerful, and when a cheque for three pounds came winging in from Edward Marsh, for the poem 'Snapdragon', Lawrence's note of thanks was almost ecstatic. Without expecting Marsh to accept, he invited him down to Kingsgate to see them. He was in luck: the civil servant was about to visit his friends the Asquiths, who had taken a house for some months at Kingsgate. Marsh promptly arranged to bring the writer and the Prime Minister's son together. 'We are quite swells,' Lawrence reported later to McLeod. 'Edward Marsh came on Sunday (he is the *Georgian Poetry* man and Secretary in the Admiralty to Winston Churchill) and he took us in to tea with the Herbert Asquiths – jolly nice folk – son of the Prime Minister.' To Garnett he wrote: 'Frieda is quite set up at this contact with the aristocracy – of course I am quite superior.'[42]

They had already met John Middleton Murry and Katherine Mansfield in London, and the meeting had been a success. Murry and Katherine Mansfield were living together as man and wife while they waited for Katherine's divorce, so they were in the same position as Lawrence and Frieda, which helped to cement the friendship. The Murrys lived at Chancery Lane, where they had a small flat, and had been running their magazine from there. Alas, this had now collapsed. Katherine Mansfield greeted the visitors from the floor of a rather bare room, where she sat, wide-eyed, by a bowl of goldfish. Intrigued, Frieda befriended the young woman at once, enlisting her help in her efforts to make contact with her children. Lawrence and Frieda looked gay, if poor, in their straw hats, and when they went off in a bus to eat in Soho, Frieda was delighted to see Katherine and Murry pulling faces at each other.

Sitting on the beach at Kingsgate, surrounded by 'fat fatherly Jews and their motor cars and their bathing tents', Lawrence soon began to wonder what on earth he was doing there. He set to work on the Murrys by letter, trying to persuade them to come: 'Come for the weekend, and bathe. We've got a tent in a little bay on the foreshore, and great waves come and pitch one high up, so I feel like Horace, about to smite my cranium on the sky. I can only swim a little bit and am a clown in the water, but it's jolly.'[43] When they came, Katherine swam superbly and Murry himself was good. Not to be outdone, Lawrence darted in and out of the waves, sprightly as a schoolboy. It was twilight, growing chilly. They rubbed themselves dry and went back to the flat and devoured a big supper of fried steak and tomatoes.

Almost immediately, Lawrence wanted to know all Murry could tell him about his life. Then he waded in decisively among the details, sorting them out. There was the mess of the magazine's failure, for instance. Lawrence assured the bewildered couple that this was of no importance, they should congratulate themselves on being rid of it. It was obvious to him that they needed a fresh start somewhere else. Why not get out of England altogether, and join him and Frieda when they reached Italy again? And he gave them an enchanting picture of their six months on the Garda. All this was not only alarming, it was excruciating: the Murrys had nourished for years their own dream of living somewhere abroad, but Murry knew very well that his survival as a reviewer depended on his remaining in London. Lawrence was a creative writer, he could live anywhere, and didn't appreciate their position. Also, Murry was unnerved, to say the least, by this man's terrifying 'immediacy of contact'. Sitting in the train on the return journey to London, he decided that Lawrence was 'a really new experience', and began to read the copy of *Sons of Lovers* their new friend had given them. The opening pages flooded him, he wrote later, 'with warm rich darkness'.[44]

Murry was a handsome, soulful-looking young man, four years younger than Lawrence. Katherine Mansfield looked frail, with her pale, set face under a fringe, her big, dark eyes and boyish figure. The ardent admiration of these two was a sure sign that the young generation had been alerted by the author of *Sons and Lovers*. What exactly was it about the novel that made them look on him now as the coming man? 'It is natural to point out', wrote Richard Aldington, 'that the book was one of the first, if not the first, of English novels to illustrate the psychological theories of Freud, then just coming into vogue in England.'[45] Another convert, Ivy Low, expressed more fulsomely her discovery of the novel: 'The next morning I bought half a dozen post cards and wrote on them: "Discovered a genius!" "Be sure to read *Sons and Lovers*!" "This is a book about the Oedipus complex!" "The most marvellous novel I have ever read!" "I have found a classic by a living author!" "Don't talk to me about Joseph Conrad!" . . . I addressed them haphazard to my friends – first of all to the Meynells, who were the nucleus of one of London's foremost literary cliques.'[46] Lawrence had evidently arrived.

Nevertheless, he was still poor, and before long he heard that the book had actually failed to make a profit. Meanwhile, the time had come to return to Germany. At the end of July they made their way back to the same small wooden house among the firs. With Frieda more settled in her mind about the children – she knew they were safe, and she had managed to remind them of her existence, at least – Lawrence felt they now had a chance, as they turned their backs resolutely on England. And it was good to escape, to be able to breathe and to see things distinctly, to have a broad landscape around you and not to be banging your head against the sky. He sharpened and shone inside himself, in accord with the climate. As soon as it was autumn, they would break camp again and set out for his beloved Italy and the Mediterranean.

Frieda's birthday was in August. This was her homeland, and she celebrated the occasion according to the Bavarian custom, dressing in a beautiful peasant costume and standing solemnly on the little verandah to receive presents from her nephews and nieces. The children trooped in a line up through the meadow, crowned with flowers and carrying baskets of fruit, boxes of sweets, and perfumes. 'Then Peter, aged seven, recited some birthday verses, and Frieda blew on a mouth organ.'[47]

Eager to maintain his new contacts in England, Lawrence opened a correspondence with Cynthia Asquith, who had become Lady Cynthia during that summer. Unsure about this, he added a postscript: 'Are you Honourable or aren't you? How does one address your letters?' His letter betrayed some social unease, as if he were straining to impress her with his newly acquired sophistication: 'We live in a little wooden house (but genuine Dürer engravings and Persian rugs) in a corner of a pine forest. But it rains – oh, Lord! – the rain positively stands up on end. Sometimes one sees the deer jumping up and down to get the wet out of their jackets, and the squirrels simply hang on by their tails, like washing.' Soon they would be going to Italy, probably Lerici, he told her: – 'Shelley and Byron tradition. It might be good for my rhythms.'[48]

Good news came from Austin Harrison, editor of the *English Review*, who was going to publish the 'Honour and Arms' story. The hypnotic summer landscape of the opening of that story – later to be called 'The Prussian Officer' – was all around him again now, with its huge skies: 'On either hand, the valley, wide and shallow, glittered with heat; dark green patches of rye, pale young corn, fallow and meadow and black pine woods spread in a dull, hot diagram under the glistening sky. But right in front the mountains ranged across, pale blue and very still, snow gleaming gently out of the deep atmosphere.'

He had swept everything else aside now to concentrate on 'The Sisters', which he had decided to begin again on 'a new basis altogether'. This time, he promised Garnett, it wouldn't be so 'damned flippant'. But before he could roll up his sleeves and attack it, there was the transfer to Italy to be accomplished. Lawrence was all for walking through Switzerland again, but Frieda had had enough of such hardships. So it was agreed that she should visit her parents and then meet him in a fortnight, in Milan.

He set off alone with his rucksack and his fragile health, a very respectable vagabond, going down the Rhine by steamer to Schaffhausen. The boat journeyed between its 'high, mysterious, romantic banks, which were high as hills', 'the Germany of fairy tales and minstrels and craftsmen',[49] until it reached the ugly factories waiting for him at Schaffhausen.

Switzerland he liked even less than before: he had forgotten how intolerable the 'average ordinariness' of it was, like a dreadful blight falling on everything equally. When he reached Zürich, he found the place like the most ordinary person in the world dressed in a picturesque costume. Two hours were as much as he could stand. He got on a steamer and went down the lake. It began to rain. He thought he would 'rather be in fiery Hell than in this dead level of average life.'[50]

He hated Lucerne, and its lake which was 'like the wrapper round milk chocolate'. He got on a steamer and went right to the end of it. At a German inn he met a fellow-countryman eating bread and milk from a bowl, whom at first Lawrence took for a German. Then he was startled by the young man's London accent: 'It was as if one suddenly found oneself in the Tube.'[51]

He had the painful, English reserve, Lawrence noticed, and hated to be questioned, but it seemed he was on a gruelling walking holiday, forcing himself up and down the mountains in a sort of self-torture. He was half dead with fatigue, but glowing with triumph, as he kept to the punishing schedule he had set himself. He was a London clerk, and this was his fortnight's holiday: that was why he had to keep going. Soon he would be home, riding in the Tube, sitting in his office. He had done a hundred miles in four days, battering along like a machine, 'with no language but English at his command, and his purse definitely limited. Yet he wanted to go among the mountains, to cross a glacier. So he had walked on and on, like one possessed, ever forward. His name might have been Excelsior, indeed.'

This Excelsior, who came from Streatham, certainly had plenty of guts: Lawrence gave him full marks for that. But what was the point of it, what was the poor devil trying to prove? When Lawrence got up in the morning, the young clerk had gone. Lawrence looked up his name in the register. There it was, 'written in a fair, clerkly hand'.[52]

He went on again, through the mountains of the Alps, climbing slowly all day, like an insect crawling under the great shadows of the peaks. He marvelled at the villages perched on the slopes and ledges, high up, dominated by the enormous shadowy mountains, looking down into sheer drops to the valley below. The thought of living in these precarious villages made him shudder, and push on faster. It was all too inhospitable, awesome, deathly. The snowy peaks and the rushing icy water and the collapsing rocks on the vast slopes all seemed to menace the 'little temporary squattings of outcast people.'

Somewhere beyond Andermatt he met a youth from Basel who was heading in the same direction, another clerk on holiday. They set off through the heather and rocks. Emil was properly equipped, wearing hob-nailed climbing boots, and Alpine hat and knee-breeches. They marched along together, and Emil told him that once over the Gothard, he intended to get on a train and travel back to Göschenen, and then carry on with his round trip. He had one week of holiday left.

Over the top and down the south side they went, and now Lawrence was elated to be within striking distance of Italy. Descending, they increased their pace. Now they could see Airolo far below, the track of the railway disappearing into the tunnel, the valley itself 'like a cornucopia full of sunshine.'[53]

Down in the streets, they went into an Italian shop that was hollowed out like a dark cave, and bought sweet black grapes. Emil, a town youth, rolled down his shirt-sleeves and buttoned his shirt at the neck, because he was in streets again. They went together to to the station and had a meal at the restaurant. The boy ordered bread and sausage, and Lawrence, realising how poor his companion was, divided his large amount of beef and vegetable in two, and found an extra knife, fork and plate.

When Emil had gone, Lawrence turned down the Ticino valley, heading for Bellinzona. The new road, bringing the industries and lodging houses to Italy from the world of industrial squalor beyond, depressed him horribly. It was an ugly reminder of England, which he thought he had escaped. 'But there is nothing, in England', he wrote in *Twilight in Italy*, 'to the terror one feels on the new Italian roads, where these great blind cubes of dwellings rise stark from the destroyed earth, swarming with a sort of verminous life, really verminous, purely destructive.'

Bellinzona, when he got there, was somewhat better, the old world still fundamentally intact. But the road out had the same 'evil' aspect, its houses flung down like raw crystals.

Even the peasant girl he saw working in the fields as he passed by on the high road, her 'handsome naked flesh that shone like brass', seemed to him to personify the callous new order. He paused a moment to admire her, and she shouted out something in a raucous voice that he couldn't understand.

He stayed the night at Lugano, and the next day walked by the lake, then went by steamer the rest of the way. Walking again, he got on a tram at Chiasso and rode to the Lake of Como. Fashionable town women looked askance at his dishevelled appearance, mistaking him for a navvy. Lawrence didn't realise this, however, until it was time to get off and he noticed that a girl, climbing down ahead of him, had left her parasol behind.

'*Pardon, Mademoiselle*,' he said, and she turned on him haughtily, to hear what this dirty individual could have to say to her. Seeing the parasol, she grabbed it 'with a rapacious movement'. As she hurried off, in her white kid boots, Lawrence muttered '*bourgeoise*' under his breath.

Another steamer floated him down to Como, where he stayed the night 'in a vast old stone cavern of an inn'. Then he got on a train to Milan. On a Saturday afternoon, he sat in Cathedral Square and waited for Frieda. Sipping Campari and watching the bustling city life, he decided that here the steady disintegration of the past was at least vigorous, 'centred in a multiplicity of mechanical activities that engage the human mind as well as the body. 'But always,' he noted with disgust, 'there was the same purpose stinking in it all, the mechanizing, the perfect mechanizing of human life.'[54]

When Frieda arrived, they went on together to Lerici, across the gulf from La Spezia. There they found a small hotel by the sea, and began to search for a cottage. Soon they discovered one at Fiascherino: to get there, you had to row yourself round the headland in a boat, or get one of the rare steamers.

Fiascherino was only a few miles from Shelley's San Terenzo. The pink, four-roomed cottage was cheap, and the rent included a servant woman who washed and cleaned, coming to and fro from the next village. Lawrence wrote off at once to tell Garnett the glad tidings. 'You run out of the gate into the sea, which washes among the rocks at the mouth of the bay. The garden is all

vines and fig trees, and great woods on the hills all round.' And
Felice, the old servant, sixty if she was a day, she was something to
crow about, striding around barefoot, proud as a queen with
great loads of charcoal on her head, 'her petticoats kilted up and a
gleam of triumph in her eye.' She brought the soup tureen like
'the Queen of Sheba taking spice to Solomon.' Her girl, Elide,
came sometimes and acted as maid, but according to Lawrence
she'd never seen a scrubbing brush in her life, and the 'exquisite'
cottage was filthy when they came to look inside. So Lawrence,
Puritan conscience blazing and braces knotted round his waist,
'went for it. Lord, to see the dark floor flushing crimson, the dawn
of deep red bricks rise from out of this night of filth, was enough
to make one burst forth into hymns and psalms.' As for Elide,
exclaiming behind him about fresh air and clean rooms, 'She
might as well have said nectar and ambrosia, for all she knew of
'em.'[55]

Lawrence went swimming often, though he was a poor swim-
mer and Frieda told him more than once that he would end up by
following Shelley's example. He took no notice of her. The only
way he could be a poet, she yelled after him, was by drowning like
one.

For perhaps the first time in his life he felt no compulsion to
work. 'If I'd got the smallest income,' he wrote to Edward Marsh,
'I should be delighted to loaf for ever.' But if this was a hint, it
didn't produce a response. Marsh was now amiably guiding him,
so he thought, down the straight and narrow path of poetry.
Lawrence resisted this in his own way, by demolishing, one after
the other, Marsh's current favourites. There was 'poor' W. H.
Davies, for instance: 'I think one ought to be downright cruel to
him, and drive him back: say to him, Davies, your work is getting
like Birmingham tin-ware; Davies, you drop your 'h's, and everybody is tempering the wind to you, because you are a shorn lamb;
Davies, your accent is intolerable in a carpeted room; Davies, you
hang on like the mud on a lady's silk petticoat. Then he might
leave his Sevenoaks room, where he is rigged up as a rural poet,
proud of the gilt mirror and his romantic past: and he might grow
his wings again, and chirrup a little sadder song.'[56]

But it was difficult to work oneself up into a temper here, with
the water glittering among the rocks, and ripe figs falling in the
garden. Writing to Lady Cynthia he did manage one or two
octopus-squirts of inky rage, as he recalled the 'stupid' mountains
of Switzerland, 'always in the way', and then Milan, 'its imitation
hedgehog of a cathedral, and its hateful town Italians, all socks
and purple cravats and hats over the ear'. Then he relaxed, and

rejoiced again at his great good luck in finding such a cottage in such a place, where you could bathe naked and think of London in amazement, 'all smoke a long way off'.

Writing to Edward Garnett, he mentioned a short story, 'Once', that he thought might go well with the two soldier stories already taken by the *English Review*. He wondered, though, if Harrison would think it too strong. 'Once' has a good deal of Frieda, and Frieda's younger sister, in it. The heroine, Anita, an aristocrat's daughter married to 'a brute' of an officer who neglects her, has begun to take lovers. The narrator of the story is her latest lover, and in the story she torments him, half unconsciously, with her past. He probes obsessively for more details, and then hates her for her shamelessness in telling him. Laughing with pleasure, she remembers a young officer who came to her once in her hotel room, as she lay on her bed, and threw a whole armful of red and pink roses on her. This was magnificent, but she loved him even more for the way he unbuckled his belt with all its jingling paraphernalia and flung it down, before making love to her. Listening to this description, the narrator burns with jealousy and thinks he will never be able to trust her, if her passion depends on anything so proposterous. But she is a superb creature, and, like it or not, he loves her.

The story is full of the sensual delight in a woman's body that Lawrence was now experiencing for the first time, with Frieda. Her naked flesh, like her uninhibited nature, still startled him. 'She was so natural! She was dressed in a transparent lacy chemise, that was slipping over her shoulder, high boots, upon one of which her string-coloured stocking had fallen. And she wore an enormous hat, black, lined with white, and covered with a tremendous creamy-brown feather, that streamed like a flood of brownish foam, swaying lightly.' Such a picture of wickedness – and how thankfully Lawrence embraced it! Yet this story is the nearest he ever came to owning directly to a fascination that was far from being a commitment.

In another tale of this period, 'New Eve and Old Adam', the protagonists, clearly Frieda and Lawrence, are engaged in that battle 'so many married people fight, without knowing why.' At the end, the relationship founders because neither will yield to the other. 'She crouched between his knees and put her arms round him. She was smiling into his face; her green eyes, looking into his, were bright and wide. But somewhere in them, as he looked back, was a little twist that could not come loose to him, a little cast, that was like an aversion from him, a strain of hate for him.' And he too was flawed: 'he seemed only like an instrument

for his work, his business, not like a person at all. Sometimes she
thought he was a big fountain pen which was always sucking at
her blood for ink.' This deadly image signals more grievous
battles to come. She may tell him, in bed, that he is her lord, but to
him this is mere childish indulgence on her part. It doesn't mean
that she submits to him.

At Fiascherino there was a lull of happiness. Whatever was in
store for them, they were irrevocably bound to each other now.
Again and again their letters reflected it. They might have violent
flaming rows, and nearly tip themselves out of the rowing boat on
their way to Lerici, but they could laugh these quarrels out of the
window afterwards. Fundamentally they were together as never
before. Lawrence freely admitted now that his big new novel,
'The Sisters', afterwards called 'The Wedding Ring' and finally
The Rainbow, was founded on his life with Frieda, 'of me and of
her', as he told Middleton Murry. The final title was Frieda's
inspiration, and it expressed the hope and the triumph they both
felt at the firm establishment of their relationship at last. It had
survived the deluge, the darkness and the flood, and now they
would be married. It was permanent.

A kind of sympathetic letter came from Cynthia Asquith.
Responding warmly to it in her rather muddled, breathless
English, Frieda gave her letter to Lawrence, who interlarded her
sentence with comic contradictions before posting it:

21 December, 1913

(In D.H.L's hand: 'The shortest day.' Frieda's: 'his temper
short as well.')

Dear Mrs Asquith,
    You wrote me such a frightfully nice letter, don't be too
sympathetic, I warn you, or I shall come and weep to you
when we are in England. Don't be too sorry either, after all
we are very happy too, (I'm not – DHL) and I believe in the
miracle too; (I don't – DHL) only it's hard, I miss them so,
like one would miss a leg (L: one wouldn't, after a fortnight).
It's still gorgeous here (L: it isn't – it's cold and dark). I know
such a lovely little villa with torrino here 'with a beautiful,
beautiful' view for you. We hear of you through Eddie
Marsh, a Kipling performance was the last. Barrie wrote
such a nice letter to L. (L. – he didn't) This is to wish you all
three a Merry Christmas. L. must write, being an 'autore', he
does it so much better than yours, (L. – what a hateful way of
ending)   Frieda.

They were not so isolated at Fiascherino as they had been at Gargano. A social period began for them. There was a small English colony at Lerici, people like the English consul at La Spezia, and the Chaplain, keen to meet the author of *Sons and Lovers*. Soon, stray visitors from England were seeking out the Lawrences; but when a quartet of Georgian poets descended out of the blue, Lawrence found it hard to make the adjustment from his Italian neighbours to the small group of cultured Englishmen. Two of them, W. W. Gibson and Lascelles Abercrombie, he liked a great deal – Gibson especially. Abercrombie he thought sharp rather than lovable, very much the intellectual. This 'very rare air' made him literally stagger, after the thick-blooded Italian life. But, so he told McLeod, the wine at the time was 'running very red', so he could have been tipsy.

Just before the arrival of this party, Frieda suddenly conceived a passion for a piano she had seen in La Spezia. Why couldn't they hire it? Lawrence went off obediently to grapple with the formidable transport problems involved. First it had to be put on one of the workmen's steamers as far as Lerici, manhandled into a rowing boat and steered past the rocks in the rough November sea to their small bay, then dragged up all the steps to their cottage. He came back empty-handed, after hours spent among Italians all flapping their hands and squawking excitedly with their heads on one side. Now, he told Lady Cynthia, he detested Italians for their stupidity. The 'cursed' piano would have to come overland and he would end up paying 'a regiment' to do the job. A few letters later, he told Will Hopkin that he was 'very fond of the Italians', and by this he meant their little maid Elide, whose quaint ceremoniousness delighted him. He approved, too, of her cousin, the beautiful Luigi, who came sometimes in the evening and played his guitar.

Some of Lawrence's letters home during this period were on Frieda's crested stationery, and often carried a note to say that Frieda's mother gave them a lot of this paper – 'please excuse it'. He still liked to impress certain people, such as the Asquiths, with the fact that his 'wife's' father was a baron: using the stationery was a nice way of rubbing it in without appearing to care one way or the other.

Entrenched in his newly won security, Lawrence now proceeded to set about Murry and Katherine Mansfield, analysing their situation in a letter to Murry so savagely frank and hectoring that it must have stung for weeks afterwards. This outburst was in response to a letter from Murry explaining why he couldn't bring himself to live off Katherine's allowance, as Lawrence had suggested. Katherine, said Murry, weakly, needed her distractions and her little luxuries, and he couldn't bear to deprive her of them – yet he was too poor to provide them himself.

Brutally, Lawrence told him: 'If you must work yourself sterile to get her chocolates, she will most justly detest you – she is *perfectly* right. She doesn't want you to sacrifice yourself to her, you fool. Be more natural, and positive, and stick to your own guts. You spread them on a tray for her to throw to the cats.' Supremely confident, he went on to explain to the 'fool' that 'a woman unsatisfied must have luxuries.'[57] This, of course, was before Frieda had demanded her piano, but he would doubtless have argued successfully that Frieda had given up everything to go with him in the first place and had therefore earned her piano. Not that such apparent contradictions ever bothered him in the slightest. He was, and indeed he had to be, irrefutably right always, for hadn't his mother taught him never to forget that he was a Lawrence and that the Lawrences of Eastwood were special? This particular moral onslaught finally ended, several pages later, with a renewal of Lawrence's invitation to the Murrys to join him in Italy, where the living was so cheap and easy, and where they could be called '*Signoria*' into the bargain. Meanwhile, he would be glad of a few books, as Frieda was out of reading matter again.

Christmas came, and it was a social time for Lawrence and Frieda. They were invited to the homes of rich new friends in the colony, the Cochranes and Pearses and Huntingdons, all of whom had read *Sons and Lovers* with admiration, according to Lawrence. They went as Mr and Mrs Lawrence, hoping that no one had heard of their 'dark history', or read of it in the London papers. But despite this social activity, he didn't neglect to maintain contact with his roots. To Will Hopkin he wrote: 'I *was* glad to get that letter from you, full of good old crusty Eastwood gossip. Always write to me like that.' And in the new year (1914) he wrote a long letter to Jessie's sister, May Holbrook, asking for all her news, skilfully touching his descriptions with nostalgia for her benefit. 'In the rocks by the sea,' he told her, 'the little white and yellow narcissus, such as one buys off Rowley's greengrocer cart in Eastwood, are twinkling away in the sunshine.'[58]

He had sent Edward Garnett yet another version of the big novel he kept tussling with, now called 'The Wedding Ring', warning him that it was so different from *Sons and Lovers* that it was like another language. Anticipating his friend's reaction, he added bluntly that he was finished now with his *Sons and Lovers* manner, 'that hard, violent style full of sensation and presentation'.[59] Obviously he expected trouble from Garnett.

When the editor's criticisms arrived he considered them carefully, point by point. Garnett was disappointed and censorious. Richard Aldington has summed up his attitude in these words: 'After two exciting but not quite integrated early novels Lawrence had produced in *Sons and Lovers* a masterpiece of very high achievement. Among the qualities which had attracted readers were its mingling of precise reality with poetic imagination, its truth to ordinary life and high aspiration, its clear presentation of character and the clash of deep but completely understood emotions, its vivid writing from beginning to end. And he was still in his twenties. Naturally, Garnett's expectations of the next novel were high, especially as Lawrence had written rather boastfully of it. Imagine Garnett's disappointment when he found that Lawrence had dropped all this for a rather solemn saga of generations where character was analysed so far back to common elements that there was some difficulty in sorting out the people and remembering them. It was at once rustic and psychological, as if it were a Russian novel written by George Eliot.'[60]

Defending himself with a new obstinacy, Lawrence went to great pains to explain why it was absolutely essential for him to write differently. He was quite prepared, if Garnett felt disappointed with the second half also, to jettison the whole thing, 'put all this novel in the fire', because he knew he was going through a transition stage, and his 'spring' would eventually come. In this early version of the novel, the Ursula of *The Rainbow* and *Women in Love* was still called Ella Templeman. Putting it aside a week later, he reported to McLeod with extraordinary fortitude: 'I have begun my novel again – for about the seventh time. I hope you are sympathising with me. I had nearly finished it. It was full of beautiful things, but it missed – I knew that it just missed being itself.'[61]

Although he was still some way from the bisexual themes of *Women in Love*, the character of Birkin had already been conceived, and before Christmas he had written an exploratory letter to Henry Savage on the nature of homosexuality. 'I should like to know', he asked, 'why nearly every man that approaches greatness tends to homosexuality, whether he admits it or not: so that he loves the *body* of a man better than the body of a woman – as I believe the Greeks did, sculptors and all, by far. I believe a man projects his own image on another man, like on a mirror. But from a woman he wants himself reborn, reconstructed. So he can always get satisfaction from a man, but it is the hardest thing in life to get one's soul and body satisfied from a woman, so that one is free from oneself. And one is kept by all tradition and instinct from loving men, or a man – for it means just extinction of all the purposive influences.' Becoming incoherent, he dismissed the difficult subject in exasperation: 'Again I don't know what I'm talking about.'[62] But he had voiced for the first time in his letters the dire, secret need of his life, which was for a man friend. 'If only you'd been a man, things might have been perfect,' he once said to Jessie Chambers. His letter to May Holbrook had ended with a sad postscript, asking for news of Jessie.

One night in January there was a heavy snowfall. Elide didn't turn up in the morning, so Lawrence got up and built a roaring fire 'and proceeded to wash the pots, in a queer, silent, muffled Fiascherino.' Looking out, he saw a weird, Japanese-like scene, the pines standing dark on the headland, over the 'lead-grey' sea. The colour had run out of everything, the sea sliced a sharp, clean curve on the snowy beach. Lawrence saw it as a 'Japanesey' wash drawing, with 'no distance, no perspective, everything near and sharp on a dull grey ground.' Mino the cat, sunk in the snow outside the door, was mewing piteously, but fled when they tried to get him into the house.

The olive trees on the hillside, bent under the weight of the snow, were creaking and crashing to the ground. Soon many trees were smashed, and villagers running to and fro excitedly, lamenting their loss.

By the end of February the spring had transformed everything with its violets and anemones, wild narcissi and primroses, the ground foaming like the sea. The olives were ready for gathering, and a great triumphant activity began. Men came with long canes to beat down the olives, leaving the small black fruit on the ground for the peasant women to gather in panniers and carry down to the village on their heads. Lawrence and Frieda kept getting invitations to dinner, and more visitors from England, such as Ivy Low. Miss Low was a novelist herself, a friend of another of Lawrence's new admirers, Catherine Carswell. This gushing and affected girl's first impression of the famous young author was that he was 'a darling', but when he asked her what she thought of him, her words soon disenchanted him. She told him that he was like a working man, 'full of life', sitting in the corner of a third-class compartment, with the tools of his trade in a straw bag on the floor; then she sat enjoying her remorse at the look of pain on his face. But it was all right, she decided, for he was soon looking at her admiringly again, 'with his soul in his eyes'.

After a week of her company, the honey in the conversation stopped flowing, as she trailed down the paths with Lawrence and naïvely unburdened herself, talking about everything from writing problems to her friendship with Viola Meynell. Frieda remarked cattily that all she saw of the pair of them was their jaws opening and shutting, and, more pointedly, that Lawrence would rather walk with the dullest person than go alone. Taking his cue from Frieda, Lawrence now let rip with his own brand of malice. The trouble with Miss Low was that she deluded herself: she was wasting her time trying to become a good writer. As for her friendship with Viola, in his opinion it didn't exist; if it did, she wouldn't be carting that big framed photograph everywhere she went. Poor Ivy Low was bewildered, but Lawrence had hardly got into his stride. In the next few days he fired off volleys of criticism, much of it stinging and personal. She walked clumsily, she talked too much, she never offered to help in the kitchen, and she had an absurd way of lengthening her vowels. Lawrence mimicked her speech after a visit by the poet Sturge Moore, just to ensure that she knew what she sounded like. It was funny, accurate, cruel. She went back to England badly shaken, and with very mixed feelings about 'the greatest living English author'.

By now Lawrence had had his fill of visitors, especially the female of the species. 'And my God,' he exclaimed to Henry Savage, 'how weary I am of women, women, eternal women.' The spring had entered his veins and he felt restless: he wanted to turn his back on writing and on people, to walk out of the house and into the hills and just disappear. They went on a picnic, high above the sea, and could see Carrara, and 'great white slits of the quarries', and mountain peaks in the distance. It tore at him intolerably, the great longing to wander again, let his feet follow the road. From where they sat they could see the coast curving, towns scattered along it 'like handfuls of shells', the sails of ships 'like butterflies in mid-air'. Up there on the untamed hillside he spoke to an old man who was a charcoal-burner and slept under a sort of tent of branches he had made for himself. Lawrence felt hemmed in, he wanted to free himself, go off somewhere alone. The whole earth was about to give birth, and he felt his own spring surging nearer, underground, in the earth of his flesh. He had begun his novel yet again.

12

'And The Rainbow Stood on The Earth'

That day on the hills had been symbolic. After it, in letters to his few friends in England, Lawrence made it clear that he had also reached a peak inside himself. If all went well, he and Frieda would be in England by the summer, and married. But the battle on that front was far from over: Frieda's 'old figurehead of a husband plays marionette Moses, then John Halifax, Gentleman, then Othello, then a Maupassant hero tracking down his victims, one stock piece after another, with amazing energy. He is a fool. I wish the worms would eat him up.'[1]

The recipient of this aside was Middleton Murry, to whom he was now 'getting rather sermony'. Murry had, amazingly, not taken offence at the onslaught of Lawrence's last letter. Even Lawrence was surprised by this. He had expected Murry and Katherine to accuse him of being 'an interfering Sunday-school superintendent sort of person', he confessed. What he was, in fact, was a thorough-going Nonconformist with a passion of impatience, who had fought the good fight and henceforth would preach the virtues of being oneself and having faith in oneself: in other words, having the guts to stand alone, against the entire world if necessary.

This was the substance of his sermon now to Murry. He told him, after a few skipping sentences of easy guilt-shedding: 'At present, I do believe in trying to give what moral support one can. I call it, helping people to have *faith*. I am rather great on faith just now.' Already, in this letter, he had started to make the first of his impassioned pleas for *real* friends, and to hint at persecution. 'They are all against one. I feel Marsh against me with the whole of his being: and Campbell would like to be, for he is a perverse devil.' But they, the Murrys, would get on famously with him and Frieda, he wrote emphatically, 'and we'll be jolly'. It was a determined overture of friendship, with his coming visit to England very much in mind.[2]

In his letters during this resurgent season, he declared outright war on the traditionalists, sounding the battle-cry whenever he wrote to one of their representatives. His attitude towards Garnett's endless carping about *The Rainbow* suddenly hardened. Dropping the note of sad resignation he normally used, he turned militant, referring angrily to the other's previous gibes about Lawrence's 'commonness' and telling him bluntly: 'You know how willing I am to hear what you have to say, and to take your advice and to act on it when I have taken it. But it is no good unless you will have patience and understand what I *want* to do. I am not after all a child working erratically.' This was plain speaking indeed, and it marked a turning point in their relationship. Lawrence continued, even more significantly: 'But primarily I am a passionately religious man, and my novels must be written from the depth of my religious experience.'[3] With this extraordinary statement he lifted the argument out of the confines of literature altogether. Garnett was first and foremost a literary man: hence their insurmountable differences.

Lawrence's firm stand was made possible by the new economic freedom he was beginning to feel. A leading agent, Pinker, together with Curtis Brown, had made offers for the next novel when it was ready, so that he was no longer dependent on Garnett's firm, Duckworth, for money. The loss that Duckworth had made on the publication of *Sons and Lovers* was yet another determining factor for Lawrence. He would rather a big commercial publisher took the gamble on him, he told Garnett: then he wouldn't feel such personal qualms.

This stand established, Lawrence turned next to Edward Marsh, who still insisted on plodding up and down before him as a sort of policeman of poetry. Once more attacking Marsh's poets rather than the man himself, he tore into the 'red nose and rough-spun cloak' brigade of Masefield, Gibson, and now Lascelles Abercrombie: Lawrence had just seen the second issue of *New Numbers*. 'I hate and detest', he wrote, 'his [Abercrombie's] ridiculous imitation yokels and all the silly hash of his bucolics; I loathe his rather nasty efforts at cruelty, like the wrapping frogs in paper and putting them for cartwheels to crush; I detest his irony with its clap-trap solution of everything being that which it seemeth not; and I hate that way of making what Meredith called Cockney metaphors: moons like a white cat and meteors like a pike fish.'[4] Some of this furious loathing for Abercrombie had been whipped up by the poet speaking of *Sons and Lovers* as being 'all *odi et amo.*' Unable to control his rage, Lawrence condemned the poetry and the man as 'cheap and wicked', 'mean and rather sordid', 'full of rancid hate', 'corrupt and dirty', and wondered finally if something was 'going bad in his soul'.[5] The insult had been returned with interest, and the amiable Marsh must have been stunned by this torrent of disgust expressed in moral terms.

In May, Lawrence wrote again to Murry, badgering him to stop struggling with his wretched problems and just 'get well physically'. This fresh blast of advice was delivered like an order. Murry should give in, be dependent on Katherine, and evidently on Lawrence too. But Lawrence was also in need of staunch friends himself. About to come to London, his novel finished yet again, he had begun to divide the world into those for and those against him. Referring to the novel, he wrote: 'Don't get sick and leave me in the lurch over it. Can you understand how cruelly I feel the want of friends who will believe in me a bit? People think I'm a sort of queer fish that can write; that is all, and how I loathe it. There isn't a soul cares a damn for me, except Frieda – and it's rough to have all the burden put on her.'[6] Here was his second direct appeal for the other's friendship. And Murry was a fine critic, rising fast in the literary world: he would be a valuable ally.

Other, less likely allies at this time were the futurists, in particular Marinetti and Paolo Buzzi, though neither of these contemporaries even knew of Lawrence's existence. Lawrence had been reading their essays and manifestos avidly, in search of a system of ideas with which to confront men like Garnett who were critical of the new direction his novel had taken. He saw that he had to stiffen his defence, and in any case he shrank from delivering up the naked body of his book to a literary world which he knew would be hostile to it. These Italian futurists were at least boldly modern, though their pseudo-scientific jargon didn't really deceive him. 'They want to deny every scrap of tradition and experience, which is silly,' he told McLeod. 'They are very young, college-student and medical-student at his most blatant.'[7] But he resembled them in at least one respect, and that was in the quest for a new approach, a new attitude that would take the artist beyond the existing moral scheme and on to a consideration of what Marinetti called 'the physiology of matter'. That fascinated him, and he loved the way it cut one free from the 'beastly' sentimental and the old-fashioned manufacturing of characters who could only develop in accordance with fixed human laws. The futurists, 'crassly stupid' though they were, smashed a hole through the cardboard and let in the inhuman. Putting this revolt in terms he personally found acceptable, he told Garnett, 'I don't so much care about what the woman *feels* – in the ordinary usage of the word. That presumes an *ego* to feel with. I only care about what the woman *is* – what she IS – inhumanly, physiologically, materially . . .'[8] No doubt realising how shocking this would be, Lawrence then tried to formulate a metaphysic from it that would stand up to an almost scientific scrutiny, having the same irreducible quality as the basic elements themselves. 'You mustn't look in my novel,' he warned, 'for the old stable *ego* – of the character. There is another *ego*, according to whose action the individual is unrecognisable, and passes through, as it were, allotropic states which it needs a deeper sense than any we've been used to exercise, to discover are states of the same single radically unchanged element.'[9]

This must have been sheer gibberish to the conservative Garnett, but Lawrence went on very earnestly with his attempt to interpret the vision embedded deeply in the novel which he thought he had at last completed. It was necessary to establish a bridgehead, ready for the next advance. The futurists' jargon wearied him almost as soon as he had made use of it, but to express his ideas in terms of physics like this was at any rate more respectable than talking about Freud and the Unconscious. Later on he would make a more sustained effort to erect 'pollyanalytics' on the evidence 'derived from his novels and poems', as he put it.

Keeping to their plan, Lawrence and Frieda headed north in June, but they went in different directions. Frieda got on the train for Baden-Baden, to call on her parents en route for England, while Lawrence joined up with a man named Lewis, who worked at the Vickers-Maxim factory at La Spezia, and the two set off on foot across Switzerland and towards France. From Aosta he sent a postcard to his sister, Ada, to say that he and Lewis were going over the St Bernard Pass. It was tough going, and after climbing part of the way through snow which was three feet deep in places, they slept in the monastery, in 'a lovely little panelled room'. By the end of June Lawrence and Frieda were together again, staying in Selwood Terrace, Kensington with a young Irish barrister, Gordon Campbell, to whom Murry had introduced them the year before.

On the day of his marriage, 13th July, 1914, Lawrence wrote to Sallie Hopkin: 'Frieda and I were married this morning at the Kensington registrar's office. I thought it was a very decent and dignified performance. I don't feel a changed man, but I suppose I am one.'[10] The Murrys and Campbell were witnesses. Both Katherine and Murry had had pleurisy, and, for various reasons, they were in poor shape psychologically. In their own uncertain state, they were bound to have mixed feelings about the marriage. Murry says solemnly in his reminiscences that Lawrence took the ceremony very seriously because he and Frieda had lived together for some time, and so knew 'the reality of the bond that binds a man and a woman'. And Katherine was so impressed by Lawrence's insistence on the permanence and importance of marriage that she jettisoned there and then her allegiance to women's rights and announced that she would wear a wedding ring. Frieda impulsively gave her friend the wedding ring of her former marriage, as she had no further use for it. Katherine put it on, and she wore it for the rest of her life.

The Lawrences had many visitors at Selwood Terrace. One of the first was Catherine Jackson (afterwards Carswell), a fervent admirer who managed to meet with Frieda's approval from the beginning. Mrs Jackson had already heard rumours of the beauty of Frieda, but the reality disappointed her. For one thing, she thought her clothes were unsuitable. 'She wore a tight coat and skirt of horse-cloth check that positively obscured her finely-cut, rather angry Prussian features.' Lawrence, however, impressed her at once 'with his deep-set jewel-like eyes, thick dust-coloured hair, pointed underlip of notable sweetness, fine hands, and rapid but never restless movements.'[11] Soon she was asking him to read the manuscript of her first attempt at a novel. The letter she got from him was far from sweet: he had decided that the best way he could help her was by giving her a severe trouncing at the outset. He told her: 'You have very often a simply *beastly* style, indirect and round-about and stiff-kneed and stupid. And your stuff is abominably muddled – you'll simply have to write it all again.'[12] Like the willing disciple she already was, she took this slap in the face without a murmur, and trotted round humbly to discuss all the points he had raised. To her astonishment, she found that this meant getting down to four hours of hard work that very afternoon, with Lawrence sitting tensely beside her at the table, 'quiet and teacher-like'. Throughout the session, she felt he was darting to and fro in spirit like a bird – and a bird with a painfully sharp beak. Yet he managed to be charming, and endlessly encouraging, in spite of all his strictures. She discovered that once he was assured of her seriousness, he took it for granted that she was on an equal footing with him, and treated her accordingly. This startling evidence of his patience and humility quite overwhelmed her.

Freudian psychoanalysts, alerted by the Oedipus theme in *Sons and Lovers*, now began to seek Lawrence out. The first to do so was Dr David Eder. Murry would call round to find the two men discussing sex with an intensity and seriousness which baffled the young literary critic. Ignorant of Freudian doctrine, Murry was bewildered by Lawrence's insistence on its importance, and he resented the implied criticism of himself and Katherine which he felt Lawrence was levelling. Why *should* they be tormented lovers, with complexes and repressions, just because Lawrence and Frieda were? To Lawrence this was childish, not to say flippant. Katherine retaliated by spitefully poking fun at what Murry called 'Lawrence's Freudian entourage', which now included Dr Eder's wife, Edith, and her sister, Barbara Low, herself to become a psychoanalyst. But the real reason for their irritation lay elsewhere, for Lawrence's insistence on an intimate relationship between him and the Murrys had led them to regard him as their special friend. Now it seemed that everyone wanted to know him. There was a veritable crowd of new friends in Hampstead, for instance, and the Murrys regarded them with a mixture of jealousy and suspicion. Murry admitted that he himself preferred one or two close friends and was devoid of social aptitude, and Katherine often felt 'like a cat among tigers' at parties; whereas Lawrence sometimes enjoyed company, and Frieda, warm and expansive by nature, could be positively gregarious.

A comic incident soon emphasised these incompatibilities. Campbell, Katherine, Murry and the Lawrences took the tube to Hampstead one sunny July afternoon, to picnic on the Heath. Emerging at Hampstead Station, they started up the hill, with Frieda and Lawrence in the lead. All at once Ivy Low appeared from nowhere, screaming 'Lawrence!' and running down the hill towards them, arms stretched wide in extravagant welcome. The Murrys and Campbell took one horrified look at the vision and fled, leaving Lawrence to face the girl alone. When Lawrence accused them later of making him look a perfect fool, Katherine tried to articulate her neurotic fear of being rushed at by gushing females. Calming down, Lawrence admitted that probably no one had seen them melt away: certainly he hadn't.[13]

His literary affairs were now in the hands of J. B. Pinker, the agent, and through him he accepted an advance of three hundred pounds from Methuen for his new novel. In September, getting desperate for money, he asked Pinker to 'extort' the first half of this advance from Methuen, though by this time he had begun work on the eighth version of *The Rainbow*. Whether this was at the request of the publisher, or because of his own continuing dissatisfaction with it, is not clear.

By now his poetry had attracted the attention of editors in America, and both Harriet Munroe and Amy Lowell were after him for poems. At the end of July he heard that Harriet Munroe had taken 'Grief', 'Memories', 'Weariness', 'Service of All the

Dead', 'Don Juan', 'Song', and 'Ballad of Another Ophelia'. But she wanted to 'cut the tail' off the ballad, and he vigorously objected. He ordered her to 'use it whole or not at all.'

Amy Lowell was in London that summer, drumming up recruits for the Imagist movement and endeavouring to wrest the leadership from Ezra Pound. Partly to capture Lawrence, she gave a dinner at the Berkeley and invited him. It was the end of a sunny July day on the eve of the war. Just before Lawrence came into Amy's private room, Richard Aldington, sitting by an open window with his American wife, the poet H.D., looked down over the Piccadilly traffic at the news-stand by the Ritz, with its poster: 'British Army Mobilised'.

Incredibly, no one took the news very seriously. Then Lawrence entered, and Aldington saw for the first time this slim young man 'with a lithe, springing step'. He noticed particularly his brilliant blue eyes, and remembered long afterwards his opening words to the company: 'I say, I've just been talking to Eddie Marsh, and he's most depressing. He says we shall be in the war.'

There was a silence. Marsh, as a secretary in the Admiralty, surely knew what he was talking about. But the company was in no mood for such boring nonsense. Dinner was served by the Austrian waiters 'with ominous quiet deftness'. Sitting as guest of honour next to the Bostonian's massive figure, Lawrence looked even thinner than he actually was. Aldington didn't appreciate at the time, he said later, the sight of 'the coal miner's son sitting at the right hand of a Lowell.'[14] But there was no condescension on her part or uneasiness on his. They liked each other.

Immediately after this encounter, Lawrence escaped the London whirl and went off to tramp over the Westmorland moors with three other men. Apparently the trip was suggested by a man named Norne, who was at the Russian Law Bureau, and he brought along a colleague, Koteliansky with him. This swarthy, intelligent Jew from Kiev, who had only been in England a few years, soon became one of Lawrence's most devoted admirers. Rananim, the pet scheme which focused Lawrence's hopes for a new, clean life somewhere far away from the world of 'war and squalor', was a name provided by Koteliansky.

War was declared while Lawrence was away in the North. This is how he described it to Lady Cynthia Asquith: 'I had been walking in Westmorland, rather happy, with water-lilies twisted round my hat – big, heavy, white and gold water-lilies that we found in a pool high up – and girls who had come out on a spree and who were having tea in the upper room of an inn, shrieked with laughter. And I remember also we crouched under the loose wall on the moors and the rain flew by in streams, and the wind came rushing through the chinks in the wall behind one's head, and we shouted songs, and I imitated music-hall turns, while the other men crouched under the wall and I pranked in the rain on the turf in the gorse, and Koteliansky groaned Hebrew music – *Ranani Sadekim Badanoi.*

'It seems like another life – we *were* happy – four men. Then we came down to Barrow-in-Furness and saw that war was declared. And we all went mad. I can remember soldiers kissing on Barrow station, and a woman shouting defiantly to her sweetheart – "When you get at 'em, Clem, let 'em have it," as the train drew off – and in all the tramcars, "War". Messrs Vickers-Maxim call in their workmen – and the great notices on Vickers' gateways – and the thousands of men streaming over the bridge.'[15]

Back in London, he looked around for a cheap cottage, and located one near Chesham in Buckinghamshire. It was a bad choice, a damp, depressing hole, and Lawrence's health soon began to suffer. Some time after they moved in, Compton Mac-kenzie called on them, and later used both the place and the Lawrences as material for his novel, *The South Wind of Love*:

'The cottage which had been lent to the Rayners was a dreary little structure of crimson brick and blue slates standing in a decayed orchard overgrown with nettles. Inside it was furnished with some striving after pettifogging arty picturesqueness but no attempt at all at comfort.

'When they arrived Rayner in an apron was on his knees scrub-bing the floor of the living room, which owing to the encroach-ment of the nettles on the windows and the shade of the moulder-ing apple trees had the dim greenish look of an aquarium tank.

'Rayner rose to his feet and in a broad Midland accent told them that he was taking the chance of Sunday afternoon to give the damned place a jolly good clean-up . . .

'John took an immediate liking to this frail young man whose pale face but for his stubby little reddish moustache which hardly concealed his vivid lips would have had a pierrot look. He had wavy reddish hair and exquisitely delicate white hands which he was wiping on his discarded apron.'[16]

Badly off, and already feeling 'seedy', Lawrence looked out at the autumn rain and the windfalls in the grass. The water drip-ped into the rotten water-butt. Everything, from the weather to the world, disgusted him. His answer was to grow a beard. 'I think I look hideous,' he told Catherine Carswell in October, 'but it is so warm and complete, and such a clothing to one's nakedness, that I like it and shall keep it. So when you see me don't laugh.'

He was now so hard up that he qualified for a grant of £50 from the Literary Fund. This brought his capital up to £70. But he owed £145 to the solicitors for his divorce costs, and £20 elsewhere. The divorce costs could go hang, he told Catherine, and added truculently: 'Have I not earned my whack – at least enough to live on – from this nation?'[17]

All his visitors reported bad moods and depressions at the cottage called The Triangle in Bellingdon Lane. Murry was to speak later of the 'desperate quarrels which were raging between Lawrence and Frieda' there, but this didn't prevent him from cycling round the area and finding a cottage only three miles away for himself and Katherine. For nearly a fortnight they lived with the Lawrences, going to and fro on daily pilgrimages across the wet fields to clean out their place and decorate it. Lawrence, though obviously ill, had to have a hand in this. Murry's slowness with the paintbrush irritated him, so he snatched it from his friend and daubed away 'in a kind of berserk fury'.

The Murrys were now able to witness at close quarters the 'spectacular' unhappiness of Lawrence and Frieda, though they themselves were miserable enough at this time. The conflict raging and waning was more than just a clash of two powerful personalities. In fact, Lawrence could be extremely timid, and painfully shy and uncertain; but this was combined in him with an overriding conviction of his superiority. What the Murrys were witnessing was essentially a battle for mastery,' his mastery, and her refusal to be mastered; it was a struggle that had them at each other's throats with great violence, time and time again. The catalyst was often Frieda's fiercely maintained link with her children, but what was really at issue was Lawrence's frantic need for adoration, endlessly supplied by his mother and now strenuously denied by this young aristocrat who was herself quite accustomed to being worshipped. For a sickly miner's son to assert dominance over her was too ridiculous for words, and she never missed an opportunity to rub this in. But she failed to grasp the significance of those repeated, agonised attempts by Lawrence, in *Sons and Lovers*, to tear himself free from his mother and make himself into a man, almost by an act of will. And this killing struggle did not stop at his mother's death. It was a continuous process of assertion, whereby he raised himself to be the equal, not only of her, but of the whole world of men he now had to face alone. Some form of domination was therefore indispensable to a man so cripplingly handicapped from childhood. And sexuality, with its shedding of the ego and its promise of release from the endless strivings of the will, was of paramount importance to him.

It was even a means of staying sane. Each time he engaged in sexual activity he triumphed, for he broke the bonds with his mother. But now he had exchanged a strong mother, who had humiliated and almost destroyed him, for an even stronger wife who was also a mother. The irony was rich and inescapable.

There were many compensations. From *Sons and Lovers* onwards, Frieda's influence on his work was supreme. Her forceful and generous nature flowed into it at all points; not because she was a literary collaborator like Jessie, but simply because she was solidly there at the back of him, a flesh-and-blood reality. Also, she brought with her a dowry of half-understood but immensely relevant ideas from Germany. And he began to expand. As soon as she had joined herself to him, and he knew beyond doubt that she was fully committed, his confidence in his own powers became absolute, and there seemed no limit to his vitality. Thus she freed him from his mother in a way that no other woman had been able to do. *Sons and Lovers*, the novel in which Lawrence analysed and liberated himself in one and the same creative act, was perhaps as much Frieda's victory as his own. But she was so unaware of this herself, so impatient with the flickering ghosts of his past – and one could hardly blame her for being jealous – that she swept the book aside almost contemptuously, as if its achievement had nothing to do with her at all. In a letter to Edward Garnett from Fiascherino, she declared: 'The novel is a failure, but you must feel something at the back of it struggling, trying to come out. You see, I don't really believe in *Sons and Lovers*; it feels as if there were nothing *behind* all those happenings, as if there were no *Hinterland der Seele*, only intensely felt fugitive things.'[18]

Lawrence's hatred and fear of Frieda's mother-love was, at least in part, a transference of his growing resentment of his mother, and the years of bondage she represented. But undoubtedly, too, Frieda's realisation that Lawrence was sterile must have been a cruel spear in the side of his male superiority, such as it was. If she goaded him with this, sometimes, in the heat of violent outbursts – and she may well have done – then his seemingly insane rages, acts of jealousy, and appalling cruelty to her in front of their friends, could have been as much her fault as his. But whoever was more at fault, they were both capable of snatching up any weapon that happened to be at hand and using it in the blind fury of the moment.

What kind of woman *was* Frieda? How did other women regard her, and how did they see Lawrence's relationship with her? Catherine Carswell had this to say:

'Sometimes it seemed to us that he had chosen rather a force of nature – a female force – than an individual woman. Frieda was to Lawrence by turns a buffeting and a laughing breeze, a healing rain or a maddening tempest of stupidity, a cheering sun or a stroke of indiscriminate lightning. She was mindless Womanhood, wilful, defiant, disrespectful, argumentative, assertive, vengeful, sly, illogical, treacherous, unscrupulous and self-seeking. At times she hated Lawrence and he her. There were things she jeered at in him and things in her that maddened him – things that neither would consent to subdue.'[19]

Murry and Katherine Mansfield could not have been a more complete contrast. Their dilemma, or a good deal of it, had been brought about by Murry's chronic inability to assert himself. From the moment that Lawrence realised this, he never stopped urging Murry to 'be a man' and take charge of his affairs. Then, he told him, Katherine would respect him and their troubles would be over. But in fact it was her will-power and self-confidence that gave Murry the security he so badly needed. At these times he was afflicted by what was virtually a paralysis of the will. Many of his characteristics went later into the creation of Gerald in *Women in Love*, just as Lawrence himself was projected into the character of Birkin. Gerald and Birkin's relationship too resembles that of Lawrence and Murry, with their mutual dependence, and the weaker of the two becoming more and more bemused by the other's fierce demands. Lawrence loved strong men, but he longed even more to be strong himself. The situation was ironic, for if Lawrence's strenuous efforts to put some backbone into his friend had succeeded, it would not have suited Lawrence at all. Right from the start of their friendship, Lawrence sought to impose his will on Murry. As it became clearer that he would never be able to dominate Frieda, his need grew to appear strong for Murry. This was what lay behind the crushingly domineering advice he hurled again and again at the hapless younger man. And Murry, for his part, very much wanted a strong Lawrence to admire.

Until Lawrence came along, Murry had been bolstered up by Katherine Mansfield. Now she was threatening to desert him, and Murry fastened on to Lawrence like a leech. From time to time Lawrence would try irritably to throw him off, yet without ever admitting the extent of his own dependence. Most likely he had no idea how incapable he was of developing a real friendship. He demanded allegiance, and when this was not forthcoming, he quarrelled. Murry lasted longer than most because of his inability to fight back.

Murry had once suffered a mental breakdown, which could have been caused by the strain of study at Oxford. A poor boy, he had gone there on a scholarship, and had done brilliantly. On the threshold of a career, he found himself unable to decide on any course of action, and lost confidence in himself completely. His academic development had landed him in a sort of no-man's land between his family in south London and the very different world of the intelligentsia which lay before him. As if illustrating a classic case of neurosis, he couldn't move in either direction, forwards or backwards. Then he met Katherine Mansfield. Her strength of character enabled him to propel himself into literary journalism.

Katherine Mansfield was the *nom de plume* of Katherine Beauchamp, a New Zealand girl whose father was President of the Bank of New Zealand. Sir Harold had sent his daughter to England to be educated, and, more important, to become a lady. Four years later, Katherine felt that she would die if she couldn't escape from Wellington and return to her life of freedom in London. But it took her two years to convince her parents, and indeed the venture would have been impossible without their financial support. In 1908, at nineteen, with an allowance of one hundred pounds a year, she arrived in England again, determined now to be a writer.

She felt crippled by her lack of experience. One solution was to plunge into love affairs. She became pregnant by one man and married another, leaving him the next day. Fleeing to Germany, she lost the child. By the time Middleton Murry met her she had published her first book, a collection of sketches entitled *In a German Pension*.

Now she and Murry were living close to the Lawrences at Chesham, repelled by the violence of the rows they witnessed. Nevertheless, if one reads between the lines of Murry's accounts, there seemed to be a horrible fascination in it all. For two people to carry on in this manner, in what looked like a savage fight for survival, there could be only one explanation, and that was that they were incompatible. It was behaviour completely outside Murry's experience, and ran counter to his innermost nature. He looked on, horrified, certain that he was about to see actual slaughter take place. In this period, as he says, he was very hostile to Frieda. All his sympathy went to Lawrence. But this certainly didn't mean that he wanted them to split up. The very thought of having to cope with Lawrence on his own terrified him, and on one occasion he was instrumental, or so he believed, in reconciling the warring pair. Either he or Katherine had been foolish enough to mention Frieda's children. Frieda burst into tears, and Lawrence turned pale and exploded with fury. Frieda would have to clear out, he yelled – now! He tore upstairs to fetch their money and share it out between them. Coming down, he banged sixteen sovereigns down on the table for her. Frieda already had her hat and coat on, and she stood by the door, crying bitterly.

Usually these explosions left Murry in a state of shock, unable to move a muscle: Katherine always refused to participate. This time, however, Murry amazed himself by launching into a long 'theatrical speech', aimed at reconciling the Lawrences. It seemed to work, which bewildered him even more. Before he left, Lawrence and Frieda were smiling together.[20]

Another time, Koteliansky, who always disliked Frieda, was staying at the cottage. They all had lunch and then Frieda left. Outside it was raining hard. Suddenly the door opened and Katherine stood there, with her skirts tucked into her Wellingtons. She was wet through.

'Frieda has asked me to come and tell you that she will not come back,' she said.

'Damn the woman,' bawled Lawrence in a rage, 'tell her I never want to see her again.'

Katherine had a curious detachment, and Koteliansky, who had never seen her before, remembered it. On this occasion she didn't utter a word, but simply turned on her heel and went back the way she had come.[21]

Although Murry's instinct was to recoil from these blazing scenes, he liked it no better if he happened to be in the room watching Lawrence become more and more absorbed in Frieda, sitting there the whole evening quite happily trimming one of her hats. Murry felt nauseated by this. 'Rightly or wrongly,' he wrote later, 'it seemed to me that Lawrence did not serve Frieda as a person, or an individual, but as a sort of incarnation of the Female principle, a sort of Magna Mater in whom he deliberately engulfed and obliterated himself.'[22] This could have been mere jealousy on his part, but on the other hand he may have been witnessing something that Lawrence had begun to do quite consciously now, as a matter of principle. Before leaving Italy he had told McLeod in a letter: 'I think the only re-sourcing of art, revivifying it, is to make it more the joint work of man and woman. I think *the* one thing to do, is for men to have courage to draw nearer to women, expose themselves to them, and be altered by them.'[23] Even more explicit was his declaration to Gordon Campbell: 'I believe there is no getting of a vision, as you call it, before we get our sex right: before we get our souls fertilised by the female.'[24]

This was fine by Frieda, so long as she remained indisputably the female in question, but Lawrence had now begun to offer his soul, tentatively at least, to one or two other notable ladies for fertilisation. In January the Lawrences escaped from Chesham and moved into a long, narrow cottage, once a barn, in Greatham in Sussex. The place belonged to Viola Meynell, who lived nearby. Soon Lawrence and Frieda were receiving visitors, among them Lady Ottoline Morrell and Lady Cynthia Asquith. Ford Madox Hueffer also came, and Ivy Low, and of course Murry, very despondent now because he and Katherine had temporarily split up.

Robert Lucas points out, in his biography of Frieda, that Cynthia Asquith was the first *grande dame* Lawrence had met. Frieda responded warmly to her, comparing her beauty to that of Botticelli's Venus. For Lawrence, she was 'a feminine idol, and from the time of their meeting he worshipped her like a troubadour, platonically.'[25] This is how he described his 'unattainable ideal of womanhood' in a short story, 'The Thimble': 'She was a beautiful woman, tall and loose and rather thin, with swinging limbs, one for whom the modern fashions were perfect. Her skin was pure and clear, like a Christmas rose, her hair was fair and heavy. She had large, slow, unswerving eyes, that sometimes looked blue and open with a childish candour, sometimes greenish and intent with thought, sometimes hard, sea-like, cruel, sometimes grey and pathetic.' She also had a sense of humour. Lawrence sent her the story in manuscript, and she commented in her diary: 'I *was* amused to see the word-picture of me. He has quite gratuitously put in the large feet.'

She was twenty-six when she met Lawrence at Kingsgate. She had married Herbert Asquith, the second son of the Prime Minister, and her authoritarian father, a high Tory who was the eleventh Earl of Wemyss, strongly disapproved. They had a retarded son, but only their close friends ever knew of his existence.

Ottoline Morrell was an equally impressive but very different woman. Her home as a child had been Welbeck Abbey in Nottinghamshire, so at their first meeting they were able to talk together about a countryside they both knew intimately from childhood. Her husband was Philip Morrell, the Liberal M.P., who had just bought a large house outside Oxford, Garsington Manor.

This extraordinary woman, whose eccentric dress and strange horsey profile made people stop and stare after her in the street, attracted the portrait painters and the writers in equal measure. Celebrities were as common as peacocks in the grounds of her five-hundred-acre estate. Philip Morrell, as a pacifist, was an added attraction for the intellectuals. And there was no denying Lady Ottoline's generosity when it came to the encouragement of the arts, though the gossips maintained that it was the artists she was primarily interested in. She dyed her hair 'the colour of dark marmalade', as Bertrand Russell put it, and could be seen walking in the middle of London with a flock of Pekingeses, all fastened by coloured cords to her upraised shepherd's crook.

When Lawrence came to write *Women in Love* he transferred Ottoline to Derbyshire, renamed her Hermione, and called her 'the most remarkable woman in the Midlands'. He described her appearance with more than a touch of cruelty in his opening pages: 'Now she came along, with her head held up, balancing an enormous flat hat of pale yellow velvet, on which were streaks of ostrich feathers, natural and grey. She drifted forward as if scarcely conscious, her long blanched face lifted up, not to see the world. She was rich. She wore a dress of silky, frail velvet, of pale yellow colour, and she carried a lot of small rose-coloured cyclamens. Her shoes and stockings were of brownish grey, like the feathers on her hat, her hair was heavy, she drifted along with a peculiar fixity of the hips, a strange unwilling motion.'

There was much worse to come. But her initial response to him was generous. She remarked on his naturalness, his flame-like mind, and thought how much he resembled the portraits of Van Gogh she had seen. On that first meeting she went with him and Frieda to a vantage point on the Downs, looking towards Arundel and the coast. It was late January and the trees were bare, but delicate red buds were visible on the twigs. Lawrence pointed them out to her, delighted, and said, 'See, here is the little red flame hidden in Nature.'[26]

The war had not yet affected him deeply, but the very thought of it enraged him, and to have his escape to Italy, or even Ireland, cut off by it, was almost a personal affront. 'The war makes me depressed,' he told Campbell, 'The talk about the war makes me sick, and I have never come so near to hating mankind as I am now.'[27] In reaction, he absorbed himself in thoughts of Rananim, a fantasy place which had in a sense originated in Eastwood while his mother was still alive. Then he had imagined a big house, into which he would put his mother and a few friends, and live a communal life with other men. This dream had been lying dormant during his two years with Frieda: now it was resurrected with a vengeance. Lawrence went about drumming up members for it like a recruiting sergeant. So far the only stalwart supporters were Koteliansky and the Murrys, and in their joint imaginings Rananim was located on an island somewhere. Katherine would call this escapist activity 'talking the Island', but by January, 1915, she had begun to have reservations. In her journal she wrote: 'It is quite real except that some part of me is blind to it. Six months ago I'd have jumped . . .'

In the same month, Lawrence reached out for Willie Hopkin, crystallising his dream into a vision of primitive Christianity in his effort to win over the little socialist:

'I want to gather together about twenty souls and sail away from this world of war and squalor and found a little colony where there shall be no money but a sort of communism as far as necessaries of life go, and some real decency. It is to be a colony built up on the real decency which is in each member of the community. A community which is established upon the assumption of goodness in its members, instead of the assumption of badness.'[28]

Lawrence went on brooding and elaborating on his concept, while Murry too began to have second thoughts. The enchantment of Rananim was being gradually eroded, thought Murry, by something alien, and it amounted to a dangerous denial of individuality. All must be surrendered 'to some great and all-inclusive religious purpose. Each was to be "the angel of himself in a big cause", and this "angel of himself" was mysteriously to arise out of the acknowledgement and fulfilment of the "animal of himself".' Murry now suspected Lawrence of building certain elements into this evolving creed of his, such as the need for sexual experience, and the need for gregarious male friendship, which had been his personal preoccupations for much of his life. 'Lawrence, it should never be forgotten, was a Puritan, and even something of a Manichee.'[29]

But Murry kept these growing suspicions to himself, partly because he was only dimly aware of them at the time, and also out of fear. He couldn't afford to lose Lawrence's affection now, for he had just lost Gordon Campbell's, and also, it seemed, Katherine's. One raw February day he arrived at Lawrence's Greatham cottage in the dark. He had walked through the pouring rain from Pulborough, and was aching in every joint with influenza. Lawrence took one look at him and told him he must go to bed. Before Murry could object, he was being undressed and put between the sheets. Lawrence kept him there for three days, nursing him as if he were a child. It was exactly, said Murry afterwards, like the treatment of Aaron by his friend Lilly in *Aaron's Rod*. As soon as he showed signs of recovery, Lawrence gave Murry a vicious 'right-and-left', telling him brutally what a damn fool he was to lose Katherine. She had had enough of the intellectual probings that went on interminably between Campbell and Murry, declared Lawrence, and it served Murry right if she had gone off to look for someone who would give her what she wanted. As it happened, the man she sought out in Paris, Francis Carco, failed her miserably, and she soon returned.

Now Lawrence had met Ottoline Morrell, he not only saw her, amazingly, as a potential recruit for his Rananim, but as a person eminently capable of housing and feeding the whole colony on her estate. Richard Aldington in his biography suggests that pressing financial difficulties, soon to be aggravated by the war, forced Lawrence to look around for alternative ways of surviving, and that for this reason the Rananim notion was doubly attractive. Whatever his motives, Lawrence set out to woo Ottoline with a passionate and eloquent letter. After meeting her, he said, his heart felt 'quite big with hope for the future', and he proceeded without more ado to drop his 'pet scheme' into her lap:

'I want you to form the nucleus of a new community which shall start a new life amongst us – a life in which the only riches is integrity of character . . . Let us be good all together, instead of just in the privacy of our chambers, let us know that the intrinsic part of all of us is in the best part, the believing part, the passionate, generous part. We can all come croppers, but what does it matter?' Pages later he was still struggling to clarify his dream: 'It is communism based, not on poverty but on riches, not on humility but on pride, not on sacrifice but upon complete fulfilment in the flesh of all strong desire, not in Heaven but on earth.'[30]

Lady Ottoline's answer was to introduce Lawrence to Bertrand Russell. Such an extraordinary juxtaposition of opposites may have been prompted by a simple desire to get herself off the hook, but more likely she had been misled by Lawrence's loathing of the war into thinking that he was, like Russell and her husband, a pacifist. In her eyes at least, the two men had a great deal in common.

At first it did seem as though she was right. Ideas, schemes and discussion proliferated, and Russell invited Lawrence to come to Cambridge and plan a campaign.

Before he went, Lawrence met E. M. Forster, a man he always liked, but who exasperated him with his neutrality. Forster stayed for three days with the Lawrences, and he and Lawrence were 'on the edge of a fierce quarrel' during the whole of that time. According to Lawrence, the other man 'seized a candle' and went off to bed without even saying goodnight. But he must surely have had a lot to put up with: Lawrence was now in full prophetic flood, boiling with plans to revolutionise the state, to make a clean sweep and clear the ground for the regeneration of man's body and soul. This he saw as the real burning need. Let others deal with the practical business of getting rid of the existing rottenness: then he could begin his work. As Aldington points out, Lawrence had now got into the habit of making declarations beginning 'Let there be', 'There must be' and 'We shall', like Ruskin and Carlyle before him, and he seemed to believe for a time that his words would magically transform themselves into actions. This, says Aldington, was 'cheating himself with the fairy money of ideas'. His honesty and his poet's insights had temporarily deserted him. Immensely hopeful, radiating goodwill and 'positive' thinking, he held up poor Forster as an example of the educated Englishman's predicament, in a remarkable letter to Russell on 15th February, 1915:

'But why can't he act? Why can't he take a woman and fight clear to his own basic, primal being? Because he knows that self-realisation is not his ultimate desire.' Lawrence had grasped something of fundamental significance, and he developed it at great length, reiterating his points like a schoolmaster and quite oblivious of the irritation he was causing at the other end. What he was at such pains to hammer home in this letter was the predicament of modern man who was now unable to progress, to realise his potential, to take a woman and voyage on richly from there, because he sensed that his discoveries would only be thrown in his face by a crippled, suffering, cynical humanity. This tragic wastage Lawrence saw as leading to sodomy, with the man, short-circuited and unable to go forward, using the woman instead for masturbation. A man like Forster, with 'too much honour for the other body – man or woman', turns aside and 'remains neutral, inactive'. Which to Lawrence was only another symptom of the passivity, stagnation and despair of the whole country, and especially the 'educated class'. So what was to be done?

'There must be a revolution in the state,' Lawrence proclaimed. 'It shall begin by the nationalising of all industries and means of communication, and of the land – in one fell blow. Then a man shall have his wages whether he is sick or well or old – if anything prevents his working, he shall have his wages just the same.'

In a fury of impatience to get going, he swept all practicalities aside. Things had come to a standstill, the whole of society was in a state of neurosis, it was necessary to 'smash the frame'. He saw the problem essentially in terms of himself, and could never forget his own years of chronic immobility, until he broke out of the shell and achieved his rebirth. Yet it was incomplete, and he would have to go on repeating the process for the rest of his life. The smell of sex in his books was in reality the odour of birth. 'There comes a point when the shell, the form of life, is a prison to the life,' he wrote to Russell. It was a sentence full to the brim with autobiography. The enormous accession of well-being and power he had experienced on achieving manhood through Frieda was something which lay behind every word he now wrote to Russell. He ended touchingly, 'You must have patience with me and understand me when my language is not clear.'

Russell was certainly mystified by much of his language, but he admired the energy and passion, and above all the belief. All this he called later Lawrence's 'fire'. This fiery little Midlander had affected him more deeply than Lawrence ever realised.

The momentous visit to Cambridge, a civilisation in itself, drew nearer, and Lawrence's nervousness increased. What would they make of him there? Flattered, and at the same time intimidated, he was in an agony of indecision as the day approached. In a final appeal to Russell he confessed his fear of the occasion, of feeling 'so clumsy, so clownish', and begged the mathematician not to force too many people on him at once, 'or I lose my wits. I am afraid of concourses and clans and societies and cliques . . .'[31]

Maynard Keynes, one of the men Russell wanted Lawrence to meet, said later that perhaps Lawrence's feelings about Cambridge had some foundation in fact. The economist was able to detach himself from the scene sufficiently to see Cambridge as a collection of 'water spiders, gracefully skimming, as light and reasonable as air, the surface of the stream without any contact at all with the eddies and currents underneath.'[32] But Lawrence's 'ignorant, jealous, irritable, hostile eyes' must have observed more than this, one would imagine, for him to have been so repelled. He summed up his passionate distaste in a single sentence, writing to Barbara Low: 'I went to Cambridge and hated it beyond expression.' After dinner in the hall of Trinity College with Russell, G. E. Moore, and G. H. Hardy, the mathematician, Lawrence stayed with Russell in his rooms in Nevile's Court. Keynes met him there for the first time and the three of them had breakfast together. Lawrence sat morosely on the sofa in front of the fire 'in rather a crouching position', and the two friends encouraged him, without success, to participate in the conversation. This moment was for Lawrence 'one of the crises' of his life.

The original proposal was for Russell and Lawrence to lecture in some sort of loose collaboration, but as letters went on being exchanged after the Cambridge meeting, Russell soon became aware of serious differences between them. Dismissing Russell's firmly held democratic beliefs, Lawrence told him flatly: 'I don't believe in democratic control. I think the working man is fit to elect governors or overseers for immediate circumstances, but for no more . . . The thing must culminate in one real head, as every organic thing must – no foolish republics with foolish presidents, but an elected King, something like Julius Caesar.'[33]

To Russell this was arrant rubbish, and meant that Lawrence was calling for a dictatorship to be established, with himself as dictator. 'This', said Russell, 'was part of the dreamlike quality of all his thinking. He never let himself bump into reality.' Russell was also beginning to suspect that Lawrence was not interested in pacifism either – or even in the civilised interchange of ideas. For Lawrence an idea was something to be seized and acted upon at once, and he fully expected others to follow his example. Those who questioned or resisted were immediately accused of treachery, or else dismissed as unworthy. But the truth of his feelings about pacifism lay in a positive rather than a negative direction. Murry, a more perceptive critic than Russell, understood at least something of the subtlety of Lawrence's craving for destruction when he wrote: 'It was mysterious to me, and frightening, as though he hated this war only because it was not war enough, and was in some sort a further frustration of the animal rather than a satiation of it. It was partly in the name of essential war that he repudiated this grim parody of war.'[34]

At any rate, Russell soon came to the conclusion that Lawrence's ideas had no merit whatsoever. Towards the end of his life he even expressed doubts as to whether they were Lawrence's ideas at all, and put the blame for their incipient Fascism on Frieda: 'Somehow she imbibed prematurely the ideas afterwards developed by Mussolini and Hitler, and these ideas she transmitted to Lawrence, shall we say by blood-consciousness. Lawrence was an essentially timid man, who tried to conceal his timidity by bluster.' Crude though this was, it drew attention to a curious trait in Lawrence's character which certainly existed. Russell came much nearer to the mark when he said that Lawrence was 'a sensitive would-be despot who got angry with the world because it would not instantly obey.' And, even more significantly: 'His excessive emphasis on sex was due to the fact that in sex alone he was compelled to admit that he was not the only human being in the universe. But it was because this admission was so painful that he conceived of sex relations as a perpetual fight in which each is attempting to destroy the other.'[35]

Russell was here describing a particular authoritarian type, the kind of man who has to be always right, who holds women in contempt and identifies every manifestation of kindness as weakness. Indeed, Russell noted that Lawrence always lost his temper if one spoke of having kindly feelings towards others, and when Russell objected to the suffering produced by war, he was accused of hypocrisy. It was this devastating attack by Lawrence which brought Russell to the brink of suicide: 'For twenty-four hours I thought that I was not fit to live . . .'[36]

Russell might have had other revealing things to say if he could have contained his impatience instead of dismissing Lawrence out of hand as a forerunner of Fascism. Russell came to know at first hand, for instance, Lawrence's habit of swerving violently from passionate attachment to the most violent hatred. Freud, another precocious child who became his mother's favourite, said once: 'An intimate friend and a hated enemy have always been indispensable to my emotional life.' And sometimes, as with Lawrence, 'friend and enemy have coincided in the same person.' Again, like Lawrence, Freud was made aware of his uniqueness at an early age by his mother, and the memory of this burden of favouritism led him to remark later: 'A man who has been the indisputable favourite of his mother keeps for life the feeling of a conqueror.'[37]

Anthony Storr, in his book, *The Dynamics of Creation,* points out that creative activity is a natural way for the schizoid individual to express himself, and he defines this kind of individual as one in whom feelings of inferiority and omnipotence can co-exist. 'First,' says Storr, 'since most creative activity is solitary, choosing such an occupation means that the schizoid person can avoid the problems of direct relationships with others. If he writes, paints or composes, he is, of course, communicating. But it is a communication entirely on his own terms.' And he goes on to quote D. W. Winnicott's illuminating remark: 'In the artist of all kinds I think one can detect an inherent dilemma, which belongs to the co-existence of two trends, the urgent need to communicate and the still more urgent need not to be found.'

Lawrence at Greatham was now suffering the extremes of rage and depression which would afflict him, at intervals, for the rest of the war, and carry him at times to the edge of insanity. Indeed, he seemed to have a premonition of this. Commenting on a life of Van Gogh he had been reading, he told Ottoline Morrell: 'He couldn't get out of the trap, poor man, so he went mad.' Whenever Murry came to see him, they talked about the Revolution – or rather, Lawrence did – and the necessity of forming a revolutionary party. Expounding the Revolution in a series of weekly pamphlets was now more important to Lawrence than publishing novels. What was the point of writing novels, without first changing the conditions so that people could hear? After *The Rainbow,* he said, he would write one more novel and that would be all. He spoke strangely, and with sadness, and as far as Murry was concerned incoherently, about himself as a forerunner, a kind of John the Baptist preparing the way for Christ, and seemed to hint at the possibility of Murry succeeding him. A 'philosophicalish' book he had been writing, ostensibly on Hardy, he now wanted to rewrite in pamphlet form. It would be a truly revolutionary utterance and he would perhaps call it 'The Signal'. And he still insisted, even after sampling the 'marsh-stagnancy' of Cambridge, that he wanted to lecture on 'Eternity' or 'Immortality' while Russell lectured on Social Reconstruction; and he kept pounding away at Russell in letters to win him over.

But it wasn't true that he had abandoned novels or thought them irrelevant. As he sat back and looked at his finished novel, the protracted struggle to give birth to it at last behind him, he felt very excited, 'like a bird in spring that is amazed at the colours of its own coat.' And he told his agent sternly: 'I hope you are willing to fight for this novel. It is nearly three years of hard work, and I am proud of it, and it must be stood up for.'[38]

The nightmare of the war had now begun to oppress him. He went with Frieda to Bognor one day in March, and the white, powerfully crashing sea frightened him. He saw a soldier with one leg amputated, his face 'brown and strong and handsome', affecting the women because he was a war hero but not yet fully aware of his condition. Lawrence imagined this shocked, confused young man under chloroform, and then had a vision of ghostly legions of the dead marching in over that icy white sea towards him, wave after wave, as he stood on the pier.

He may well have been in a similar phantom-haunted mood when David Garnett and a friend named Birrell arrived, at Lawrence's invitation, to spend a night with him and Frieda at Greatham. They came in a train packed with young, sunburnt soldiers in their new uniforms, who were smoking Woodbines and looking out of the windows with good-tempered interest at everything. It was only mid-April, but exceptionally warm.

Frankie Birrell and Garnett and Frieda talked together noisily over supper, and at first all was well. Then Garnett became intimidated by Lawrence's silence, and realised that 'something dreadful was going on inside him.' Lawrence sat there in acute tension, and seemed to crouch into himself with the unbearable effort of trying to deal with whatever was afflicting him. Not knowing what to say, Garnett and Birrell went off to bed.

In the middle of the night David Garnett woke up to hear someone banging about outside the door of the bedroom. It was Birrell, in his pyjamas, pointing dumbly at his mouth. His tongue had swollen to a huge size, half choking him. Disturbed by the commotion, Frieda and Lawrence came out of their room to investigate. Eventually Birrell was allowed to crawl into bed again to 'await a doctor.'[39]

Next morning, to everyone's amazement, Birrell's tongue was back to normal, and the young man felt no after-effects of any kind. After the two visitors had departed, Lawrence wrote to both Ottoline Morrell and David Garnett. He told Lady Ottoline on the 19th April that Birrell had driven him mad with his endless irreverent chatter, 'and never, never a good thing said. They are cased each in a hard little shell of his own and out of this they talk words.' These encapsulated egos made him dream of black beetles. It was pure horror. He had killed one beetle in the dream, but, horror of horrors, it came back again.

His letter to David Garnett used the same imagery, but was so offensive that it put an end to their friendship. He ordered: 'Never bring Birrell to see me any more. There is something nasty about him like black beetles. He is horrible and unclean.' He urged young Garnett to break with these beetle-like friends of his, not only Birrell but Duncan Grant and Keynes too. He had had a similar beetle dream in Cambridge, and 'it sent me mad with misery and hostility and rage.'

Everything now tended to drive Lawrence further into misanthropy, as many witnesses have testified. Writing to Lady Ottoline about a bird on the wall outside his window, he confessed: 'I wish I was a blackbird, like him. I hate men.'

One way or another, Lawrence managed to create plenty of trouble for himself in 1915. His novel, *The Rainbow*, a book he had fought so hard to deliver cleanly – spending long years on it and sustained only by an absolute belief in its final arch of triumph – was to be published in September and then suppressed after only five weeks. But even before this, Lawrence was busily making enemies of members of the Garsington-Cambridge-Bloomsbury set by his jealous outbursts and his indiscretions, either not understanding, or caring, how influential these people were in England's literary and intellectual circles. It would perhaps be truer to say that he was well aware of their influence as individuals, but failed to appreciate the power they wielded as a group. Their solidarity was such that, once Lawrence had fallen foul of them, they were able to make sure that he was either ignored or denigrated for many years to come. Much of this animosity he brought on himself, of course, by the kind of letter he wrote to David Garnett and by treacherous portraits, in short stories and novels, of those who had befriended him. It could be argued that his need for enemies was as characteristic of him as his hunger for a few real friends. His whole dynamic seemed to originate in the constant interaction of opposites within himself. As he became more aware of these inner divisions, Lawrence's work – in *The Rainbow,* and in philosophical essays he was writing at this time – increased in depth and complexity, while his surface behaviour was often inexplicably unbalanced and cruel. Anthony Storr, in his reflections on the apparent similarities between the behaviour of the neurotic and that of the creative person, remarks succinctly: 'Artists who are primarily in love with their creative power are, of course, less vulnerable on this account, since they are less affected than most of us by the bestowal or withdrawal of love. They are also less agreeable; since most of the pleasantness of ordinary human beings is related to their need for approval and affection, which makes them anxious to please, and reluctant to offend, their fellows.'[40]

Frieda, too, had been doing some characteristically straightforward offending on her own behalf, hurling abuse at Ford Madox Hueffer's uniform, for instance, when he came to Greatham to see the Lawrences. He had brought Violet Hunt and H. G. Wells with him, and, to be fair to Frieda, it was Violet Hunt who had started the row with some remark sparked off by the sight of Belgian refugees at Charing Cross Station. What she called her 'tiny word of reproach forced from an over-charged heart' almost brought the roof down on her head.

'Dirty Belgians! Who cares for them!' Frieda shouted in her German accent.

Fordie fled to an outhouse while the two women fought it out verbally over tea and cakes. Violet Hunt, flinching and retaliating, understood after a while that the 'Valkyrie' meant her no harm and merely thought her foolish and sentimental, but in the gracious exchanges at the door she nevertheless managed to have the last word: 'Goodbye. It is you who are charming but I hope we shall *never* meet again.'[41]

This was the first public manifestation of Frieda's sporadic pro-Prussianism. Lawrence was soon being bracketed with her as pro-German, whether he remained tactfully silent or not. It was one thing to be anti-war – and there were so many Bloomsburyites who were conscientious objectors, or pacifists of the Morrell kind, that it was almost fashionable to be so – but quite another to have a German wife who expressed herself outspokenly and naïvely on the subject. All this would be stored up and used against him, with disastrous results, in the not too distant future.

In August 1915 the Lawrences moved again, this time to Hampstead; but first they had a few days by the sea at Littlehampton. In a letter to Viola Meynell, thanking her for the use of her cottage, Lawrence was in a gentle mood. He and Frieda had had lunch on the beach, and the only other people in sight, a young, poor family nearby, had saddened him, they were so resigned, submissive and abstract. He watched the tiny group with their faces turned to the sea, the mother sitting still, the young father playing with the baby. He was just a youth in a cap, sitting there like a condemned prisoner, a symbol for the nice clean English people everywhere who knew they didn't stand a chance. Lawrence always grieved for those caught in the trap: in a sense it was a lament for Eastwood, and his own trapped youth.

As always, moving and making a new, if transitory home cheered him up immensely. He thought the war might be over by the autumn, and *The Rainbow* was due out in September, which meant he would be solvent again. Then they could escape to America. Meanwhile, Frieda wanted to be near her children in London, so they took a flat in Byron Villas in the Vale of Health at Hampstead. It was on the ground floor of a small red-brick house with panes of frosted glass in the front door. Catherine Carswell called to help them furnish it with second-hand bits from Praed Street and the Caledonian Market, and Lawrence was at his best, gay and careless, full of ardour about the details of living. 'Proudly he showed me the new pots and pans which were to be kept clean, not merely on the inside, as the Christians do, but on the outside, as the Pharisees use.'⁴² To Dollie Radford, whom he had met whilst staying at Greatham, Lawrence reported wryly: 'The infinite is now swallowed up in chairs and scrubbing brushes and waste paper baskets, as far as I am concerned.'

The change in Lawrence's appearance, compared to 1914, was startling: it was as if he were trying to differentiate himself and also keep pace with his inner changes. Now he wore a bohemian-looking velvet jacket, kept his reddish hair parted in the middle, and of course he had let his beard grow. The beard made him look either vulpine or messianic, according to the eye of the beholder.

Now he had delivered up his novel, he lost interest in it. He

became engrossed in obtaining passports for himself and Frieda
in readiness for the journey to America. All he had by way of
destination was some vague promise of 'a cottage in Florida', but
that didn't deter him. He felt so desperate now about getting away
that he would have gone almost anywhere. He wrote to Cynthia
Asquith: 'I feel like knocking my head against the wall: or of
running off to some unformed South American place where
there is no thought of civilised effort. I suppose I could learn to
ride a horse and live just by myself for myself.'[43]

It was while he was living at Hampstead that he saw his first air
raid. Guns opened fire, bombs exploded, and looking up he saw
the Zeppelin in the clouds, quite beautiful, a fantastic vision 'like a
bright golden finger', calmly drifting and disappearing.

He linked up again with the Murrys, who were living now in St.
John's Wood, and between them they hatched the idea for a little
magazine to be called *Signature*. To bring out six numbers at
fortnightly intervals they would have to raise thirty pounds in
subscriptions. In the event, only fifteen pounds came in. But the
32-page pamphlet was launched, and for a few shillings a week
they rented a room off Red Lion Square, to use as an office and
for holding small weekly meetings. Lawrence helped to scrub this
room and colour-wash the walls, and for furniture they got a long
table and some Windsor chairs from the Caledonian Market.
They were in business, if not for long. Only three numbers saw
the light. But the venture produced, as well as short stories by
Katherine Mansfield and an autobiographical piece by Murry, an
extraordinary essay by Lawrence called 'The Crown'.

'The Crown' is aptly named. Murry admitted that at the time it
was too difficult for him to penetrate. Years later, when he did
profess to understand it, he had become hostile to Lawrence and
so rejected its doctrine. Even so, it is clear that he was still deeply
impressed by its profundity. Now that we are able to stand back
and look with detachment at the whole range of Lawrence's work,
'The Crown' emerges as possibly the summit of his achievement.
It is pure vision from start to finish.

The essay was his second big attempt to forge a philosophy
which would incorporate 'my essential beliefs, the ideas I struggle
with.' There is no doubt that he was in deadly earnest about the
necessity for this, if he was to survive at all in his spirit. His
desperation shows itself, with greater and greater urgency, in
most of his letters during this period. He told Cynthia Asquith:
'My head feels like a hammer that keeps hammering on a nail.'

Not so very long after Lawrence's death, Viktor Frankl, an
existentialist philosopher who survived the concentration camps,

266

wrote in an essay: 'Meaning sets the pace of being. Existence falters unless it is lived in terms of transcendence towards something beyond itself.'[44] The statement is so in accord with Lawrence's convictions that it could easily have been written by him. But Lawrence's language was the language of symbols. Only through symbol could he reach the most profound truths, and also play the artist's game of simultaneously revealing and hiding himself.

Prior to 'The Crown', he had used the pretext of a study of Thomas Hardy to try and achieve the same purpose, but had fallen into incoherence. He tried at least once more, during the war years, and produced 'The Reality of Peace', another sustained and beautiful essay on the same theme of the marriage of opposites. Not so dense as 'The Crown', it uses a similar symbolism, but substitutes the rose for the crown. The shaman-like language has the same deliberate intention, urging on us in a kind of circling subtlety the 'peace in that perfect consummation when duality and polarity is transcended into absorption.' This has nothing to do with the hated Christian goal of reconciliation, which nullifies the opposites instead of allowing them to exist in 'pure polarity'. The moment of peace comes for the doe when she is 'torn and scattered beneath the paws of the leopard, like a quenched fire scattered into the darkness.' For man, peace comes when he admits his divisions: 'I am given up into universality of fellowship and communion, I am distinguished in keen resistance and isolation, but so utterly, so exquisitely, that I am I and I am not at once; suddenly I lapse out of the duality into a sheer beauty of fulfilment. I am a rose of lovely peace.'

We are in the world of symbols again with *The Rainbow*. The natural horizontals of land and sky are contrasted with man's spiritually ascending Gothic arches, and the more earth-bound Norman arch, doggedly leap-frogging forward, with its promise of the rainbow to come.

The Rainbow is Lawrence out in the open for the first time, openly making use of the more than usually overt bisexuality within himself. It is a proud, glowing, immensely confident book, created by a man who is now fully conscious of all his powers. Strongly influenced by Frieda's nationality as well as by her femaleness, Lawrence's evocation of a yeomanry intimately connected with the soil is as much mystically German as it is English, and as reminiscent of Gottfried Keller and Ernst Wiechert as of Thomas Hardy. But the dynamism, rooted in puritanical Eastwood, is peculiarly Lawrence's. And whereas the German influence evident in his Wagnerian *The Trespasser* had been transmitted at second hand, now Lawrence was able to draw on personal memories of Frieda's world of Silesian fields and forests and medieval villages. The Polish widow whom Tom Brangwen marries could just as easily have been a German.

To an England still firmly stuck in the moral climate associated with Queen Victoria, the heavily sexual imagery of parts of *The Rainbow* must have come as a shock. Lawrence had not only admitted the woman in himself and allowed her to speak, he had gone on to celebrate Woman, in all her irrefutability. The men are virtually eclipsed. The theme is announced right at the beginning in words of ringing triumph, even exultation:

'There was a look in the eyes of the Brangwens as if they were expecting something unknown, about which they were eager. They had that air of readiness for what would come to them, a kind of surety, an expectancy, the look of an inheritor.'

The time of the woman was about to come. It was enough for the men to be forever turned 'to the heat of the blood, staring into the sun, dazed with looking towards the source of generation, unable to turn round.' But not the women: 'The women were different', they were looking outside the circle of the family, beyond. And the book, spanning three generations, sets out to chart and explore their quest for another form of life.

And finally Ursula emerges full-blown, in all her singleness, born of generations of discontent, ushered in by the new century. This eternally dissatisfied modern woman, superficially based on Louie Burrows but clearly speaking for Lawrence's feminine side – and sounding often like Frieda – soon becomes a half destructive, insatiable figure who asks:

'Love – love – love –what does it mean – what does it amount to? . . . as an end in itself, I could love a hundred men, one after the other. Why should I end up with a Skrebensky?'

Skrebensky falls back, aghast, from her terrible embrace, obliterated. 'He felt as if the knife were being pushed into his already dead body.'

A new ferocity has been unleashed. What are its demands? Who will be able to contain it? No wonder that Birkin, who crops up in earlier versions, is pushed right out of this furious, tender, female-dominated novel by a mounting tide of motherhood, female sexuality, female will and female restlessness which floods out inexorably from the opening earth, with its 'sky and harvest and beast and land'. *Women in Love,* in spite of its title, will restore the balance and be as dominated by men as *The Rainbow* is by women. Even here, however, the dialectical cut and thrust ends finally with the triumph of the female principle, while Gerald, and the world of men he represents, is swept aside. Birkin's true role – like Lawrence's – is thus seen to be that of a priest in the service of Woman, fashioning ideology from her female life-material. He is an intermediary, no more. He educates. His spirit wavers, subtle but untrustworthy, in the end external to the field of force. The force itself comes undeniably from the world of the female, the earth and the sun, and it is unstoppable.

This secondary role for man has already been assigned, and quite explicitly, in the 'Foreword to *Sons and Lovers*', at a time when Frieda's influence was supreme. Ursula herself is without doubt a Lawrence–von Richthofen creation. Lawrence nearly always sought to collaborate with his women, making himself so receptive in the process that he became curiously passive, virtually sliding out of himself and into the psyche of the other person. *The Sisters* is such a collaboration, as profound as any that took place during the long liaison with Jessie, and infinitely more fruitful, as it turned out, in terms of Lawrence's development. Never again would Frieda have her deepest, most powerful instincts for the destiny of womanhood – and of herself as its representative – so totally confirmed.

The Rainbow begins in the guise of a dense saga of family life. At the finish there is only this singular woman, Ursula Brangwen, sharp and separate as a star, who has been called the first free soul of the English novel. And what a dangerous freedom she possesses! She blazes with freedom and contempt, 'free as a leopard that sends up its raucous cry in the night.'

The bomb which was Lawrence's novel went off on 30th September, 1915, detonated in all innocence by Methuen. The critics fell on *The Rainbow* and slaughtered it – since they were unable to get at the perpetrator of the outrage. Robert Lynd, in the *Daily News* for the 5th October, headed his notice 'The Downfall', and said that the book was 'like Strindberg trying to write a novel in the manner at once of Pierre Louys and of Miss Victoria Cross.' Most of the book he found 'windy, tedious and nauseating', the men and women like 'cattle who chronically suffer from the staggers', and he issued a warning to 'ordinary readers' to beware of wandering into this 'monotonous wilderness of phallicism'.

This squawk of indignation from a distinguished reviewer encouraged coarser hands to reach for the axe, and soon James Douglas and Clement Shorter were swinging wildly at the novel. Shorter in the *Sphere* pronounced it an 'orgy of sexiness' that left out 'no form of viciousness, of suggestiveness'. 'By a singular irony,' wrote Aldington later, 'an Irishman, a Scotsman and a Jew combined to vilify the most original English writer of his generation.'

John Galsworthy gave vent to his disgust in a letter sent to Lawrence's agent, in the autumn of 1915, that went as follows: 'Frankly – I think it's aesthetically detestable. Its perfervid futuristic style revolts me. Its reiterations bore me to death.' But what really disturbed him, apparently, was what he called 'the sexual aspect'. The sexual instinct was such a strong one that 'any emphasis upon it drags the whole being of the reader away from seeing life steadily, truly and whole.' These reflections led him to conclude: 'I much prefer a frankly pornographic book to one like this. That at all events achieves what it sets out to do; and does not leave on one the painful impression of a man tragically obsessed to the ruin of his gifts.'[45]

But the hostility shown to *The Rainbow* did have one positive result: it intensified Lawrence's longing to get out of the country as quickly as possible. There was the vile war, and the detestable Bottomley of *John Bull* busily undermining the 'softly foundering' Asquith government, and now in addition there was this personal insult to be swallowed. From now on his mood veered between the valedictory and the grimly black. Rananim flowered lushly again in reaction, and the theme of resurrection, a perennial one for Lawrence, blossomed anew in his story 'The Thimble', later transformed into 'The Ladybird'.

He took pride in his still flourishing friendship with Ottoline Morrell, seeing her more often now: but Frieda had very mixed feelings about this swooping, gushing woman, who crooned over her husband because he was a 'genius', and made her feel a mere appendage. Did Ottoline know what it was like to live with a 'genius'?

Lawrence wrote to Ottoline: 'I always wanted us to be friends, real friends in the deep, honourable, permanent sense', and she in turn confided in her journal that 'Lawrence is the spirit of flame.' At Garsington they would put their heads together in earnest discussion. It all sickened Frieda, who called it so much 'soul-mush'. Lawrence's spiritual 'affair' with Cynthia Asquith she found easier to stomach, probably because Cynthia, unlike Ottoline, didn't make her look a fool in front of others.

At Garsington, Lawrence got to know a number of young artists who seemed eminently suitable for enrolment in his Rananim. The leading lights were still to be Ottoline and Russell, but some others temporarily won over by Lawrence's sense of urgency included the composer Philip Heseltine, Aldous Huxley,

Michael Arlen, and the painter Dorothy Brett. This motley crew was urged to prepare for imminent departure on a tramp steamer bound for the West Indies and Florida. The details were delightfully vague, but Lawrence's eloquence swept aside any objections. Dorothy Brett needed no persuading in any case, and young Heseltine, who had been in a state of chronic depression for years, was also ripe for the scheme. He told his friend Delius: 'I feel that I am, and have been for years past, rolling downhill with increasing rapidity into a black, shiny cesspool of stagnation . . .'[46]

Suddenly there was a hitch, and Russell ceased to be a candidate for the presidency of Rananim. He had written an article full of peace and goodness and sent a copy to Lawrence. This struck Lawrence as so loathsome that he wanted nothing more to do with the man, and promptly told him so. In an attack fairly seething with hatred, he wrote to Russell: 'You are simply *full* of repressed desires, which have become savage and anti-social. And they come out of this sheep's clothing of peace and propaganda. As a woman said to me, who had been to one of your meetings: "It seemed so strange, with his face looking so evil, to be talking about peace and love. He can't have *meant* what he said."' And to make doubly sure that Russell had got his message, he added: 'The enemy of all mankind, you are, full of the lust of enmity.'[47]

Russell must have assumed, after such an onslaught, that this was the end of their association. But a few months later, Lawrence, after firing off a few more accusations, calmly suggested to Russell that when he made his will he could leave some provision for him, at least sufficient to live on. Russell has commented dryly that although he didn't oblige, he immediately stopped feeling suicidal about his 'evil' tendencies.

In this year, too, Lawrence added Dorothy Brett to his entourage. She was destined to be the only survivor. In 1915 she was already a strange bird, with her trousers and her bobbed hair. Her father was Viscount Esher, but Dorothy had fled the aristocracy and fluttered now among the London artists, staring hard at people because she was deaf. She was a painter herself, and painfully shy, but this didn't prevent her from adapting skilfully to the scandalmongering habits of her circle. Lawrence 'in due course himself became a scandalmonger of finished eloquence', as Aldington puts it, and he was learning now to guard his enthusiasms. When he and Dorothy Brett met for the first time they enjoyed themselves by dismantling Ottoline Morrell, until even Brett feared they had gone too far: 'We sit drinking tea, tearing poor O. to pieces. We pull her feathers out in handfuls until I stop, aghast, and try to be merciful, saying, "We will leave her just one feather." You laugh at that, a high, tinkling laugh, mischievous, saying, "We will leave her just one draggled feather in her tail, the poor plucked hen!"'[48] Lawrence may have improved on his technique by listening to Katherine Mansfield, whose ruthless mockery at his own expense 'made him smile rather crookedly.'

Brett was so nervous of meeting Lawrence alone that she took the painter Mark Gertler along to Byron Villas with her. Gertler then was like something out of Botticelli, with his delicate face, elongated eyes and thick curly hair. Gertler and Lawrence were already friends, and Gertler had been urging Brett for some time to come with him.

On the day they arrived, Murry was there, and came scuttling out as they went in. Brett remembered afterwards the brightly burning fire in the tiny room, and 'a large woman', who turned out to be Frieda. Lawrence, sensitively aware of his visitor's spasms of nervousness, coaxed her gently into conversation.

A few days later she threw a studio party in Lawrence's honour. Also present were Gertler, Koteliansky, the Murrys, Dorothy Carrington, a friend of Katherine Mansfield named Estelle Rice, and, of course, Frieda. Carrington and Gertler were both friends of Brett from her Slade days. Carrington, another denizen of bohemia, 'sidled' rather than walked, wore some brick-red material which made her look like an Augustus John girl, and her heavy gold hair fell around her face. She looked from under it with 'two sly blue eyes'.

Koteliansky looked massive and powerful, his black hair 'brushed straight up "en brosse"', his gold eye-glasses giving him an air of distinction. Beside him, Katherine must have seemed even more delicate and bird-like than usual, dressed in black, her sleek, dark hair fitting her head like a cap, her forehead dangerously pale. Her eyes twitched about, missing nothing. But Murry's gaze was strangely unseeing, as he came rolling in 'with the gait of a sailor', his handsomeness enhanced rather than spoiled by his crooked broken nose.

The party was soon ruined by gate-crashers, over twenty of them, half drunk, with bottles shoved in their pockets. Not knowing what to do, Brett played the pianola faster and faster, while Gertler and Carrington had one of their interminable rows and Katherine sat on the sofa embracing a stranger. In the early hours, after it was all over, Murry was discovered sitting quietly among the wreckage, blind drunk but amiable.

Brett's only memory of Lawrence that night was of him talking

19. Lady Ottoline Morrell   20. Lady Cynthia Asquith, c. 1916

21. Lawrence at Mountain Cottage,
Middleton-by-Wirksworth, Derbyshire, 1918

22. Higher Tregerthen, Zennor, Cornwall

to Iris Tree; but Lytton Strachey, apparently one of the uninvited guests, said later that he had 'rarely seen anyone so pathetic, miserable, ill, and obviously devoured by internal distresses.'

Not long before this, *The Rainbow* had been suppressed. Lawrence had no idea that the police were acting against the book until W. L. George noticed that Methuen's advertisements of the book had stopped appearing, and rang the publishers to find out what was happening. On 3rd November, Detective Inspector Albert Draper from Scotland Yard went to Methuen's offices and confiscated the 1,011 copies of the novel still at the publishers. On 14th November, the case came to Bow Street Magistrates' Court, and was reported by the *Daily Express* under the headline: OBSCENE NOVEL TO BE DESTROYED – WORSE THAN ZOLA. A man named Muskett who represented the police said in court that the novel was 'a mass of obscenity of thought, idea and action throughout, wrapped up in a language which he supposed would be regarded in some quarters as an artistic and intellectual effort.' No defence was presented by the publishers, who apologised abjectly and agreed with the magistrate that their reputation had been 'soiled by the publication of this work'. The magistrate fined them ten guineas and ordered the book to be destroyed.

The damage done to Lawrence was incalculable. He now owed his publishers the advance on the book; he was publicly branded as 'obscene', which meant that nobody would touch any work of his for years to come: a book on European history for schools had to be published under a pseudonym. But more damaging than any of these things was the psychological shock of being castigated in public like a common pornographer. Lawrence expressed his complete disgust in a very few words to his agent, Pinker: 'I am not very much moved: am beyond that by now. I only curse them all, body and soul, root, branch and leaf, to eternal damnation.'[49]

Emile Delavenay, in his recent book on Lawrence, argues persuasively that *The Rainbow* prosecution was politically rather than sexually motivated, even though the novel was banned officially for implications of lesbianism. Whatever the reasons, reverberations were still being felt fifteen years later. The day after Lawrence died, a journalist wrote in the *Daily Telegraph*: 'Alas, the kink in the brain developed early and he came to write with one hand always in the slime. . . . His later books and poems were rightly banned by the censor, like the unspeakable pictures which were brazenly exhibited in London last summer, till the attention of the police was pointedly drawn to them in these notes and the disgusting show was closed.'[50] Two days later, a civil servant saw an advertisement of the uniform pocket edition of Lawrence's works, snipped it out and attached it to an official memo form on which he had written: '*The Rainbow* is included among D. H. Lawrence's published works, but in 1915 proceedings were successfully taken by the police for the destruction of the book. I have not seen *The Rainbow,* but there was no doubt, according to the press reports, of its obscenity according to the standards of 15 years ago, though of recent years opinion has moved very rapidly away from anything like a conventional standard. I think the attention of the police should be called to the matter.'[51]

Nothing happened, but only because a higher official thought it unwise to give further publicity to 'the works of Lawrence'.

The rallying cry of America, Florida, Rananim, sounded now in nearly all his letters, but it soon became clear that his dream of staking out an advance-post in the New World would have to be abandoned for the present: the authorities seemed to have developed 'an insane determination' to keep him in the country. But, damn them, he refused to sit there in London and rot. Just before Christmas he went with Frieda to spend a few days in Derbyshire with his younger sister. He had given up the tiny flat in Hampstead, stored away some bits of furniture and got rid of the rest, and they were '*Vogelfrei,* thank God – nothing but the trunks to bother us – no house nor possessions.' By the end of the year he was in Cornwall – a place as remote and unknown to him as Florida. He called it a new beginning.

13

Cornwall:
The Crow's Nest

Christmas in Derbyshire had plunged Lawrence back into his boyhood and youth. The experience was painful. Curiously, he recoiled at once from the mindlessness of the life up there. It was terribly strange to him now; their minds were shut to everything except industrial strife and the issues of 'wages and money and machinery'. It led straight to a mean socialism which reduced his Eastwood friends and his brother to the lowest terms. He knew them and he loved them, but he hated the way they were spitting on their passionate nature, getting ready to sell it in the shoddy bargain basement of industrialism. Even his elder brother had gone over to it. Lawrence argued bitterly with this 'radical nonconformist', until he saw it was hopeless. The process must go on, it was implacable, irreversible. It made him want to scream, to get right away to Cornwall.

Three days later he was there with Frieda. J. D. Beresford, the novelist, had lent them his cottage-house at Porthcothan, Padstow, 'for which may the gods shower blessings and much money on him', and at once he perked up, his letters radiating cheerfulness and hope, as the wild Cornish winds rushed round the house and blew the sea half up the cliffs like a bombardment. He hadn't reached Florida, but he felt he had got himself well clear of England at least, and parasitic London, and the clashing, mechanical destructiveness of the Midlands. He wrote exultantly to tell Koteliansky that it was possible to create a new life here among the 'good peace' and the 'good silence'. The cardinal sin now was the endless 'analysis and introspection and individualism': one must jettison that, and inherit this wild, big, blowing space, brimming with light and air.

A week later he was laid up in bed with what he euphemistically called his 'wintry inflammation', yet still scattering letters to all and sundry. Ottoline Morrell sent him a soft orange jersey, which went with his beard and made him look like an 'orange-breasted robin in the springtime'.

Two Café Royal habitués joined him, one after the other: first Heseltine, and then Michael Arlen. Both brought the jarring atmosphere of London, and for some reason were antagonistic both to Lawrence and to each other. For once Lawrence managed to restrain himself, not allowing the situation to work on his nerves. Heseltine was dangerously restless, hankering after his 'Puma', a girl who was a model, and, he said, a whore. Nevertheless, he wanted her, and despised himself for it.

Stimulated by the bare, yellowish landscape descending to jagged black rocks and a 'torn' sea, Lawrence sent out a call for books. He wanted things like 'Norse literature, or early Celtic, something about Druids (though I believe it's all spurious) or the Orphic religions, or Egypt, or on anything really African, Fetish Worship or the customs of primitive tribes.'[1]

His 'inflammation' kept him in bed for weeks. Finally he was scared enough by its persistence to allow a doctor friend, Maitland Radford, to examine him. The most frightening thing was a numbness, like a paralysis, down his right side, affecting his arm so badly that he found it difficult to hold a pen. Slowly he recovered, trying to lie still and peaceful, as the doctor had ordered, while he waited and listened for spring, the 'profound spring' of the world which he rehearsed so poignantly, again and again, within himself.

The Cornish people barely impinged on him, he was so dominated by the landscape during those first months. But he saw they were very different. The women attracted him so much that he thought he would like to be married to one: they were 'so soft and so wise and so attractive – so soft and unopposing, yet so true: a quality of winsomeness and rare, unconscious Female soothingness and fertility of being.'[2] This sounds like a reaction to the boisterous assertiveness and well-being of Frieda, who could be anything but soothing at times. His impression of the men was far from favourable – 'detestably small-eyed and mean – real cunning-nosed peasants mean as imbeciles.'[3]

For all that, he liked very much the 'curious softness and intimacy' of the Cornish. Theorising wildly, he thought they had somehow escaped Christianity, and had no social love, social structure, 'only the immediate intimate self. 'That's why they're generally disliked.' This had made them 'wreckers and smugglers and all antisocial things', he went on, glad to turn them into outlaws. For this was how he now saw himself, as an outlaw who had cleared out of 'the whole social ship'.

Much as he loved the savagery of North Cornwall, there is plenty of evidence that it wore on his nerves unbearably and only prolonged his illness, which was as much psychological as physical. After the profound shock of *The Rainbow* prosecution he sorely needed 'soothingness'.

Though he was frequently in bed that winter, he was inwardly as ' restless and active as the wind outside, collecting poems together for a new volume – he had recovered a lost manuscript from Fiascherino – and correcting the proofs of *Twilight in Italy*. He wanted to remake his 'philosophy' too, and there was the second part of *The Rainbow* waiting, which he was beginning to envisage as a clean act of passionate destruction to be set against the unclean horror of the war, a great river of dissolution swirling through to a new, unimagined health. He wanted to compose a hymn to death, 'beautiful destructive death', to sing the virtual death of civilisation, and in the same creative act to plant the seeds for a resurrection. As he began work on it, these themes became inextricably bound up with the necessity to come to terms with the potent, dark underworld of his father's mine, always half horrible to him, and to destroy, once more, his mother's values above ground. There was also the sexual impasse of his own marriage to be resolved, a trap he had already sought to escape by universalising it in his 'Two Principles' philosophy. With his parents' example constantly before him, Lawrence was obsessed, like his hero Birkin, by the idea that in a sexual relationship one partner must inevitably triumph over the other, unless, as he wrote in *Women in Love*, 'the root is beyond love'. In Birkin's case, this meant a marriage to Ursula which was not exclusive, but left room for an additional, homosexual relationship. To make all this, not only credible, but transcendental, was the immense task that Lawrence, sick and isolated, had begun to set himself at the age of thirty. The result would be 'a terrific abstraction', like the primeval shore of Cornwall, and it would mark the end of an epoch.

Meanwhile, virtually without resources, Lawrence was entering the most impoverished period of his life. The extent of his destitution can be seen in his letters to a friend in London, asking for his meagre belongings to be sent to Cornwall. 'I should like the kitchen table, but if it will cost very much to come (the man from the G.W. Ry. will advise you), then don't send it: if it will cost more than 8/-.'

To cope with the everyday world he knocked together a sort of Robinson Crusoe philosophy of survival for himself, just as he would make a dresser or put up a shelf or paint a chair. He did it by sinking back into his soul and sitting there, 'as in a crow's nest out of it all'. Then he could grin, and turn his back. He did it, too, by looking at seagulls. 'The seagulls here are so wonderful, large and white, with strong bent shoulders in the light of the sun. Why should one care, or will?'

Again, from an instinct of self-preservation, he refused to worry about money. 'Something in me is asleep and doesn't trouble.' He was turning himself into a castaway.

But his nerves couldn't take any more of the 'black and terrible' winds that never stopped and the enormous waves exploding on the black rocks, flinging up a great ghost of spray to stand on the sea. And anyway, the house was only borrowed. He and Frieda set out to look for a modest place in the Redruth district. At the beginning of March they were at the Tinner's Arms, Zennor, using it as a base while they kept searching. With next to no money, and little prospect of any, they deliberately avoided big places. They found a two-roomed cottage, unfurnished, with a long galley of a scullery, for 4/- a week. As soon as their bits and pieces came from London, they moved in, 'like foxes under the hill'.

And it was spring. The transfusion ran straight into his veins, circulating in his blood. The triumph he felt was always a personal one, as if the spring was his creation, brought forth from within his own body, miraculously. In his letter to Cynthia Asquith he wrote a valedictory to winter.

'It really is our turn to begin to dance round the fountains. This morning, the world was white with snow. This evening the sunset is yellow, the birds are whistling, the gorse bushes are bristling with little winged suns.'[4]

Lawrence was buoyed up, now, by a project of Heseltine's, broached and discussed while he was staying with the Lawrences at Porthcothan. This was a scheme to print and publish *The Rainbow* privately. If successful, he would then bring out a philosophical work of Lawrence's called 'Goats and Compasses'.

The Murrys were piqued at this intrusion by Heseltine, who wasn't even a writer or publisher, into their domain, and Lawrence hastened to placate them. There was no need for them to be jealous: Heseltine was very young and enthusiastic, and, more to the point, he had a small private income. He had gone off to London to get a pamphlet and subscription form printed, so for God's sake, he told Murry, don't get into a state. His friendship with Heseltine didn't affect theirs in the least: it was entirely different. 'Don't get silly notions. I've waited for you for two years' now, and am far more constant to you than ever you are to me – or ever will be. Which you know.'[5] Heseltine, they must understand, was in a queer state, split between two women. Lawrence liked him for his generosity and enthusiasm. He thought he was one of those people born to be 'conveyors of art' rather than artists.

But Heseltine, after living with Lawrence for seven weeks, had had more than enough. Lawrence had tried to sort out Heseltine's love affairs without permission, and had nearly landed him in 'a fearful fix'. *The Rainbow* scheme fizzled out: there were only thirty replies to six hundred circulars. 'Goats and Compasses' – according to Cecil Gray a psycho-philosophical treatise dealing largely with homosexuality – was destroyed: 'Lawrence himself destroyed the one,' wrote Gray, 'while the other, which Philip had in his possession, was gradually consumed by him some years later, leaf by leaf, in the discharge of a lowly but none the less appropriate function.'[6] Thus Philip Heseltine had his revenge on the man who acted on him 'like a subtle and deadly poison. Later in the same year he was in the Café Royal with Michael Arlen, jeering at a copy of Lawrence's 'Amores' and reading poems aloud from it. Katherine Mansfield happened to be at a nearby table. She rose and went over to the two men, picked up the book and walked away with it, 'all down the brilliant room, between the tables, in her measured fashion. It was some moments before anybody realised what was happening.' The passage in the chapter called 'Gudrun at the Pompadour' in *Women in Love* describes the incident exactly.

Now that Lawrence had a tiny base of his own again, his spirits rose. He could sit like a brigand among the stone fields at the edge of the peacock sea and let the rest of the world go to the devil. He wrote seductively to the Murrys, who were living none too happily at Bandol on the French Riviera, urging them to join him immediately in establishing a small company of brave souls at Zennor, where they would be 'like a little monastery'. He sketched the layout of the group of cottages, tucked under the moors, five miles from St. Ives and seven from Penzance. Next to the Lawrences was a block of three cottages knocked into one, with 'a funny little tower at one end . . . I call it already Katherine's house, Katherine's tower.' How could they resist his eloquence, his ability to coo like a dove when he wanted something badly enough? They were charmed. And Murry, as it happened, needed little persuading. His alliance with Katherine seemed to be crumbling yet again. In a crisis he tended to drift hopelessly and lose what strength he had, whereas Lawrence, like Frieda, thrived on adversity. A risen Lazarus, Lawrence brimmed with hope and energy. He announced proudly that he had made a dresser and book-shelves with his own hands and painted them royal blue. The walls of his cottage were pale pink inside, the ceiling and beams white. Outside were the skipping lambs, stone walls, boulders half as big as cottages sunk in the rough grass, and the sea dawdling beyond. What more did anyone want? It could be their Rananim.

That name Rananim should have warned them, but they came, Katherine trailing disconsolately in a farm cart with the goods and chattels. Coming down to Cornwall with Murry she had been more and more depressed. Everything was wrong: the sky was steely, the sea too grey, the cry of the gulls simply awful. After the warm South, she could see nothing enchanting in this gaunt northern landscape, scoured bare by the winds.

Thus poor Murry was undermined at the outset. Oblivious, Lawrence set to work furiously alongside his friend in the cold, slaty April weather, getting the second cottage ready. This was the sort of situation Lawrence loved, rolling up his sleeves and putting his back into a task, absorbing himself in ordinary things. He hitched on his rucksack and marched over the hill and down into St. Ives with Murry, on the hunt for cheap bits of Victorian furniture, imparting country lore on the way and informing the whole enterprise with an intimacy that Murry found irresistible. But Murry was only too aware of Katherine's ill-concealed misery, and soon began to sink with her, in sympathy. The chairs he had bought at St. Ives came up on the cart early one morning, and he set to work painting them in the sunshine. When Lawrence and Frieda came out of their cottage, they were 'comically dismayed' to see the colour he had used: a dull funereal black. Katherine grimly approved of this touch of doom. And in May her mood was still the same: she wrote in a letter: 'Today I can't see a yard, thick mist and rain and a tearing wind with it. Everything is faintly damp. The floor of the tower is studded with Cornish pitchers catching the drops.'[7]

Even more unpleasant than the weather was having her literary talent virtually ignored by Lawrence, whose obsessions had now carried him far beyond such considerations. For one thing, he was engaged in a 'fight to the death' with Frieda, who was stubbornly refusing to yield precedence to him as the man. One night Frieda came screaming into the Murrys' cottage, pursued by a white-faced Lawrence who was yelling, 'I'll kill her! I'll kill her!' as he tore round the room and knocked chairs aside. Murry grabbed the lamp, to save it, then sat down, terrified. Katherine sat still, utterly indifferent. Suddenly Lawrence collapsed in a chair by the fire and Frieda crept away. The day after this, Murry peered nervously into the Lawrences' cottage, and there the couple sat, perfectly content, while Lawrence decorated one of Frieda's hats.[8]

There was worse to come for Murry. Not long before their arrival, Lawrence had discovered *Moby Dick,* 'a very odd, interesting book'. It could have been there that he got the idea of blood-brotherhood after reading of the relationship between Ishmael and Queequeg. It was already one of the themes in *Women in Love,* though presumably Murry was not to know this. Now Lawrence began to persecute his baffled friend with a theory that, for some strange reason, he thought it unnecessary to explain, though he was stating it clearly, repeatedly, and with intense seriousness in the novel. There, Gerald is destroyed after marrying Gudrun instead of forming an alliance with Birkin first. 'The other way', wrote Lawrence, 'was to accept Rupert's offer of alliance, to enter into the bond of pure trust and love with the other man, and then subsequently with the woman.' This was what Lawrence wanted for himself, and he had decided that it was what Murry needed too, for the salvation of his relationship with Katherine.

Things came rapidly to a crisis when Murry, acting weakly on Katherine's insistence, told Lawrence that they had decided to move to the southern, 'kindly' side of Cornwall. It was a way of escaping from the intolerable pressure that he felt mounting to danger point as he kept up his evasions. But to Lawrence this desertion stank of betrayal, and it brought on his nightmares. Murry heard him calling out one night: 'Jack is killing me! I hate his love. *I hate him.* He's an obscene bug, sucking my life away.'

By now Katherine was complaining virulently in her letters to Koteliansky: 'I don't know which disgusts me worse, when they are loving and playing with each other or when they are roaring at each other and he is pulling out Frieda's hair and saying "I'll cut your bloody throat, you bitch."' And to Gordon Campbell: 'Once you start talking, I cannot describe the frenzy that comes over him. He simply *raves*, roars, beats the table, abuses everybody. But that's not such great matter. What makes these attacks insupportable is the feeling one has at the back of one's mind that he is completely out of control, swallowed up in an acute, *insane* irritation. After one of these attacks he's ill with fever, haggard and broken.'[9]

Murry hurried off in search of another cottage for them, and found one at Mylor, near Falmouth. They lost no time in making a getaway. Katherine went on by train and it was left to Murry to say the final farewells. Lawrence helped him to rope his belongings to the cart, working in gloomy silence. Then Murry got on his bicycle and rode away, feeling he had said goodbye for good.

This wasn't the first time that Lawrence's apparent disconnection from external reality had landed him in trouble, and it wouldn't be the last. It was becoming more and more difficult for him to keep the strands of his life and his work separate, and indeed he refused to allow any such distinction. About another mauled friend, Heseltine, soon to be a dangerous enemy, he wrote in a letter:

'Perhaps he is very split, and would always have the two things separate, the real blood connection and the real conscious or spiritual connection. . . . For these people I really believe in two wives. I don't see why there should be monogamy for people who can't have full satisfaction in one person, because they themselves are too split, because they act in themselves separately.'[10]

Here was a resurrection of the startling proposal he had once put to Jessie; he was now transferring it from himself to Heseltine. But it remained Lawrence's psychosexual impasse too. In his attempt to deliver himself from it, he had, after shattering misadventures, married Frieda, who combined, as he thought, both the light and the dark that Heseltine wanted and went shuttling back and forth between his two girls, Mlle and Puma, to find. To his horror, Lawrence now half believed that his marriage to Frieda had landed him with a 'devouring mother', a Magna Mater who required him to 'cast himself as it were into her womb',[11] as he confided to Katherine Mansfield. This was a kind of incest, horribly reminiscent of his mother's desire and gratification. Now he fought madly to get out, and the nearest, most obvious escape for him was through the creation of new schemata (and the destruction of the old) in a work of art. Biographers have commented on his pathological outbursts against Frieda and Middleton Murry in Cornwall without making the connection between these 'fits' and his bloody struggle with *Women in Love*. The murderous shrieks and groans and the insane frenzies reported by Murry were as much outbreaks from within the structure of the novel, torn out of Lawrence as the tensions convulsed him, as they were cries of fury from a man who could never bear to be opposed or afford to be let down. A man of death and life (like the transitional types he so often wrote about), stuck agonisingly with his head and shoulders out and his lower body still in the womb, only half created, he strove simultaneously to shed the old dying world and give birth to the future. One could say that he had no choice. This single-handed effort, in complete isolation, was nearly killing him, as he was perfectly well aware. 'The book frightens me,' he wrote to Catherine Carswell, 'it is so end-of-

the-world. But it is, it must be, the beginning of a new world
too.'[12]

Maurice Capitanchik, in a review of a book by Emile Delavenay
which seeks to identify the sources of Lawrence's ideas, remarks
pertinently that 'in his mythology connubial love was really a goal,
the culmination of an extraordinarily complex effort,'[13] and
entailed the virtual sacrifice, for her own good, of the woman to
the man. Thus his father's defeat could be revenged, his potency
redeemed.

Lawrence was now plunging further into the forbidden depths
of himself than ever before. For this reason alone, *Women in Love*,
so disintegrative in parts, had to be also as powerful a call for
integration as he could make it, strong enough to challenge
the world's 'stupendous assertion of not-being' and at the same
time overcome the phobic divisions within himself. Its fertile
ambiguities could only have originated in a man so drastically
split that he longed for union with every fibre of his being.
Birkin's bisexuality, revealed in the original first chapter or Prologue to the novel, makes this character the most significant of
Lawrence's self-projections. Compton Mackenzie remembered
Lawrence saying to him once: 'I believe that the nearest I've ever
come to perfect love was with a young coalminer when I was about
sixteen.'[14] To see how close Lawrence came to active homosexuality, and how he struggled against it, one has only to read between
the lines of the Prologue, published for the first time in 1968. Its
pages blaze with secrets, with desires kept in check by a reserve 'as
strong as a chain of iron'. Why, Birkin asks himself repeatedly,
did the *beauté mâle* torture him so abominably, with such subtlety
and refinement? How could he escape the insufferable bondage
of it, and the destruction of real love that was taking place in him?
He knew that in order to love at all he had to somehow unite the
two halves of himself. But his will was no match for his desires:

'It might be any man, a policeman who suddenly looked up at
him, as he inquired the way, or a soldier who sat next to him in a
railway carriage. How vividly, months afterwards, he would recall
the soldier who had sat pressed up close to him on a journey from
Charing Cross to Westerham; the shapely, motionless body, the
large, dumb, coarsely-beautiful hands that rested helplessly upon
the strong knees, the dark brown eyes, vulnerable in the erect
body.'

He would think he had overcome it; forget all about it. 'But
then, inevitably, it would recur again. There would come into a
restaurant a strange Cornish type of man, with dark eyes like
holes in his head, or like the eyes of a rat, and with dark, fine,

rather stiff hair, and full, heavy, softly-strong limbs. Then again Birkin would feel the desire spring up in him, the desire to know this man, to have him, as it were to eat him, to take the very substance of him.'[15]

Like Lawrence in early life, Birkin recoiled from the incestuousness of physical contact with a woman. Yet his deep hunger for unity stopped him from being homosexual: that, and the iron-like reserve in him, the refusal to acknowledge the secret even to himself. He never fully accepted the desire, never faced the question.

Now, in Cornwall, it was being faced at last. It was at the very root of Lawrence's mad irritability. He was inflamed to the point of madness by it at times. But he understood at last that any solution to his very complex problem could only be reached within the context of a larger complexity, namely the death and rebirth of society itself. And how else could this be achieved satisfactorily, in other words at once, except through the flexibility and freedom of a novel, by the construction of a world impregnable to attacks by Frieda and by society? Once constructed, it could never be brought down. The vision it embodied would triumph over the life of here and now which so disgusted him. 'I know it is true, the book,' he wrote to Ottoline Morrell. 'And it is another world, in which I can live apart from this foul world which I will not accept or acknowledge or even enter.'[16]

Of course he omitted to tell her that she herself was depicted in the book as Hermione Roddice, in a setting suspiciously like that of her own home at Garsington, or that the full-length portrait of her contained such details as: 'Ursula resented Hermione's long, grave, downward-looking face. There was something of the stupidity and unenlightened self-esteem of a horse in it.' Waspishness of this kind incensed Lady Ottoline to the extent of threatening libel action if Lawrence went ahead and published the manuscript. Two years after his death, she told Koteliansky that the novel was 'horrible . . . a wicked chaotic spiteful book.'

She was by no means the only victim in this 'book of retaliation', as Aldington has called it. Bertrand Russell appeared briefly as 'a learned, dry baronet of fifty', and there were merciless caricatures of Philip Heseltine and his Café Royal crowd. But no one is more ruthlessly treated than the author himself. Lawrence showed uncanny knowledge of his own character – even if he seldom acted on it – in this description of Birkin by Hermione-Ottoline: 'He is frail in health and body, he needs great, great care. Then he is so changeable and unsure of himself – it requires the greatest patience and understanding to help him . . . He lives an *intensely* spiritual life at times . . . And then come the reactions . . . He is so uncertain, so unstable – he wearies, and then reacts . . . That which he affirms and loves one day – a little later he turns on it in a fury of destruction. He is never constant, always this awful, dreadful reaction.'[17]

And comment that was a good deal more vitriolic comes from Ursula's mouth – presumably direct from Frieda – in the chapter called 'Excurse'. Lawrence knows it is well earned, and reproduces it with absolute veracity and no ill-will at all:

'You go to your women – go to them – they are your sort – you've always had a string of them trailing after you – and you always will. Go to your spiritual brides – but don't come to me as well, because I'm not having any, thank you. You're not satisfied, are you? Your spiritual brides can't give you what you want, they aren't fleshy and common enough for you, are they? So you come to me, and keep them in the background! You will marry me for daily use. But you'll keep yourself well provided with spiritual brides in the background. I know your dirty little game.'[18]

However, her changes of front are as disconcerting as his, and after this virulent denunciation she returned with a piece of heather as a peace offering. Taking it, he says, 'Pretty!' and smiles. It is like a scene from childhood.

Aldington has remarked sensitively that this was invariably the exclamation of the mother when Lawrence brought her a gift as a boy and she wanted to express her love. We are prepared for tenderness by the 'tree-like, tiny branch', but the word 'pretty' transfers the boundless tenderness of mother-love to the woman.

The summer had come, the gorse flamed, there were 'graceful little companies of bluebells everywhere on the moors', and sea-pinks down by the water, and primroses on the cliffs 'like settling butterflies'. The foxgloves would soon be out, that the Cornish called 'high poppies' and Jessie had once called 'Red Indian braves'. Whenever Katherine Mansfield saw foxgloves, she thought of the Lawrences, of peering between the daffodil curtains of their cottage to see the 'great sumptuous blooms' set in pitchers against the whitewashed walls, and Lawrence and Frieda sitting in the middle of them 'like blissful prisoners'.

Outwardly it was idyllic, and impossible to imagine the terrible carnage at Verdun and on the Somme. But the Lawrences, without even knowing it, were being suspected and hated. Frieda attracted attention, walking into St. Ives to do her shopping in her orange-and-pink or yellow-and-green stockings. They saw this blonde Brunhilde lying brazenly on the rocks to sunbathe, and noticed the strange bearded visitors coming and going. General conscription had been introduced in January, and the hatred for Germany and all things German was mounting. The slaughter reached into the villages of Cornwall. People went about in mourning for their sons cut down in France or torpedoed and drowned at sea. Frieda was German, and sometimes openly sympathetic towards the U-boat crews in the Channel. After all, she might know some of the men, might have grown up with them. As for disguising her nationality for the sake of expediency, as some Germans in England were doing – how ridiculous! Tales had begun to circulate against the Lawrences.

In June, Lawrence was called for his first medical examination. To his horror he found that this meant going to Bodmin and living in the military barracks there for a night as a conscript, before being rejected the next morning. It was like being in a gang of convicts, he wrote later, in 'The Nightmare' chapter of *Kangaroo*. The ignominy of it unfuriated him. They had herded him into a barracks yard, with a little terrier of a sergeant yapping at his ankles. What a shock it all was. And the glamour of camaraderie, of Homer, that he had secretly hankered after for so long – what a humiliation in reality! He asked Dollie Radford to picture the scene: 'Thirty men in their shirts, being weighed like sheep, one after the other – God!' And he added comically, 'They have such impossible feet.'[19] So much for the *beauté mâle* in the cold light of a barracks.

That night he slept in his long woollen pants, and was ashamed because they had patches on the knees and betrayed his poverty to the world. His mother had brought him up to regard himself as a gentleman, and he never forgot it. The little sergeant, next morning, turned out to be a gentleman, for he recognised Lawrence's own gentlemanliness by making him relinquish the heavy broom to another man. The doctor, too, asking him where he lived, 'as a gentleman asks', met with his approval.

Whereas the youth in the next bed fascinated him, though he was obviously no gentleman. He had an Apache look to him, 'a degenerate sort of handsomeness', standing there stupidly without a word to say for himself, his straight black hair hanging over his eyes. He fumbled for a long time with his clothes, and finally stood there in his white shirt, which came down below his knees like a nightshirt.

Rejected as C3, Lawrence went back to Zennor. He had finished his novel – it had come out 'in a rush' – and as he had no money he was going to type it himself. He tried, but it got on his nerves so much that he put it aside. What did it matter? – there was no publisher for it. He would wait. Not too fit, he drifted about rather emptily, in a peculiar state of abstraction. Autumn crept nearer and he was still suspended, as it were. Frieda wanted to go to London for the usual reasons, but the thought of masses of people frightened him now, he had turned so far away. Wandering on the moor alone, he saw 'the few visionary temptations: heather and blackberries on the hills, a foamy pool in the rocks where one bathes, the postman with barbed letters.' He was a St. Anthony in the wilderness, tempted but not deceived by what he called 'the disordered hallucinations of temporal reality'.[20]

He refused to go out of Cornwall: he felt safe there. The outer world was mad. He drifted on to the land, helping a neighbouring farmer, William Hocking, with whom he had made friends. Hocking, a man of Lawrence's age, had a younger brother, Stanley, and two sisters Mabel and Mary. Lawrence became fond of them all – in a way it was like The Haggs all over again. He wore old clothes, an old hat, and could have passed for a working man. It was as if he wanted to go drifting back to his origins. Frieda felt deserted.

A police constable rode up on his bicycle to ask for Lawrence's birth certificate. He was apologetic: Bodmin had demanded it. The penniless author's nationality was now in question. He had German relatives, a German wife; he had sent letters to Germany regularly, and he received replies.

The implication outraged him. At the end of his patience, Lawrence, 'one of the most intensely English little men England ever produced',[21] now talked openly against the war to the Hockings, mocked at the propaganda in the newspapers and sang German folk songs at the top of his voice with Frieda.

One afternoon, he and Frieda were coming home across the cliffs with a knapsack full of shopping. Two army officers stopped them and examined their goods, groping around among the rice and soap and candles. Finding a block wrapped in brown paper, they insisted it was a camera. The senior officer tore off the paper. It was a pound of salt. Before they got out of earshot, Frieda laughed loudly: 'The poor innocent salt!' Another black mark went down against them.

They knew now that they were being watched, but Frieda would often either forget or just not care. Once she danced about on the cliff in a gay mood, letting her white shawl blow in the wind. 'Stop it, stop it, you fool!' Lawrence cried in a panic. 'Can't you see they'll think you're signalling to the enemy?' By instinct he used the word 'enemy', like a good patriot.

As an author, he hardly existed: he had published one poem

287

during the whole of 1916. To keep going he was reduced to 'precarious borrowing' from his agent, from Ada, who never deserted him, and from a few friends in England and America. 'There isn't any particular news,' he told Lady Ottoline. 'I feel like one who lies in wait and prepares.'

Somebody sent him Swinburne. The poems moved him deeply and reminded him of Shelley, always a favourite, a fiery spirit whose life, like Lawrence's, was one of perpetual motion.

His discovery of Melville had put him on the track of classic American literature. He sent ten shillings off to Koteliansky and asked for cheap copies of *The Last of the Mohicans*, *The Pathfinder*, *Omoo* and *Typee*. A little later, after reading some Turgenev and then *The Deerslayer*, he told Catherine Carswell: 'No, enough of this silly worship of foreigners. The most exquisite literature in the world is written in the English language.'

In January, 1917, he decided to make another attempt to get to America. He applied for reindorsement of their passports to New York, and listed his reasons as follows:

1. Ill-health.
2. Failure to make any money at all over here.
3. Necessity to place short stories, and literary articles, and poems, and to arrange with a publisher the publications of *The Rainbow*, which is ready for press but has been deferred, and of the novel *Women in Love*.[22]

While he waited, he tore himself apart emotionally, going through imaginary agonies of parting. But he needn't have bothered: the Foreign Office kept the passports and didn't bother to answer his application.

It was a bitter blow, even though he might have expected it. Somehow he could never get used to the idea that he was now listed as a suspect. And then another blow fell: news came through of the collapse of Asquith and the rise of Lloyd George. This made him feel so ill that he had to get out of the cottage, on to the moor. He wanted to go on walking, get right away. 'Canaille, canaille, all the lot of them.'

He loved this west corner of Cornwall now more than ever before, with its shaggy moors and its huge boulders bulging out of the ground like monsters. He loved it because it was pre-human: the invincible earth, which endured forever.

He believed now that if the war went on much longer there would be a real shortage of food, so he set about teaching himself to garden. Writing to his faithful old supplier, Koteliansky, he asked for a sixpenny gardening book, *The Culture of Profitable*

23. View across fields from Cossall to Ilkeston. 'Whenever one of the Brangwens in the fields lifted his head from his work he saw the church tower of Ilkeston in the empty sky.' *The Rainbow*

24. Felley Mill Lane, near Eastwood

Vegetables in Small Gardens. And while his friend foraged for it in London, he painted a picture of the death of Procris, 'which fills me with great delight.'

The stealthy spying on him and Frieda continued. As he described it in *Kangaroo*: 'Harriet could not hang out a towel on a bush, or carry out the slops, in the empty landscape of moors and sea, without her every movement being followed by invisible eyes. And at evening, when the doors were shut, valiant men lay under the windows to listen to the conversation in the cosy little room.'[23]

When Frieda went to London in April to see her children, he stuck it out alone for a day or two, then went off himself to see his people in the Midlands. It was a long journey up through the glamorous spring West country to Plymouth, on to Bristol and Birmingham, and up to Derby. He got into Derby quite late on Saturday, and had to transfer to a bus for the last few miles. Derby was, unfamiliar, hostile. He sat in a bus packed solid with half-drunk young miners that went lurching into the black Saturday night, as if heading straight for Hell. He felt murder in the air. Once all this violence broke loose there would be no stopping it, he told himself.

Breaking his return journey in London, he fell ill, and struggled back to Cornwall. There he found Frieda woefully stricken with colitis. He occupied himself with nursing her, though his own condition was very shaky. As soon as he felt a renewal of strength he made a new garden, above the small one he had cultivated already, and with the help of William Hocking ploughed and planted a corner of a potato field, to provide them with vegetables.

Summer came early, the weather 'hot and lovely'; he went about dressed only in a thin shirt and trousers, trying to keep the lambs and sheep out of his newly created garden. He rushed to erect barricades of gorse and blackthorn, and cursed 'the filthy lambs' for eating his broad beans. Gardening made him blissful, as well as appealing to the peasant in him. 'It is so lovely here, now,' he wrote, 'my seeds have come up, there is a strange joyfulness in the air. For those of us who can become single and alone, all will become perfectly right.'

But the 'war wave' submerging England was now breaking over Cornwall, that had resisted the English spirit for centuries. Things were moving to a climax for the Lawrences. At Christmas they had been humiliated by a policeman banging on the door in the pouring rain: he had been sent to examine the papers of their two American guests, one of whom was Robert Mountsier, later to be Lawrence's agent in America. Mountsier was harassed further by the police when he returned to London, and advised to go back home.

The gardening was a way of staying sane. Lawrence gazed with a satisfaction that was half practical, half mystical, at the beautiful rows of broad beans and peas, 'to say nothing of endive and beet and spinach and kohlrabi and all the rest.' By mid-summer he had fat marrows, 'on plants that seemed as if they were going to roam till they encircled the earth.' Nor had he forgotten the flowers: sweet peas and nasturtiums winding upwards, and in the little garden pansies and columbine and fuchsia, mixed in with the vegetables. Then in August the rain and wind smashed it all to the ground. It was a foretaste of another storm soon to break.

In the heat of the summer, Lawrence spent more and more time in the fields with the Hockings. He went about like a labourer, abandoning Frieda in her cottage, and when he returned in the evenings he would be speechless, as if he resented her. She attacked him bitterly for this neglect, and he hated her. He stayed away from her for longer periods. William Hocking, he said, was a dear friend with whom he loved to talk half philosophical stuff about the mysteries of the seasons and the planets 'and the mysterious effects of sex on a man'. They lay in the bracken together and talked, waiting for the girls to bring their snack in a wicker basket. And these girls intrigued him. 'Right or wrong was not fixed for them as for the English: it was still mysterious. Their black eyes would be fixed on his face, as if trying to read the ethics of an issue, and they would ask quickly: "Now do 'ee think it right?"'[24]

Frieda came out to the fields once or twice to join their picnics, but because she was so obviously a lady, she made them uneasy. Lawrence's natural intimacy with them was beyond her: she would have said beneath her. It had been the same in Fiascherino.

Lawrence would pride himself on being able to tackle any job, slogging away manfully with his shirt gaping. But his thin body tired quickly, and he couldn't keep going all day like the rest of them. Neither could he cut corn with a scythe. And when it came to binding the sheaves, he insisted on using the Midland method he knew, probably because he was unable to master the Cornish knot. 'We had a method of tying it,' said Hocking, 'and twisting it and shoving it in with a bang which, if it's done properly, you could never undo.'[25]

Now, when Lawrence came home late to the cottage, he was like an enemy, imbued with 'the pregnant malevolency of Cornwall'. Frieda hated the change in him, and hated William Hocking for bringing him down in the world, when he so obviously wasn't one of them. But she knew she only had to wait. He would react, back to her, as he always did in the end.

An unidentified visitor, presumably a girl, has provided a vivid picture of him at this time, cooking on an open fire in his spotlessly clean stone cottage, living the life of a frugal workman with his 'big rosy German' wife:

'His head seems too heavy for his very slim body and hangs forward. The whole expression of his figure is of extreme fragility. His movements are quick and sure . . . He has very large, wide-apart grey eyes, a long slender face with a chin that is out of proportion long, a defect that is concealed by the aforesaid beard. His under lip protrudes from the dainty decoration of the beard in a violent red that makes his beard look pink. In the midst of all this, is a podgy, almost vulgar, certainly undistinguished nose.'

Of his character she writes: 'Lawrence is a Puritan really, and his intellectual reaction against it is so violent that he hurls himself against it with all of himself, destroying himself as he does it. In the marvellously sweet side of his nature, he is inarticulate.'[26]

The arrival of a friend of Heseltine's, Cecil Gray, broke his isolation somewhat. Gray, a young composer, took a house on the coast about four miles to the west of Zennor and began to make regular visits and to invite the Lawrences to his house, 'Bosigran'. Earlier in the year, Philip Heseltine had turned up again in the area and taken a bungalow, between Penzance and Zennor. He seemed friendly, but this time kept his distance. Murry too made friendly overtures, but was curtly rejected. 'You shouldn't say you love me,' Lawrence replied, in the brutally direct style he reserved for Murry. 'You disliked me intensely when you were here, and also at Mylor.'[27]

He brought Dollie Radford up to date on his literary news, such as it was, telling her that Chatto had a new book of poems which they would bring out some time. This was the volume he called *Look! We've Come Through!* To a new correspondent, Waldo Frank, an American, he announced that he was writing a set of essays on 'The Transcendental Element in Classic American Literature', and admitted that he believed in 'Paradise and Paradisial beings'. Writing about America was the next best thing to going there. Now he wanted to go further west than Florida – to California, to San Francisco. He wanted to see the Pacific. His Isle of the Blest was no longer called Rananim, but Typee. He had no illusions about 'Uncle Samdom', he told Frank. 'But there is a quality in your sky, a salt in your earth, that will, without the agency of man, *destroy you all*, and procreate new beings – not men, in our sense of the word.'[28] As for Europe, it was 'a lost name, like Nineveh or Palenque'.

A gentleman by the name of Wilbur Lucius Cross, then editor of the *Yale Review*, invited Lawrence to write forty or fifty pages on contemporary English novelists. Much as he needed the money, Lawrence couldn't face the task. He replied testily: 'I don't care a rush for any of them, save Thomas Hardy, and he's not contemporary . . .'

It was October, and the corn was harvested. Frieda made embroidered caps, to give away as presents at Christmas. She had been laid up for nearly a month with neuritis in her leg, but now she was better.

They went to spend a weekend with Cecil Gray at his house. One evening the three of them sat in front of the fire in Gray's music-room and tried to enjoy themselves, but Gray was melancholy, and this seemed to make Lawrence irritable. He sang German folksongs so badly that he set Gray's teeth on edge. There came a loud hammering on the front door and a gang of uniformed men burst in, led by an officer. A light had been seen upstairs from a window looking out to sea.

A few days after this incident the Lawrences had their cottage searched while they were out. The next morning they were visited by an army officer and three policemen. The cottage was ransacked once more, notebooks and papers were confiscated, and they were handed an expulsion order, giving them three days in which to leave Cornwall. On reaching their new place of residence they had twenty-four hours to report full details to the police.

Before he left, Lawrence burned a pile of old manuscripts – which probably included his own copy of 'Goats and Compasses'. Then he wrote a letter to Lady Cynthia Asquith, telling her what had happened, and that they had no money and nowhere to go.

They made for London and Dollie Radford. The train was crammed with soldiers and sailors travelling up from Plymouth. Frieda felt almost happy: she had been terrified of being interned as an alien. But Lawrence 'sat there feeling he had been killed: perfectly still, and pale, in a kind of after-death, feeling he had been killed.' The face that so horrified Frieda, when she looked at him, he described later in *Kangaroo*. It was that of a man who, despite everything, had stubbornly continued to care, to maintain a kind of belief. Now that belief was dead.

When Lady Cynthia saw him, he was still in a state of shock, and looked very ill, 'as though every nerve in his body was exposed.'[29]

14

Departure

Dollie Radford was frightened, but she stuck by them. The police continued to watch them. Dollie, a frail, plucky thing, had once seen William Morris arrested for making a speech. Now she upheld them staunchly, and said they could share her small house in Hampstead. But she had children; it was all too crowded. Richard Aldington's American wife, Hilda Doolittle, came to the rescue and lent them a room in Mecklenburg Square, her husband being in the army. Food and fuel were included with the room, and Lawrence and Frieda moved in gratefully.

Friends cautiously made contact again with the suspects: 'the starry genius of our time', as Murry called him, never failed to exert a magnetic attraction. They may have had misgivings, but they came. And the 'Island' of escape surfaced again in Lawrence's imagination. Dr Eder, the psychoanalyst, had relatives with big estates in Colombia, so that now the plan was to head for these plantations in the Cauca Valley of Colombia. The departure date was fixed for spring: finances were to be provided by Cecil Gray, who, according to Lawrence, had a thousand pounds. But the whole thing was a pipe-dream and soon foundered. By the time the magical spring arrived, his sacred band of followers was sacred no more. He told Gertler: 'I truly wish I were a fox or a bird – but my ideal now is to have a caravan and a horse, and move on for ever, and never have a neighbour . . . I feel like a wild cat in a cage – I long to get out into some sort of free, lawless life . . . I feel horribly mewed up. I don't want to act in concert with any body of people. I want to go by myself – or with Frieda – something in the manner of a gypsy, and be houseless and place-less and homeless and landless, just move apart.'[1]

Certainly they looked the part, this raggle-taggle pair, with their home-made shrunken clothes and their bare feet in sandals. Cecily Lambert met them for the first time in Berkshire, and was amazed by the spectacle of Frieda 'hurrying along, panting and rather dishevelled, trying vainly to catch up with the man in front, who sped along on his toes almost as if he were being propelled by an invisible force and appeared as if he were trying to escape from the woman.'²

Shortly after a visit to her farm, which became the setting for Lawrence's story 'The Fox', they were lent a cottage nearby. It belonged to Dollie Radford, who had bought it for her daughter, 'the impossible Margaret Radford'. This was the snag, for Margaret descended on them from time to time, forcing them to leave and go to friends until the coast was clear.

But it was spring again, always a consolation and a triumph. He found some big cowslips, whose scent was 'a communication direct from the source of creation – like the breath of God breathed into Adam.' The blackthorn was in blossom, 'white and wet, its tiny amber grains burning faintly in the white smoke of blossom.'

Another great satisfaction was reading Gibbon's *Decline and Fall of the Roman Empire* – 'the emperors are all so indiscriminately bad.' And books on occultism interested him, though his final feeling was one of aversion.

Money was an everlasting curse. For months now he had been at the end of his resources, unable to raise the wind at all. Koteliansky, down to his last ten pounds, loyally offered it. Fortunately there was Ada, who consistently baled him out. She had found them a bungalow in Derbyshire, and would pay sixty-five pounds towards the year's rent. It was pleasant, with a rough field attached, on the rim of a steep valley at Middleton, near Wirksworth. Lawrence looked forward to being among his own people again, and within reach of Willie Hopkin and the others. Instead, when he reached there he felt bitterly that he was a stranger among these northerners who seemed to live only for coal and iron. In his end-of-the-world mood he turned back to Gibbon and his old Roman emperors, who 'just did as they like, and *vogue la galère*, till they were strangled.'³ And he ploughed his way through a couple of massive tomes on Africa by Frobenius, a ponderous German who theorised about a West African civilization before Egypt and Carthage.

There he sat, more or less living on his sister, applying 'with a black and angry heart' to the Royal Literary Fund for another meagre hand-out. The only work he could bring himself to do was episodic stuff, apart from his essays for the book now entitled 'The Mystic Import of American Literature'. He had begun, without enthusiasm, 'another daft novel': this was *Aaron's Rod*, which he had started the previous December and then put aside. Aaron Sisson, picking up his flute – his self-sufficiency, his phallus

– and shoving off alone into the rainy Midlands night, is dark with Lawrence's end-of-the-tether distress and desperation. 'It goes slowly – very slowly and fitfully,' he told Gertler. 'But I don't care.' Earlier he had asked: 'Do you think you might know of somebody who would give us something to keep us going a bit? It makes me swear – such a damned, mean, narrow-gutted, pitiful, crawling, mongrel world, that daren't have a man's work and won't even allow him to live.' He felt desperate, ready for anything. 'Nowadays one can do nothing but glance behind to see who now is creeping up to do something horrible to the back of one's neck.'⁴

His forebodings were justified. In September, 1918, the Military dragged him into Derby for another medical. It was a foul experience, and left him speechless with fury. The full story is told in *Kangaroo*. Frieda had gone into town with him, and he eventually found the recruiting office in a sort of basement. There, 'old military buffers' wielded power over two naked men, a youth bravely puffing out his chest and a big, gaunt collier whose nakedness was somehow gruesome. Lawrence was next.

What infuriated him was the joking that went on between the desks at the sight of his scarecrow emaciation. When these jokers fingered his private parts and made him bend over while they peered up his arse, taking their time over it, he could have killed them.

He spat out his loathing in a letter to Cynthia Asquith: 'I'm out on a new track – let humanity go its own way – I go mine. But I *won't* be pawed and bullied by them – no.'

Six weeks later the war was over.

Lawrence's androphobia was now extreme, as acute as it had been in July 1916, when, after finishing *Women in Love*, he had expressed feelings to Koteliansky that were frankly murderous: 'When I see people in the distance, walking along the path through fields to Zennor, I want to crouch in the bushes and shoot them silently with invisible arrows of death.' If only one could have 'a great box of insect powder and shake it over them, in the heavens, and exterminate them.'⁵

On Armistice Day he happened to be in London with Frieda. He forced his way through the half-drunken crowds rejoicing in the streets, screaming, singing, copulating in doorways, bawling hymns, crowding into taxis and taking over buses. The Lawrences were making for a house in Bloomsbury, Montague Sherman's, and when they got there it was full to the doors. The Sitwells were there, Keynes, Diaghilev, Massine, Duncan Grant, and David Garnett. Frieda greeted Garnett with a warm embrace, but Lawrence, looking wretched, delivered a jeremiad that went something like this: 'I suppose you think the war is over and that we shall go back to the kind of world you lived in before it. But the war isn't over. The hate and evil is greater now than ever. Very soon the war will break out again and overwhelm you.'[6]

He took himself back to live among the dark folds of Derbyshire, 'the navel of England', and went one weekend to see Ada at Ripley, then on to Eastwood. He didn't hate Eastwood, as he thought he might, but it haunted him. On the train on Saturday night, he looked out at the ironworks at Butterley, 'a massive roar of flame and burnt smoke in the black sky, flaming and waving again on the black water round the train'. On the platform, he saw a man who didn't look human at all: 'I could write a story about him.'

In this queer, dislocated mood, in almost total despair about human relationships, he wrote some of the brilliant, acrid stories of *England, My England*: 'Wintry Peacock', 'Monkey Nuts' and 'Tickets Please'. To earn some immediate money he struggled with a European history for schools, which a publisher had offered to commission. But he didn't want to do it, didn't see why he should write anything. Life was too vile.

He was still keeping Murry at arm's length, but he had made his peace with Katherine Mansfield, who saw him in London, and wrote afterwards to Dorothy Brett: 'We kept to things like nuts and cowslips and fires in woods and his black self was not. Oh, there is something so lovable about him and his eagerness, his passionate eagerness for life – that is what one loves so.'[7]

In the winter of 1918 he fell ill, so seriously that Frieda took fright and got him transferred to his sister's home. It was partly influenza, the epidemic of 1918–19, and partly his old lung trouble. When he returned to Middleton in mid-March, still feeble but recovering, he burst out against Frieda in a letter to Koteliansky: 'She really is a devil – and I feel as if I would part from her for ever – let her go alone to Germany, while I take another road. For it is true, I have been bullied by her long enough. I really could leave her now, without a pang, I believe.'[8] He knew, of course, that this puffing and blowing would be music in the ears of his friend, but as much as anything the outburst was an admission of Lawrence's continuing dependence on her, and his resentment that this should be so.

The winter dragged on. It had been a mistake to come so far north. At the end of March the snow was falling as thickly as ever. Occasionally the postman brought a newspaper, and he read the national news with disgust. 'It seems as if the dear old regime of happy industrial England is slowly and greasily melting like a dead thaw.'

Murry, now the newly appointed editor of the *Athenaeum,* wrote to ask Lawrence for a contribution. Lawrence responded with one of his most beautiful essays, 'Whistling of Birds', ostensibly a nature piece, but in reality a call for 'a new world of spring'. Still improving in health, he ended a letter to Katherine Mansfield with the wistful: 'I wish it was spring for us all.'

Frieda, worried about her sister in Munich and her elderly mother in Baden-Baden, was now in a state of constant agitation. Letters from home sounded dreadful and reduced her to tears. From time to time she sent off food parcels, while she and Lawrence waited for the signing of the peace treaty and the clearance of their passports. Lawrence of course wanted to make for America, but in the end it was decided that he would start for Italy, while Frieda went to Germany to see her family. Frieda left first.

He saw her off on the Harwich–Hook of Holland express, then hung about for a few weeks in London and Berkshire. At last he made his way to Folkestone and got on the boat. He would never live permanently in England again.

England had rejected him, the England he had loved and hated so bitterly. Now he turned his back on it. But first he had to see it sinking into the sea behind him like a corpse, 'with her dead grey cliffs and the white, worn-out cloth of snow above.' He looked back from the boat and felt loose, broken-off, adrift. 'The ties were gone,' he wrote three years later, in *Kangaroo,* and trembled helplessly at the memory of it. All the never-ending 'battle-battle' in his soul that had torn his frail body, grieving his mother and shattering Jessie, was gone now with the people and the land. The nightmare of the war years had cut him clear of the past, and there was no going back. His England had died in the war and he no longer belonged there. He had no home. The immense ferment of his youth was over.

In his essay, 'Whistling of Birds', he had written: 'We may not choose the world. We have hardly any choice for ourselves. We follow with our eyes the bloody and horrid line of march of extreme winter, as it passes away. But we cannot hold back the spring. We cannot make the birds silent, prevent the bubbling of the wood-pigeons. We cannot stay the fine world of silver-fecund creation from gathering itself and taking place upon us. Whether we will or no, the daphne tree will soon be giving off perfume, the lambs dancing on two feet, the celandines will twinkle all over the ground, there will be a new heaven and new earth.'

Notes to the Text

1

Eastwood: The Heritage

1 Letter to Rolf Gardiner, 3rd December 1926
2 'Return to Bestwood', *Phoenix*, Vol. II
3 A. L. Rowse, *The English Past*
4 *Sons and Lovers*, Chapter I
5 ibid.
6 William Hopkin, quoted in Harry T. Moore, *The Intelligent Heart*, Part One, Chapter 1
7 *Sons and Lovers*, Chapter I

2

Families: The Father

1 'Nottingham and the Mining Countryside', *Phoenix*
2 ibid.
3 *Sons and Lovers*, Chapter I
4 ibid.
5 ibid.
6 ibid.
7 ibid.
8 ibid.
9 ibid.
10 ibid.
11 ibid.
12 ibid.
13 'The Miner at Home', *Phoenix*
14 *Sons and Lovers*, Chapter I
15 ibid.
16 ibid.
17 ibid.
18 Ada Lawrence and G. Stuart Gelder, *The Early Life of D. H. Lawrence*
19 'Nottingham and the Mining Countryside', *Phoenix*
20 ibid.
21 ibid.
22 *Sons and Lovers*, Chapter I
23 ibid.
24 ibid.
25 ibid.

3

The Skinned Rabbit

1 *Sons and Lovers*, Chapter II
2 ibid.
3 ibid.
4 ibid.
5 Harry T. Moore, *The Intelligent Heart*, Part One, Chapter 1
6 Ada Lawrence and G. Stuart Gelder, *The Early Life of D. H. Lawrence*
7 Stephen Spender ed., *D. H. Lawrence; Novelist, Poet, Prophet*
8 Autobiographical Sketch in Edward Nehls, *D. H. Lawrence: A Composite Biography*, Vol. 1, Chapter 1
9 ibid.
10 ibid.
11 ibid.
12 ibid.
13 *Sons and Lovers*, Chapter IV
14 'Nottingham and the Mining Countryside', *Phoenix*
15 'Rex', *Phoenix*
16 Richard Aldington, *Portrait of a Genius, But . . .*, Part One, Chapter 1
17 Jessie Chambers, *A Personal Record*, Chapter I
18 Harry T. Moore, *The Intelligent Heart*, Part One, Chapter 2
19 Jessie Chambers, op. cit., Chapter I

4

The Rise of Ernest

1 *Sons and Lovers*, Chapter III
2 ibid.
3 Richard Aldington, *Portrait of a Genius, But . . .*, Part One, Chapter 1
4 *Sons and Lovers*, Chapter III
5 ibid.
6 op. cit., Chapter IV
7 ibid.
8 Harry T. Moore, *The Intelligent Heart*, Part One, Chapter 2
9 *Sons and Lovers*, Chapter V
10 op. cit., Chapter VI

5

Farm and Factory

1 Letter to Rolf Gardiner, 3rd December 1926
2 Letter to J. D. Chambers, 14th November 1928

3 *Sons and Lovers*, Chapter VI
4 ibid.
5 Graham Hough, *The Dark Sun*
6 *The White Peacock*, Chapter VII
7 J. D. Chambers, quoted in Bridget Pugh, *The Country of my Heart*
8 *The White Peacock*, Chapter VI
9 *Sons and Lovers*, Chapter VI
10 J. D. Chambers, 'Memoir of D. H. Lawrence as a Boy'
11 Jessie Chambers, *A Personal Record*, Chapter I
12 ibid.
13 *Sons and Lovers*, Chapter VI
14 op. cit., Chapter V
15 A. L. Rowse, *The English Past*
16 Bridget Pugh, *The Country of my Heart*
17 Autobiographical Sketch in Edward Nehls, *D. H. Lawrence: A Composite Biography*, Vol. 1, Chapter 1

6

The Invalid, and Mother Love

1 *Sons and Lovers*, Chapter VI
2 ibid.
3 ibid.
4 George Neville, Interview with Harry T. Moore, *The Intelligent Heart*, Part One, Chapter 3
5 *Sons and Lovers*, Chapter VI
6 Letter to Edward Garnett, 14th November 1912
7 J. D. Chambers, in lecture to students in Albuquerque, New Mexico, December 1964
8 Jessie Chambers, *A Personal Record*, Chapter I
9 Ada Lawrence and G. Stuart Gelder, *The Early Life of D. H. Lawrence*
10 *Sons and Lovers*, Chapter VII
11 'Love Among the Haystacks'
12 Mrs Mary Brice, BBC Third Programme's 'Son and Lover', 8th May 1955
13 Jessie Chambers, *A Personal Record*, Chapter I
14 *Sons and Lovers*, Chapter V
15 Richard Aldington, *Portrait of a Genius, But . . .*, Part One, Chapter 2
16 'Autobiographical Fragment', *Phoenix*
17 *The White Peacock*, Chapter VIII
18 ibid.
19 Letter to Blanche Jennings, 30th July 1908
20 'Love Among the Haystacks', Part Two
21 op. cit., Part Three
22 Letter to Blanche Jennings, 30th July 1908
23 'Love Among the Haystacks'

24 Letter to Blanche Jennings, 30th July 1908
25 ibid.
26 Letter to Blanche Jennings, 15th April 1908
27 *The White Peacock*, Chapter II
28 op. cit., Chapter VIII
29 ibid.

7

Jessie

1 *Aaron's Rod*, Chapter 1
2 *The Rainbow*, Chapter XIII
3 ibid.
4 ibid.
5 Jessie Chambers, *A Personal Record*, Chapter II
6 J. D. Chambers, 'Memoir of D. H. Lawrence as a Boy'
7 Jessie Chambers, op. cit., Chapter II
8 Ford Madox Ford, *Portraits from Life*
9 *The Rainbow*, Chapter VII
10 *Sons and Lovers*, Chapter VII
11 Jessie Chambers, op. cit., Chapter I
12 *Sons and Lovers*, Chapter IX
13 Jessie Chambers, op. cit., Chapter V
14 ibid.
15 *Sons and Lovers*, Chapter VII
16 op. cit., Chapter VIII
17 Jessie Chambers, op. cit., Chapter II
18 *Sons and Lovers*, Chapter X
19 Jessie Chambers, op. cit., Chapter II
20 ibid.
21 ibid.
22 ibid.
23 ibid.
24 op. cit., Chapter IV
25 *Sons and Lovers*, Chapter IX
26 Letter to Edward Garnett, 8th March 1912
27 Letter to Edward Garnett, 30th October 1912
28 *Sons and Lovers*, Chapter VII
29 ibid.
30 Jessie Chambers, op. cit., Chapter V
31 ibid.
32 ibid.
33 *Sons and Lovers*, Chapter VII
34 Ford Madox Ford, *Portraits from Life*
35 *The Rainbow*, Chapter XV
36 'Nottingham's New University'
37 Jessie Chambers, op. cit., Chapter IV
38 'A Fly in the Ointment'

39 *Sons and Lovers*, Chapter IX
40 ibid.
41 Jessie Chambers, op. cit., Chapter V
42 ibid.
43 ibid.
44 op. cit., Chapter IV
45 Richard Aldington, *Portrait of a Genius, But . . .*, Part One,
   Chapter 4
46 William Hopkin, quoted in Edward Nehls, *D. H. Lawrence: A
   Composite Biography*, Vol. 1, Chapter 1
47 E. Delavenay, in *Revue Anglo-Américaine, XIII* (February 1936)
48 Letter to Blanche Jennings, 31st December 1908
49 Letter to Blanche Jennings, 25th June 1908
50 Harry T. Moore, *The Intelligent Heart*, Part One, Chapter 5
51 Jessie Chambers, op. cit., Chapter V

8

The Teacher in London

1 'Last Hours'
2 Jessie Chambers, *A Personal Record*, Chapter V
3 ibid.
4 P. F. T. Smith, a memoir, quoted in Harry T. Moore, *The
   Intelligent Heart*, Part Two, Chapter 1
5 A. W. McLeod, a memoir, quoted in Harry T. Moore, op. cit.,
   Part Two, Chapter 1
6 'The Best of School'
7 'Discipline'
8 ibid.
9 Letter to Louie Burrows, 23rd October 1908
10 Letter to Louie Burrows, 28th February 1909
11 ibid.
12 Letter to Blanche Jennings, 28th January 1910
13 'Letter from Town: The Almond Tree'
14 Jessie Chambers, op. cit., Chapter IV
15 ibid.
16 Stewart A. Robertson, article in *Glasgow Herald*, 8th March 1930
17 Letter to Louie Burrows, 7th October 1908
18 William Hopkin, quoted in Edward Nehls, *D. H. Lawrence: A
   Composite Biography*, Vol. 1, Chapter 1
19 F. D. Chambers, in a letter to Edward Nehls, 17th May 1955
20 Jessie Chambers, op. cit., Chapter VI
21 ibid.
22 Ford Madox Ford, *Portraits from Life*
23 Violet Hunt, *I Have This to Say*
24 Letter to Blanche Jennings, 8th May 1909
25 Ford Madox Ford, op. cit.

26 Jessie Chambers, op. cit., Chapter VI
27 Ford Madox Ford, op. cit.
28 ibid.
29 William Hopkin, quoted in Edward Nehls, *D. H. Lawrence: A Composite Biography*, Vol. 1, Chapter 1
30 Jessie Chambers, op. cit., Chapter VI
31 ibid.
32 ibid.
33 Violet Hunt, quoted in Edward Nehls, op. cit., Vol 1, Chapter 1
34 Ford Madox Ford, op. cit.
35 Jessie Chambers, op. cit., Chapter VI
36 ibid.
37 Letter to William Heinemann, 15th December 1909
38 Letter to Blanche Jennings, 28th January 1910
39 Helen Corke, *Neutral Ground*
40 Ford Madox Ford, op. cit.
41 Letter to Sydney S. Pawling, 27th April 1910
42 Letter to Helen Corke, 21st June 1910
43 Letter to William Hopkin, 24th August 1910
44 ibid.
45 Enid C. Hilton, quoted in Harry T. Moore, *The Intelligent Heart*, Part Two, Chapter 2
46 Irene Clephane, *Towards Sex Freedom*
47 Enid C. Hilton, quoted in Harry T. Moore, op. cit., Part Two, Chapter 2
48 ibid.
49 Harry T. Moore, *The Intelligent Heart*, Part Two, Chapter 2
50 'Goose Fair'
51 Letter to Jessie Chambers, August 1910
52 From Lawrence's introduction to Edward D. Macdonald, *A Bibliography of the Writings of D. H. Lawrence*, reprinted in *Phoenix*
53 *Sons and Lovers*, Chapter XV
54 op. cit., Chapter XIV
55 Letter to Rachel Annand Taylor, 3rd December 1910
56 ibid.
57 Jessie Chambers, *A Personal Record*, Chapter VII

9

Collapse and Recovery

1 Jessie Chambers, *A Personal Record*, Chapter VII
2 Letter to Mrs S. A. Hopkin, 26th April 1911
3 Letter to Jessie Chambers, early 1911
4 From the rejected preface to *Collected Poems*, in *Phoenix*
5 Letter to Jessie Chambers, Spring 1911
6 Letter to Ada Lawrence Clarke, 8th March 1911
7 Letter to Ada Lawrence Clarke, 27th March 1911

8 Letter to William Hopkin, 20th February 1911
9 Letter to Louie Burrows, 6th April 1911
10 Letter to Martin Secker, 12th June 1911
11 Letter to Edward Garnett, 18th December 1911
12 Jessie Chambers, op. cit., Chapter VII
13 ibid.
14 Letter to Louie Burrows, 7th April 1911
15 Letter to Louie Burrows, 10th April 1911
16 Letter to Ada Lawrence Clarke, 26th April 1911
17 Letter to Ada Lawrence Clarke, October 1911
18 Letter to Edward Garnett, 4th December 1911
19 Letter to Edward Garnett, 17th December 1911
20 Jessie Chambers, op. cit., Chapter VII
21 Letter to May Chambers Holbrook, 7th January 1912
22 Letter to Jessie Chambers, January 1912
23 Letter to Edward Garnett, 19th January 1912
24 Letter to Louie Burrows, 12th January 1912
25 Letter to A. W. McLeod, 24th January 1912
26 Letter to Edward Garnett, 29th January 1912
27 Letter to Helen Corke, 1st February 1912
28 Letter to Louie Burrows, 4th February 1912
29 Jessie Chambers, op. cit., Chapter VII
30 ibid.
31 Letter to Edward Garnett, 10th February 1912
32 Letter to Edward Garnett, 3rd April 1912
33 Letter to Edward Garnett, 10th February 1912
34 Letter to Edward Garnett, 3rd April 1912
35 Letter to Edward Garnett, 12th February 1912
36 Jessie Chambers, op. cit., Chapter VII
37 *The Trespasser*, Chapter 15
38 Letter to Edward Garnett, 24th February 1912
39 Letter to Edward Garnett, 6th March 1912
40 Jessie Chambers, op. cit., Chapter VII
41 George Neville, article in *The London Mercury*, XXIII (No. 137, March 1931)

10

Frieda

1 Jessie Chambers, *A Personal Record*, Chapter VII
2 Letter to Jessie Chambers, Spring 1911
3 Jessie Chambers, op. cit., Chapter VII
4 Frieda Lawrence, *Not I, But the Wind . . .*
5 Frieda Lawrence, *The Memoirs and Correspondence*
6 ibid.
7 ibid.
8 ibid.
9 Frieda Lawrence, *Not I, But the Wind . . .*

10 ibid.
11 Letter dated 11th April 1912 in Frieda Lawrence, *The Memoirs and Correspondence*
12 Letter dated 13th April 1912 in Frieda Lawrence, op. cit.,
13 Letter to Frieda, ?30th April 1912
14 Letter.to Edward Garnett, 3rd April 1912
15 Letter to Edward Garnett, 29th April 1912
16 Letter to Frieda, ?30th April 1912
17 Letter to Frieda, 2nd May 1912
18 Letter to Edward Garnett, 9th May 1912
19 Letter to Frieda, ?6th May 1912
20 Letter to Frieda, ?7th May 1912
21 Letter dated 10th May 1912 in Frieda Lawrence, *The Memoirs and Correspondence*
22 Letter to Frieda, 9th May 1912
23 Letter to Frieda, 8th May 1912
24 Letter to Frieda, 9th May 1912
25 Letter to Frieda, ?13th May 1912
26 Letter to Frieda, 14th May 1912
27 Letter to Frieda, ?15th May 1912
28 Letter to Frieda, 16th May 1912
29 Letter to Mrs S. A. Hopkin, 2nd June 1912
30 ibid.
31 Frieda Lawrence, *Not I, But the Wind* . . .
32 ibid.
33 Letter to Edward Garnett, 2nd June 1912
34 Frieda Lawrence, op. cit.
35 Letter to Edward Garnett, 11th June 1912
36 ibid.
37 Letter to Edward Garnett, 29th June 1912
38 ibid.
39 Letter to Edward Garnett, 3rd July 1912
40 Letter to Edward Garnett, ?22nd July 1912
41 Letter to Edward Garnett, 4th August 1912
42 Postcard to Jessie Chambers, May 1912
43 Jessie Chambers, *A Personal Record*, Chapter VII
44 Letter to Edward Garnett, 4th August 1912
45 David Garnett, *The Golden Echo*

11

Wandervögel

1 Letter to Mrs S. A. Hopkin, 19th August 1912
2 'A Chapel and a Hay Hut Among the Mountains'
3 Letter to Mrs S. A. Hopkins, 19th August 1912
4 Letter to A. W. McLeod, 2nd September 1912
5 Richard Aldington, *Portrait of a Genius, But* . . ., Part Two, Chapter 3

6 Letter to Edward Garnett, ?16th September 1912
7 Letter to Edward Garnett, 30th October 1912
8 Frieda Lawrence, *Not I, But the Wind* . . .
9 Letter to A. W. McLeod, 6th October 1912
10 ibid.
11 Frieda Lawrence, op. cit.
12 Jeffrey Meyers, 'D. H. Lawrence and Homosexuality', *The London Magazine*
13 Letter to David Garnett, 19th December 1912
14 *Twilight in Italy*, 'On the Lago Di Garda', Chapter 4
15 Letter to Edward Garnett, 14th November 1912
16 Letter to David Garnett, 19th November 1912
17 Letter to Ernest Collings, 24th December 1912
18 Letter to Edward Garnett, 12th January 1913
19 Frieda Lawrence, *The Memoirs and Correspondence*
20 Robert Lucas, *Frieda Lawrence*
21 *Burns Novel* fragments, published in Edward Nehls, *D. H. Lawrence: A Composite Biography,* Vol 1
22 Letter to Edward Garnett, 12th January 1913
23 *Twilight in Italy*, 'On the Lago Di Garda', Chapter 7
24 'Both Sides of the Medal'
25 'Everlasting Flowers'
26 'Why does She Weep'
27 'All Souls'
28 'Spring Morning'
29 Letter to Ernest Collings, 12th January 1913
30 Letter to Edward Garnett, 1st February 1913
31 Letter to Jessie Chambers, February or March 1913
32 Jessie Chambers, *A Personal Record*, Chapter VII
33 Letter to Edward Garnett, ?18th April 1913
34 Letter from Frieda Lawrence to Edward Garnett, late May or early June 1913
35 Frieda Lawrence quoted in Harry T. Moore, *The Intelligent Heart*, Part Two, Chapter 5
36 Letter to Helen Corke, 29th May 1913
37 *The Lost Girl*, Chapter 4
38 Letter to A. W. McLeod, 26th April 1913
39 Robert Lucas, *Frieda Lawrence*
40 From a memoir published in Edward Nehls, *D. H. Lawrence: A Composite Biography*, Vol 1, Chapter 3
41 Frieda Lawrence, *Not I, But the Wind* . . .
42 Letter to Edward Garnett, ?28th July 1913
43 Letter to J. M. Murry, ?22nd July 1913
44 John Middleton Murry, *Between Two Worlds*
45 Richard Aldington, *Portrait of a Genius, But* . . ., Part Two, Chapter 4
46 Ivy Low Litvinoff, *Harper's Bazaar*, No. 2818, October 1946
47 Letter to William Hopkin, 11th August 1913

48 Letter to Lady Cynthia Asquith, 17th August 1913
49 *Twilight in Italy*, 'Italians in Exile'
50 *Twilight in Italy*, 'The Return Journey'
51 ibid.
52 ibid.
53 ibid.
54 ibid.
55 Letter to Lady Cynthia Asquith, 23rd October 1913
56 Letter to Edward Marsh, 28th October 1913
57 Letter to J. M. Murry, ?Autumn 1913
58 Letter to May Chambers Holbrook, 22nd February 1914
59 Letter to Edward Garnett, 30th December 1913
60 Richard Aldington, *Portrait of a Genius, But . . .*, Part Two,
    Chapter 5
61 Letter to A. W. McLeod, 9th February 1914
62 Letter to Henry Savage, 2nd December 1913

12

And the Rainbow Stood on the Earth

1 Letter to J. M. Murry, 3rd April 1914
2 ibid.
3 Letter to Edward Garnett, 22nd April 1914
4 Letter to Edward Marsh, 24th May 1914
5 ibid.
6 Letter to J. M. Murry, 8th May 1914
7 Letter to A. W. McLeod, 2nd June 1914
8 Letter to Edward Garnett, 5th June 1914
9 ibid.
10 Letter to Mrs S. A. Hopkin, 13th July 1914
11 Catherine Carswell, *The Savage Pilgrimage*
12 Letter to Catherine Carswell, ?29th June 1914
13 John Middleton Murry, *Between Two Worlds*
14 Richard Aldington, *Life for Life's Sake*
15 Letter to Lady Cynthia Asquith, ?31st January 1915
16 Compton Mackenzie, *The South Wind of Love*
17 Letter to Catherine Carswell, 21st October 1914
18 Robert Lucas, *Frieda Lawrence*
19 Catherine Carswell, *The Savage Pilgrimage*
20 John Middleton Murry, *Between Two Worlds*
21 Leonard Woolf, in *New Statesman and Nation*, No. 1248, 5th
    February 1955
22 John Middleton Murry, op. cit.
23 Letter to A. W. McLeod, 2nd June 1914
24 Letter to Gordon Campbell, 21st September 1914
25 Robert Lucas, *Frieda Lawrence*
26 Ottoline Morrell, in *The Nation and Athenaeum*, No. 25, 22nd
    March 1930

27 Letter to Gordon Campbell, 21st September 1914
28 Letter to William Hopkin, 18th January 1915
29 John Middleton Murry, op. cit.
30 Letter to Lady Ottoline Morrell, 1st February 1915
31 Letter to Bertrand Russell, 2nd March 1915
32 John Maynard Keynes, *Two Memoirs*
33 Letter to Bertrand Russell, 26th July 1915
34 John Middleton Murry, op. cit.
35 Bertrand Russell, *Portrait from Memory and Other Essays*
36 ibid.
37 Ernest Jones, *Sigmund Freud, Life and Work*
38 Letter to J. B. Pinker, 23rd April 1915
39 David Garnett, *Flowers of the Forest*
40 Anthony Storr, *The Dynamics of Creation*
41 Violet Hunt, *I Have This to Say*
42 Catherine Carswell, *The Savage Pilgrimage*
43 Letter to Lady Cynthia Asquith, 16th August 1915
44 Viktor Frankl, an article in *Phenomenology, Pure and Applied*
45 John Galsworthy letter quoted in Keith Sagar, *The Art of
   D. H. Lawrence*
46 Philip Heseltine letter to Delius, 15th December 1915
47 Letter to Bertrand Russell, 14th September 1915
48 Dorothy Brett, *Lawrence and Brett*
49 Letter to J. B. Pinker, 6th November 1915
50 Hugh Hebert, an article in *The Guardian*, 28th July 1972
51 ibid.

13

Cornwall: The Crow's Nest

1 Letter to Lady Ottoline Morrell, ?21st January 1916
2 Letter to Barbara Low, 5th January 1916
3 ibid.
4 Letter to Lady Cynthia Asquith, 9th March 1916
5 Letter to J. M. Murry and Katherine Mansfield, 24th February
   1916
6 Cecil Gray and others, *Peter Warlock, A Memoir of Philip Heseltine*
7 Katherine Mansfield, *Letters*
8 John Middleton Murry, *Between Two Worlds*
9 Katherine Mansfield, op. cit.
10 Letter to Lady Ottoline Morrell, 15th February 1916
11 Letter to Katherine Mansfield, 21st November 1918
12 Letter to Catherine Carswell, 7th November 1916
13 Maurice Capitanchik, review, *D. H. Lawrence: The Man and his
   Work* by Emile Delavenay in *Books and Bookmen*, November 1972
14 Robert Lucas, *Frieda Lawrence*
15 'Prologue to *Women in Love*', Phoenix, Vol. II

16 Letter to Lady Ottoline Morrell, 3rd October 1916
17 *Women in Love*, Chapter XXII
18 op. cit., Chapter XXIII
19 Letter to Dollie Radford, 29th June 1916
20 Letter to Lady Cynthia Asquith, 1st September 1916
21 *Kangaroo*, Chapter XII
22 Letter to J. B. Pinker, 29th January 1917
23 *Kangaroo*, Chapter XII
24 ibid.
25 Edward Nehls, *D. H. Lawrence: A Composite Biography*, Vol 1, Chapter 4
26 Anonymous memoir quoted in Mabel Dodge Luhan, *Lorenzo in Taos*
27 Letter to J. M. Murry, 23rd May 1917
28 Letter to Waldo Frank, 15th September 1917
29 Lady Cynthia Asquith, *Remember and Be Glad*

14

Departure

1 Letter to Mark Gertler, ?16th March 1918
2 Cecily Lambert Minchin quoted in Edward Nehls, *D. H. Lawrence: A Composite Biography*, Vol 1, Chapter 4
3 Letter to Cecil Gray, 18th April 1918
4 Letter to Mark Gertler, 16th February 1918
5 Letter to S. S. Koteliansky, 4th September 1916
6 David Garnett, *Flowers of the Forest*
7 Katherine Mansfield, *Letters*
8 Letter to S. S. Koteliansky, ?14th March 1919

Bibliography

In the writing of this volume the undermentioned books provided essential information:

(a) D. H. LAWRENCE

All works by him

The Letters, edited and with an introduction by Aldous Huxley, Heinemann, London, 1932; The Viking Press, New York, 1932

Collected Letters, edited by Harry T. Moore, Heinemann, London, 1962; The Viking Press, New York, 1962

Lawrence in Love: Letters to Louie Burrows, edited by J. T. Boulton, University of Nottingham, 1968

Letters to Bertrand Russell, ed. Moore, Gotham Book Mart, 1948

The Quest for Rananim, D. H. Lawrence's Letters to Koteliansky, 1914–1930, edited by George J. Zytaruk, Montreal, McGill Queen's University Press, 1970

Phoenix: The Posthumous Papers of D. H. Lawrence, edited by E. D. Macdonald, Heinemann, London, 1936, 1961; The Viking Press, New York, 1936

Phoenix, Volume II, edited by W. Roberts and Harry T. Moore, Heinemann, London, 1968

A Bibliography of D. H. Lawrence, Warren Roberts, Hart-Davis, 1963

(b) WORKS ON D. H. LAWRENCE

Richard Aldington: *Life for Life's Sake*, Cassell, London, 1968; The Viking Press, New York, 1941

Richard Aldington: *Portrait of a Genius, But . . .*, Heinemann, London, 1950; Duell, Sloan and Pearce, New York, 1950

Dorothy Brett: *Lawrence and Brett*, Secker, London, 1933

Edward Carpenter: *The Intermediate Sex*, Swan, Sonnerschein, 1908

Edward Carpenter: *Love's Coming of Age*, (1896) sixth edition, Swan, Sonnerschein, 1909

Catherine Carswell: *The Savage Pilgrimage*, Secker & Warburg, London, 1932

Jessie Chambers (E. T.): *A Personal Record*, Cape, London, 1935; reprinted by Frank Cass, London, 1965

Colin Clarke: *River of Dissolution*, Routledge, London

Helen Corke: *D. H. Lawrence, The Croydon Years*, Austin, University of Texas Press, 1965

Helen Corke: *Neutral Ground*, Barker, London, 1933

Emile Delavenay: *D. H. Lawrence; The Man and His Work*, Heinemann, London, 1972; Southern Illinois Press, 1972

Emile Delavenay: *D. H. Lawrence and Edward Carpenter*, Heinemann, London, 1971

Ford Madox Ford: *Portraits from Life*, Houghton Mifflin, Boston, 1937; *Mightier than the Sword*, Allen & Unwin, London, 1938

BIBLIOGRAPHY

David Garnett: *The Flowers of the Forest*, Chatto & Windus, London, 1955; Harcourt, Brace, New York, 1956

David Garnett: *The Golden Rule*, Chatto & Windus, London, 1953; Harcourt Brace, New York, 1954

Cecil Gray and others: *Peter Warlock; A Memoir of Philip Heseltine*, Cape, London, 1938

Martin Green: *The Von Richthofen Sisters: The Triumphant and the Tragic Modes of Love*, Weidenfeld & Nicolson, London, 1974

Graham Hough: *The Dark Sun*, Duckworth, London, 1970

Violet Hunt: *I Have This To Say*, Boni & Liveright, New York, 1926

Ernest Jones: *Sigmund Freud, Life and Work*, Hogarth Press, London, 1954

John Maynard Keynes: *Two Memoirs*, Augustus M. Kelley, New York, 1949

Ada Lawrence and G. Stuart Gelder: *The Early Life of D. H. Lawrence*, Orioli, Florence, 1931

Frieda Lawrence: *The Memoirs and Correspondence*, edited by E. W. Tedlock, Heinemann, London, 1961; Knopf, New York, 1964

Frieda Lawrence: *Not I, But the Wind . . .*, Heinemann, London, 1935; The Viking Press, New York, 1934

Robert Lucas: *Frieda Lawrence*, Secker and Warburg, London, 1973

Compton Mackenzie: *My Life and Times, Octaves IV and V*, Chatto & Windus, London, 1965

Compton Mackenzie: *The South Wind of Love*, Dodd, New York, 1937

Katherine Mansfield: *Letters*, edited J. M. Murry, Knopf, New York, 1932

Harry T. Moore: *The Intelligent Heart*, Heinemann, London, 1955 (revised as *The Priest of Love*, 1974); Farrar, Straus, New York, 1955

John Middleton Murry: *Between Two Worlds*, Cape, London, 1935; Messner, New York, 1936

Edward Nehls: *D. H. Lawrence: A Composite Biography*, Vol. 1, Wisconsin, 1957

Bridget Pugh: *The Country of My Heart*, a local guide to D. H. Lawrence, Nottinghamshire Local History Council, Nottingham, 1972

A. L. Rowse: *The English Past*, Macmillan, London, 1951

Bertrand Russell: *Portraits from Memory and Other Essays*, Simon and Schuster, New York

Arthur Schopenhauer: *Essays*, trans. by Mrs Rudolph Dirks, Walter Scott, 1903

Anthony Storr: *The Dynamics of Creation*, Secker & Warburg, London, 1972

(c)   ESSAYS AND ARTICLES IN PERIODICALS

Maurice Capitanchik: review of *D. H. Lawrence; The Man and His Work*, by Emile Delavenay, in *Books and Bookmen*, London, November 1972

J. D. Chambers: 'Memoirs of D. H. Lawrence as a Boy', in *The Listener*, 7th October 1948

Viktor Frankl: an article in *Phenomenology, Pure and Applied*, ed. Erwin Straus, Duquesne, 1964

Ivy Low Litvinoff: in *Harper's Bazaar* (No. 2818, October 1946)

Jeffrey Meyers: 'D. H. Lawrence and Homosexuality', *London Magazine*, Vol 13, No. 4, Oct/Nov 1973

Ottoline Morrell: in *The Nation and Athenaeum* (No. 25, 22nd March 1930)

George Neville: 'The Early Days of D. H. Lawrence', in *The London Mercury*, XXIII (No. 137, March 1931)

Stewart A. Robertson: article in *Glasgow Herald*, 8th March 1930

Leonard Woolf: in *New Statesman and Nation* (No. 1248, 5th February 1955)

Index

314

Nottingham High School, 58
Nottingham, University College, 121–2

Pidsley, Miss, 60
Pinker, J. B., 242, 246, 273
Porthcothan (Cornwall), 275, 278
Pound, Ezra, 149, 150, 151, 247

Radford, Dollie, 265, 286, 291, 292, 293, 294
Rhys, Ernest, 151
Richthofen, Else von. See Jaffe, Dr. Else
Richthofen, Johanna von, 183, 185, 190, 208
Richthofens, the von (family), 183, 188, 201
Riva (Austria), 207, 208
Robertson, Stewart, 137
Rowse, A. L., 18, 75
Ruskin, John, 43, 100, 215, 258
Russell, Betrand, 255, 257–62, 270, 271, 284
Rutherford, Mark, 123, 217

Savage, Henry, 238, 240
Schopenhauer, Arthur, 127
Seaman, Mrs Elsa, 226
Secker, Martin, 166, 179
Shelley, Percy Bysshe, 53, 136, 232, 233, 288
Shorter, Clement, 269
Smith, Philip, 133, 169
Stendhal, 173
Stevenson, Robert Louis, 43, 100

Strachey, Lytton, 273
Strindberg, August, 210, 214

Taylor, Rachel Annand, 137, 161
Trier (Germany), 191, 201
Turgenev, Ivan, 137, 288

Underwood (Notts.), 17, 19

Van Gogh, Vincent, 255, 261
Verlaine, Paul, 49, 99, 136
Victoria Street (Eastwood), 18, 28

Waldbröl (Germany), 192–3
Walker Street (Eastwood), 43, 72, 78, 94
Weekley, Barbara: See Barr, Mrs Barbara
Weekley, Elsa. See Seaman, Mrs Elsa
Weekley, Ernest, 182–5, 188–91, 194, 200, 212, 216, 218, 241
Weekley, Frieda. See Lawrence, Frieda
Weekley, Montague, 226
Wells, H. G., 100, 137, 142, 151, 177, 210, 225, 264
Whitman, Walt, 43, 99, 156
Wiechert, Ernst, 267
Wight, Isle of, 144, 153
Wingfield Manor (Derbyshire), 103
Wright, Miss, 60

Yeats, W. B., 151

Zennor (Cornwall), 278–81, 286, 295